MICHAEL FIELD

Series in Victorian Studies
Series editors: Joseph McLaughlin and Elizabeth Miller

MICHAEL FIELD

DECADENT MODERNS

Edited by

Sarah Parker and

Ana Parejo Vadillo

OHIO UNIVERSITY PRESS   ATHENS

Ohio University Press, Athens, Ohio 45701
ohioswallow.com
© 2019 by Ohio University Press
All rights reserved

Printed in the United States of America
Ohio University Press books are printed on acid-free paper ⊗ ™

29 28 27 26 25 24 23 22 21 20 19   5 4 3 2 1

Library of Congress Cataloging-in-Publication Data

Names: Parker, Sarah, 1985- editor, author. | Parejo Vadillo, Ana, 1969-
editor, author.
Title: Michael Field : decadent moderns / edited by Sarah Parker and Ana
Parejo Vadillo.
Description: Athens : Ohio University Press, [2019] | Series: Series in
Victorian studies | "This collection of essays in part originates in
'The Michael Field Centenary Conference' that was held on July 11-12,
2014, under the auspices of the Institute of English Studies,
University of London" -- Acknowledgments. | Includes bibliographical
references and index.
Identifiers: LCCN 2019043331 | ISBN 9780821424018 (hardcover) | ISBN
9780821446928 (pdf)
Subjects: LCSH: Field, Michael--Criticism and interpretation. | Lesbianism
in literature. | Desire in literature. | Poetry, Modern--19th
century--Themes, motives. | Lesbians' writings--History and criticism.
Classification: LCC PR4699.F5 Z75 2019 | DDC 821/.8--dc23
LC record available at https://lccn.loc.gov/2019043331

Contents

CONTENTS

Illustrations

Acknowledgments

This collection of essays in part originates in "The Michael Field Centenary Conference" that was held on July 11–12, 2014, under the auspices of the Institute of English Studies, University of London. The editors would like to thank the staff at the Institute of English Studies for administering the conference. We are most grateful to the organizer, Birkbeck College, University of London, and particularly the Birkbeck Centre for Nineteenth-Century Studies for providing invaluable assistance and generous funds that made the conference possible. The editors would like to thank especially the Bingham Hotel, Michael Field's home in Richmond from 1899 to 1914, for facilitating rooms for the keynote and for holding the memorable conference dinner. Since Michael Field often made a point of writing down the menu of dinners they held for special guests, we record here that the dinner consisted of asparagus salad or heritage tomato tarte fine, followed by salt marsh lamb or courgette blossom. For dessert, there was summer berry trifle followed by tea, coffee, and petit fours.

The editors and the contributors would like to thank all of the collectors, copyright holders, librarians, and publishers who have made it possible to reproduce the illustrations in this volume. Every effort has been made to secure permissions for reproductions where copyrights are still active. If we have failed in any case to trace a copyright holder, we apologize for any apparent negligence on our part and will make the necessary arrangements at the earliest opportunity. Figure 3.3 is reproduced courtesy of Dennis Jarvis, Wikimedia Commons (CC-BY-SA-2.0). Figures 10.1 and 10.2 are reproduced courtesy of the William Andrews Clark Memorial Library, UCLA. The publisher would like to thank Oxford University Press for granting kind permission to reprint in part Catherine Maxwell's "Michael Field's Fragrant Imagination" in chapter 6 of this volume.

The editors are especially grateful to the contributors for the patience, cooperation, and support during the time that it has taken to bring this volume together.

INTRODUCTION

Michael Field

Decadent Moderns

SARAH PARKER AND ANA PAREJO VADILLO

And so closes the Victorian epoch.—~~It is~~ an epoch already yesterday: it is for us, England's living, & yet unspent poets to make all things new. We are for the morning—the nineteenth century thinks it has no poets—nothing to lose—verily it has nothing: for we are not of it—we shake the dust of our feet from it, & pass on into the 20th century.

—Michael Field, "Works and Days" (October 12, 1892)

I ~~still~~ do not yet realise where <u>modernity</u> is taking me; I am moving with it as if down a stream, not using it enough for ~~as a~~ motive force like a ~~mill wheel~~ water fall turning a mill. But I do not get frightened—I maintain a resolute patience. I cannot ~~yet~~ define my position to Law & Anarchy—though I am certain that we are doing an unnatural & destructive thing if you allow the claims of others to mar the freedom of self-realisation as the central need of our lives—& the condition of happiness.

—Michael Field, "Works and Days" (December 31, 1893)

THE TWO ENTRIES THAT SERVE HERE AS EPIGRAPHS—
the first by Katharine Bradley, the second by her beloved niece and life
partner Edith Cooper, with whom she wrote and published under the pseudonym "Michael Field"—are taken from the poets' unpublished joint diary "Works
and Days" in 1892 and 1893, respectively. Bradley writes following the funeral
of Alfred, Lord Tennyson—a symbolic death for Victorian poetry. But as her
diary account suggests, Bradley did not identify as a "Victorian poet" herself.
Neither did Cooper. For as we see in the second quotation, written after seeing
Ibsen's play *The Master Builder*, Cooper felt at one with modernity, embracing
its possibilities and its perils. This is indeed the very definition of modernity
in our own time, if we are to accept Marshall Berman's influential discussion
of modernity in industrial capitalist societies. And it is worth noting that his
definition was deeply influenced by the decadent philosophy and writing of the
European fin de siècle, from Charles Baudelaire and Walter Pater to Karl Marx
and Fyodor Dostoyevsky.[1]

But Cooper's conundrum with regard to individualism pertains also to the
question of modern selfhood. How, Cooper wonders, do self-realization and
happiness happen when in a partnership? What is the limit of individuality
in the context of the social and communal? In her insightful analysis of modern social relations at the turn of the century, Regenia Gagnier suggests that
new models of society were stimulated at the fin de siècle by what she calls
"individuals-in-relation," a concept that recognizes "that people are both socially
constituted and individually unique."[2] Michael Field, like other social dissidents
of this period (socialists, New Women, anarchists), found in their very "unnatural" partnership a form of social experimentation, whose limits in terms of
"Law" and "Anarchy" Bradley and Cooper felt in their own skins because it was
so often directed publicly toward their collaborative writings, which made them
vulnerable at times to the point of social ostracism.

Perhaps for this reason the poets viewed themselves as outmoded, altogether out of time, and belonging to the future. Bradley and Cooper found
models of partnership and inspiration in the past. Yet, even as they tried to
create new literatures that combined historical themes and aesthetics with their
own contemporaneity, they were aware that their readers were in the future.
Bradley once noted, "It is we who bring the harmonies, not time."[3] This may
seem paradoxical, but there are many paradoxes that characterize the modern
life of Bradley and Cooper and that encapsulate their oeuvre as a whole. It also
makes impossible a unified reading of Michael Field's works, and this is the
reason why their writings attract a stunning range of scholarly approaches. The
poets were prolific—publishing more than thirty-three books of poetry and

verse drama during their lifetime and under different names—yet their works were frequently critically disparaged and eventually neglected, even by their closest friends. They were poets, with markedly different personalities, composing separate poems and eventually almost entirely separate works—yet they were also one, operating defiantly under the aegis of "Michael Field" even when this identity was revealed to be a collaboration.

They were obviously female and feminine (at the cutting edge of dissident fashion, while favoring elegant hats and gowns)—yet their use of a male pseudonym and their circle of predominantly male friends and mentors marked their allegiance with masculinity. Their lives and works are suffused with homoerotic desire and their union was also incestuous—yet they were often viewed by their contemporaries (and posthumous biographers) as a pair of sexless spinsters. They themselves spoke of belonging to a group of celibates (Charles Ricketts, Charles Shannon, and Thomas Sturge Moore), but their sensual relationships to men and women are closer to what we would today call polyamory. They talked of their writing as "queer."[4] And if their friend Mary Costelloe disparaged them, she also described them as "poets like Dante and Ariosto and Tasso."[5] Persian, Hellenistic, Roman, Renaissance, modernist: they were both too antique and too modern—yet the criticism of the early twentieth century viewed them as stuffy, hopelessly fin-de-siècle, a product of enervated decadence.

Rather than playing down these contradictions, paradoxes, and complexities, *Michael Field: Decadent Moderns* seeks to elucidate them and expand on them by exploring the qualities that make Michael Field such an experimental and unique writer both within their own time and our own—indeed what made them distinctly modern. The focus of this book is interdisciplinary, highlighting Michael Field's energetic engagements with a range of fields: ecology, perfume, tourism, art history, sculpture, formalism, Classics, and book history, among others. For Michael Field's partnership functioned as a workshop in which they sought to collaborate with different groups of artists and intellectuals; their aims in some fashion closer to the all-encompassing power of a Renaissance artist. This book examines the breadth of Michael Field's writing, extending into the twentieth century. In doing so, *Michael Field: Decadent Moderns* aims to highlight the modernity, radicalism, and relevance of their work, for their modernity—with all its complexities—mirrors our own modernity.

"Biography" of "Michael Field"

We can reconfigure "Michael Field's biography" through the various domestic environments the women lived in and the communal utopian life of letters they created for themselves, which evolved from traditional notions of Victorian domesticity to the radical community of two that "Michael Field" represented. For once, Oscar Wilde perhaps was wrong in suggesting "be yourself, everyone else is taken," for Bradley and Cooper excelled in the mythmaking of creating and recreating their very individualities and poetic personalities. Katharine Harris Bradley was born in 1846 in Digbeth, Birmingham. Her father, Charles Bradley, was a tobacco manufacturer who died when she was two years old. She had one older sister, Emma Harris Bradley, her senior by eleven years. Since her sister was frail and often in poor health, Bradley and her mother (also Emma Harris Bradley) moved to Kenilworth to live with Emma and her husband, James Robert Cooper. In 1862, Emma gave birth to a daughter, Edith Emma Cooper. As Emma Donoghue writes, "[T]aking her niece into her arms, Katherine [sic] burst into tears, but she could have had no idea that this tiny creature, christened Edith, would eventually become the love of her life."[6] Two years later, Emma gave birth to a second daughter, Amy. This difficult birth rendered her a permanent invalid, and Bradley became increasingly attached to Edith, taking over the role of mother, aunt, teacher, and educator.

In 1868, Bradley's own mother died, and she embarked on a trip to Paris to study languages and literature at the Collège de France. During this pivotal trip, she fell in love with her friend's brother, Alfred Gérente. Gérente died suddenly shortly after their meeting, a devastating loss that for Bradley seemed to confirm her destiny as a spinster. On returning to England, Bradley continued her education at Newnham College in 1874 and began to compose the poems that would be published as *The New Minnesinger and Other Poems* (1875). As she later reflected, "I came to Newnham empty-headed, with vague ambition, vague sentiment—the pulpy lyrics of the N.M. in my brain."[7] These poems were published under the pseudonym of "Arran Leigh," which critics agree is a reference to Elizabeth Barrett Browning's earlier *Aurora Leigh* (1856). However, this pseudonym also contains an edge of gender ambiguity that foreshadows "Michael Field." Like Barrett Browning's poem, the poems of *The New Minnesinger* asserted women's right to claim their place as poets and singers. Indeed, the "Minnesinger" is a term for a German singer or troubadour of courtly love lyrics, a role that Bradley defiantly claims for the woman poet.

As Marion Thain and Ana Parejo Vadillo note, "It is no accident that Bradley's introductory poem to *The New Minnesinger* is 'To E.C.'"[8] As the 1870s progressed, and Edith Cooper entered her teenage years, she and her aunt Bradley grew ever closer, artistically and romantically. In 1879, the whole family moved to Bristol, and Bradley and Cooper attended classes at University College, Bristol, in subjects such as classics and philosophy that would ultimately inform their poetic works. They were becoming scholars and poets. As their early biographer Mary Sturgeon writes, during this period the poets were noticeably "aesthetic"; they "joined the debating society of the college and plunged into the questions of the moment," including vivisection and women's rights, and both women "wore wonderful flowing garments in 'art' colours, and dressed their hair in a loose knot at the nape of the neck."[9] During this time, they also developed an interest in pagan religion, eschewing the conventions of Christianity in favor of freedom and nature worship, expressed through their construction of Bacchic altars and pagan rituals, later described in their diaries. Foreshadowing their later striking religious transitions, Bradley had angered her early mentor John Ruskin in December 1877 by declaring that the acquisition of a terrier had converted her from Christianity to paganism. An enraged Ruskin responded, "[T]hat you should be such a fool as coolly to write to me that you had ceased to believe in God—and had found some comfort in a dog—this is deadly."[10] While Bradley's original letter may have been partly flippant in tone, dogs did indeed play a pivotal role in their belief systems, with the later death of their beloved Whym Chow precipitating a Catholic conversion in 1907.

Living and studying together in Bristol, Bradley and Cooper began to develop their creative collaboration. Their first collaborative work was entitled *Bellerophôn* (1881). This work was a historical closet drama, inspired by an eponymous Greek hero. The volume concluded with poems, also on Greek subjects. As Ana Parejo Vadillo shows in the present volume, this initial experiment in collaboration was the product of studying sculpture at the British Museum. It was published under "Arran and Isla Leigh," a gender-ambiguous pseudonym that, as Yopie Prins observes, suggests "various possible relationships . . . a pair of siblings, a parent and child, a married couple."[11] These relationships, and a variety of others, structured the collaborative dynamic between Bradley and Cooper. As Bradley later explained to John Gray, "To me a relation is like this. / lover & loved / mother & child / server & served."[12] In their relationship, Bradley and Cooper played a variety of roles, often shared between them. But their relationship was not without opposition. Letters from 1885 suggest that Cooper's mother had reservations about their increasing closeness. For example, Bradley writes to Cooper, "Mother must have a heart of stone if after this she keeps you from me."[13] Cooper replies, reassuring but pleading for more time to placate her parents, "I will come & heaven favouring, we will indeed be happy. . . . But wait a little for dear little Pussie's sake. She is getting better & parents want her to have a full week at Weston now the lovely weather is here. Let her have this."[14] Bradley's tone in these letters becomes increasing frustrated: "Tell Mother she is a real scamp. . . . Tell her to beware: her hand is on the lion's mane."[15] The tensions are articulated in the women's correspondence for the 1880s that was made available by Sharon Bickle in her groundbreaking edition of the letters in *The Fowl and the Pussycat* (2008). The women's relationship in this earlier period is explored by Kate Thomas's essay in the present volume, in which she shows how nature becomes a symbol for their intergenerational, incestuous love.

Bellerophôn was not well received. In a negative review in the *Academy*, the reviewer complained that the poets were too Greek and too clever.[16] But the extraordinary *Bellerophôn* was the pillar on which they constructed their vision for the collaborative poetics that would become Michael Field. Critical success came in 1884 with another Greek book, their verse drama *Callirhoë*. This play occupies a unique place in the Field oeuvre as the first literary work published under the "Michael Field" pseudonym. It was well received by critics, many of whom compared this new "male" playwright to Shakespeare. For example, T. W. Higginson suggested that Michael Field be awarded the title of poet laureate on the strength of this play.[17] Many readers assumed that Michael Field was a man, with writers such as A. Mary F. Robinson and Oscar Wilde writing admiring letters to "Michael Field Esqre." The sexologist Havelock Ellis tried to guess the gender of the author. The press was also onto the pseudonym: a review in the *Athenæum* (July 5, 1884) revealed that the author was a "she."[18] The following month, in his review for *To-Day*, L. O. Streeter (pseudonym of George Bernard Shaw) noted that "Michael Field" was a "woman" and that some of the scenes in *Callirrhoë* could only have been written by a woman.[19] Robert Browning was involved in these speculations and eventually became an influential supporter of the women. As he wrote to Cooper in admiration after receiving a copy of *Callirhoë* and *Fair Rosamund*, bound together, "[I]t is long since I have been so thoroughly impressed by indubitable poetic genius,—a word I consider while I write, only to repeat it, 'genius.'"[20] The women finally confessed their joint and female authorship to him. Cooper explained their method of collaboration:

> My Aunt & I work together after the fashion of Beaumont &
> Fletcher. She is my senior by but 15 yrs. She has lived with me,
> taught me, encouraged me & joined me to her poetic life. . . . Some
> of the scenes in our plays are like mosaic work—the mingled,
> various product of our two brains. . . . This happy union of two
> in work & aspiration is sheltered & expressed by "Michael Field."
> Please regard him as the author.[21]

But despite such instructions, Browning eventually gave the secret of Michael Field's joint and female authorship away. Bradley expressed her anxieties that this would affect the reception of their work:

[I]t is said *The Athenaeum* was taught by you to use the feminine pronoun. . . . I write to you to beg you to set the critics on the wrong track . . . the report of lady-authorship will dwarf & enfeeble our work at every turn. . . . We have many things to say the world will not tolerate from a woman's lips. We must be free as dramatists to work out in the open air of nature—exposed to her vicissitudes, witnessing her terrors: we cannot be stifled in drawing-room conventionalities.[22]

In hindsight, it is surprising that Bradley was more worried about the feminine pronoun than about the composite nature of their authorship. It is difficult to determine how far this revelation of female authorship affected the reception of their work. As Holly Laird and Jill R. Ehnenn have shown, Bradley and Cooper had as much to fear from prejudice against joint authorship—collaboration unseating the model of lone genius—as from that against female authorship. While joint authorship in drama was not too unusual, joint lyric female authorship was troubling, this genre being associated even more with lone male consciousness and the expression of inward feeling (partly due to the legacy of Romanticism). Michael Field's authorship thus combined a number of elements disturbing and difficult to explain to Victorian readers.

In April 1888, the Cooper family, along with Bradley, moved to Reigate, Surrey. This placed the women nearer to London, facilitating networking with publishers such as John Lane and providing better access to the British Library and National Gallery. At this same moment, Bradley and Cooper began their joint diary, later entitled "Works and Days." This diary eventually extended to twenty-eight volumes, covering the years 1888 to September 1914—the last entry was written four days before Bradley's death. The early volumes of the diary chart their poetic success.

In 1889, Bradley and Cooper published *Long Ago*, the first volume of lyric poems under the Michael Field pseudonym. This volume was inspired by Henry Thornton Wharton's 1885 translations of the fragments of the ancient Greek poet Sappho, along with "selected renderings" by other poets. Michael Field took Sappho's suggestive and oblique fragments and composed their own poems around them, combining their collaborative lyric voice with Sappho's to enter the poetic field.[23] How much this volume owes to their first collaboration, *Bellerophôn*, we are only beginning to appreciate today. *Long Ago* attracted critical praise, being the first volume by Michael Field that sold out. In the *Academy*, John Miller Gray wrote:

From the first her [Michael Field's] work has been informed with intensity and passion, has evinced sufficient native force and freshness to assure its reader that a new and original poetic personality has grasped the pen.... [T]he present book will take a permanent place in our English literature, as one of the most exquisite lyrical productions of the latter half of the nineteenth century.[24]

Gray's words "intensity" and "passion" immediately located Michael Field within a very particular group of writers and intellectuals. Those words echo Walter Pater's controversial 1873 collection of essays, *Studies in the History of the Renaissance*. Pater, who was sent the volume by the women, very much enjoyed the work and asked to meet the "author," whom he suspected to be a "woman."[25] Pater would prefer their lyrical poetry to their lyrical dramas, and in this subtle but key difference lies Michael Field's fracture with the most prominent decadent writers of the period. Drama was for Michael Field the writing of the future, but Pater and others thought poetic drama was, despite its Romantic origins, a dead genre, not the live thing that Michael Field believed it to be.[26]

Michael Field's next work, their poetic drama *The Tragic Mary* (1890), attracted some enthusiastic contemporary reception, but it marked a new turn in the response to Michael Field's work, with some bad reviews. This retelling of the life of Mary, Queen of Scots, whose story fascinated many Victorian writers, poets, and dramatists, demonstrates Michael Field's distinctive approach to historiographical reinterpretation: depicting Mary as a feminist heroine. In addition to its content, *The Tragic Mary* was admired for its appearance. Sixty copies were commissioned of a fine edition, with a cover by the artist and designer Selwyn Image. This beautiful thistle design led the volume to become celebrated as an aesthetic object, with Wilde declaring it one of the "two beautiful books (in appearance) of the century," alongside Dante Gabriel Rossetti's poems.[27] Many of Michael Field's books were designed with painstaking care and detail—from the white vellum of *Long Ago*, embossed with a cameo of Sappho, to the russet suede of *Whym Chow, Flame of Love*. Michael Field's role as a "book sculptor" is discussed in Vadillo's essay in this volume.

A few months after the publication of *Long Ago*, Cooper's mother (and Bradley's sister) died of cancer. This left the women free to travel and pursue their aesthetic ambitions. In June 1890, they embarked on their first European trip, arriving first in Paris. In the Louvre, they met the art historian and critic Bernard Berenson. He quickly became an influential mentor (Browning had died in 1889 and, as Margaret D. Stetz explains in this volume, Bradley and Cooper were constantly on the hunt for male mentor figures to admire and worship). During this pivotal trip, they toured the galleries of Europe, gathering notes for the volume that became *Sight and Song* (1892). This volume exhibited the influence of Berenson and Pater in its emphasis on artistic impressions, although Michael Field sought to capture "what chosen pictures sing in themselves" through their ekphrastic translations of paint into song.[28] This volume received mixed reviews; W. B. Yeats compared it unfavorably to their earlier works, writing that it was an "unmitigated guide-book": "'Sight and Song,' following as it does 'The Tragic Mary,' is enough to make us turn our eyes forever from the 'false dawn' we believed to be the coming day."[29]

These early European tours were significant for other reasons, too. While in Germany in August 1891, Cooper contracted scarlet fever. Recovering in a Dresden hospital, with her hair clipped short, Cooper was reborn as "Heinrich": "She looks very pretty in her short boy's hair & fresh cotton jacket."[30] As Martha Vicinus has argued, the figure of the boy was one of identification and desire for Michael Field and other fin-de-siècle women writers: "his protean nature displayed a double desire—to love a boy and to be a boy."[31] During this period, these associations also became concentrated in the figure of the young Berenson. For Cooper, Berenson was a faun with whom she both identified and whom she desired. As Vicinus has argued, intimacy with Berenson brought complications and tensions to the Field partnership. As the 1890s progressed, Bradley and Cooper's friendship with Berenson and his partner Mary Costelloe, also an art historian, became increasingly intimate. Indeed, as Sarah Parker has suggested, *both* Bradley and Cooper found rich poetic inspiration in this young art historian—and his lover Costelloe—a passion that is expressed in poems found in their volume *Underneath the Bough* (1893).[32]

Underneath the Bough can be read alongside the *Rubáiyát of Omar Khayyám* (translated by Edward FitzGerald in 1859) as well as Elizabethan-inflected sequences of love lyrics and the Biblical "Song of Songs." This volume is suffused with various semiautobiographical narratives—the death of Cooper's mother, the threat of Cooper's illness, their unrequited passion for Berenson. The poet Augusta Webster, in her unsigned review for the *Athenæum*, noted that

> The two great thoughts, Death and Love—with Sorrow for the inner name of both—are in fact almost the sole inspirations of the whole, but there is no monotony. . . . A peculiarity of these poems is that while they are of antique mould, ancestral not merely in form but in expression, they are in feeling distinctively modern.[33]

This is the sense that several chapters in this volume emphasize. Critics have frequently observed that Michael Field's work is often paradoxically both forward and backward looking. As Joseph Bristow remarks in the present volume, nowhere is this more apparent than in their dramas, which, through their Elizabethan blank verse and strikingly modern subject matter, exhibit a "double temporality . . . at once antiquated and avant-garde."[34] In 1893, the first and only performance of their plays during their lifetime took place. On October 27, 1893, *A Question of Memory* was performed at the Independent Theatre Society.[35] The next day, the poets awoke to critical derision:

> It seems more natural to be dead than alive. We wake to the surprise of finding every morning paper against us. . . . Not a flower had any one sent us yesterday, not a flower was given to us. No word, no letter, no visit, only the execrations of the Press! . . . We are hated as Shelley was hated by our countrymen blindly, ravenously.[36]

Nonetheless, they persisted with drama, and it was their drama that would attract modernist experimental dramatists in the twentieth century. As discussed by Bristow in this volume, Bradley and Cooper hoped that *Attila, My Attila!* (1895) would prove more of a success, though this was not to be.

The negative response they received from Costelloe and Berenson caused a break in their friendship. To an extent, though, Michael Field had simply replaced one collaborating couple with another. From early 1894, Bradley and Cooper had developed a close friendship with Charles Ricketts and Charles Shannon—a pair of artists, designers, and aesthetes who were also, like themselves, a collaborating homosexual couple. This friendship fostered aesthetic collaborations between the couples, such as the Roman Trilogy—three plays by Michael Field (*World at Auction*, 1898, *The Race of Leaves*, 1901, and *Julia Domna*, 1903) with covers designed by Ricketts and jewelry designed by Ricketts for the women.[37]

The year 1897 was particularly difficult, as Cooper's father James died while mountaineering. Bradley and Cooper comforted themselves by acquiring a chow dog that they named Whym Chow after the explorer Edward Whymper, who had led the search for Cooper's father. In 1899, at the encouragement of Ricketts, Bradley and Cooper moved to 1, The Paragon, in Richmond, London. This was the first time they had lived together alone, without the interference of family members. This home became a work of art in its own right, as their early biographer Mary Sturgeon records:

> Their rooms were not less flawless than their poems. . . . The silvery clear lithographs of their friend, Mr C. H. Shannon, were hung all together in a cool northern room. . . . [I]n another room the golden grain of the walls, alike with the Persian plates that glowed on the table as if they were rich, large petals, seemed to find

their reason for being there in the two deeply and subtly coloured pictures by Mr Charles Ricketts on the walls. But always there was the same feeling of inevitable choice and unity everywhere; in a jewelled pendant that lay on a satinwood table, in the opal bowl of pot-pourri nearby on which an opal shell lay lightly.[38]

As the century drew to a close and the new century began, Bradley and Cooper concentrated on their verse drama, including the Cornwall-set masque *Noontide Branches* (1899), discussed by Alex Murray in this volume; the Roman Trilogy; and *Borgia* (1905), which was published anonymously. As Donoghue notes, this "simple trick worked on the critics brilliantly. *Borgia* . . . though one of their worst plays, was the first for many years to get reviews, and a few good ones at that."[39]

In 1906, disaster struck. Their beloved dog Whym Chow died of meningitis. The devastating and transformative effect of this on both Bradley and Cooper cannot be overstated. Cooper wrote, "Today I have had the worst loss of my life—yes, worse than that of beloved Mother or tragic father. . . . My Whym Chow, my little Chow-Chow, my Flame of Love is dead."[40] For Whym Chow was metaphorically and poetically both their muse and their child. Their bereavement ultimately led to both women's conversion to Catholicism in 1907. However, Bradley and Cooper were by no means unique in turning from Pagan decadence to Roman Catholicism during this period. As Ellis Hanson and other critics have shown, many aesthetes converted to Catholicism in the years following the Wilde trials of 1895, including Wilde himself, Marc-André Raffalovich, Ernest Dowson, and John Gray. The latter—an erstwhile decadent poet and rumored inspiration for Dorian Gray—even became Cooper's priest. Indeed, as Ruth Vanita notes, with the conversion to Catholicism, the content of Michael Field's work did not alter substantially.[41] Instead, they had simply found a slightly different set of tropes through which to express their desire for one another. A key volume that captures this gradual transformation is *Wild Honey from Various Thyme* (1908), which crosses the Christian and Pagan divide with poems combining imagery of Christ and Dionysus. This volume expresses the complex dualities of Michael Field's career—looking back to their Bacchic worship and forward to Catholic devotion.

One of the reasons behind Bradley and Cooper's Catholic conversion is that they hoped, through doing so, to be together in the afterlife. Thus, their newfound religious beliefs provided some comfort when Cooper was diagnosed with bowel cancer in February 1911. Despite being in considerable pain, Cooper managed to write Catholic poems that were published as *Poems of Adoration* (1912). Bradley published her own volume of religious poems, *Mystic Trees* (1913). These works are discussed by Jill R. Ehnenn and Leire Barrera-Medrano in this volume. On December 13, 1913, Cooper died. Bradley had secretly been suffering from cancer herself. She managed to prepare and publish a volume of poems devoted to their beloved dog, *Whym Chow: Flame of Love* (composed mostly by Cooper in 1906 but published in 1914) and a volume of Cooper's poems, *Dedicated: An Early Work of Michael Field* (mostly composed in 1900, published in 1914). Bradley died just under a year after her beloved partner, on September 26, 1914.

Critical Reception: Twentieth Century to the Present

During their lifetime, Michael Field's poetry and drama received an increasingly mixed reception. Bradley and Cooper began to feel that their works would never be critically appreciated. As Cooper wrote despairingly in 1893, "We are desperately alone in a world that shuns us. . . . We are boycotted in the papers, by the men, . . . & by even literary society."[42] Some of Michael Field's contemporaries recognized that although their works might be derided in the present, they would be appreciated in the future. As George Meredith reassured them in 1899, "[Y]our noble stand for pure poetic literature will have its reward, but evidently you will have to wait."[43] During their lifetime, Michael Field's fame was often linked to the rise and fall of decadence. For example, "Michael Field," claimed the *Academy* in 1898, "are two clever ladies, but they will not do much until they get . . . out of this hothouse of decadent chronicle."[44] But this is ironic given that Bradley and Cooper had a markedly ambivalent relationship to decadence. For example, they refused to contribute to *The Yellow Book*, writing, "The best one can say of any tale or any illustration [in *The Yellow Book*] is that it is clever—the worst one can [say] is that it is damnable."[45] They requested that Henry Harland return the manuscript of their poem "Rhythm," concluding triumphantly, "This means a break forever with the hated Bodley Head—it is like a noisome dragon dropping from one dead."[46]

But in spite of such ambivalence, their association with the 1890s did not help when this period of decadence fell out of favor in the early twentieth century, becoming reconfigured as an epoch of enervation and degeneration—Yeats's twilight generation—in comparison with the new energies of literary modernity. For one can only be modern in the rejection of the most recent past. For example, one twentieth-century reviewer wrote that within Michael Field's diaries, "The nineties pour forth their dead finery and dusky fragrance."[47] The 1916 *Cambridge History of English Literature* was even more dismissive, comparing their work to the "machine-made verse which usually comes late in great periods of poetry."[48] Though poets such as Margaret Sackville (1910) saw in Michael Field's poetry the foundational aesthetics of modernity—"Michael Field's is one of the strongest women's voices of the present day . . . it is of to-day in spirit and expression"—by the time of the women's death, modernism had buried deep Michael Field's experimental writing, both lyric and dramatic.[49]

Even the gargantuan efforts of their friend, the poet Thomas Sturge Moore, until well into the 1930s failed to ignite interest in the poets. He brought to print a number of Michael Field's poems (*A Selection from the Poems of Michael Field*, 1923) and unpublished verse dramas, and perhaps more importantly, published his selections from the women's multivolume diary, *Works and Days: From the Journal of Michael Field* (1933).[50] He was part of a number of modernist circles (Yeats was a close friend), but these posthumous publications were received more as a reminder of a Victorian past than as indicative of the radical experimentation with which critics are finally beginning to connect Michael Field. Robert Lynd, for example, entitled his 1933 review of the women's diary "Eminent Victorians through the Eyes of Two Women"—managing in one phrase both to consign Bradley and Cooper to the dusty past *and* to suggest that their words are merely a conduit to more "eminent" (male) Victorians.[51]

For the bulk of the twentieth century, Michael Field remained mostly forgotten. Nonetheless, biographers and critics continued to work to recover Bradley and Cooper's texts and personal history, contributing studies that remain useful to Michael Field scholars today. In 1930, a new volume of verse, *The Wattlefold*, based on the unpublished later poetry of Michael Field, post Catholic conversion, was published (edited by Emily C. Fortey, with preface by Vincent McNabb, Bradley's priest). Mary Sturgeon published the first full-length biography of Michael Field in 1921. In the 1960s, Ursula Bridge also worked on a biography of Michael Field that has remained unpublished but proved useful to scholars in discovering this unusual writer.[52] By the 1970s, a number of scholars were rediscovering Michael Field and discussing their work from different critical and methodological perspectives. For example, Henri Locard (1979) considered the significance of their life writing; Kenneth R. Ireland wrote one of the earliest journal articles on poetry and painting in *Sight and Song* (1977); and Jan McDonald considered the drama *A Question of Memory* (1975).[53] In 1981, Lillian Faderman included Michael Field in her path-forging study of female romantic friendship, *Surpassing the Love of Men*, opening up future studies that considered Bradley and Cooper's life and work in light of gender, sexuality, and queer theory.

As with the fin-de-siècle period in general, the 1990s saw an intensifying of interest in Michael Field. Motivated by an urgent need to revise the masculinist conceptions of Victorian poetics, critics such as Isobel Armstrong, Virginia Blain, Joseph Bristow, Holly Laird, Angela Leighton, Yopie Prins, Martha Vicinus, and Chris White recovered Michael Field's poetry for nineteenth-century studies. In their different ways, each of these critics highlighted Bradley and Cooper's innovative experiments with lyric voice, interrogating their multivocality, their complex expressions of sexual and gendered identities, their entangled relationship to earlier poetic traditions (of the poetess, ekphrasis, the love lyric, the poetic drama), and their deft manipulations of form and meter.[54] *Long Ago* (1889) attracted particular interest during this period of criticism, both for its negotiations of sexuality (including Sappho's rumored lesbianism) and its use of polyvocal lyric voice. Holly Laird (1995, 2000), Virginia Blain (1996), and Yopie Prins (1999) took up different but equally influential positions on questions of unity and dissonance within the "Michael Field" pseudonym, as focused through their collaboration with Sappho. Meanwhile, in 1995, Ian Small and R. K. R. Thornton issued a reprint of *Sight and Song* and *Underneath the Bough*, making these volumes accessible for a new scholarly audience. In addition, Michael Field's poems were increasingly included in anthologies, such as Angela Leighton and Margaret Reynolds's *Victorian Women Poets* (1995) and Virginia Blain's *Victorian Women Poets: An Annotated Anthology* (2001).

Simultaneously, a fascination with the collaborative nature of Michael Field's authorship and their sexual relationship meant that biographical studies of the women began to appear, feeding into larger questions of nineteenth-century women's lives and the sexual politics of the period. One of the first key publications was Emma Donoghue's brief and informative biography, *We Are Michael Field* (1998), which was published in the same year as Ivor C. Treby's *Michael Field Catalogue: A Book of Lists*, the most comprehensive bibliography of Michael Field's writings to date. Critical essays on the women's poetry continued to grow, as a number of unpublished writings by Michael Field were brought to print by Treby.[55] As a result of this scholarship, Michael Field has emerged as one of the most fascinating writers of the fin de siècle.

Following the groundbreaking revisionist scholarship of the 1990s, the last twenty years have seen a major resurgence in work on Michael Field, which has coexisted with (and further ignited) the galvanized interest in fin-de-siècle studies today, fueled by our own twenty-first-century decadent moment. The first-ever conference on Michael Field—"Michael Field and Their World"— was organized by Margaret D. Stetz and Mark Samuels Lasner and was held at the University of Delaware in 2004. It confirmed that this resurgence during the first decade of the twenty-first century had opened up multiple avenues of scholarship for critics interested in Michael Field, including discussions of the pseudonym and constructions of authorship, considerations of ekphrasis in *Sight and Song*, and reassessment of the Catholic poetry and of Bradley and Cooper's various literary networks, among other varied topics. This diversity is captured in the conference proceedings published in 2007 by Riverdale Press (*Michael Field and Their World*, edited by Margaret D. Stetz and Cheryl Wilson). The proceedings were published the same year as the first modern scholarly monograph on Michael Field's poetry, Marion Thain's *"Michael Field": Poetry, Aestheticism, and the Fin de Siècle* (2007). These two significant publications were soon followed by Sharon Bickle's edition of the women's love letters, *The Fowl and the Pussycat: Love Letters of Michael Field, 1876–1909* (2008), and the first scholarly anthology of Michael Field, *Michael Field, The Poet: Published and Unpublished Manuscript Materials* (2009), coedited by Marion Thain and Ana Parejo Vadillo. The same year, the *Michaelian* journal was founded, which though short lived was helpful in providing a forum for new work on the poets.[56] These publications have effectively consolidated studies on Michael Field, confirming Bradley and Cooper's own belief that their work would not be appreciated until sometime in the distant future. Finally, with the rise of social media and new technologies, Michael Field's "outmodedness" has allowed a fluid, global engagement with the works, which is both playful and political. Thain has written about the digitization of their manuscript diaries, and Rob Gallagher and Ana Parejo Vadillo have explored the possibilities of creating experimental editions via GIFs and HIVE.[57] Digitally speaking, their time is now.

Michael Field: Decadent Moderns

Michael Field: Decadent Moderns brings about a major shift in the direction of Michael Field's research by focusing on Michael Field's decadent modernity seen through the eyes of a number of scholars who write expertly about the different parts of the women's history and their writing. One of the unique characteristics of their work is that their poetry and dramas were always thoroughly researched, exhibiting a phenomenal amount of knowledge of all kinds of literature and arts and of all periods, from Greek, Roman, and Renaissance writings to the most up-to-date critical study of the subjects that interested them. Equally, with the rise of modern interdisciplinary criticism alongside the new formalism, Michael Field's writings have begun to be opened up to reveal the complex world their poetics created, whose fabric (aesthetic, politic, formal) was the literatures, arts, and criticisms of the past.

Michael Field used the metaphor of the mosaic to speak about their collaboration. *Michael Field: Decadent Moderns* is also an exercise in mosaic composition and presents us with a complex poet whose writings were deeply embedded in a number of disciplines. The scholarly nature of their work and the range of their publications in different fields require the vision and the disciplinarity of different types of scholars and scholarship. This book offers analysis and discussions on previously unexplored writings, encompassing interdisciplinary perspectives relating to poetry, verse drama, theatre studies, ecology, travel writing, disability, art history, women's and gender studies, queer studies, material culture, and cosmopolitanism. In doing so, this volume highlights the variety and significance of Michael Field's work, moving beyond a focus on the nineteenth century and poetry to encompass the full range of Bradley and Cooper's oeuvre and to place them in the context of twentieth-century modernity, as well as that of fin-de-siècle aestheticism and decadence.

Michael Field: Decadent Moderns elucidates and opens up Michael Field's radical decadent modernity for the first time by amplifying the concept of decadent poetics (key to the revisionist work carried out in the 1990s and 2000s) to include other genres (autobiographical writing, prose, and verse dramas) and artistic manifestations (art history, sculpture, book art). This book pays particular attention to Michael Field's writings before 1884 and after 1900, aligning them with modernist aesthetic transformations and reconfiguring Michael Field as an experimental writer. Our collection therefore also contributes to the current significant turn in modernist studies that emphasizes continuities rather than breaks with fin-de-siècle decadence, while also producing new lines of inquiry into what it means to be modern.[58]

The chapters in this collection highlight Michael Field as an intellectual writer whose importance can be gauged by the diversity and productivity of their engagement with various literary forms and ideas, reconnecting Michael Field's modernity in their time with ours. The chapters are arranged to be roughly chronological, alighting on key moments in Michael Field's complex and varied oeuvre. However, in a manner appropriate to Michael Field's own experiments with time and chronology—what Kate Thomas refers to as their "ebullient deconstruction of 'chrononormativity'"—one can trace multiple connections and continuities between and across the chapters in this volume.[59] Indeed, we encourage readers to seek out thematic and formal connections across the chapters (from ecology and animal activism to marble aesthetics, from art criticism to the language of sculpture, from Paganism to Catholic dissidence, from chrononormativity to disability, from formalism to feminist poetics, from Italian, French, and Spanish poetry to Elizabethan poetic theory), as this will enable them to discern the complex aesthetic philosophy that plays across the whole body of Michael Field's work, as Bradley and Cooper often returned to and reworked tropes and forms as their ideas evolved.

Our collection begins with Kate Thomas's provocative essay on queer ecology, "Vegetable Love." Thomas's chapter looks at how Michael Field used imagery of fruit, flowers, weeds, and vegetables in their verse and life writing. This fondness for nature may perhaps be surprising given other aesthetes' vocal declarations against nature. Thomas reads such vegetal imagery alongside theories of becoming and queer temporality, in order to argue that Michael Field did not "queer" nature but instead recognized "the already-queerness of the vegetal," emphasizing this in their work.[60] For example, Thomas discusses how Bradley and Cooper adopted the bramble-bough symbol for their union—combining the fruit and flower as a symbol of their intergenerational, incestual, and queer relationship, as well as their collaborative creativity. Fusing queer with ecological criticism, this chapter catalyzes one of the many salient new readings of Michael Field proposed by this volume: the green aesthetics of Michael Field.

Michael Field's multisensory conceptualization of desire weaves through a series of motifs and topics, including plants, perfume, and animals. Catherine Maxwell's chapter, "Michael Field's Fragrant Imagination," emphasizes the importance of perfume, both floral and vegetal, in Michael Field's work. Linking to Thomas's chapter, Maxwell confirms that Bradley and Cooper had specific knowledge of the significance and symbolism of their favorite flower scents, including myrtle (symbolic of Aphrodite), musk, and rose. As Maxwell argues, "Bradley and Cooper's use of the rose is no poetic commonplace but arises out of a deep love and knowledge of the flower."[61] Maxwell's chapter concludes with a new reading of "The Grand Mogul" (published in the 1898 edition of *Underneath the Bough*). Maxwell notes that previous analyses of this poem have overlooked the particular rose that serves as Michael Field's inspiration. By paying attention to this, Maxwell asserts, what emerges is the suggestive image of a cross-dressed feminine flower, exuding hints of "tobacco, leather, brass"—the "essence of Michael Field."[62]

Maxwell's chapter also draws attention to Bradley and Cooper's important relationship with their male mentor figures, Charles Ricketts and Charles Shannon. Margaret D. Stetz's chapter elucidates Michael Field's significant relationships with the men around them. Through her reading of an underanalyzed poem from *Long Ago* about the nymph "Dryope," who was raped by Apollo, Stetz explores Bradley and Cooper's conception of inspiration. Comparing their work to that of other late nineteenth-century women writers—such as Katharine Tynan and George Egerton, who tend to portray literary inspiration as arriving early in girlhood—Stetz contrasts this with Bradley and Cooper's vision of an adult Dryope who is set apart by her daring and autonomy. Stetz suggests that this vision of being overcome and transformed by masculine power is provoked by two male muse/mentor figures with whom Bradley and Cooper were entangled at the time of writing the poem—Robert Browning, who read and admired drafts of *Long Ago*, and Havelock Ellis, who had previously praised Michael

Field's work while writing of another poet, Thomas Ashe. Ashe had written his own "Dryope" poem, and Stetz suggests that Michael Field's poem is an attempt to rewrite Ashe's poem, to reconceptualize Dryope as an empowered, inspired figure, not a conventional Victorian maiden, wife, and fallen woman.

Michael Field's relationship with their male mentors also features in Sarah Parker's chapter. However, Parker seeks to highlight Bradley and Cooper's complex relationship with the female art critic Mary Costelloe. While critics have traced Michael Field's relationship with the art connoisseur Bernard Berenson, their equally significant relationship with Berenson's collaborator Costelloe had yet to be explored. Parker redresses the balance by tracing the women's evolving friendship with Costelloe. In doing so, she compares Michael Field's ekphrastic lyrics in *Sight and Song* with Costelloe's own art historical writings. As the relationship developed, Bradley and Cooper fantasized about stealing scopic authority from both Costelloe and Berenson. The desires and tensions of these relationships are expressed in lyrics in *Underneath the Bough*. In Parker's essay, Michael Field emerge as art critics too, as she demonstrates the ekphrastic lyric as intrinsically critical. In their emphases on Michael Field's influences, inspirations, and networks, all of these chapters reject the image of intellectual aridity and isolation Michael Field have often been associated with, showing that they were involved in collaborative aesthetic experimentation and exchange with their fin-de-siècle peers, whether male mentors or overlooked female influences.

Beyond Michael Field's work in lyric, *Michael Field: Decadent Moderns* contains three essays on Michael Field's verse drama. As Joseph Bristow has noted elsewhere, "the tendency in recent criticism to focus on Michael Field's poetry rather than their verse-plays has produced a skewed understanding of their considerable achievements."[63] Essays by Bristow, Alex Murray, and Ana Parejo Vadillo recuperate the importance of verse drama for understanding modernism and modernist theater. Vadillo's chapter examines Bradley and Cooper's first joint publication, *Bellerophôn*, to argue that this first verse drama is an exploration of collaboration based on the concept of the antique sculptural fragment. The vision offered in this first poetic drama is one of a decadent modernity built on fragments of the past. Vadillo's essay is also the first to take into account Michael Field's engagement with sculpture. She examines how antique sculpture formed their youth, enabling them to carve their authorship and to articulate their passion for each other. Focusing on what she calls the "marble period," a period marked by the production of white books, she presents Michael Field as a book artist and as a sculptural poet. This essay thus recovers the early work of Bradley and Cooper, while it also opens up two new fields of research in Michael Field studies: sculpture and book art.

Bristow's chapter discusses Bradley and Cooper's attempts to negotiate and find success on the London stage. Through the disastrous production of *A Question of Memory* at the Independent Theatre Society in October 1893, Bradley and Cooper gained experience of the difficulty of translating their modern and ambitious play (dealing with the Hungarian Revolution of 1848) to the stage. However, as Bristow shows, they were undeterred by their experience and sought again to create a "modern" play with *Attila, My Attila!* (1895). Although this play is characteristically archaic in style, Bristow argues that it was strikingly modern in theme, representing the heroine Honoria as "the New Woman of the fifth century," and affirming the importance of desire for women.[64] But once again, critics attacked the women, sneering at the thought of spinsters writing about sexuality.

Alex Murray's chapter addresses Michael Field's verse drama and their little-discussed prose works in the context of late nineteenth-century tourism. As Murray recounts, Bradley and Cooper traveled in the 1890s in France, Italy, and Scotland, often on literary pilgrimages. Distaining the behavior of other tourists, however, Cooper's prose sketches of "For That Moment Only" (1893–95) and the diary writings capture the women's attempts to forge a vision of Bacchic travel, in opposition to the growing fin-de-siècle tourist industry. Murray's chapter concludes with an analysis of Michael Field's Cornwall-set masque *Noontide Branches* (1899), a play that signals the pull of Catholicism over paganism, attempting to "translate the quotidian experience of travel into a dynamic commingling of the Christian with the Pagan."[65]

Michael Field's Catholic poetry provides the basis for the next two chapters in the volume. As Jill R. Ehnenn observes in her chapter, Michael Field's work post-Catholic conversion remains underanalyzed, despite the complexities of its engagements with theology, Catholic literary tradition, and the body and its complex eroticism. Indeed, Ehnenn argues that Michael Field's Catholic poems exhibit internal intricacies that have been overlooked by the few critics who *have* discussed this work. She identifies a shift in their poetics between Catholic poems written before Cooper's diagnosis with cancer in 1911 and those written after. In the first part of her chapter, Ehnenn recounts Bradley and Cooper's attempts to become Catholic poets, following the principles set out by influential Christian poets such as John Keble, who emphasized reverence, the use of natural analogy, and measured, regular use of meter to instill a sense of reserve. However, Ehnenn shows how the meter employed in poems like "A Crucifix" is actually more ambiguous than it first appears and, when carefully analyzed, reveals the submerged homoeroticism of Michael Field's depiction of Christ. Eventually, Cooper moves from worshipping to identifying with religious martyrs as her illness takes hold, finding in Christ's suffering an eroticized and aestheticized embodiment of the pain she was herself experiencing.

Michael Field: Decadent Moderns moves away from a strictly "British" literary tradition in Michael Field's aesthetics to an engagement with cosmopolitan thinking and other European literary traditions. Leire Barrera-Medrano's chapter shows that the Michael Field partners were indebted to Spanish mystic poetry, represented by St. John of the Cross and St. Teresa of Avila. Barrera-Medrano suggests that Spanish mystic writers' imagery often connected sacred and profane love in ways that expressed an entwined sensuality and spirituality. This was inflected with a suggestive homoeroticism that was inspiring to both Bradley and Cooper and to their friend, the priest John Gray, who first introduced them to the writings of St. John of the Cross. Through readings of *Mystic Trees* (mostly authored by Bradley), Barrera-Medrano demonstrates that Bradley was influenced not only by the imagery but also by the forms of Spanish mystic poetry (such as the five-line stanza, *quintilla*). Michael Field found even greater inspiration in the figure of St. Teresa, whose pierced heart—or "female-male wound"—captured their own sense of sexual ambiguity and sensual response to religious ecstasy. Barrera-Medrano concludes by arguing that Michael Field's work entwines aestheticism, modernism, and Catholicism and suggests that their engagement should be read alongside the usage of the Spanish mystics by modernists like T. S. Eliot, Ezra Pound, and Gertrude Stein.[66]

This links to our endeavor in this volume to expand the time frame for Michael Field's work, contextualizing their writings in the first two decades of the twentieth century rather than just the last decades of the nineteenth century. In her chapter, Kristin Mahoney highlights Michael Field's connections with the controversial artist Eric Gill, usually conceived as a "modernist" figure. Beginning with Michael Field's letter to Gill regarding a gift of his *Madonna and Child* statuette (1912–13), Mahoney explores the links between these figures, including their mutual friendships with William Rothenstein, Marc-André Raffalovich, John Gray, and Vincent McNabb, a priest who heard both Bradley's and Gill's confessions and wrote an introduction to Michael Field's posthumous collection of poetry *The Wattlefold* (1930). Mahoney speculates that Gill may have recognized within this volume a vision of queer Catholic kinship that mirrored his own sexually dissident practices. Mahoney meditates upon the connections between Michael Field and Gill to show the rich afterlife of aestheticism in the modernist period.

Finally, Sarah Kersh's chapter explores one of Michael Field's most unusual symbols for desire and faith: their dog *Whym Chow*, eulogized in the posthumous volume *Whym Chow, Flame of Love* (1914). Kersh discusses these complex poems as engaging with long-standing poetic traditions of the elegy and the amatory sonnet sequence, using Chow as a complex metonymic figure for both desire and grief, unity and separation. Comparing the Whym Chow poems with Elizabeth Barrett Browning's *Sonnets from the Portuguese* (1850), Kersh shows how Michael Field's poems radically break down the I/thy binary of the love sonnet, in the process exploding the sonnet form itself, predicated on the division between self/other. In the poems to Whym Chow, marriage or "two-ness," unity (as "Michael Field"), and the Holy Trinity are all invoked, and the poems ultimately encapsulate the radical slippiness of Michael Field's lyric positioning, seen throughout their oeuvre as a whole.

From the immateriality of perfume as decadent sensoria to the materiality of the book as an art object, Michael Field emerges in this book as a writer whose aesthetics radiate in our cultural moment, illuminating diverse areas of current scholarship. Bradley and Cooper's engagement with a wide variety of fields continues to resonate today, when divisions between "art" and "science" are increasingly broken down, and conversations between disciplines are encouraged. Michael Field had interesting things to say about a dizzying variety of subjects; their writings illuminate diverse areas of inquiry, from ecology to theology. In this sense, their work reflects our own contemporary aspirations to a broad perspective on the world. *Michael Field: Decadent Moderns* highlights the range and multidisciplinarity of Michael Field's aesthetics. These essays effectively confirm a new phase in Michael Field's scholarship, a phase that is not only challenging traditional boundaries between fin-de-siècle and modernist studies but also firmly connecting Michael Field to other disciplines and to our own cultural moment.

Notes

Epigraphs: Michael Field, "Works and Days," BL Add MS 46780, fol. 228v (October 12, 1892) [K.B.]. Michael Field, "Works and Days," BL Add MS 46781, fols. 104r–v (December 31, 1893) [E.C.].

1. Marshal Berman, *All That Is Solid Melts into Air: The Experience of Modernity* (London: Verso, 1983), 15.

2. Regenia Gagnier, *Individualism, Decadence and Globalization: On the Relationship of Part to Whole, 1859–1920* (Basingstoke, UK: Palgrave Macmillan, 2010), 4.

3. Michael Field, "Works and Days," BL Add MS 46779, fol. 24r (March 6, 1891) [K.B.].

4. Katharine Bradley writes thus about *Sight and Song* (1892): "We have written the queerest little book in the world. Our teeth chatter with fear." See Michael Field, "Works and Days," BL Add MS 46780, fol. 89v (May 19, 1892) [K.B.].

5. Mary Berenson, *A Self-Portrait from Her Diaries and Letters* (New York: Norton, 1893), 53.

6. Emma Donoghue, *We Are Michael Field* (London: Bello, 2014), 8.

7. Michael Field, "Works and Days," BL Add MS 46779, fol. 15r (February 13, 1891) [K.B.].

8. "Introduction," in *Michael Field, the Poet: Published and Manuscript Materials,* ed. Marion Thain and Ana Parejo Vadillo (Peterborough, Ontario: Broadview, 2009), 34.

9. Mary Sturgeon, *Michael Field* (London: Harrap, 1922), 20, 21.

10. John Ruskin to Bradley, December 30, 1877, in Thain and Vadillo, *Michael Field, the Poet,* 308.

11. Yopie Prins, "Greek Maenads, Victorian Spinsters," in *Victorian Sexual Dissidence,* ed. Richard Dellamora (Chicago: Chicago University Press, 1999), 55.

12. Bradley to John Gray (1907), qtd. in Marion Thain, *Michael Field: Poetry, Aestheticism and the Fin de Siècle* (Cambridge: Cambridge University Press, 2007), 58.

13. K.B. to E.C., April 13, 1885, in Thain and Vadillo, *Michael Field, the Poet,* 300.

14. E.C. to K.B., April 1885, in Thain and Vadillo, *Michael Field, the Poet,* 300. Pussie (or Persian Puss) is one of Edith Cooper's many nicknames. She refers to herself in third person here.

15. K.B. to E.C., April 1885, in Thain and Vadillo, *Michael Field, the Poet,* 303.

16. "Review of *Bellerophôn,*" *Academy* (September 10, 1881): 196.

17. T. W. Higginson, "Women and Men: Women Laureates," *Harper's Bazaar* (June 17, 1893); see Thain and Vadillo, *Michael Field, the Poet,* 363–67.

18. "Review of *Callirrhoë: Fair Rosamund,*" *Athenæum* (July 5, 1884): 24–26.

19. George Bernard Shaw, "Recent Poetry," in *Bernard Shaw's Book Reviews,* vol. 2: *1884–1950,* ed. Brian Tyson (University Park: Pennsylvania State University Press, 1996), 22–28.

20. Robert Browning to E.C., May 28, 1884, in Thain and Vadillo, *Michael Field, the Poet,* 309.

21. E.C. to R.B., May 30, 1884, in Thain and Vadillo, *Michael Field, The Poet,* 310.

22. K.B. to R.B., November 23, 1884, in Thain and Vadillo, *Michael Field, the Poet,* 311.

23. See Yopie Prins, *Victorian Sappho* (Princeton, NJ: Princeton University Press, 1999), 74–111.

24. John Miller Gray, *Academy* (June 8, 1889): 359–61.

25. Arthur Symons to K.B. See Ana Parejo Vadillo, "Walter Pater and Michael Field: The Correspondence, with Other Unpublished Manuscript Materials," *Pater Newsletter* 65 (2014): 35.

26. Vadillo, "Walter Pater and Michael Field," 35.

27. Wilde, quoted in Sharon Bickle, "Michael Field: Fifty Books from Fifty Years," *Monash University Library Exhibition,* http://www.lib.monash.edu.au/exhibitions/fifty-books-fifty-years/virtual-exhibition/photos/photo4.html, accessed May 12, 2016.

28. Michael Field, "Works and Days," BL Add MS 46780, fol. 47r (February 14, 1892) [E.C.]. For more on Pater's influence on Michael Field, see Ana Parejo Vadillo, "*Sight and Song:* Transparent Translations and a Manifesto for the Observer," *Victorian Poetry* 38, no. 1 (2000): 15–34.

29. Yeats, *The Bookman* (July 1892), in *Michael Field, the Poet,* 363.

30. Michael Field, "Works and Days," BL Add MS 46779, fols. 98r–99r (August 30, 1891) [E.C.].

31. Martha Vicinus, "The Adolescent Boy: Fin de Siècle Femme Fatale?" *Journal of the History of Sexuality* 5, no. 1 (1994): 91.

32. Sarah Parker, *The Lesbian Muse and Poetic Identity, 1889–1930* (London: Pickering and Chatto, 2013), 43–70, and Parker's chapter in this volume.

33. Augusta Webster, "*Underneath the Bough: A Book of Verse*. By Michael Field," *Athenæum* (September 9, 1893). Rpt. in *Michael Field, the Poet*, 367–69.

34. See Bristow's chapter in the present volume.

35. The play was performed by the New York Airmid Theatre group in 2008.

36. Michael Field, "Works and Days," BL Add MS 46781, fols. 86v–87r (October 28, 1893) [E.C.].

37. Displayed at the exhibition *Queer British Art 1861–1967*, Tate Britain, 2017.

38. Quoted in Sturgeon, *Michael Field*, 52.

39. Donoghue, *We Are Michael Field*, 103.

40. Michael Field, "Works and Days," BL Add MS 46795, fol. 14r (January 28, 1906) [E.C.].

41. See Ruth Vanita, *Sappho and the Virgin Mary: Same-Sex Love and the English Literary Imagination* (New York: Columbia University Press, 1996).

42. Michael Field, "Works and Days," January 26, 1893 [E.C.], in *Michael Field, the Poet*, 258.

43. George Meredith, "To Michael Field, November 16, 1899" in *The Collected Letters*, 1341.

44. "Gibbon and Water," *Academy* (July 30, 1898), 103.

45. Michael Field, "Works and Days," BL Add MS 46782, fol. 38r (April 17, 1894) [E.C.].

46. Michael Field, "Works and Days," BL Add MS 46782, fol. 95r (July 17, 1894) [E.C.].

47. Shane Leslie, "Works and Days," *Times Literary Supplement* (February 15, 1934): 105.

48. *Cambridge History of English Literature*, vol. 13: *The Nineteenth Century*, ed. A. W. Ward and A. R. Waller (Cambridge: Cambridge University Press, 1916), 181.

49. Margaret Sackville, *A Book of Verse by Living Women* (London: Herbert & Daniel, 1910), xx.

50. See Michael Field, *Deirdre; A Question of Memory; Ras Byzance* (London: Poetry Bookshop, 1918); Michael Field, *In the Name of Time* (London: Poetry Bookshop, 1919); and Anon. [by Michael Field], *Above Mount Alverna, Iphigenia in Arsacia, The Assumption* (Oxford: Basil Blackwell, 1930). Michael Field, *Works and Days: From the Journal of Michael Field*, ed. T. and D. C. Sturge Moore; introduced by William Rothenstein (London: John Murray, 1933).

51. Robert Lynd, "Eminent Victorians through the Eyes of Two Women," *News Chronicle* (1933).

52. Ursula Bridge, "The Diary of Michael Field: A Biographical Study of a Forgotten Poet" [six parts; incomplete] [1966], MS. Eng. misc. d. 983 and d. 984. Bodleian Library, University of Oxford.

53. Henri Locard, "Works and Days: The Journals of 'Michael Field,'" *Journal of the Eighteen Nineties Society* 10 (1979): 1–9; Kenneth R. Ireland, "*Sight and Song*: A Study of the Interrelations between Painting and Poetry," *Victorian Poetry* 15, no. 1 (1977): 9–20; Jan

MacDonald, "'Disillusioned Bards and Despised Bohemians': Michael Field's *A Question of Memory* at the Independent Theatre Society," *Theatre Notebook: A Journal of the History and Technique of the British Theatre* 31, no. 2 (1975): 18–29.

54. See Selected Bibliography for references to these works.

55. These included *Shorter Shirazad: 101 Poems of Michael Field* (1999); *Uncertain Rain: Sundry Spells of Michael Field* (2003); and *Binary Star: Leaves from the Journal and Letters of Michael Field 1846–1914* (2006).

56. Now merged successfully with *Latchkey*.

57. Marion Thain, "Perspective: Digitizing the Diary—Experiments in Queer Encoding (A Retrospective and a Prospective)," *Journal of Victorian Culture* 21, no. 2 (2016): 226–41. The "Online Diaries of 'Michael Field'" can be accessed at http://tundra. csd.sc.edu/vllc/field_diaries. See Rob Gallagher and Ana Parejo Vadillo, "Animating *Sight and Song*: A Meditation on Identity, Fair Use, and Collaboration," *19: Interdisciplinary Studies in the Long Nineteenth Century* 21 (2015), December 10, 2015, https://www.19.bbk. ac.uk/articles/10.16995/ntn.754/.

58. As seen in the recent conference, Aestheticism and Decadence in the Age of Modernism: 1895 to 1945 (Senate House, London, April 2015), and recent publications such as Vincent Sherry, *Modernism and the Reinvention of Decadence* (Cambridge: Cambridge University Press, 2014) and Kristen Mahoney, *Literature and the Politics of Post-Victorian Decadence* (Cambridge: Cambridge University Press, 2015).

59. See Kate Thomas's "Vegetable Love: Michael Field's Queer Ecology," chapter 1 in the present volume.

60. Thomas, "Vegetable Love."

61. Catherine Maxwell, "Michael Field's Fragrant Imagination," chapter 6 in the present volume.

62. Maxwell, "Fragrant Imagination."

63. Joseph Bristow, "Michael Field: In Their Time and Ours," *Tulsa Studies in Women's Literature* 29, no.1 (Spring 2010): 160.

64. Michael Field, *Attila, My Attila! A Play* (London: Elkin Mathews, 1896), vi.

65. Alex Murray, "'Profane Travelers': Michael Field, Cornwall, and Modern Tourism," chapter 7 in the present volume.

66. Leire Barrera-Medrano, "'St. Theresa, I Call on You to Help': Michael Field and Spanish Mysticism," chapter 9 in the present volume.

ONE

Vegetable Love

Michael Field's Queer Ecology

Kate Thomas

> The love that breeds
> In my heart for thee!
> As the iris is full, brimful of seeds,
> And all that it flowered for among the reeds
> Is packed in a thousand vermilion-beads
> That push, and riot, and squeeze, and clip,
> Till they burst the sides of the silver scrip ...
> —Michael Field, "Unbosoming" (1893)

IN HER 1928 NOVEL *ORLANDO*, VIRGINIA WOOLF CREDITS time for "mak[ing] animals and vegetables bloom and fade with amazing punctuality," before observing that it has no such effect on people: "The mind of man, moreover, works with equal strangeness upon the body of time. An hour, once it lodges in the queer element of the human spirit, may be stretched to fifty or a hundred times its clock length; on the other hand, an hour may be accurately represented on the timepiece of the mind by one second."[1] Human lives, Woolf theorizes in her "biography" of a poet whose adventures span more than three hundred years, do not always fit into standardized temporal schemas. Animals and plants are regulated by breeding seasons. But the "queer element" of the human mind can syncopate the simple metronomics of clock time and evade the scheduling of the natural world. The contradistinction of queer time with reproductive time has been of recent interest to queer theorists, who have invested in pushing against what Elizabeth Freeman calls "chrononormativity,"[2] and whose work focuses on agents who resist the temporal regulation of lives and desires. Much of this work has centered on the child, and, in some cases, the animal.[3] But in this chapter, I would like to turn instead to Woolf's blooming and fading vegetable, using the fin-de-siècle poets and lovers Michael Field to ask whether salad is indeed punctual and whether queer time is indeed pitted against vegetable time.

Back in 2010, Tim Morton began to answer the conundrum, "Ecological criticism and queer theory seem incompatible," he writes, "but if they met, there would be a fantastic explosion."[4] Morton's point is that they have, of course, already met and that this explosion looked something like the Big Bang. Leading us back through Charles Darwin's prose, Morton shows that "The story of evolution is a story of diverse life-forms cooperating with one another," that the natural world is built on "deviations," and that "biodiversity and gender diversity are deeply intertwined."[5] Morton promises that queer ecology will "worry away at the human-nonhuman boundary,"[6] and indeed this has already come to pass. Since Morton published his article, posthumanist work on what philosopher Michael Marder calls "plant-thinking" has done much to help us understand plant life as more than inertly scenic or mindlessly growthful.[7] Marder complicates Woolf's notion that vegetables' relationship to time is one of nonqueer obeisance.[8] Marder acknowledges that plants are directed by temporalities such as "seasonal variation" that "imposes cyclical and iterable existence on perennial plants and spells out the finitude of the annual ones," but he counters the coding of this relationship as "unfreedom."[9] He writes: "Not only does this view disregard the ontic exuberance and uncontrollable efflorescence of vegetal life, but it also ignores this life's ontological potentialities, still working themselves out in various guises as animals and human beings—the variations that free it to be otherwise than it is."[10] Marder recommends that we resurrect the ancient idea of a "vegetal soul" to resist modern agriculture's wholesale efforts to regulate plant life, reducing it to calories or combustibles, and to explore instead the possibilities of plants' "fugal, fugitive mode of being."[11]

Although this "fugal and fugitive mode" expressed by plants might sound queer (polymorphous, divergent), the queer protagonist, particularly the fin-de-siècle queer protagonist, is most usually posed "against nature."[12] *Against Nature* is, after all, the English title often given to the most decadent of novels, Joris-Karl Huysmans's À *rebours* (1884), in which a tortoise is fatally bejeweled and a feast is prepared from foods that are black in hue. Think, too, of Oscar Wilde's unnaturally green carnation that he wore in his buttonhole and of Vivian's complaints in *The Decay of Lying* (1891) about the discomfort of reclining on grass: "Why, even Morris's poorest workman could make you a more comfortable seat than the whole of Nature can," he moans.[13] Wilde waves aside the live, the damp, the lush in favor of artifice, and we obediently look back at that generation and see crops and queers at odds with each other.[14]

Michael Field, however, disagreed. In 1894, we find this journal entry: "Then my Love takes me to her Oatfield, where the sheaves rest. . . . Nature, in spite of Oscar, has made a seat that is perfect—a group of oat-sheaves—it has spring & curve fit for any royal race."[15] Field likes fields. Nature, in this case edible and vegetable nature, upholds and even thrones them, making a sexy seat for their love. When seated upon this divan of harvested oats, the two women are furnished with a progenerative and inheriting, even conquering future—a "royal race." The Fields have read *The Decay of Lying*, and both this journal entry and their work as a whole counter Wilde's disdain for all things rural, proffering a wholly more botanical queer aestheticism. The botanical was so expressive for these poets that it became for them, as Chris White notes, a "meta-discourse."[16] The titles of their collections of poetry speak it loud: *Underneath the Bough; Wild Honey from Various Thyme; Mystic Trees; Noontide Branches; The Race of Leaves.* And their writing is verdant with trembling aspen leaflets, sweet basil, hops, violet banks, roses, irises, cowslips, hazels and apples, passionflowers and bees, hay making, holly hedges, azaleas, amaranth, lilies and cherries and cyclamen. Across the arc of their writing lives, the hawthorn of an English hedgerow mingles with the laurels of Olympus and the pomegranates of underworlds, with druidical twists of ivy, and the high-church fragrance of myrrh: throughout Michael Field's various incarnations—mythological, pagan, Catholic—the sensuous and transformational capacities of plant life remain the root mass of their own peculiar and peculiarly queer temporality.

So much did Bradley and Cooper identify with plant life that by 1881 they had derived from it an insignia that they described as the "emblem of our united life," and—in a neat inversion of Wilde's preference for furniture over vegetation—they had this botanical emblem carved into their mantelshelf and their study chair.[17] This emblem was the bramble-bough. A circular woodblock imprint of this image would end up on the title pages of three of their books all told: *Brutus Ultor* (1886), *Canute the Great/The Cup of Water* (1887), and *Sight and*

Song (1892).[18] When *Brutus Ultor* was published, Cooper sent a copy to Robert Browning, with these accompanying remarks:

> We have worked equally at it. My song-mate has entirely shaped Lucretia, I, mostly Brutus. You may like to know that she made the bramble-bough the emblem of our united life: that is why it is drawn on the cover. She wrote:
>
> > My Poet-bride, sweet Song-mate, do I doom
> > > Thy youth to age's dull society?
> > On the same bramble-bough the pale-cheek'd Bloom
> > Fondling by purple berry loves to lie;
> > Fed by one sap & sunshine, there is room
> > For fruit & flower in living unity.
>
> When we adopted this as our symbol, my father carved the berried and flowery sprays over our mantelshelf and we have them on our study-chair also.[19]

Figure 1.1. The "bramble-bough" woodblock, from the title page of *Sight and Sound* (1892).

Crucially, the bramble is figured in both fruit and flower. Together, the emblem and the letter are an exercise in intergenerationality. We should first remember that when Cooper is writing to Browning, she is writing to the poet whom the couple nicknamed, reverently, "the Old Gentleman."[20] If this positions Browning as an ancestor figure, that paternalism is redoubled when we learn that the emblem is carved into the Fields' furniture by Cooper's father. Then, most directly, Bradley's enclosed poem addresses the sixteen-year age difference between her and Cooper, wondering if it is—onomatopoetically— dooming and dulling.[21] She answers her own question empirically, via the evidence of the hedgerow, which allows her to confidently figure the cross-temporalization of their partnership as not deadening but sensuous: the pale and the purple lie together and the berry and the bloom "fondle" each other across both a line break and a generational divide. And, appropriate to lovers who were also aunt and niece, it is an incestuous image; the same root produces the erotic touching of blossom and fruit. It is also a pedophilic image; it recalls that Aunt Katharine actually cradled her niece Edith in her arms, first as a baby and then as a grown lover. And the erotics—of a berry that might stain a blossom—is an erotics of sweet ruination of a youth by an elder. In another description of the carvings, made in a footnote to the poem, Bradley lingers on the seductions that happen across partition: "berry & blossom are seen either poutingly apart, or bending toward and beckoning to each other; at the last close—flower & fruit in perfect unison."[22] The intervals between the song mates become, in the end, one harmonious sound. This "perfect unison" resonates with the hailing of the lover as a "poet-bride" to become a marital image, but any metaphysicality is trumped by the trollopy fleshliness of "pouting, bending and beckoning."

The poem's focus on the blossom-touching-berry or the berry-touching-blossom allows both fruit and flower to be fully sensual and fully realized. It refuses the progressivism of fruit-follows-flower and also the moral service to which metaphors of fruitfulness can easily be pressed. We find many examples of what we might call the "moral botanical" in the work of Christina Rossetti, a poet whom the Fields read and on whom they published. Bradley's worries about "dooming" Cooper's "bloom" half recalls one of Rossetti's poems about blasted blooms. "Buds and Babies" is a devastatingly slight, two-stanza verse:

> A million buds are born that never blow,
>> That sweet with promise lift a pretty head
>> To blush and wither on a barren bed
>> And leave no fruit to show.

> Sweet, unfulfilled. Yet have I understood
> One joy, by their fragility made plain:
> Nothing was ever beautiful in vain,
> Or all in vain was good.[23]

Here, Rossetti not only holds tight to a progressive blossom-then-fruit model but nips a million blossoms in the bud. I cite this poem as contrast, to show just how defiantly sensuous Michael Field's take on the botanical is. Rossetti's perspective, on the other hand, is wide angled and synoptic: "A million buds" never turn to fruit, she notes, but instead "blush and wither on a barren bed." The poem takes a redemptive turn; the blossoms may be "unfulfilled," but they prompt a universalizing ("nothing") and transtemporal ("ever") understanding: "Nothing was ever beautiful in vain, / Or all in vain was good." It is a sentiment that Michael Field directly decried. In 1895, a year after Christina Rossetti died, Michael Field published a sonnet in her memory, and it displays impatience with Rossetti's embrace of fruitlessness.[24] The poem laments less her death and more her living death, regretting that Rossetti "buried" herself while alive.[25] And the experience that her life spent in a "tomb" denied her is specifically figured as pastoral. Rossetti is not to be found, the sonnet opens, "'mid the trees."[26] She cannot, with the happy Syrinx, "murmur with the wind," nor find herself, like Daphne, "thrilled through all her mystic bloom." For Michael Field, winds and foliage are partners in and amplifiers to sensuality—murmuring, thrilling—and the poet has a right to "slip into the universe" like it is a vast sensorium. This is an elegy not for the renunciation of physical love ("Fleeing from love") but for Rossetti's failure to flee *into* the sensuousness of the "leafy."

Others were troubled by the way Rossetti herself disavowed nature as collaborator, Muse, or inspiration.[27] Scottish writer and member of the Rossetti literary group, William Sharp, recalled a social evening in Bloomsbury during which Rossetti was harangued by a woman who was taken aback that Rossetti did not find the country more poetic than the city: "But now let me ask," the woman persisted, "do not you yourself find your best inspiration in the country?"[28] Rossetti apparently replied that "inspiration" was an "inapposite" term, to be used only in its "literal and sacred sense," and continued, "I don't derive anything from the country at first hand! Why, my knowledge of what is called nature is that of the town sparrow, or, at most, that of the pigeon which makes an excursion occasionally from its home in Regent's Park or Kensington Gardens."[29] Rossetti's levity regarding day-tripping urban birds is half appreciated by Sharp, but it is also more than half deflated: he might admire how deftly she could deflect an annoying interlocutor, but he also collapses Rossetti herself into the natural world she says she scarcely knows. When Rossetti speaks, he writes, "the words came away from the mouth and lips as cleanly as a trill from a bird."[30]

Despite having showcased Rossetti's spirited shunning of the countryside, Sharp's portrait of her joins the multitude that figure her as a child of nature, an artless creature from whom poetry simply sings out. The unnamed woman wishes Rossetti to find inspiration in nature, then Sharp denigrates her very intellect as natural. They both have Rossetti completely wrong: in her oeuvre, she passes through the natural world to turn it instantly to symbol. Nineteenth-century poet and critic Theodore Watts-Dunton, who had been trained as a naturalist, noticed that Rossetti's relationship to nature was distinctly en passant. Writing in the *Athenæum* in 1895, he argues, "Her intimacy with Nature—of a different kind altogether from that of Wordsworth and Tennyson—was of the kind that I have described on a previous occasion as Sufeyistic: she loved the beauty of this world, but not entirely for itself; she loved it on account of its symbols of another world beyond."[31] An excellent example of the theological schematics to which Rossetti presses all things natural is her 1881 publication *Called to Be Saints*. A devotional reading book for saints' days, it was originally to be titled "Young Plants and Reading Corners." Each entry is headed by a natural emblem, many of them plants, and in the introductory "Key to My Book," Rossetti notes, "I think the Gospel records more lessons drawn by our Master from a seed or a plant than from a pearl. . . . Let us learn something from the grass of the field which God clothes."[32]

Rossetti's natural imagery is not rooted in a lush and present world but is always en route to a spiritual world, a world deferred. A poem that was subsequently titled "Looking Forward," but which Rossetti originally used without title as the work of her heroine in her story "Maude" (1849), envisions a kind of posthumous fecundity. The speaker in the poem is dying and—we might say—taking leave of her friends. She asks for their patience, "For soon, where you shall dance and sing and smile. / My quickened dust may blossom at your feet."[33] The word "quickened" sets up a metaphor of maternal reproduction that will crescendo in the last line and is compounded by knowing that the manuscript of this first-person poem is in Rossetti's mother's hand; it seems that Rossetti composed and dictated these lines, with her mother as amanuensis, when Rossetti was believed to be dying.[34] The narrator comforts herself: "I may yet live and grow green, / That leaves may yet spring from the withered root, / And buds and flowers and berries half unseen." She instructs those who happen to "muse on the past" to then conclude, "Poor child, she has her wish at last; / Barren through life, but in death bearing fruit." To a degree, this poem's temporality falls in line with what I have elsewhere described as Michael Field's proleptics—like them, Rossetti imagines a fruitful future, a posthumous fulfill-ment of her wishes.[35] But for Rossetti, the "buds and flowers and berries" seem to remain always imminent, never to be fully realized, only to be "half unseen." Not even half seen, but rather half *unseen*—deferral here becomes deferral doubled.[36] And Rossetti's leaves, roots, buds, flowers, and berries are cursory descriptors—unadorned, signifying rebirth, but themselves barely living. As Angela Leighton observes, "These are haunted poems, in which the chilly, fu-turistic landscapes of the grave suggest a state of mind removed from the grip of immediate experience."[37] And indeed, Rossetti takes a steely delight in turning away from a chamber made "sweet with flowers and leaves" ("A Pause") and rel-ishes a deathscape with no ebbs, no flows, "No bud-time no leaf-falling," no rip-ples of waves, beats of wings, nor "pulse of life" ("Cobwebs").[38] In a poem titled "Introspective," Rossetti refuses to cry out over physical pain and stands proud, "like a blasted tree / ... On my boughs neither leaf nor fruit."[39] She renounces reproduction with vigor.

Plant Life Black, Not Green

Michael Field had some attraction to but ultimately precious little patience for any kind of renunciation. Nor were they like the unnamed woman who wished Rossetti to turn to nature for the abstract purpose of inspiration. Rather, they found in the garden a lush and present world, a riot of intertwinings that undid the forward drive of human "progress," undid narrative thought itself, and cer-tainly undid mystical afterlives in favor of a cyclical, fleshy foreverness. Consider this diary entry, describing the time they took themselves to the Convent of the Cenacle for a religious retreat but could not stand the restrictions on speech:

> We have just been out into the Garden. The fearful roar of the
> trams has made us hysterical, & the restraint of the speechless
> breakfast is such that deep calls to deep in us to utter language—&
> we go out to cry to the flowers. The abounding charity I feel to the
> artichoke-flowerhead! The love with wh[ich] I slide kisses toward
> a mouthly rose. The intimacies we encourage with that negress-
> creature, the polished beet. How we hail the rockets shot up by
> salsify! In the garden we let out the roar within us, by degrees; so
> that the whole convent does not hear the earthquakes.[40]

So much for retreat. They are tormented by both street noise and sisterly si-lence, by both the clatter of a forward-hurtling world and the wordless antique cloistering. From these pressures they retreat in their own style, which means becoming one with the plant life. What happens in that garden is hilariously

Bacchanalian, orgiastic.[41] They swoon over the yonic furls of flowers, salute the thrustings of phallic vegetables, and only pace out their orgasmic hollerings in case they alarm the nuns. This is a vegetable interval. I borrow and modify the term, of course, from Kathryn Bond Stockton, who has written of the prevalence of what she calls the "animal interval" in queer coming-of-age stories.[42] Stockton's model theorizes how the queer subject—not allowed to grow up—identifies sideways through the animal. Michael Field, whose devotion to their dog Whym Chow had a distinctly erotic tenor, knew a good deal about animal intermediaries, but they also felt sideways via the botanical world.[43] They "cry out" not to each other exactly, but "to the flowers." Desire and ecstasy are experienced through plants that are personified and made sensual; they have heads and mouths and skin.

But what of this dark-skinned beet, the "negress-creature"? The image appears abruptly and has the potential to be confounding. The other scholar to engage this diary passage is Chris White, writing back in 1996. She reads the passage for its eroticism, especially regarding the rose, but when she transcribes the passage she cannot read the word "negress" and in its place writes "[one word indecipherable.]"[44] That I could read the word in manuscript is perhaps because I was made to take a graduate class in bibliography, or—more likely—nearly twenty years of intervening scholarship have made late nineteenth-century racial schema literally more "cipherable." We have benefited from the scholarship that has, as Jennifer DeVere Brody puts it, "mine[d] the intersection of the supposedly distinct fields of Victorian studies and African American studies."[45] And one of the things this scholarship has revealed is that nineteenth-century white Britons felt, as Gretchen Gerzina writes, that they "had defined, had described, and knew black people."[46] So when Michael Field write of "encouraging intimacies" with a "negress beet," their fantasy of cross-racial, cross-species desire draws upon a long British culture of imitating and appropriating black bodies. But for what feeling, precisely, do they turn to the "negress"? On a different occasion, Michael Field write of feeling like a "negro" and then translate what they mean; they use "negro" as a byword for abjection, for when they feel others have stamped them with "inviolable inferiority."[47] In this instance, invoking the "negro" is what might be called affective blackface, donned when the white women feel publicly ridiculed for the limitations of their gender. But the "negress-creature" does slightly different—though equally racist—affective work in the convent vegetable patch. Within this cloistered garden, the black woman is used not to explicate the bad feelings that misogyny engenders in white women but rather to usher them through blackness to desire. The beet, which is the only vegetable to be personified and gendered, allows same-sex desire into the garden. The beet's femaleness is important, but in marking the beet as a *black* woman, the beet's personification is usefully, to Field, limited. Blackness, to borrow the words of Homi K. Bhabha, is the sign of "almost the same but not quite. . . . Almost the same but not white," and that *almost* is essential to Field's poetics of vegetable love.[48] The poets do not want to turn the garden into a metaphor for love, nor an allegory nor a symbol of it. They need the beet to be woman and animal and vegetable together, metonymical of each but restricted to none of the above. Black femaleness, because of its "inviolable inferiority," its immediate connection to "creature," allows Michael Field to create a complex thicket of objectification connecting the human via the animal to the vegetable, into which the white human can somewhat disappear and out of which the vegetable possibilities of white lesbian love can somewhat emerge. Raced as black, gendered female and sliding between human, animal, and vegetable, the beet allows white same-sex desire to slip into this scene through the very profusion and proliferation of its objectification. Fetishizing the blackness of this plant life is a way for Michael Field to release restraints on their desires.[49]

To examine a contemporaneous white lesbian deployment of a black, desiring body, we can turn to Gertrude Stein's story, "Melanctha, or, Each One as She May," which was published just one year before the Field diary entry. Elizabeth Freeman has opened up the queer—and somewhat botanical—chronicities of Stein's tale.[50] Melanctha is a mixed-race bisexual woman, and her name, Freeman hypothesizes, compounds the Greek words for "black" and "flower."[51] Stein's "black flower" is, in Freeman's reading, a character who is "chronic" in the sense of stubbornly resisting "biopower's regulation of life."[52] For Freeman, Melanctha stands against some of the more inflexible dichotomies that have dominated queer and critical theory; Melanctha is neither passive nor active, neither progressive nor regressive. Her blackness serves Stein similarly to the way the beet's blackness serves Field: it insists upon the eruption of queerness from a place of nonprogress, of vegetative, iterative, chronic being. Freeman moves calmly away from ideology to a critique of Stein's racial schema. "It goes without saying," she writes, "that 'Melanctha' contains all kinds of racist imagery."[53] She asks what nonetheless can be found in the text's sedimentations and nonprogressiveness—a nonprogressiveness that is in part manifested through the "repetitions without much difference" of racism.[54]

The crux of Freeman's method is to extricate queer theory from "[a] certain conflation of the radical and the progressive-transgressive."[55] That is to say, she pulls against the way that queer theory has privileged antinormativity and celebrated eruption and transgression as a way of producing new futures. Queer studies have sometimes also made the mistake of expecting queer writers to be always radical, always resistive, and then felt betrayed, or found them illegible, when they are not.[56] Not all queer subjects are inclined to buck normalcy. Not all queer subjects are willing or, indeed, able to do so. Freeman draws on recent scholarly intersections between queer theory and disability studies to further illuminate how the queer subject producing these eruptions is presumptively *able*.[57] Antinormative queer politics and its practices (coming out, acting up, etc.) rely on the body's capacity to perform and value, above all, norm-disrupting agency. As Michael Warner complained in *The Trouble with Normal* (1999), the desire to be normal might lead us to "imagine . . . we somehow belong to the wider world, even as we stay home and make dinner for our boyfriends."[58] This is an anorectic stance. Warner characterizes consumption (commodity consumption, conflated with the consumption of boyfriend-made dinners) as inherently solipsistic, political couch-potato-ism. How else can we belong to a "wider world"? One answer might be by dancing around with potatoes. Having a moment of being, as Woolf would term it, in that potato patch. Communing with the potato teaches us that we are already part of a wider world. The Fields reject both the world that only pretends to be wide by being filled with bustling trams *and* the world that renounces width and bustle—the convent—and they turn instead to a deep and earthy world in the form of growing, fruiting vegetables. That they mark this moment as both female and lesbian via the black female body should not bump us out of the reading into a moment of scholarly regret; rather, it should shock us into recognizing the passion of their antiprogressive call to love vegetables, to vegetable love.

Berries, Blossoms, and Becoming

The temporality that Michael Field finds in that garden is neither scheduled (trams) nor in abeyance (cloistered time out). It is, instead, both riotous and producing a sense of everything in unison. This returns us to the figuration of botanical simultaneity in Field's bramble-bough insignia. When I first saw this image, I thought it was the equivalent of Wilde's green carnation. I assumed that Bradley and Cooper had queered the plant, making the flower and fruit coincident through artifice: first comes the flower, which then produces the fruit, I thought. But on a recent blackberrying adventure, I found myself buried somewhat uncomfortably in the brambles, reaching for a clutch of berries, when I saw it: the blossom *beside* the fruit. If a plant is, as Woolf imagined, obedient to seasons, why would it not produce flowers in a flowering season and then fruit in a fruiting season? I turned to a botanist colleague of mine, Ted Wong, for answers. He explained that a plant is a highly plural being that is built to deal with microenvironment variables and unpredictability: "The metameric (modular) nature of plant architecture means that whole-plant phenology is made of thousands of discrete events.... [T]he simultaneous appearance on one plant of more than one reproductive stage is a kind of phenological bet-hedging."[59] A plant is not blindly obeisant to seasons but can respond selectively and variously to seasonal prompts. When Bradley and Cooper figured the bramble-bough in flower and fruit, in other words, they were not queering anything, but they were noticing the already queerness of the vegetal. Botanical growth is a model of growth that is not simply progressive, linear, and directly mapped onto season. Plants do not grow up as much as just grow; they exist in a state of growing.

"Becoming" has long been a key term in queer studies: "To be gay is to be in a state of becoming," declared Michel Foucault in 1982.[60] Almost a hundred years earlier, Michael Field's botanical writings make an intense and intensely queer study of becoming. The moment that Bradley and Cooper's bramble-bough emblem freeze-frames, in which blossom and fruit are coincident with each other, shows full-blown fruitfulness touching immanence. It is thus an image that interrupts associations of fecundity with temporal linearity (first blossom, then fruit) by literally moving our gaze sideways, getting us to notice generational adjacency and simultaneity. The bramble-bough is, in other words, an ebullient deconstruction of "chrononormativity."[61] It is not, however, an image that deconstructs that normativity through importing a "no future" death-drive model but instead does it from noticing carefully the nature of the pulsing vitality that lies within—as it were—the bud, along the bough. Michael Field's journals testify to the attention they pay not only to plants but to the botany—the mode of growth—of plants: in 1892 Cooper writes, "I do not care for my work as I used to do—It does not grow up in me like a quickened seed—it grows from node to node like a yew."[62] Flowers are, of course, a ready lexicon for the nineteenth-century poet,[63] but I am suggesting that the Fields produce an intricate erotics of flower*ing* itself; one that reminds us that the natural world has seasonal polyphonies and matter-of-course polyamories.

Michael Field published one collection of poetry with "bough" in the title: *Underneath the Bough* was issued in three different editions, the first appearing in 1893. Joseph Bristow has detailed how this collection was almost titled "Summer Apples" or "In Winter and Summer."[64] Like the bramble-bough in fruit and flower, both these titles thematize seasons that are hand-in-hand with each other. The title upon which Bradley and Cooper finally settled is taken from Edward FitzGerald's popular translation of the Persian rubai that he titled *The Rubáiyát of Omar Khayyám* (1859). They use the same passage for their epigraph; four lines that rejoice in having "A Book of Verse" underneath a bough, together with "A Jug of Wine, a Loaf of Bread" and "thou."[65] The jug of wine—which is, like the blackberry, "fruit of the vine"—is a definite part of the pleasure: in their journals, the Fields are fabulously scathing about a temperance house, proudly declaring, of their own household, "Here the frank Bacchus lives, & we have honest cheer."[66] The epigraph is, as Marion Thain and Ana Parejo Vadillo deftly put it, "a picnic of sensual delights.[67] Picnic is the right word—the *Rubáiyát* lines portray a kind of sacramental picnic just as the bramble-bough is troped as an elemental picnic—the blossom and fruit are, Cooper writes, "Fed by one sap & sunshine."[68]

Being "fed" by sun-ripened fruits and inhaling deeply the scent of flowers are central to several of the collection's poems, which are about filling up on pleasure and becoming one with a sensual world: "Through hazels and apples" leads my love to the strawberry bed; in "Say if a gallant rose," a rose breaks free of trellising and "Toward me doth sigh her / Perfume, her damask mouth"; in "When cherries are on the bough," the fruit is raised to lips and roses are kissed, and "Cowslip-Gathering" imagines alder boughs being thrilled by cuckoo calls, the hum of bees vibrates first the cherry trees and then the lovers; "Filled us; in one our very being blent."[69] Becoming one is, of course, a central trope for these poets who wrote under a single name. Becoming one *via and with* a sensuous vegetal world is also key. And by this I mean that Michael Field tropes plant life in such a way as to work from inside the becomingness of the plant, experiencing libidinal seasonality and paying botanical attention to the polymorphous desires of plant forms. The way that Michael Field feels through plants sometimes even results in poetry emerging from out of the plant itself. A single quatrain in *Underneath the Bough* titled "An Apple-Flower" is spoken by the blossom:

> I felt my leaves fall free,
> > I felt the wind and sun,
> At my heart a honey-bee:
> > And life was done.[70]

This is the voice of sweet ruination. This poem transforms the routine death of an apple blossom into an orgasmic undoing: the bee embedded and sucking at the center of her produces a *petit morte*. The flower becomes all-sensory ("I felt . . . I felt"), and indeed all-knowing, since this is a postmortem testimony.

Jill R. Ehnenn has written on a very similar poem, "The Bee and the Flower," which Bradley wrote for Cooper's birthday in 1897. Although this version does not personify the blossom, it likewise imagines the physical pleasures of the bee feeding on the flower. Ehnenn writes of the poem's "simple, playful certitude, that the bee and flower will come together as surely as the sun will rise and fall,"[71] and she is right that these ventriloquizations of flora are a way of naturalizing (same-sex) sexual passion. They also display a wonderful libidinal egotism—Michael Field's desire is filled with the strength of the sun—powerful enough to escape the trellis of being human.

Walking in a Flowery Way

In their explorations of the queer sensuous powers of plants, Bradley and Cooper found some comradeship with other fin-de-siècle thinkers. By 1889, Bradley joined the Fellowship of the New Life, which espoused vegetarianism, pacifism, socialism, and alternative modes of sexual intimacy.[72] Lightly mocked by George Bernard Shaw as a movement of those who "wanted to sit among the dandelions,"[73] Bradley herself wrote of how much she relished the opportunity that the Fellowship offered to contemplate flora: "Yesterday I joined the Fellowship of the New Life at Merstham. . . . The scene was significant. . . . [T]he moment was appleflowertime in May. . . . [I]t was good to feel that everyone of that motley group was . . . seeking a 'better' country: and the fair land of buttercups & deep grass yielded new beauty."[74] Although Diana Maltz has described Bradley as a "marginal figure" in this movement,[75] she seems to have responded to the pantheism of the movement, and her membership means she likely read (though never contributed to) the Fellowship journal, first called the *Sower* and later *Seed-Time*. She was also therefore likely aware of the radical politics of one of its founder figures, Edward Carpenter.[76] Carpenter—a back-to-nature commune dweller—was most definitely interested in vegetal intervals. He was a vegetarian, sandal-wearing (it was he who made the fatal mistake of introducing the sandal to Englishmen), homosexual activist. Shaw quickly dubbed him "The Noble Savage,"[77] and Shaw's mockery had cultural precedent. In *Patience* (1881), W. S. Gilbert satirized the overcultivated aesthete who is "content with a vegetable love."[78] He who harbors "An attachment à la Plato for a bashful young potato, or a not-too-French French bean" and who walks a "flowery way," Gilbert's verse proposes, is sexually suspect.[79] *Patience* was the Gilbert and Sullivan production that played a large role in inventing and "canonizing" Oscar Wilde's persona, as Carolyn Williams points out.[80] D'Oyly Carte sent Wilde on a lecture tour of North America so that when the production of *Patience* followed, American audiences would know what was being satirized. Wilde was hired to seed the provinces with knowledge of what a young man who displays "the sentimental passion of a vegetable fashion" was, so that he could then profitably be lampooned. Mocking homosexuality through a vegetal tribute would, almost fifteen years after *Patience*, return to haunt Wilde. On the opening night of *The Importance of Being Earnest*, the Marquess of Queensberry left a bouquet of vegetables at the stage door . . . followed four days later by the infamous calling card, accusing Wilde of being a "Somdomite." Wilde called this bouquet "grotesque," and some have speculated that Queensberry's vegetable choices might have been phallic and suggestive of Wilde's sexual tastes.[81] But whether or not the vegetables in question were graphically explicative of homosex, there was, I am proposing, an explicit and widely understood late-century association between vegetables and homosexuality. "Vegetable love" was same-sex love. For Gilbert and Sullivan, for Wilde and for Queensberry, it was an association that was literally theatrical, to be exaggerated on stage and grotesquely mocked at stage (that is to say, *backstage*) doors. But for others, "Vegetable Love" was a philosophy and an ethics. Yes, there was affiliation between vegetable and homosexual modes of life, but for Carpenter and Michael Field, the affiliation was not shameful but instead desirably humbling.

Like Bradley and Cooper, Carpenter noticed the conquering power of the bramble. One of his essays, "Weeds: A Study of Human and Vegetable Life," is prompted by the struggle he feels as a gardener, waging war against "battalions" of weeds.[82] His thesis, though, is that we should admire the "persistence and vitality" of these abjured or wayside plant forms and recognize that they have a place in our diverse world (223). More than this, they may—in time—triumph over us: Carpenter imagines a future in which brambles and grasses and herbs seize and destroy London. He quotes lines from Dean Hole:

> What time, when Spring is due,
> > The captives dungeoned deep
> Beneath the stones of London Town
> > Grow troubled in their sleep,
>
> And wake—mint, mallow, dock,
> > Brambles in bondage sore,
> . . .
> Like Samson, blind and scorned,
> > In pain their time they bide
> To seize the roots of London Town,
> > And tumble down its pride.[83]

Unlike Bradley and Cooper, who hurl themselves into anthropomorphism, the sober Carpenter notes, "It may be very 'unscientific' to use such anthropomorphic terms as *ingenuity, experience, habit,* &c, in relation to plants," but he goes on to say that plants are so like us, we are compelled to it (221). In his account, plants have wit and adaptability, they are "vagabonds" (224) and "squatters" (225), and—perhaps like homosexuals carving out a life against the flow of history, born too soon or too late—seeds have "the instinct, the prescience, the sensitive-ness to withhold themselves from germinating in many cases when conditions are against them" (227). For it is, he writes, "notorious that many seeds will lie for years and years in the ground, through the sunshine and moisture and warmth of spring after spring, still waiting for their favourable occasion" (227). Carpen-ter's romance of the weeds admires their powers of dormancy; how receptive they are to feelings of seasonality, then how selective they are about obeying sea-sonal urges. When it is, in other words, "deep April, and the morn Shakespeare was born,"[84] the queerness of the response is not to deny seasonal feelings but to be washed over by such sensations and still be able to seize your particular pleasures and make the world your own.

My title—"Vegetable Love"—owes something to Gilbert and Sullivan and also something to metaphysical poet Andrew Marvell. He uses the image to describe persistence: his "vegetable love" contemplates growing vaster than empires, while fretting about the sensual life turning to dust. Plant life fur-nishes Michael Field with a libidinal realm and a model for triumphing over (and under) the world and establishing their own affective affiliations. One of Michael Field's most important long-term friendships was with the artists and lovers Charles Shannon and Charles Ricketts. Of this relationship Mi-chael Field wrote, "We have walked into friendship as deep as mowing grass."[85] This beautiful simile suggests friends close enough to get lost, or "blent,"[86] in each other, just as their legs disappear into the greensward. Always, Michael Field's figurations of plant life derive sensuousness from the feeling of being on a temporal edge: grass about to be mown, apple blossoms full blown, seeds "That push, and riot, and squeeze and clip, / Till they burst the sides of the silver scrip" ("Unbosoming"). This is a fertility that is overblown and—ultimately—over-taking. The future is green and made more lush by the delays and persistence of plant life. Edward Carpenter believed that the homosexual had the capacity to show society "the wealth and variety of affectional possibilities it has within itself." Michael Field's poetic perspective is made from within the straining seed pod or the trembling calyx of the flower. It is a way of figuring queer capacities and futurities. Thinking from alongside and inside the plant is a way of pro-ducing a queer and lush "evermore."[87]

Notes

Epigraph from Michael Field's "Unbosoming," in *Underneath the Bough* (London: George Bell and Sons, 1893), 77–78.

 1. Virginia Woolf, *Orlando* (New York: Houghton Mifflin Harcourt, 1928), 98.

 2. See Elizabeth Freeman, *Time Binds: Queer Temporalities, Queer Histories* (Durham, NC: Duke University Press, 2010). Freeman uses the term *chrononormativity* to describe

how "naked flesh is bound into socially meaningful embodiment through temporal regulation" (3). She explains that "people are bound to one another, engrouped, made to feel coherently collective, through particular orchestrations of time" (3).

3. Work on child-predicated temporalities cluster around Lee Edelman's denunciation of "reproductive futurism" in his 2004 polemic No Future: Queer Theory and the Death Drive (Durham, NC: Duke University Press, 2004). José Esteban Muñoz's Cruising Utopia: The Then and There of Queer Futurity (New York: New York University Press, 2009) counters Edelman's antirelational stance, arguing that not all children embody futurism; queer youth of color "are not the sovereign princes of futurity" (95). Judith Halberstam's In a Queer Time and Place: Transgender Bodies, Subcultural Lives (New York: New York University Press, 2005) unpacks the presumptive naturalness and desirability of what they call "repro-time" (5).

4. Tim Morton, "Queer Ecology," PMLA 125, no. 2 (2010): 273.

5. Morton, 276.

6. Morton, 277.

7. Michael Marder, Plant-Thinking: A Philosophy of Vegetal Life (New York: Columbia University Press, 2013).

8. The work of art historian Alison Syme also firmly yokes the vegetal and the floral with queer orientations. In "Bohemians of the Vegetable World," she describes nineteenth-century reactions to plants that seem unnatural and "exhibit a variety of improper behaviors" (in Queer Difficulty in Art and Poetry: Rethinking the Sexed Body in Verse and Visual Culture, ed. Jongwoo Jeremy Kim and Christopher Reed [London: Routledge, 2017], 10). Syme's book, A Touch of Blossom, focuses on the fin-de-siècle and queer readings of botanical reproduction, floral models of hermaphroditic sexuality, the naturalization of sexual inversion through garden metaphorics, and the erotics of hand and "back-door" pollination (A Touch of Blossom: John Singer Sargent and the Queer Flora of Fin-de-Siècle Art [University Park: Pennsylvania State University Press, 2010]).

9. Marder, Plant-Thinking, 12.

10. Marder, 12.

11. Marder, 18, 28.

12. Dennis Denisoff broke ground when he opined that "The garden of the Decadents has always been rather crowded," noting that his "correlation of Decadence with the natural environment conflicts with the standard characterization of the phenomenon . . . as insensitive to humans' links with nature." "The Dissipating Nature of Decadent Paganism from Pater to Yeats," Modernism/Modernity 15, no. 3 (2008): 431–46, 431.

13. Oscar Wilde, "The Decay of Lying," Intentions (New York: Brentano's, 1905), 4.

14. On the subject of the natural world, Wilde was, like Whitman, unafraid to contradict himself. Although Wilde scorns nature here, he elsewhere turns to it ecstatically. At the end of De Profundis, for example, Wilde tremblingly anticipates the lilac and the laburnum flowering upon his release from prison: "I know that for me, to whom flowers are part of desire, there are tears waiting in the petal of some rose" (The Complete Works of Oscar Wilde, vol. 2, ed. Ian Small [Oxford: Oxford University Press, 2005], 192). "Society" and "articulate men" have tried and sentenced him, but "Nature,

whose sweet rains fall on unjust and just alike, will have clefts in the rocks where I may hide" (193). In the same text, Wilde suggests, "It seems that we all look at Nature too much, and live with her too little" (191). This passage seems to react against press-ganging nature into representational duty, and Jeff Nunokawa agrees: "Wilde's aversion to the outdoors, his distaste for the natural, is a dislike for the coercions of desire he finds there" (*Tame Passions of Wilde* [Princeton: Princeton University Press, 2003], 47). Tim Morton suggests that decadent writing might be a "reserve of utopian energy . . . that might be strangely greener than the usual injunctions to stop reading or writing and go outside, because it conveys an overwhelming, almost unbearable intimacy" ("Queer Ecology," 280–81). We might say, then, that Wilde adores nature, he just does not want to go outside.

15. Michael Field, "Works and Days," BL Add MS 46782, fol. 120r (September 9, 1894) [E.C.].

16. Chris White, "Flesh and Roses: Michael Field's Metaphors of Pleasure and Desire," *Women's Writing* 3, no.1 (1996): 48.

17. Ivor Treby notes that the insignia was at least in currency from 1881 to 1888. Inside the cover of Katharine's black notebook, there is a note that reads "The bramble bough 1881," and then when they find their lodge in Reigate it is "named Blackboro (we hope boldly to transform the name into Blackberry)" (in Treby, *Music and Silence* [Bury St Edmunds: De Blackland Press, 2000], 43).

18. Ana Parejo Vadillo discusses this woodblock in her chapter on book sculpture in this volume.

19. E.C. to R. Browning (BL Add MS46866, fol. 43v, 1886).

20. See, for example, *Michael Field, the Poet: Published and Manuscript Materials*, ed. Marion Thain and Ana Parejo Vadillo (Peterborough, Ontario: Broadview, 2009), 233, 305.

21. "The Sign of the Bramble-Bough," in Treby, *Music and Silence*, 43.

22. Quoted by Treby, *Music and Silence*, 43.

23. From *A Pageant and Other Poems, 1881. Christina Rossetti: The Complete Poems* (London: Penguin, 2001), 321.

24. Susan Conley writes that Michael Field finds Rossetti "an unfit subject for pastoral elegy and—partly in consequence—an unfit muse for future poets." "'Poet's Right': Christina Rossetti as Anti-Muse and the Legacy of the 'Poetess,'" *Victorian Poetry* 32, no. 3/4 (1994): 365–86.

25. Conley points out that Michael Field's sonnet anticipates Gilbert and Gubar writing of Rossetti "bury[ing] herself alive in a coffin of renunciation" ("'Poet's Right,'" 370).

26. Michael Field, "To Christina Rossetti," *Academy* (April 4, 1896): 1248. All subsequent quotations are from the same page.

27. In this respect, of course, Rossetti was setting herself at odds with her brothers and the Pre-Raphaelite Brotherhood (PRB), who adopted John Ruskin's mantra "Truth to Nature" and who painted a world of flowers with what Debra Mancoff calls "the analytical eye of a botanist" (*The Pre-Raphaelite Language of Flowers* [Munich: Prestel Verlag, 2012], 7). Remembering the antiseasonality of "Goblin Market's" jumble of

fruits "All ripe together" and persuasive readings of that poem as a protest against the Brotherhood's goblinlike commodification and exploitation of young women, we might well conclude that Christina Rossetti's antibotanical eye was also a baleful one. This young female poet would not conform to either PRB or gender expectations that she write well about flowers.

28. William Sharp, "Some Reminiscences of Christina Rossetti," *Atlantic Monthly* 75 (June 1895): 737.

29. Sharp, 737–38.

30. Sharp, 737.

31. *Athenæum*, January 5, 1895.

32. *Selected Prose of Christina Rossetti*, ed. David A. Kent and P. G. Stanwood (New York: St. Martin's Press, 1998), 249.

33. *Christina Rossetti: The Complete Poems*, 708.

34. An 1898 biography of Rossetti observes, "We learn from a touching note by Mr. William Rossetti on 'Looking Forward,' a poem dated June 8, 1849, that the MS. is in his mother's handwriting, and he adds that when Christina was seventeen or eighteen years old her health was so uncertain as to lead none of her family to suppose that she would attain an average length of life" (Mackenzie Bell, *Christina Rossetti: A Biographical and Critical Study* [London: Thomas Burleigh, 1898], 19).

35. I describe Michael Field as both backward and forward looking, shaped both by antique precedents for same-sex love and their conviction that Michael Field's literary fame would be posthumous. See Kate Thomas, "'What Time We Kiss': Michael Field's Queer Temporalities," *GLQ: A Journal of Lesbian and Gay Studies* 13, no. 2–3 (2007): 327–51.

36. The botanical delays in "Looking Forward" find an echo in Keats's 1819 poem, "Ode to a Nightingale," in which the speaker "cannot see what flowers are at my feet." Both speakers are dying and both poems open with references to drowsiness and opiates. Keats, whom Shelley eulogized as a "young flower . . . blighted in the bud," was a compelling figure for Rossetti; her sonnet "On Keats" was unpublished in her lifetime, but her poetry enfolds numerous allusions to—and critiques of—his work. See chapter 2, "'Decayed Branches from a Strong Stem': Rossetti's Keatsian Heritage," in Dinah Roe, *Christina Rossetti's Faithful Imagination: The Devotional Poetry and Prose* (Houndmills, UK: Palgrave Macmillan, 2007). I am grateful to Sarah Parker for pointing out this connection.

37. *Victorian Women Poets: An Anthology*, ed. Angela Leighton and Margaret Reynolds (Oxford: Blackwell Publishers, 1995), 355.

38. *Christina Rossetti: The Complete Poems*, 747, 772.

39. *Christina Rossetti: The Complete Poems*, 796.

40. Michael Field, "Works and Days," BL Add MS 46800, fol. 174r (October 11, 1910) [E.C.].

41. We might contrast Michael Field's experience of this convent garden with Christina Rossetti's poem, "The Convent Threshold" (composed 1858, first published 1862). The Fields are fleeing *from* the confines of a convent; Rossetti's narrator flees *into* a convent. The Fields reach out to a sensorium of vegetation; Rossetti's novitiate repents her "lily feet soiled . . . with mud." And rather than luxuriating in its materiality, Rossetti

immediately turns this mud to metaphor, describing it as "scarlet" with "hope and guilt." *Christina Rossetti: The Complete Poems*, 56.

42. Kathryn Bond Stockton, *The Queer Child, or Growing Sideways in the Twentieth Century* (Durham, NC: Duke University Press, 2009).

43. Their beloved dog, Whym Chow, died on January 28, 1906, and *Whym Chow: Flame of Love*, a memorial collection of poems mostly by Cooper, edited by Bradley, was published in 1914. Bound in russet suede to mimic the dog's coat, the anthology expresses a passionate, immortal intertwining of couple and canine. As Thain and Parejo Vadillo write, "the three were united in a trinity that was both spiritual and erotic" (Thain and Vadillo, *Michael Field, the Poet*, 183).

44. White, "Flesh and Roses," 54.

45. Jennifer DeVere Brody, *Impossible Purities: Blackness, Femininity, and Victorian Culture* (Durham, NC: Duke University Press, 1998), 6.

46. Gretchen Gerzina, *Black Victorians/Black Victoriana* (New Brunswick, NJ: Rutgers University Press, 2003), 5.

47. Michael Field, "Works and Days," BL Add MS 46780, fol. 106r (June 18, 1892) [E.C.]. The passage is written on what they call "A day of blight!" caused by reading George Moore's article, "Sex in Art." This article, which was first published in the *Speaker* on June 18 and 25, 1892, accuses women of being "facile" and "trifling," incapable of "penetrat[ing] below the surface" (*Modern Painting* [London: Walter Scott, 1893], 220) and having something Moore calls "Mental nudeness" (223). Is it to express feelings of being stripped and dispossessed that the Fields compare themselves to a slave on an auction block? They pursue the trope of being blackened when they complain that the article was clever enough to be "almost convincing" and that it had the "power of blackening the sky for us, as the devil's wings do in [Flaubert's] St. Antoine."

48. Homi K. Bhabha, *The Location of Culture* (London: Routledge, 1984), 89.

49. The "polish" of the negress/beet also demands attention. It recalls figurations of black skin as "polished jet," an aestheticizing that Lisa Lowe points out is anterior to commodification (*The Intimacies of Four Continents* [Durham, NC: Duke University Press, 2015], 52). Lowe makes this argument through Aphra Behn's 1688 story, *Oroonoko*, but the trope was still available at the end of the nineteenth century: Oscar Wilde's poem "The Sphinx" features a "swarthy Ethiop whose body was of polished jet" (*Complete Works of Oscar Wilde* [New York: Harper and Row, 1989], 836). Catherine Molineux also notes that describing a black body as "glossy" has a historically "contested symbolism" (134), showing that luster could be deployed to signify either "the oppression or benevolence of British rule" (*Faces of Perfect Ebony: Encountering Atlantic Slavery in Imperial Britain* [Cambridge, MA: Harvard University Press, 2012], 125).

50. Elizabeth Freeman, "Hopeless Cases: Queer Chronicities and Gertrude Stein's *Melanctha*," *Journal of Homosexuality* 63, no. 3 (2016), 329–48.

51. Freeman points out that the name also "chimes with 'melancholy'" and with "the timid and often ill Reformation theologian Philipp Melancthon" ("Hopeless Cases," 331). She further notes that "Philipp Schwarzerdt (whose last name, meaning 'black earth' in German, was changed to 'Melancthon,' or 'black earth' in Greek, in honor of his proficiency in the latter language) was a contemporary and friend of Martin Luther" (347n2).

52. Freeman, 338.

53. Freeman, 341.

54. Freeman, 333.

55. Freeman, 333.

56. For more on this topic, see the special issue, "Queer Theory without Antinormativity," *differences* 26, no. 1 (2015), ed. R. Wiegman and E. A. Wilson.

57. See, for example, Jasbir Puar, "Prognosis Time: Towards a Geopolitics of Affect, Debility and Capacity," *Women & Performance: A Journal of Feminist Theory* 19 (2009): 161–72.

58. Michael Warner, *The Trouble with Normal: Sex, Politics, and the Ethics of Queer Life* (Cambridge, MA: Harvard University Press, 1999), 70.

59. Ted Wong, private email, July 5, 2014.

60. Michel Foucault, "History and Homosexuality," in Sylvère Lotringer (ed.), trans. Lysa Hochroth and John Johnson, *Foucault Live: Interviews, 1961–1984* (New York: Semiotext(e), 1989), 370.

61. Freeman, *Time Binds*, xxii.

62. Thain and Vadillo, *Michael Field, the Poet*, 257.

63. See, for example, Jack Goody, "The Secret Language of Flowers," *Yale Journal of Criticism* 3 (1990): 133–52; Sabine Haass, "'Speaking Flowers and Floral Emblems': The Victorian Language of Flowers," in *Word and Visual Imagination: Studies in the Interaction of English Literature and the Visual Arts*, ed. Karl Josef Höltgen, Peter M. Daly, and Wolfgang Lottes (Erlangen, Ger.: Universität-Bibliothek, 1988), 241–68.

64. Joseph Bristow, "Michael Field's Lyrical Aestheticism: *Underneath the Bough*," in *Michael Field and Their World*, ed. Margaret D. Stetz and Cheryl A. Wilson (High Wycombe, UK: Rivendale Press, 2007), 54. The collection was conceived of as a "songbook" in early titles, and Bristow shows how the final titling of the collection also likely marked a distancing from their early career association with Robert Browning, who had critiqued FitzGerald's *Rubáiyát* in "Rabbi Ben Ezra." Their turn from Browning to FitzGerald was a turn from a sage to a sensualist. One reviewer pursued the title's botanical trope a little fiercely, recommending a "severe pruning . . . 'decreasing' it to the dimensions of [a] sprig" (Bristow, 57).

65. FitzGerald published four editions, which were followed by a fifth edition containing only minor changes from the fourth, compiled after his death on the basis of manuscript revisions he had left behind. The version used by Michael Field is Quatrain XII in the fifth edition.

66. Michael Field, "Works and Days," BL Add MS 46781, fol. 25r (March 6, 1893) [E.C.].

67. Thain and Vadillo, *Michael Field, the Poet*, 112.

68. E.C. to R. Browning (BL Add MS 46866, fol. 43v, 1886).

69. Michael Field, *Underneath the Bough*, 22, 23, 58, 68.

70. Field, 17. Lyric III in *Long Ago* has a similar thematic. Taking the fragment "Neither honey nor bee for me," a lustful Sappho yearns, "Deep in thy bosom I would rest, / O golden blossom wide!" The lyric has "fiery circlets," glistening nectar and the powerful desire to "feed" (in Thain and Vadillo, *Michael Field, the Poet*, 59).

71. Jill R. Ehnenn, "'Our Brains Struck Fire Each from Each': Disidentification, Difference, and Desire in the Collaborative Aesthetics of Michael Field," in *Economies of*

Desire at the Victorian Fin de Siècle: Libidinal Lives, ed. Jane Ford and Kim Edwards Keates [New York: Routledge, 2016], 191. The full poem "Bee and Flower" is reproduced on the same page.

72. Founded in 1883, the Fellowship included Havelock Ellis, Edith Lees, Arthur Ransom, and Henry and Kate Salt.

73. Sheila Rowbotham, *Edward Carpenter: A Life of Liberty and Love* (London and New York: Verso, 2008), 90.

74. Quoted by Diana Maltz, "Katharine Bradley and Ethical Socialism," in Stetz and Wilson, *Michael Field and Their World,* 195.

75. Maltz, "Katharine Bradley and Ethical Socialism," 196.

76. It should be noted, however, that Cooper wrote scathingly of "the way of Pantheism . . . vaguely trusts in nature . . . to redeem and save and sanctify" (*Works and Days: From the Journal of Michael Field,* ed. Thomas Sturge Moore [London: John Murray, 1933], 318). But her scorn is leveled less at the power of nature and more at the ways Salvationist structures establish a parasitic relation to nature. Michael Field's writing consistently figures nature as unavailable for such harnessing. It is instead overwhelming and indifferent to humans.

77. Rowbotham, *Edward Carpenter,* 95.

78. W. S. Gilbert and Arthur Sullivan. *The Complete Annotated Gilbert and Sullivan,* ed. Ian Bradley (London: Oxford University Press, 1996), 363.

79. Carolyn Williams provides commentary on this passage of *Patience,* noting the sexual innuendo, in *Gilbert and Sullivan: Gender, Genre, Parody* (New York: Columbia University Press, 2010), 167–78.

80. Williams, 166.

81. Oscar Wilde to Lord Alfred Douglas, ca. February, 17, 1895, in *The Complete Letters of Oscar Wilde,* ed. Merlin Holland and Rupert Hart-Davis (New York: Henry Holt, 2000), 632.

82. Edward Carpenter, *Sketches from Life in Town and Country and Some Verses* (London: George Allen and Sons, 1908), 220. Subsequent page numbers are cited in the text.

83. Carpenter, *Sketches from Life,* 222–23. Samuel Reynolds Hole was an Anglican priest and horticulturalist who became dean of Rochester in 1887.

84. Michael Field, *Underneath the Bough,* 79.

85. Michael Field, "Works and Days," BL Add 46782, fol. 47r-v (22 May 1894) [E.C.].

86. "Cowslip-Gathering," in Field, *Underneath the Bough,* 68.

87. It must not be overlooked that the Fields play readily with the dual meaning of "leaf," which conflates foliage with the printed page. Hence it is "aspen-leaflets" that tremble in "A Girl," not "leaves." And Bradley writes, for example, to Browning in May of 1888, sending him poems that will become *Long Ago*: "It will be time," she writes, "to put in the sickle, & bind them in the sheaves for the printer, after they shall have received your corrections" (quoted in Thain and Vadillo, *Michael Field, the Poet,* 232). "Help us to weed *Long Ago*," Bradley asks Gray (quoted in Bristow, "Michael Field's Lyrical Aestheticism," 50).

TWO

"As She Feels a God Within"

Michael Field and Inspiration

Margaret D. Stetz

THERE IS NO QUESTION THAT MICHAEL FIELD'S POEM number LXI (titled "χελώνη" and usually translated as "A Tortoise") from *Long Ago* reflects Katharine Bradley and Edith Cooper's imaginative involvement with the ancient world of Sappho.[1] Like all the lyrics in that 1889 volume, it emerged from what Richard Dellamora has called an "exercise in recuperating Sapphic song"—an exercise meant to give voice to "a consciousness open to sexual and emotional variability"—undertaken by two late-Victorian women who were themselves exemplars of such variability.[2] Nonetheless, the writers' deep affiliation with the classical past in general—as well as with Sappho in particular, as a complex predecessor who embodied lesbian possibilities in feeling and action while, as Marion Thain points out, simultaneously representing "heterosexual passion"[3]—can account only partially for what shaped this dazzling poem. "A Tortoise" was just as closely connected to the modern world of Victorian literary men—to Bradley and Cooper's personal and professional relationships with male poets and critics and to the ways in which the two women drew inspiration from them. At the same time, the poem revealed its creators' concern with identifying the roots of inspiration itself, especially when it came to understanding the origins and manifestations of genius in women, which was an interest shared and explored by many women writers of Bradley and Cooper's generation. Thus, "A Tortoise" proved less about an imagined long ago alone and more about the literary personalities and pre-occupations of an actual here and now. The poem offered a synthesis of the poets' multifaceted engagement with present-day matters, expressed through a Greek myth about a maiden and her encounter with the shape-shifting god Apollo. Unlike most of their contemporaries, however, Bradley and Cooper daringly addressed issues present in the late-Victorian zeitgeist by means of a topic that would not (and could not) be talked about openly until more than a century later—that is, rape. They did so in the third through the fifth stanzas of their eight-stanza-long poem, while depicting in explicit detail how "Round her body backward bent / In forlorn astonishment" Apollo overpowers young Dryope, whose "breath in terror fails" at the moment when he holds her by force and takes possession of her body.[4]

As Thomas Hardy would discover in 1891 (two years after the publication of *Long Ago*), when dealing with the censorship of parts of *Tess of the d'Urbervilles* before its appearance in the *Graphic*, even to allude to rape was to risk an outraged response.[5] In "A Tortoise," Bradley and Cooper did more than merely allude to rape as a subject; they referred specifically to an episode from classical mythology of a forcible penetration by Apollo, who had assumed the form first of a tortoise and then of a snake. Sensational though the mere suggestion of rape was at the fin de siècle, it is clear nonetheless that "A Tortoise" was never primarily a poem about rape—and perhaps not actually a poem about rape at all. It was instead focused chiefly on the sorts of questions to which "New Women" writers would soon turn repeatedly throughout the 1890s: What does it mean to feel inspired? Where does inspiration come from? At what point in life does it appear? Why? Are those who experience this feeling changed by it? How? And are the answers to all of these questions different, if the one who has been inspired is a woman? Indeed, does possessing inspiration—something considered essential, since the Romantic era, to being a writer and, moreover, central to being a "genius"—prove compatible or incompatible with being a woman, at least in terms of conventional social definitions of gender?

Inspired Girls

From the outset, Michael Field's poem diverged from the standard assumption in nineteenth-century writings about inspiration, which insisted that it usually asserted its presence early and that its stirrings first made themselves known in childhood through an insistent urge—in fact, an inescapable need—to compose something, whether in the form of verse or prose. This biographical trope, as Linda H. Peterson has suggested, pervaded mid-Victorian published accounts of "genius," including those focused on women writers, such as Elizabeth

Gaskell's *The Life of Charlotte Brontë* (1857). Thus, as Peterson notes, "following the conventions of Romantic biography, Gaskell demonstrates the Brontë siblings' youthful genius and gives 'curious proof how early the rage for literary composition had seized upon'" Charlotte Brontë.[6] Even for a later generation—that is, for Bradley and Cooper's turn-of-the-century female contemporaries—interest remained strong in tying women who pursued literary careers to evidence of a special calling that first appeared in childhood. In a number of works that followed the publication of *Long Ago*, this standard pattern continued, with portraits of little girls discovering themselves among an elect group, distinguished from their peers and overmastered by the desire to express in some tangible form the inspiration that had come upon them.

In her 1894 volume of sketches *A Cluster of Nuts*, for instance, Katharine Tynan used "Rose: From an Irish Hedgerow" to pay tribute to her late friend, the Irish author and editor Rose Kavanagh (1860–91), who had died of tuberculosis at age thirty-one—or, as Tynan put the matter, amidst the glory of "her bright morning of life," Rose had "drooped and broken on her stalk."[7] Tynan described how Kavanagh had been visited in infancy by "the most beneficent of all the fairies" and then, as a small child on a farm in Country Tyrone, had written "her first little stories in the tangled orchard, and poised her rhymes sitting on the bench by the house-door."[8] These youthful outpourings were a sign that Kavanagh was, as Tynan also reported in her 1913 memoir *Twenty-Five Years: Reminiscences*, "a great soul," who belonged among other "lofty souls."[9]

Similarly, in her 1897 autobiographical short story, "The Elusive Melody," from the volume *Fantasias*, "George Egerton" (Mary Chavelita Dunne) wrote of a ten-year-old child displaying "an un-guessed-at gift" and discovering suddenly that she could, without training, play melodies on the piano, then finding later that, through no conscious effort on her own part, the "magic numbers came dancing along in rhythmic measure," but this time as poetry: "they gave her words, not tunes—words like arrows winged with silver, that never failed to hit the mark. . . . It was a downright pleasure to see how easily they rhymed."[10] Even as this talent arrived as a blessing, however, it also estranged the girl from social life in general, so that she reached adulthood knowing and caring for nothing but these moments of literary upwelling: "Unfortunately, they absorbed her so, that she forgot she was a woman, and that is a thing nature rarely pardons."[11]

Frances Hodgson Burnett's slightly fictionalized memoir, titled *The One I Knew the Best of All* (1893) described, albeit in the third person, the rapture that came upon her unbidden, at age seven. Sitting alone on a Sunday and listening to church bells ringing, she first experienced the impulse to write. In her case, it made itself known as an almost illicit desire:

But she felt very still and happy, and as if she wanted to say or do something new, which would somehow be an expression of feeling, and goodness, and—and—she did not know at all what else. . . .

. . . A delightful queer and tremendously bold idea came to her. It was so daring that she smiled a little.

"I wonder if I could write—a piece of poetry," she said. "I believe—I'll try."

No one need ever know that she had attempted anything so audacious . . . [for] no one [was] in the room but the Green Arm Chair, and it could not betray her—besides the fact that it would not if it could.[12]

If, however, the process of giving vent to such "queer" impulses were to be frustrated or suppressed, the result would be unbearable, ineluctable suffering. As the narrator of the 1897 short story "Jewels to Wear," by "John Strange Winter" (Henrietta Stannard), tells us more than once, the fictional Nancy Macdonald was "a true artist" and therefore "felt, as every true artist feels, that it was in her to do great things."[13] On reaching the age of twenty and being ordered by her mother to give up the "scribbling" she had done compulsively since childhood and to turn instead to the domestic labor that comes with being a woman, Nancy Macdonald cries out in anguish, "'I try to do everything I can to . . . help you; but these stories will come into my head. They won't be put out of it. What am I to do?'"[14] To be a girl with a "mind full of visionary beauty . . . living daily in a world of her own," but to be actively prevented from following her "blessed dreams of fancy" and kept from leaving the prescribed path of social expectations imposes both mental and physical hardship.[15] From Sarah Grand's novel *The Beth Book* (1897) to *A Writer of Books* (1898) by "George Paston" (Emily Morse Symonds), numerous texts by Katharine Bradley and Edith Cooper's fin-de-siècle contemporaries, "New Women" or otherwise, spoke of girls who became aware in childhood that theirs were no ordinary destinies and who were alienated from the conventions of social life by this early revelation of difference.

But that is not at all the situation in Michael Field's lyric about the legendary figure of Dryope and her encounter with Apollo, Greek god of poetry, truth, and prophecy, who presents himself as a tortoise before transforming into a snake. This poem is not a tale of a girl who recognizes from childhood onwards, as the fictional Nancy Macdonald does, the potential to be "a true artist"—who grows up conscious of membership in a select band of singers and visionaries. In lyric number LXI of *Long Ago*, Dryope joins this elect group only after arriving at a more mature stage of life and, in fact, after a traumatic (yet also ecstasy-inducing) experience. This event is so life altering that it instantly moves the subject of it from one category of identity into a new one. Michael Field's poem is, therefore, doubly focused on shocking, unprepared-for metamorphoses: on Apollo's voluntary transformation, first into a tortoise and then into a serpent, and on Dryope's unlooked-for transformation from a bold, playful, and adventurous figure, who happily disports herself among the female Hamadryads, to a self-exiled wanderer and an initiate into a new order of being. The climactic verses read as follows:

> 'Tis Apollo in disguise
> Holds possession of his prize.
> Thus he binds in fetters dire
> Those for whom he knows desire;
> Mortal loves or poets—all
> He must dominate, enthrall
> By the rapture of his sway,
> Which shall either bless or slay.
> So she shudders with a joy
> Which no childish fears alloy,
> For the spell is round her now
> Which has made old prophets bow
> Tremulous and wild. An hour
> Must she glow beneath his power,
> Then a dryad shy and strange
> Through the firs thereafter range.
> For she joins the troop of those
> Dedicate to joy and woes,
> Whom by stricture of his love
> Leto's son has raised above
> Other mortals, who, endowed
> With existence unallowed
> To their fellows, wander free
> Girt with earth's own mystery.[16]

We might ask why Michael Field chose not only to tell the Dryope story this way but to write about the Dryope myth at all. For Bradley and Cooper did indeed have a choice, when composing their lyric based upon a tiny fragment of text by Sappho, consisting merely of the single word χελώνη—*chelōnē* or "tortoise." There were several alternatives available, the most obvious being (especially considering that Sappho is usually depicted with a lyre) a poem that would have incorporated the legend of Hermes inventing his instrument by gutting a tortoise and tying strings across its shell. If, on the other hand, the two poets had wished to write about a woman instead, they could have composed a variation on the myth of the nymph named Chelone—again, an incident involving metamorphosis—who was turned into a tortoise herself.[17] This would have had the advantage, moreover, of highlighting the theme of female rebellion and autonomy, for her transformation into animal form was intended as a punishment by Zeus, after the nymph refused to participate in the celebration of Zeus's wedding to Hera. As, in effect, the first marriage resister, Chelone might have seemed an appealing subject for Bradley and Cooper, had they wanted to enshrine her as an antiheteronormative precursor figure from, to echo the volume's title, long ago.

Yet the question remains: Why did they use Dryope? Here, I would like to mirror Michael Field's own practice of selecting an ambiguous fragment from the past and building a text around it. Indeed, I would like to offer two possible narratives about the origins of this poem, with the second even more speculative than the first. Both owe a debt to Sarah Parker's way of looking at Michael Field's poetic process in *The Lesbian Muse and Poetic Identity, 1889–1930* (2013). As Parker states, "Almost all of their volumes are structured around a triangular dynamic in which the two poets take another being/thing as muse, while also continuing to find inspiration in each other," and "Michael Field's muses were frequently male."[18] Thus, "the art critic Bernard Berenson represents the most pivotal third term in Michael Field's career: he was their first long-term male muse."[19] Of course, Bradley and Cooper did not meet Berenson until 1890, after the publication of *Long Ago*. Manuscript letters provide us with contextual evidence suggesting that during this period the women were already using another muse—and possibly several others—in the 1880s (before Bernard Berenson came along), drawn from their set of literary acquaintances, the majority of whom were men.

Michael Field and Robert Browning

The first of the male muses responsible for the choice of Dryope was Robert Browning. As Bradley and Cooper's journals (known as "Works and Days") and correspondence in the British Library indicate, the poems later published as *Long Ago* were written over the course of at least three years, during a period when Michael Field not only worshipped Browning from afar, as a literary idol, but up close, as a mentor whom the aunt and niece couple visited in London and with whom they frequently exchanged letters. On October 14, 1886, Edith Cooper wrote to Browning, confiding in him that "we are working at a collection of songs & poems, each of which is suggested by one of Sappho's incomparable fragments."[20] The next day, Katharine Bradley followed up with a note of her own, in which she confessed, "I am glad Edith has spoken to you of the poems born of our joy in Sappho. We have written about 30—nearly enough for a tiny volume; to me they have given the most genuine delight of my life."[21] (There would eventually be sixty-nine Sapphic works, sixty-eight of them bearing numbers, with the Dryope poem as the sixty-first.) On April 4, 1887, signing as "Michael Field," they grew bolder still, soliciting Browning to act as their critic and guide for this enterprise—"We are sending you the tiny vol. of lyrics which—provisionally at least we think of calling *Long Ago*"—and entreating: "Please write freely on the opposite leaf anything that occurs to you of censure, suggestion, or comment, especially pointing out any failure in Greek directions or simplicity."[22] What followed in this same letter, however, was an extraordinarily revealing image—an explicit statement of the frightening position of vulnerability and surrender that Michael Field imagined as key to being his literary disciple: "But I cannot write more—it is too terrible to think of these poems lying helpless in manuscript in your study."[23] Lest there be any doubt about their construction of Browning, in this relationship, as a figure to whom they assigned a godlike role, setting him up both as literary arbiter and as deity, they continued: "I cannot conceive of anything more audacious than to ask you to look at them. Again I say—<u>all worship must be audacious!</u>"[24] (Michael Field would, in fact, soon echo this same statement in the published "Preface" to *Long Ago*, writing that "In simple truth all worship that is not idolatry must be audacious." There, the sentiment would be couched in the context of a correspondence with "a literary friend"—surely an allusion to Robert Browning himself.)[25]

In the April 4, 1887 letter to Browning, there is much that is striking about the personification of their poetry as "lying helpless": as separated from the female sphere in which it was created and now prostrate instead in the masculine environment of Browning's "study," abandoned to its fate and open entirely before the great man who is the subject of "worship." But it is interesting most of all as a precursor to the image of Dryope, with "her body backward bent," as "her breath in terror fails," while "Apollo in disguise / Holds possession of his prize."[26] In poem LXI, Apollo "must dominate, enthrall / By the rapture of his sway, / Which shall either bless or slay,"[27] just as Browning's judgment would either bless or slay Michael Field's attempts at Sapphic writing. Twinned this way with the equally vulnerable manuscript, Dryope seems less a victim of rape in any conventional sense—that is, of any phallic penetration—than the object of a godlike male figure's scrutiny and mastery, which has the potential to bless, rather than destroy.[28]

Evidently, Michael Field did feel as though their poems in *Long Ago* had been possessed, in many senses of the word, by Browning, and that they themselves had been as well. On May 2, 1889, while the volume was still in preparation by its publisher, George Bell and Sons, Katharine Bradley wrote to Browning to declare that "all we can say is that ~~our book~~ it is yours through ownership no other can claim. You help to make ~~the book~~ it; but beside this it is full of you in a curious, remote way that you as Poet will understand."[29] Dryope, closely held in the coils "Covetous, subduing, tight" of Apollo as a serpent, knows that a god has taken her over;[30] so Michael Field, too, is eager here to acknowledge *Long Ago* as a kind of sacralized vessel containing the presence of the godlike Robert Browning—to let him know unambiguously that it is "full of you." In fact, as Yopie Prins reports in *Victorian Sappho*, Browning received from Bradley and Cooper, at the time of publication, not merely an inscribed copy of *Long Ago* but "copy no. 2" of the "limited edition of one hundred copies."[31] This was surely their way of doing proper obeisance and making an offering to the exalted figure who had magnanimously "praised" *Long Ago* and, as Mary Sturgeon also reports, had "marked some of the pieces in the manuscript 'Good' and 'Good indeed!'"[32] (They were perhaps especially grateful for such kindly treatment when, after Browning's death, they learned through their later friendship with his son that "The Old"—as they referred to him affectionately—"was evidently intolerant of faults and forcing in his culture of virtues."[33])

Again, though, we might ask how Bradley and Cooper alighted upon Dryope, in particular, as the appropriate mythical character through whom to express this relationship, at once transgressively erotic and intimate, yet safely distant, with a male mentor from whom they drew inspiration and to whom they gave "worship." Once more, their letters to Browning prove informative. Nearly two years after they had forwarded the first group of thirty poems from *Long Ago* in spring 1887, Cooper wrote to tell him, on February 9, 1889, "We send you the last twelve lyrics from Sappho, which you have not seen"[34]—a group that would have included number sixty-one, "A Tortoise." Dinah Ward has identified this as "the only *Long Ago* poem known for certain to have been written by Cooper."[35] Indeed, it is Cooper herself who explains its origin to Browning: "χελώνη was written after you had shown to us the photograph of your son's statue of Dryope. Think of this when you read it."[36] Dryope was, therefore, a figure doubly—and very intimately—connected for Michael Field with Browning: first, as the subject of a massive bronze sculpture, "well over 6ft tall and weighing more than half a ton," titled *Dryope Fascinated by Apollo in the Form of a Serpent*, which had been completed by his son, Pen Barrett Browning, and "turned down

Figure 2.1. Robert Wiedeman "Pen" Barrett Browning, *Dryope Fascinated by Apollo in the Form of a Serpent* (1883), in C. K. S. [Clement K. Shorter], "A Literary Letter— Concerning Robert Browning," *Sphere*, August 18, 1900, 204.

. . . for the 1887 Royal Academy summer show"[37]; and then, as the image in a photograph that Robert Browning himself had shared with Bradley and Cooper on one of their visits with him in London.[38] Much as Dryope had been fascinated by Apollo, so Michael Field surely had been fascinated by Robert Browning. As they saw it, the first half of the manuscript of *Long Ago* and, by extension, the two female poets themselves, had endured the trauma of "lying helpless" in his study and being nakedly exposed, after they had sent their poems to him. All had survived the experience—not necessarily intact, but improved by his powerful embrace.

Michael Field and Havelock Ellis

That is the first of the two narratives suggested by this fragment from Michael Field's 1889 volume. The second involves another male literary contemporary, Havelock Ellis. This story of inspiration, however, is less reliant on documentation and more on speculation. In the mid-1880s, when Michael Field first engaged in correspondence with and then met him, Havelock Ellis was, unlike Robert Browning, no Apollonian embodiment of the godlike "Poet" (with a capital "P"). Indeed, he was no sort of poet—merely an eager aspirant to the title of critic. Unlike the elderly Browning, he did not embody the virtues of an admired earlier era, for he was thirteen years younger than Bradley and only three years older than Cooper. But in his role as budding literary journalist with, moreover, the advantage of being a man in a misogynist publishing environment, what he did have was access to the world of the press. Through it, he could help to shape public opinion, including the reception of Michael Field's works.

As a letter to Edith Cooper from October 1885 indicates, Katharine Bradley began the epistolary relationship with Ellis in a rather playful and even somewhat patronizing spirit. "Such a nice letter from Ellis this morning," she records. "He has been reading the book again"—referring to George Bell's 1884 publication of three plays by Michael Field—"and found *The Father's Tragedy* as splendid as ever—Rufus [meaning their drama, *William Rufus*] he likes better." She continues, "An acquaintance of his,"—who has been identified by Sharon Bickle as George Moore—"from careful examination of internal evidence, is confident that the book is written by a man and a woman—Ellis has another theory—I believe that of single female authorship; but he does not say."[39] Clearly, Bradley enjoyed coyly stringing along this new correspondent and choosing not to disabuse him of his notion that the playwright Michael Field was a lone woman. Meanwhile, Havelock Ellis's own descriptions of his earlier exchanges with Bradley, as recorded in letters to Olive Schreiner from March 1885, pointed to a certain prickliness on his part; he accused Bradley of "man-like affectation" and added, "I never like women who take a man's name (!!!)," emphasizing his distaste with three exclamation marks.[40]

In later years, Bradley and Cooper would become friends not only with Ellis but with his sister Louisa (known as "Louie") and, to a lesser degree, with his wife, the lesbian feminist Edith Lees. They would have felt particularly encouraged to form a closer bond with Ellis himself, however, after he did them a good turn—the sort that male critics, in particular, were so well positioned to do. What made this kindly gesture not only welcome but also rather surprising was its almost offhand character. The April 1886 issue of the *Westminster Review*, one of the most established and influential of Victorian periodicals, contained Ellis's lengthy, unsigned appreciation of the work of Thomas Ashe (1836–89), occasioned by the recent publication of the volume *Poems by Thomas Ashe: Complete Edition*, a book that also happened to be a production of Michael Field's own publisher, George Bell and Sons. Unlike most members of the poetry-reading public, Havelock Ellis responded positively to some quality in Ashe's verse, which had been appearing regularly in print since the early 1860s but had never secured a wide audience. Thus, Ellis began by writing,

> Even among those who love poetry[,] how many have never even
> heard of Thomas Ashe? And yet he is a singer who within his own
> range has no rival among contemporary English poets. . . . He is
> of no school, though we catch faint echoes of other singers. Just
> as Blake caught up the divine mystery of song from Shakespeare's
> lips, and as again to-day Michael Field incarnates something of the
> elementary energy of the minor Elizabethan dramatists, so this
> singer, with no trace of imitation, sometimes recalls a poet from
> whom he is in most respects far removed—Heine.[41]

The compliment to Michael Field was seemingly gratuitous and also brief, but by no means negligible. To find themselves spoken of in the same sentence with Blake and Shakespeare and to be associated publicly with Elizabethan drama at this early stage in their publishing career, when they had begun issuing work under the name of "Michael Field" scarcely two years earlier, would have been cause for celebration. No doubt, this public expression of admiration advanced their relations with Ellis and smoothed over some of the original tension between him and Bradley.

Michael Field and Thomas Ashe

But who was this poet Thomas Ashe—who happened still to be alive and active in 1886, at the time of this glowing review? Did Michael Field even know his work, or care to do so? Or did Bradley and Cooper dismiss this laudatory article about him and consider it an occasion merely for their acquaintance, Havelock Ellis, to bring favorable notice to their own literary efforts? This is where the discussion must move from the realm of demonstrable fact to the hazy sphere of speculation and imaginative projection. Bradley and Cooper were in the position of having discovered that someone in their social circle, who thought well of their writing, also thought highly of Thomas Ashe—of the "sincerely rendered personality" and the "delicate vein of classic feeling" in his poetry.[42] Ashe's collected works, as it turned out, had been issued by the same publisher responsible for bringing out their own poetic dramas. It is, therefore, not much of a stretch to assume that the two women would have been interested in reading at least a few of those poems. Indeed, as Bradley and Cooper were already beginning, in 1886, to compose lyrics on Sapphic fragments (as we know from the letter to Browning about their efforts in October of that year), it seems entirely plausible that the two women might well have started with one of Ashe's poems on Greek themes. By happy coincidence, Havelock Ellis had mentioned one of these in the *Westminster Review*—not once, but twice: first as part of the title of an early book in Ashe's oeuvre, "'Dryope and other Poems' in 1861,"[43] and then again in the course of praising Ashe's choice of subjects: "He has sung of many things: of his own sad or glad moods; sometimes of old far-off dreams of love—Dryope, Plectrude, Hildegard, Yseult."[44]

This was where Bradley and Cooper would have been likely to begin their reading of Thomas Ashe's work—with his 1861 narrative poem on a Greek subject, "Dryope," in the slightly emended form that it assumed in the 1886 volume. To suggest that they were, in effect, writing against Ashe's version of the Dryope myth, when Cooper later composed "A Tortoise" (after seeing the photograph of Pen Browning's sculpture), and thus were implicitly setting up a challenge to Havelock Ellis—inviting him to recognize their superiority as interpreters of the same episode involving a Greek maiden and the god of poetry—in no way negates the centrality of Robert Browning to their poem. If anything, it merely adds a second layer of complexity. Sarah Parker rightly identifies Bradley and Cooper's favorite poetical maneuver as triangulation with a male muse. In this case, I would like to claim for Michael Field the creation of an even more complicated and transgressive geometrical configuration—not exactly a hexagon, but two intersecting triangles—or perhaps three triangles, if we put Thomas Ashe, whom the two women would have known only through his work, at the apex of another one. This is a Polygon That Dare Not Speak Its Name.

What might Michael Field have discovered in Thomas Ashe's "Dryope" to write back to or against in the sixty-first lyric from *Long Ago*? Placing the two poems side by side suggests some possibilities. First, there was Ashe's emphasis on the conventionally pretty physical appearance of the figure whom he called, perhaps a touch condescendingly,

> Sweet Dryope! bright little Dryope!
> So like a rose-leaf fallen upon the grass!
> New, rounded, flush'd with youth's fresh rosy hues;
> And soft with colour, like an evening cloud![45]

This is Dryope at the time when the Hamadryads come upon her and decide to raise her as one of their own. They do so not because of any special quality of mind or spirit that they sense in her, but purely because of the appeal of her infantile beauty. Unlike the female figures who were later to populate works by "New Women"—girl children who showed intimations of genius at an early age—Ashe's protagonist demonstrates no such promise. She is a decidedly feminine character—a Victorian Womanly Woman—and a lovely one at that, who grows up "a perfect woman pure," although "anything she look'd on sadden'd her" (35). Why is she so sad? Because, we hear, "She pined for love, and knew not why she pined" (35). Yet sometimes, she would have intimations of what it was for which she longed:

> Mysterious whispers wild, oracular,
> Moved in her, as the priestesses are moved:
> And image of Apollo came in dreams. . . .
> And at the last, when she could bear no more
> The hope and fear, Apollo was reveal'd.

> (35)

In other words, for Thomas Ashe, Apollo's assault upon Dryope was no rape, for—to put this in the crudest misogynist terms—she was asking for it: Apollo arrived in answer to her longing for him. When faced with the phallic transformation of the tortoise into an uprising serpent, she appears to lack the capacity to be thunderstruck with either wonder or horror: "She could but see how beautiful it was, / With glistening, glazed, mild eyes" (36).

Ashe's version then effects a second metamorphosis, so that there is no terrifying and physiologically-impossible-to-imagine penetration here by a serpent's body or phallus—merely a scene instead that domesticates and normalizes the encounter, with a god who is recognizably and unmistakably human in form and who is, moreover, an especially attractive specimen of masculinity:

> And while she watch'd arose a mist again.
> And dimly, beautifully, from their shroud,

> Uncoil'd the white fair flesh and human limbs
> Of manhood. Life and beauty in the light
> Took form, with subtle curves of cloudy joy.
> And then the last film of the transient veil
> Roll'd heavenward: she beheld him: he was come.
> O untold glory of his manliness!
> O heavenly god, reveal'd in earthly guise!
> O symmetry of perfect parts, and pride
> Of graceful strength!
>
> (36)

Having gotten all that she had wished for, what can this Dryope do but faint (as well as pretend to faint again), as any proper Victorian lady would, when overcome with gladness? Thus, "she swoon'd," and, after coming to her senses and finding "Apollo's arms were round her," with her "dizzy head" lying on "his breast divine," she "being happy, feign'd to swoon the more" (36).

Just as Ashe's Dryope is the perfect Victorian heroine, so his Apollo is equally the perfect gentleman. Since a gentleman would never take advantage of a lady, Apollo must go about securing explicit consent for his next move and must wait until she is both conscious and ready to give it:

> He spake holier words
> Than most lovers speak. He pleaded for
> Communion, which true spirits have, who keep
> Pure and unspotted from the soiling world.
> And thus he told his passion, and she clasp'd
> Her arms around him, and the bond was seal'd.
>
> (36–37)

But this is no mere affair based on lust, nor is it a fleeting encounter in which the god Apollo seizes his prey and moves on. A monogamous, romantic relationship follows, lasting throughout the change of seasons, from one summer to the next:

> Many a pleasant month
> Drew out its days, and wore its leaves of joy.
> And they were happy lovers, with no pain
> Or grief at all. And love made for them both
> A rich Elysium: crown'd with sunny heights
> Of fancy: sloping into vales of bliss
>
> (38)

What destroys the idyll of this perfectly suited, well-behaved, and genteel heterosexual couple, who have chosen to live together in what the Victorians would have called a free union? Here, Thomas Ashe turns to the latter part of the Dryope myth, which Michael Field's "A Tortoise" deliberately omits. In the original tale, Dryope, who is pregnant after her rape and abandonment by Apollo, gives birth and marries a human man. Her eventual fate is to turn into a poplar tree, although one version of the myth has her doing so to escape a second violation by Apollo, while another makes her transformation the result of poor maternal judgment, as a consequence of plucking a flower to give to her son from the lotus tree that was formerly the body of the nymph named "Lotis."

The variation that Ashe, however, works on this material has Dryope being abducted from her forest paradise and forced to wed a human prince. So distraught is she that she physically declines: "Her beauty wither'd in a morn, and fell / Away like tinsel; and the warm, soft flesh / Shrank into wrinkled leanness in a day" (39). Seeing this, her captors eventually allow her to escape to the forest. But Apollo, meanwhile, uncharitably assumes that her disappearance must have been voluntary and that she has been unfaithful by choice. The poem's speaker comments, "'Twas pity that he wrong'd her. 'Twas her doom" (40). Dryope winds up as an ordinary Fallen Woman, and an abandoned one at that. To lessen her suffering, the Dryads kindly transform her—"They softly breathed on her, and she became / A lotus, and her womanhood was changed"—so that she can live with the Dryads, enjoying their sort of unreflective, unfeeling existence: "She had that airy happy health of theirs, / That came of living in the air and winds" (39). Yet she can never wholly erase the consciousness of being exiled from the Edenic company of her lover:

> And once she met Apollo: but he knew
> His friend no longer. And a shudder came
> Across her for a flitting minute's space:
> And then the truth flash'd on her, clear as day,
> And she knew well it was in vain to sigh.
>
> (40)

Thus concludes Ashe's "Dryope," with a hapless female figure, disempowered and caught forever in a liminal state, after being discarded by the one she had loved and to whom she had freely given her virginity.

It would not be difficult to enumerate all the reasons why Bradley and Cooper might have found this poem offensive, for Ashe trivializes, while he subtly modernizes (and flattens), Dryope's character, plight, and fate. Michael Field's poem number sixty-one from *Long Ago*, on the contrary, restores to the figure of Dryope her dignity, even as it insists upon the unfathomable mystery and incomprehensibility of the experience to which she is subject in Apollo's presence. In Michael Field's version, Apollo singles out Dryope not for her beauty but for her unfeminine daring, as she is the sole member of the Hamadryads' band to approach and to stroke the tortoise, which all the others fear; she even boldly brings its shell up to her face. With her readiness to embrace rather than to shrink from strangeness and danger, and with her ease of overstepping limits—even before Apollo's "spell is round her" and before she assumes her new identity as a participant in sacred mysteries—Michael Field's Dryope demonstrates the *potential* to join the band of poets and prophets whom "Leto's son has raised above / Other mortals."[46] Already possessing something of the Apollonian spirit, she can, therefore, recognize who and what holds her, amidst "the wonder that has chanced, / As she feels a god within / Fiery looks that thrill and win."[47] Apollo, after all, is not in his godlike form here but in the lowly shape of an animal—a mere serpent; despite this, she *feels* his identity as a god.

That particular line ("As she feels a god within / Fiery looks that thrill and win") is a fascinating one, for it opens up multiple possibilities and forecloses none of them. Is the poem informing us that Dryope senses Apollo's godliness thanks to her superior inner vision, in effect seeing it "within" his "Fiery looks," which are directed at her? But what about that line break—the pause that it invites after the word "within"? Does Dryope, despite her sexual inexperience, innately know, from *within* her body, that a god—not a serpent or even a phallus, per se—is the thing that is upon her? Or alternatively, while Apollo holds her and compels her to acknowledge the "joy / Which no childish fears alloy"[48] of being mastered by the embodied spirit of poetry and prophecy, does *she* "feel a god within"? In other words, does she, in this process of initiation into her new identity as an elect being, feel *herself* to be godlike? Is this what it means to experience inspiration, which seems to arrive inexplicably and unexpectedly but which fills one from within with a sense of exaltation, whether it arrives in childhood (as in the fiction by "New Women" writers) or in later life?

If that is what is occurring to Michael Field's Dryope, then "LXI" from *Long Ago* is not a poem about rape, which must necessarily involve loss and violation; instead, it is about an indefinable encounter beyond the boundaries of law, nature, or any rational explanation that results in Dryope becoming aware of her own power. Afterwards, Dryope leaves the geographically fixed social world of the female Hamadryads, where gender exists in the form of conventionally feminine behavior and where the chief activity consists of childish games. Now Dryope "joins the troop of those / Dedicate to joy and woes," who have no need of gender and gender roles or of place, but who instead enjoy absolute liberty, and, "endowed / With existence unallowed / To their fellows, wander free / Girt with earth's own mystery."[49] It is difficult to conceive of a more bewildering yet wondrous image than the central one of "A Tortoise" for the equally extraordinary condition of becoming conscious, as were Bradley and Cooper themselves, of the status of being "raised above / Other mortals"[50]—of being inspired and, thanks to this inspiration, of possessing poetic genius.

It seems easy to imagine why Michael Field might have wanted to lay their rival version of the Dryope myth before Havelock Ellis. In doing so, perhaps they also wished to demonstrate why they, rather than Thomas Ashe, deserved an entire article in the *Westminster Review* devoted to their work, rather than merely a single favorable mention. It is equally easy to understand why Ellis, nonetheless, might have gone on preferring Ashe's work. As a radical social reformer dedicated to effecting change in the sphere of the actual, Ellis could not have failed to be charmed by Ashe's straightforward defense of free love and free unions or by his portrait of a desiring female subject who unashamedly seeks and accepts "communion" with a high-principled man (and who then proves lost and disconsolate without him). Less clear is what he would have made of a poem such as "A Tortoise," which depicts a female figure who accesses her own sense of power and eschews the social world entirely, leaving the sphere of heterosexuality and of gender itself, to "wander free / Girt with earth's own mystery."[51]

As we learn from an undated letter that Ellis wrote to Bradley, Michael Field did indeed send him a copy, after publication, of *Long Ago*. His response to this offering was by no means an expression of unalloyed admiration: "But I am sure you will let me tell you how much I have been enjoying 'Long Ago,'" he began, "more, I think, than I expected, for I certainly think that blank verse is M. F.'s proper medium."[52] Then, he felt it necessary to produce his rankings of the poems: "I divided those I liked into three classes—a X (positive) class, a XX (comparative) & XXX (superlative) class." It seems that "A Tortoise" earned the equivalent of a grade of A– or B+: "The XX /class\ is of higher degree & only contains four poems—8, 48, 61, 62."[53] But he definitely did not place LXI among the desirable triple XXXs; only two poems made that cut. In total, a mere twenty out of the nearly seventy poems wound up in any of these three favored classes at all, as good enough to be among "those . . . [he] liked."

Through their rewriting of the Dryope myth, Michael Field had given readers such as Ellis the chance to experience the awe that accompanies inspiration and the act of being initiated into the company of the elect—and to "feel" this viscerally and mysteriously from "within," as women did. Ellis nonetheless chose to ignore this new knowledge, or at least not to value the vehicle that transmitted it. By temperament a critic, rather than a fellow poet, he would not, it seems, even for an "hour" agree to "glow beneath" the "power"[54] of their verse and surrender himself, as Bradley and Cooper had surrendered themselves to Browning; on the contrary, he stood apart, making lists and bestowing marks. Like most Victorian men, he would not accept a posture of submission before women's work. But unlike Browning—who, alas, was dying in 1889—he was not up to the alternative role of an all-knowing Master, only of a fussy schoolmaster.

Altogether, Havelock Ellis proved to be rather a disappointment as a male muse. No wonder Bradley and Cooper moved on, almost immediately, to Bernard Berenson. At the same time, they continued, after publishing *Long Ago*, "Through the firs thereafter" to "range" and to revel in an "existence unallowed / To their fellows."[55] However much their literary contemporaries failed to live up to their expectations, Bradley and Cooper knew that they could always find inspiration—and even ecstasy—in writing to and with one another. It was their own unorthodox erotic and emotional communion, rather than any conventional version of an artistic relationship with a masculine mentor, that had first unleashed their genius and would continue to do so.

Notes

1. Michael Field, "LXI: χελώνη," in *Long Ago* (London: George Bell and Sons, 1889), 111–13.

2. Richard Dellamora, "The Sapphic Culture of Michael Field and Radclyffe Hall," in *Michael Field and Their World*, ed. Margaret D. Stetz and Cheryl A. Wilson (High Wycombe, UK: Rivendale, 2007), 134.

3. Marion Thain, *Michael Field: Poetry, Aestheticism and the Fin de Siècle* (Cambridge: Cambridge University Press, 2007), 53.

4. Field, "LXI," 112.

5. For more about this controversy, see J. T. Laird, "Developments in the Printed Versions," in *Thomas Hardy, Tess of the D'Urbervilles, An Authoritative Text: Hardy and the Novel Criticism*, 2nd ed., ed. Scott Elledge (New York: W. W. Norton, 1979), 370–77; William A. Davis Jr., "The Rape of Tess: Hardy, English Law, and the Case for Sexual Assault," *Nineteenth-Century Literature* 52, no. 2 (1997): 221–31; James A. Nye, "Thomas Hardy," in *Censorship: A World Encyclopedia*, ed. Derek Jones (London and New York: Routledge, 2001), 1029–30.

6. Linda H. Peterson, *Becoming a Woman of Letters: Myths of Authorship and Facts of the Victorian Market* (Princeton, NJ: Princeton University Press, 2009), 146.

7. Katharine Tynan, *A Cluster of Nuts, Being Sketches among My Own People* (London: Lawrence and Bullen, 1894), 221.

8. Tynan, 220, 223.

9. Katharine Tynan, *Twenty-Five Years: Reminiscences* (New York: Devin-Adair, 1913), 358.

10. George Egerton, *Fantasias* (John Lane: Bodley Head, 1898), 38, 41–42.

11. Egerton, 42.

12. F. H. Burnett, *The One I Knew the Best of All* (London: Frederick Warne, 1893), 172.

13. John Strange Winter, "Jewels to Wear," in Winter, *Princess Sarah and Other Stories* (London: Ward, Lock, 1897), 281–82, 284.

14. Winter, 273.

15. Winter, 277–78.

16. Field, "LXI," 113.

17. "Chelone," in *A Dictionary of Greek and Roman Biography and Mythology*, ed. William Smith (Boston: Little, Brown, 1867), 693.

18. Sarah Parker, *The Lesbian Muse and Poetic Identity, 1889–1930* (London: Pickering and Chatto, 2013), 50–51.

19. Parker, 51.

20. Edith Cooper to Robert Browning, October 14, 1886 (BL Add MS 46777, vol. 2); *'Michael Field' & Fin-de-Siècle Culture and Society: The Journals, 1868–1914, and the Correspondence of Katharine Bradley and Edith Cooper*, thirteen microfilm reels (Marlborough, UK: Adam Matthew, 2003), reel 2 (hereafter cited as *'Michael Field'*).

21. Katharine Bradley to Robert Browning, October 15, 1886 (BL Add MS 46777, vol. 2); *'Michael Field,'* reel 2.

22. "Michael Field" to Robert Browning, April 4, 1887 (BL Add MS. 46777, vol. 2); *'Michael Field,'* reel 2.

23. "Michael Field" to Robert Browning, April 4, 1887.

24. "Michael Field" to Robert Browning, April 4, 1887.

25. Michael Field, "Preface," in *Long Ago*, n.p.

26. Field, "LXI," 112–13.

27. Field, 113.

28. Katharine Bradley would return to and rework this image of a vulnerable and open work of art in the poem "Aridity," likening the "Soul" to a book that awaits the scrutiny of God: "A book of His dear choice, / That quiet waiteth for His Hand, / That quiet waiteth for His Eye, / That quiet waiteth for His Voice." Michael Field, "Aridity," in *Mystic Trees* (London: Eveleigh Nash, 1913), 133.

29. Katharine Bradley to Robert Browning, May 2, 1889 (BL Add MS 46777, vol. 2); *'Michael Field,'* reel 2.

30. Field, "LXI," 112.

31. Yopie Prins, *Victorian Sappho* (Princeton, NJ: Princeton University Press, 1999), 76.

32. Mary Sturgeon, *Michael Field* (London: George G. Harrap, 1922), 90.

33. Michael Field, *Works and Days from the Journal of Michael Field*, ed. T. and D. C. Sturge Moore (London: John Murray, 1933), 216.

34. Edith Cooper to Robert Browning, February 9, 1889 (BL Add MS 46777, vol. 2); *'Michael Field,'* reel 2.

35. Dinah Ward, "Interpreting Female-Female Love in the Early Poetry of Michael Field" (PhD diss., University of Sheffield, 2008), 68.

36. Edith Cooper to Robert Browning, February 9, 1889; *'Michael Field,'* reel 2.

37. Maev Kennedy, "Browning's Dreamy Snake Girl Goes on Sale," *Guardian* (UK), January 23, 2006, https://www.theguardian.com/culture/2006/jan/23/art.

38. Cooper refers explicitly to this, when telling Browning that the poem "was written after you had shown to us the photograph of your son's statue of Dryope." Letter from E. C. to Robert Browning, February 9, 1889.

39. Katharine Bradley, "Letter to Edith Cooper [Stoke Green] [Oct. 1885]," in *The Fowl and the Pussycat: Love Letters of Michael Field, 1876–1909*, ed. Sharon Bickle (Charlottesville: University of Virginia Press, 2008), 167.

40. Havelock Ellis, "H. E. to O. S. Friday Night. [13 Mar 85]," in *"My Other Self": The Letters of Olive Schreiner and Havelock Ellis, 1884–1920*, ed. Yaffa Claire Drazmin (New York: Peter Lang, 1992), 319.

41. [Havelock Ellis], "Art. V.—Thomas Ashe's [sic] Poems," *Westminster Review*, April 1886, 417.

42. [Ellis], 428.

43. [Ellis], 420.

44. [Ellis], 422.

45. Thomas Ashe, "Dryope," in *Poems by Thomas Ashe: Complete Edition* (London: George Bell and Sons, 1886), 34. Subsequent page numbers are cited in text.

46. Field, "LXI," 113.

47. Field, "LXI," 112.

48. Field, "LXI," 113.

49. Field, "LXI," 113.

50. Field, "LXI," 113.

51. Field, "LXI," 113.

52. Havelock Ellis to Katharine Bradley, n.d. [1889?], in *Michael Field, the Poet: Published and Manuscript Materials*, ed. Marion Thain and Ana Parejo Vadillo (Peterborough, Ontario: Broadview, 2009), 349.

53. Thain and Vadillo, *Michael Field, the Poet*, 349.

54. Field, "LXI," 113.

55. Field, "LXI," 113.

THREE

Sculpture, Poetics, Marble Books

Casting Michael Field

ANA PAREJO VADILLO

THIS IS HOW PLINY THE ELDER RECOUNTS THE ORIGINS
of sculpture:

> Boutades, a potter of Sikyon, discovered, with the help of his
> daughter, how to model portraits in clay. She was in love with a
> youth, and when he was leaving the country she traced the outline
> of the shadow which his face cast on the wall by lamplight. Her
> father filled in the outline with clay and made a model; this he
> dried and baked with the rest of his pottery, and we hear that it
> was preserved in the temple of the Nymphs[.][1]

Boutades's daughter was the 650 BC Greek painter Kora of Sikyon, in some
sources also identified by the name of Callirrhoë.[2] Most art historians agree that
this story, which has circulated widely from antiquity, is probably apocryphal
but that it has endured because it has served a fundamental purpose: what the
story asks continuously of its readers is if sculpture, as a manufactured object,
is to be understood as a replacement for the missing original. In Deborah Tarn
Steiner's reading, the terra-cotta object functions "as a substitute for the depart-
ing lover, representative of the absent and the dead." The object, she adds, seems
to stand in "for the lost party" and exists to maintain "communication between
those separated by time and space."[3]

This collaboration of two generations of artists, father and daughter, curiously mirrors the unique artistic partnership that was "Michael Field." Katharine Bradley and Edith Cooper's first play published under the Michael Field pseudonym was based on another Callirrhoë, the priestess whose self-sacrifice inaugurated the beginning of the cult of Dionysus in Greece.[4] *Callirrhoë* (1884) ends with 'white troops' of maenads stealing away through the moonlight and with the promise of statues for worship. But Pliny's anecdote allows another comparison, for Michael Field's poetic practice was shaped by the arts of painting and *sculpture*. As we know, critics have confined their analysis of Michael Field's ekphrastic poetry to painting, focusing in particular on their 1892 volume of verse *Sight and Song*, while the influence of sculpture on their poetics has not been documented.[5]

And yet, the imprint of sculpture on Michael Field was profound and significant: it was a primal force in the production of their art. This chapter narrates how Bradley and Cooper developed a sculptural aesthetic that encompassed their poetic practice and, particularly in the early years, the very casting of their authorship. In their poetry, sculpture would function as a complex metaphor for their modern, dissident poetics, a metaphor for the sexual and sensual body, for the intellect and ideal, for their decadence, and for the very concept of their fragmented authorship. Their lyrics also conjured sculpture as a plastic art, intervening in Michael Field's concept of both the poem, which acquired a three-dimensional quality, and the poetry volume, the materialized book of poems. Indeed, the full implications of Michael Field's engagement with sculpture converge in their book production, their books being objets d'art—sculptures in their own right. The intellectual agility with which they engaged with sculpture thus invites a new reading of Michael Field as poet-sculptors and conceptual book artists.[6]

The focus of this chapter is on Michael Field's writings from the marble period, from ca. 1878 to 1890. I call those years "the marble period" because during these years, what Cooper called "white sculptural thought" produced a number of "marble books"—that is, books bound in white: *Callirrhoë. Fair Rosamund* (1884); *The Father's Tragedy. William Rufus. Loyalty or Love?* (1885); *Canute the Great. The Cup of Water* (1887); *Long Ago* (1889); and *The Tragic Mary* (1890). It may be argued that this first marble phase culminates with the publication of their essay "Effigies" (1890), a meditation on a sculptural walk around the colored wax effigies of Westminster Abbey.[7]

The year 1890 marks a watershed in Michael Field's life and work. In this year, the poets met the aesthetic critic Bernard Berenson. Heavily influenced by Berenson and, as Sarah Parker shows in the next chapter, by his partner Mary

Costelloe, Michael Field's poetics turned toward the painterly, the most significant example of which is, of course, *Sight and Song* (1892). This is not to say that Michael Field turned their back to sculpture, only that their writings became more heavily indebted to the art of painting in what we might see as a second poetic phase post-1890. This is particularly evident in their book art, with no books after 1890 bound in white.[8] A renewed interest in sculptural poetry began to reemerge around 1894, when the poets befriended the painter, book artist, and sculptor Charles Ricketts and his partner the painter Charles Shannon. Michael Field's relationship with "the artists," as the poets would nickname them, would cause a major revolution in the form of their books, with sculpture resurging again and manifesting itself in their poetic thinking and book production. In their final years, in a religious phase of sculptural writing, Michael Field's conversion to Roman Catholicism led them to the work of the modernist Catholic sculptor Eric Gill. Their relationship with Gill is discussed by Kristin Mahoney in this book.

My thesis here is that in the marble period, 1878–90, sculpture was the touchstone of Michael Field's poetics, providing their lyrics with uncensored emotional energy and caressing forms. Using their correspondence, diaries, and early poetry, I chart how sculpture came to represent for Michael Field the art of creation: the origin of form, the unity of life and work, and the casting of their modern poetry. The starting point of my discussion is Bradley and Cooper's early fascination with sculpture and how their intellectual and sensory response to sculpture enabled the beginning of their collaboration. I then move on to examine their first coauthored book, *Bellerophôn* (1881), to argue that this poetic drama, whose plot was inspired by the broken sculptures of the Parthenon that the poets studied at the British Museum, is an experiment in fragmented authorship. My line of argument here is that Bradley and Cooper's play suggests a model of decadent poetics rooted in the concept of the fragment, or, to put it differently, a decadence articulated around archeological ruins of the past. The chapter then moves on to argue that sculpture became a metaphor for writing in collaboration, examining in particular Bradley's self-representation as a potter. The chapter ends with a reformulation of the book as a sculptural object, as a statue.

"The Language from Thy Fair Greek Mouth": Sculptural Formations

Katharine Bradley and Edith Cooper's sculptural poetic practice predates the "birth" of "Michael Field" but is at the heart of the poetical construct that would become "Michael Field." Early on in their lives, they fostered poetic channels of communication through the art of sculpture, drawing creativity and interpretation from this engagement as they developed a long-standing passion for this art, their art, and for each other. This is not surprising considering that Cooper's father, with whom the poets would live until his death in 1897, was a wood-carving artist. And it is worth noting that Bradley and Cooper would always live and write surrounded by sculptures: the furniture in their writing room would be carved by Cooper's father, where he replicated the image of the bramble-bough from the woodblock he had created for their books; they would own sculptures by Ricketts and Gill; would buy photographs of sculptures to decorate their writing room; and would collect casts, mostly replicas of ancient Greek and Roman statues. In other words, Bradley and Cooper's personal and intellectual history was always from the start closely linked to sculpture.

Bradley's first forays into sculptural writing occurred in Paris in 1868. She fell in love with the Parisian sculptor and stained glass artist Alfred Gérente, who died before she was able to convey to him her feelings. A few days after his death, Bradley visited his atelier with his sister Eliza (Bradley's companion in Paris). The sculptures that she saw during this visit to his studio are meticulously detailed in her Paris diary for 1868. She writes with frisson of "the lovely statuettes by Michael Angelo" and "the delicate, finely wrought fragments of sculpture" lying around in the studio: "a little block of a pillar," a "broken ornament," "the head of a Madonna," "a cowering Satan, with vindictive finger pressed close upon his passion compressed lips." "[S]ome odd clumsy English toys among all that antique beauty" disrupt the flow of her lingering thoughts.[9] She fixes her eye on "a bust & the hand of the mother, taken after death." "How very precious to have such relics," she observes. "I have seen my likeness," she continues, "what I shall have, a glorious head."[10]

Consciously or unconsciously, Bradley was grasping their beauty in the same way as her contemporaries were interpreting the sculptures of the past: the influence of Michelangelo, the fascination with antique Greek sculptures, satyr figures, broken pieces. These annotations foreshadow how sculpture would model Michael Field's sculptural poetics, capturing in particular an inclination for the fragmented object. They seem to suggest that fragments mattered to Bradley because they embodied classical ideals of beauty while being symbols of a decayed past. (Auguste Rodin, for example, would speak of the "unity of the fragment," noting that one could see the entire Acropolis in a broken piece.[11]) In this sense, Bradley's early engagement with sculpture was evidently aesthetic, but her comments also reveal her fetishization of sculpture as a symbolic object of desire. She morbidly enjoyed these objects because they symbolized the material sensuality of her beloved; it was a kind of fetish because only ultimately in death, through sculpture, did she get to connect intimately with her Platonic love.

And from the start, Bradley theorized sculpture for the purpose of writing. After Gérente's death, she visited the Père Lachaise Cemetary to see a "beautiful Gothic cross" "designed by Henry [his brother] and sculptured by Alfred." Her comments help us elucidate the links the poet Michael Field will set up between writing, sculpture, and collaboration. She writes, "No other tomb at all equal to it in beauty. All that art could do was done; but no blessed words were traced on that delicate sculptured stone."[12] One can in retrospect see that the poetry she would cowrite with Cooper would also be a "fraternal" union aiming to produce "blessed words" on the sculptured book; the cross of Henry and Alfred, a somewhat matching image of the as yet unimagined future union of Bradley and Cooper as joint producers of art.

It would be in the late 1870s when sculpture would emerge as a collaborative mode of thinking for Bradley and Cooper, a period the poets themselves termed "art's early days." Their writings of this period show that they are consonant with an emergent group of decadent artists and poets who in the late 1870s began to be interested in antique Greek sculpture. John Addington Symonds's "The Lotus-Garland of Antinous," written most probably in 1868 but first published in 1878 in *Many Moods* in Bristol, where the poets were then living, is a good (and better-known) example. In a letter to Cooper of 1880, Bradley writes to confirm "that the Antinous we worshipped in 'art's early days' at the Bath Museum is a copy of the Antinous of the Capitol."[13] In another letter of the same year, written after visiting the British Museum, Bradley states: "I went back to my beloved Elgins. Most sorely did I miss the Persian, *Persian Puss*; especially as I passed the vine-clad head that she loved so well."[14] Studying together ancient Greek sculptures clearly formed them as artists. Stimulated by the power of the sculptural, Bradley and Cooper began to use male statues (often of Dionysus) to identify themselves as poets. And they would also use male statues to articulate their passion for each other. In 1891, for example, after cutting her hair like a boy, Cooper would compare herself with Antinous, the beautiful boy beloved of Emperor Hadrian.[15]

One of Edith Cooper's first poems is "To Apollo—The Conqueror," written at the age of sixteen, in 1878. As Stefano Evangelista notes, this extraordinary poem, which remained unpublished during Bradley and Cooper's lifetime, is an ode to poetry and to the origins of her own poetry, the result of her writing partnership with Bradley, to whom the poem is dedicated.[16] It is worth pausing to examine Cooper's first-known sculptural poem. We can safely identify Cooper's "Apollo" with the statue of Apollo Belvedere; the poem's reference to the arrows makes this clear. Replicas of this statue were widely available in the nineteenth century, and we know that Cooper owned at least one replica, a gift

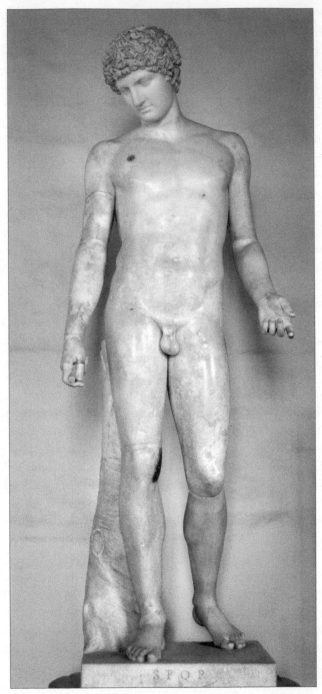

Figure 3.1. The Capitoline Antinous, marble, Roman copy, AD 2, of a Greek bronze representing Hermes. Wikimedia Commons.

from Bradley, though this may have been a later gift, from 1880.[17] The poem is about poetry and sex: indeed, poetry *is* sex. The speaker, "a priestess," watches in adoration Apollo's "sculptural form" as her heart "guesses / the awful beauty" of his "aureate life." She asks for his lips, for she is bidden the language from his fair Greek mouth. The poem then describes their sexual union:

> Dower me with thine own lips!—Am I not bidden
> The language from thy fair Greek mouth to take
> To wing thy conquering arrows, till they wake
> The heavy world & in its heart are hidden?
> Thy hands, no more destroying, I have seen
> With thrilling touch, like lute-strings sweet & keen,
> Laid on my brow to dedicate & bless;
> [...]
> I feel within a joyful, onward-leaping
> Like to a horse turned homeward, like the sea
> That springs on to the far rocks joyfully.
> The wind of inspiration downward sweeping
> Lawlessly scatters all earth's thoughts aside.
> In golden death, like dead leaves scattered wide.
> —He stays with me.—Birth from his presence springs,
> I am a mother to all beauteous things.[18]

The priestess sees Apollo's poetic inspiration as a sexual encounter in which she gets impregnated and becomes a poet, a mother of beauteous things. She is "alone," the poem ends, yet "conquered, wedded, made One" with the divinity. In this transgressive poem, Apollo is a statue and the beloved, the embodiment of Bradley, a heterosexual intercourse encoding an incestuous lesbian relationship. Bradley is indeed represented, metaphorically speaking, as the sculptor who "with thrilling touch" sculpts the priestess, the young initiate, into a poet.

Bradley and Cooper would look back to this poem as a point of origin, a sort of omphalos of their decadent modern poetics. Visiting Rome in 1880, Bradley would run madly to see the marble statue of Apollo Belvedere.[19] Two years later, in 1882, as she was rereading the poem, Bradley wrote to Cooper that after the "mighty" cares of the drama "to go back to these early lyrics is like a gt. stateman's return to his native village" to see "the village girl who first got his fancy."[20] This poem is the seed of much of Michael Field's sculptural poetics, by which the male sculptural form through its very sensuousness embodies the poetical ideal. "Kissing the fair lips" of Apollo—*kissing* statues, as we will see—would become part of their aesthetic, sexual, and intellectual approach to sculpture, a source of inspiration for their joint decadent poetics. Sharon Bickle has suggested that the women might have engaged in some form of marriage ceremony involving the gift of a cast of Apollo.[21] In 1885, a year after their first joint book of poems as "Michael Field," Cooper wrote thus to Bradley, who was unwell and not with Cooper: "We have been wo [sic] fully married this year, save for that brief dear time of wh: my adored Apollo is the pledge. Ah, dear, that was a spiritual gift, the one gt. gift to *me*. I 'hug' it instead of you and or rather through it I am never parted from you in truth."[22] Cooper's intense attachment to Apollo reminds us of the story of Pliny the Elder. As we can see in this letter, Cooper's Apollo, god of the lyre and Greek ideal of beauty, whether poem or sculpture—perhaps poem *and* sculpture—"stood in" for Bradley's absent beloved, Cooper.

More importantly in the context of their coming together as poets and lovers, what clearly emerges from these early writings is that sculpture was an intense aesthetic experience that functioned as a strategy for fulfilling sexual desire. And we can also see that they interpreted and theorized sculpture for the purpose of creating poetry.

Chiseling *Bellerophôn*: Decadence in Fragments

Concrete ideas about sculptural poetics were coalescing around 1880, thanks to visits to London and, later in the year (as we see in the next section), to a trip made by Bradley to France and Italy. During the spring of 1880 they regularly studied sculpture at the British Museum as part of the research for their first coauthored work, the poetic drama *Bellerophôn*, published a year later by C. Kegan Paul under the double pseudonym "Arran and Isla Leigh." The book contained in addition to the poetic drama eleven lyric poems, most of which were also on Greek subjects and topics. Their play was based on Euripides's 430 BC drama of that title (but without the accents), which survives in fragments. It was a play known in the ancient world for praising paganism: in Euripides's drama, Bellerophon doubts the existence of the gods.[23] Bradley and Cooper sought advice from John Wesley Hales, literature professor and journalist. He read drafts and encouraged Bradley to study in situ the sculptures at the British Museum, presumably to improve the play's characterization, environment, and architectonics. Bradley told Cooper that Hales thought that she "ought to bathe [herself] a little more in the folk-lore of Lycia, and be steeped in the stories of the local divinities."[24] On a couple of occasions, he would join Bradley to study the Elgin Marbles and the Lycian Room, where sculptures of Bellerophon could be seen. Hales also recommended the reading of the work of Johann Winckelmann.

How much of Winckelmann's writings on sculpture did the poets know before Hales suggested him? It seems difficult to imagine that the poets would not have read Winckelmann before 1880. Bradley and Cooper knew Hegel's works well, and in his writings of art, Hegel had written profoundly on Winckelmann.[25] Also, well known among aesthetic circles was Winckelmann's particular fascination (which was both sensual and aesthetic) with the statue of Apollo Belvedere.[26] Hales must have surely recommended Winckelmann's *Reflections on the Painting and Sculpture of the Greeks* (1755) and *History of the Art of Antiquity* (1764). Both works include references to the figure of Bellerophon. The illustration at the end of the dedicatory letter of his *History of the Art of Antiquity* is a relief of Bellerophon accompanied by Pegasus.[27] In 1901, Charles Ricketts would make for Michael Field the stunning pendant, "Pegasus Drinking from the Fountain of Hippocrene," a gift from Bradley to Cooper. This piece of jewelry is decorated with a low relief of Pegasus, which was inspired by a sard intaglio from the Marlborough Collection of the British Museum but echoes the relief found in Winckelmann's book. This pendant reminds us of the importance of this play for Michael Field.

But before moving more directly to a discussion of the Leighs' play—and, in the context of Winckelmann, Pater, and Bradley and Cooper's engagement with nineteenth-century theories of sculpture—it is important to note at this moment that this renewed interest in Winckelmann and, more generally, in Greek and Renaissance sculpture in the last quarter of the nineteenth century, coincided with the rise of the "New Sculpture" in Britain. And it is also worth impressing an often-unrecognized fact: that Bradley and Cooper would get to know and visit the atelier of some of its members—Robert Wiedeman Barrett Browning (Pen Browning) and, most notably, Edward Onslow Ford.[28] As recent research by has shown, one of the key texts of the New Sculpture movement was Pater's influential 1867 essay "Winckelmann." The Winckelmann essay would later be reproduced in his *Studies of the History of the Renaissance* (1873), which also included other essays on sculpture, most notably "The Poetry of Michelangelo" (first published in 1871) and "Luca della Robia" (first published in 1872). We know for certain that Bradley and Cooper were reading Pater's work in 1886 and that in 1889 Cooper was working intensely on his essays on sculpture, "The Marbles of Aegina" (1880) and "The Beginnings of Greek Sculpture" (1880).[29] The dates of these two later articles are significant. Again we see that Michael Field's work on sculpture coincides with the works of other decadent writers and artists. Auguste Rodin spent 1881 in London to study the Elgin Marbles at the British Museum. Michael Field's first play was contemporaneous with Pater's 1880s writings on sculpture. And these two 1880 essays would be used in 1889 by Cooper to compose her essay "Effigies" (1890).

Bradley and Cooper's early work shows that they were influenced by Winckelmann's vision of Romanticism in Greek sculpture, both directly and indirectly, by way of Pater (they would have read his *Studies in the History of the Renaissance* [1873] by 1880).[30] In sculpture, as we have already seen, they found passion and physical excitement, sculptural objects often symbolizing their sexual and intellectual friendship. What is certain is that during this early phase of their writings, during the 1880s, Bradley and Cooper were acquiring a wide knowledge of sculpture. By 1890, they would be studying Rodin, visiting his studio in Paris, and discussing his sculptures with Arthur Symons for an article Symons was writing for the *Art Magazine*.[31] In the context of the aesthetics of fragmentation and brokenness that would represent *Bellerophôn*, it is no surprise that Bradley and Cooper would love Rodin's *The Walking Man* (1877–78), a bronze of a man walking without a head, which they saw in Paris in 1890, calling it a "masterly figure."[32]

What Symons said of Rodin, in a language so evocative of Pater—"other sculptors turn life into sculpture, he turns sculpture into life"—matters in our analysis of Michael Field's sculptural poetics.[33] Their poetry aimed to turn sculpture into life. Bradley's visits to the British Museum were fruitful, forcing her to consider and make "archaeological" changes to the manuscript of *Bellerophôn*: "[T]he reclining statues often had *garlands* in their hands. I think I shall have to give up the orb, and substitute a chaplet in the Elgin Marbles passage," she writes in one letter.[34] In another letter, also from London, Bradley continues her examination of sculptures for *Bellerophôn* at the museum, in particular the extraordinary Lycian Room.[35] The Lycian marbles came from Xanthos, Turkey, and had belonged to the Persian, Greek, and Roman Empires. They had been transported from Turkey to England at the beginning of the nineteenth century and included three tombs: the Merehi (the Chimaera Tomb), the architectonic assemble of the Nereid Monument, and the Harpy Tomb. The Nereid Monument (actually sea nymphs) was constructed in honor of Erbinna, the king of Lycia, and had been modeled on the Temple of Athena Nike (Athens). The relief on the roof of the Chimaera Tomb was thought to be Bellerophon attacking the Chimaera.[36]

In science, the study of organic decay and decomposition is referred to as taphonomy, from the Greek work *taphos*, meaning tomb. Bradley and Cooper's collaborative decadent sculptural poetics began with the Chimera Tomb; and they wrote with relish of the decayed relics of the past. Bradley writes thus to Cooper: "As the Professor had predicted, I had already 'spotted' Bellerophon on his arrival just before three." The letter continues:

Figure 3.2. The Roof of the Tomb of Merehi. © The Trustees of the British Museum.

> Oh Persian [Cooper] the Lycian Court is the very first on
> entrance, only we did not know we did not consider, when we
> were there. First two immense tombs (actually dug up and
> brought from Zanthus about 400 BC) on one of wh[ich] Bell is
> represented combating Chimaera in a quadriga; Chimaera looking
> like a rather discomforted boar-lion; not the "tri-parte malignity"
> *we* know about. Then round the walls are fragments of a beautiful
> temple from Zanthus, of which there is a complete model and
> lovely torsoed figures of Nereids, that were placed between the
> columns of the temple. Bell. must have seen these; and there ought
> to be some allusion to them.[37]

Thus encouraged, Hales and Bradley requested to see "a second Bellerophon" at
the museum:

> There is no Chimaera visible *to us*; but to Pegasus with his pricked up
> ears, and angry head, and to Bellerophon with his set lips and intent
> stedfast [*sic*] eyes, he is clearly visible. This Bell is no "quadriger" no
> fair-charioted steed, but on his own winged horse. I was obliged to
> confess that our Bell was much weaker, and frailer; but of course in
> the moment of intense struggle, even his gentle irresolute face wd. be
> firm and fired too. The Prof. and I staid and studied every point.[38]

Cooper and Bradley transformed their research into an embodied mythological drama imagined through the three-dimensionality of sculpture. Almost every character in the play is based on the sculptures that they saw in the Lycian Room: the Nereids, for example, appear as nymphs; Erinna is the queen of Lycia, who falls in love with Bellerophôn. Their language is sculptural too: tragically in love with Bellerophôn, Anteia adores him as "marble statue that one dares not mar / It looks so worshipful."[39]

Bellerophôn is fierce and strong in battle, but he is—like Euripides's hero—a decadent philosopher plagued with doubt and eager to break with the past.[40] Key to the drama is the passage regarding the Elgin Marbles. In this monologue, which echoes Keats's ekphastic poem "Upon Seeing the Elgin Marbles," Bellerophôn explains why he is attacking the Olympus. He compares humanity to broken pieces of sculptures as he fiercely charges against the gods for being the "thwarted sculptors of the universe." The passage is worth quoting at length:

> Yet needly must I trace about mankind
> Marks of a masterpiece that, unashamed
> Of his own craft, Zeus might contemplate;—now
> It lies in torsoed ruin!—Piteous
> To any wanderer 'mid the broken forms
> The lovely breast-swell of the headless trunk,
> The falling vesture pliant to the pant
> Of the soft breathing side and slumb'rously
> Swathing the wearied limbs; but where the brow
> Should crown the perfect image of respose,
> The mutilate jagged column of the neck!
> The hero's fistless arms, the majesty
> Of some grand couchant royalty, profaned
> By lack of the foot's pedestal, provoke
> The gods to irony of their own art,—
> A most unsightly wreck, a travesty
> Not to be borne. They will not touch the stones,
> Those thwarted sculptors of the universe,
> And man can only wonder and lament,
> Piecing a little fragment here and there,
> But impotent with chisel to conclude
> The interrupted dream, to carve a block
> Meet for conjuncture with the grand essays,
> Half-shattered, of benign omnipotence.

> Oh to provoke these languid Potencies
> To reconstructive toil: be this my task.[41]

The gods are forgetful, uncaring, and sarcastic. They have abandoned humanity, leaving humans in a mutilated, incomplete state. Men and women remain impotent sculptors, unable with the chisel to conclude the dream. Though an invincible hero capable of slaying monsters, Bellerophôn is nonetheless a plaything of the gods. A human Prometheus, his defiance of the gods is punished with blindness and exile followed by death and, he presumes, oblivion.[42] The reader knows, however, that his memory will live on to be found in fragments of writings and in damaged pieces of sculpture.

In *Bellerophôn* we see Bradley and Cooper's decadent sculptural poetics at work. The poets used the decayed, broken sculptures of the British Museum to immerse themselves in the life and culture of the period. For this reason the play was able to convey successfully the sense of that time, of that space, their three-dimensional experience allowing them to write in time and space the body of their characters. It is easy to imagine this monologue (and most moments in the play) in a three-dimensional way; the drama takes the reader for a walk around the sculptures of the Parthenon and the Lycian Room just like Bradley and Cooper must have walked the room, or indeed as they imagined Bellerophôn did, time past, in Xanthos. But more fundamentally, *Bellerophôn* is a play about fragmentation and assemblage. At a metacritical level, the poetic drama is an exercise in reappraising Euripidean fragments or parts. The drama asks quite literally, How do we find the ideal in decayed parts of the past? How can we construct a modern individual out of a damaged torso? We do not see the hero in action—against the Chimaera or against the gods—we are given instead lyric moments of enlightenment and of human subjectivity. As we have seen, *Bellerophôn* was conceived as an ekphrastic experiment. And just like the sculptures of the Parthenon, the play highlights the challenges facing the collaborative nature of their dual authorship: How do two writers give life to the broken dreams of others? The decadent modernity of *Bellerophôn* resides in bringing to life the story contained in those fragments, for *Bellerophôn* presents decadence as a study of fragmentation.

"White Sculptural Thought": Toward a Theory of Sculptural Writing

As they were completing the drama and lyrics of *Bellerophôn*, Bradley embarked on a trip to France and Italy with two friends, Jane Scott and Emily Blythe, while Cooper continued her studies in England. The letters the poets exchanged during this European trip offer further insights into the complexity of their thinking about sculpture and their sculptural poetics. What we see in this correspondence is an exploration of different methodologies of writing brought to the fore through the erotic language of sculpture. How to read sculpture aesthetically and how to reproduce what sculpture does poetically are questions that emerge in their correspondence because of their need to think through and experiment with fragmented authorship. Would they be creating poetry through the assembling of parts, as ancient sculptures sometimes were made, by modeling in clay and then chiseling or by casting? What method would work better for the composite that they were becoming?

Sculpture, so prone to touch and thus so intimate and personal, was sympathetic to their sensibility as artists and aesthetes. And as Bradley and Cooper explored each other's poetic individualities, they also needed to negotiate their personal incestuous relationship. They did so using sculpture, which became a medium through which to explore their sexuality. Consider, for example, the following letter from Bradley to Cooper, written in Genoa, which describes her reaction to the "The Venus of Milo" in Paris:

> Yet that Venus! Oh, Persian. I never saw her till the other day—
> the perfect woman—perfect in and of hers[e]lf—with no thought
> of man, no entreaty for his love; yet with breasts so sweet one
> longs to drink from them, and all the lovely circles of the girl
> moon in Pan and Luna. A lovely creature, not Cupid's Mother,
> not Adonis' bride; "das ewig weibliche" the eternal womanlie act is
> what she expresses! I am so glad to have seen her, and to descend
> from her to the Venuses of the Pitti and the Capitol.[43]

With great skill, Bradley consciously adopts the poetic language of Robert Browning's poem "Pan and Luna," published earlier that year, in 1880.[44] Browning's poem explicitly talks about drinking from a "stone chalice" filled to the brim with "fresh-squeezed" "fast-thickening poppy-juice" that "turns marble to the touch."[45] By comparing the Venus de Milo to Browning's Maid-Moon ravished or seduced by Pan (Browning's poem is open to interpretation), Bradley writes sculpture as poetry, relating both arts to homosexual desire, an echo of Cooper's early poem, "To Apollo—The Conqueror." Vicky Greenaway has recently examined Browning's work as that of a poet and a sculptor.[46] Often it has been argued that the link between Browning and Michael Field was their Greek aesthetics, but as we can see in this instance, Michael Field and Browning had also in common a fascination with the art of sculpture. This explains, as Margaret Stetz's chapter in this book shows, why Michael Field would think of *Dryope*, one of the sculptures of Browning's son, to write the poem "A Tortoise" in *Long Ago*.

Figure 3.3. Alexandros of Antioch, Venus de Milo, ca. 130–100 BC., marble, Louvre Museum, Paris. Wikimedia Commons.

But Bradley's letter continues thus: "I think of writing 3 sonnets one to each Venus. I shall twine your Shelley verses round your flowers and bear them faithfully to the grave. They are [in need of] the slightest bit re-casting—I may add a word or two, and slightly recast: we shall see."[47] The Shelley poem is "Apollo's Written Grief," one of the lyric poems included in *Bellerophôn* (1881). This poem takes its title from a quotation in Shelley's *Prometheus Unbound*. Presenting himself as a bisexual god, Apollo narrates his grief for his lover using sculptural language: "And it shall be my wrong this bitter shame," he explains, "Wrought on the rosy sculpture of the gods / Bright manhood's marbled limbs." "My Hyakinthos of the ivory breast," he calls him.[48] In fact, quite crucially, this letter articulates Bradley's theorization of two distinct but intertwined ideas about lyric composition. The first relates to the lyric as ekphrasis: poetry is provoked or inspired by the beauty of sculpture—that is, the writing of sonnets. The second is that joint poetic composition is, in this instance, thought of as a form of "casting" and "recasting." The method known as "casting" is the pouring of liquid (i.e., metal, plaster, concrete) into a mold of the desired frame, which then solidifies; the solidified piece, once stripped of the mold, is also called "casting." Bradley's use in this letter of Browning's poem and the reference to Cooper's poem on Shelley indicates that she is considering the method of "casting" as a metaphor for their poetic composition, a kind of "fast-thickening of the poppy juice turned into marble": their art as an interfusion of their liquid-lyric individualities solidifying as poetry, with the final poem itself understood as "casting," a piece of sculpture.

Bradley and Cooper's sensuous reaction to sculpture, however, needs to be addressed here. Consider this letter by Cooper written to Bradley, continuing her response upon seeing the Venus de Milo:

> The thought of consecrating a sonnet to Each fair manifestation
> of Venus delights me. If you have bent before the "Eternal
> Womanhood" at the Louvre, this morning you will Kiss the
> perfect woman at Lucca, and thank God for having sent her on
> Earth and Jacopo della Quercia for having Kept her there. I have
> sent a pilgrim-Kiss; may it reach you in time to be pressed by your
> lips on her shrine![49]

Bradley accepted the role-play and in her next letter to Cooper from Florence she confessed with great excitement:

> I bear on my lips the marble of Ilaria's brow! I walked straight to
> the left transept, and saw her, and by and bye they *all* left me, and
> I kissed her on the calm forehead, the tremulously sweet lips, the

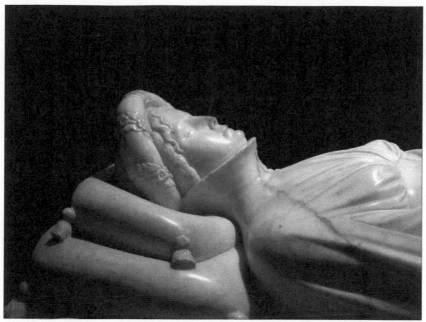

Figure 3.4. Detail of *Ilaria del Carretto* in Lucca, Cathedral of San Martino. Wikimedia Commons.

sweet round chin. And I saw the breast "heaving like a low wave of
the sea," the softly-folded hands[.][50]

The reference here is to Ruskin, who in "Three Colours of Pre-Raphaelitism"
(1878) writes thus of the tomb: "As a soft, low wave of summer sea, her breast
rises; no more."[51] Compared to Ruskin's observations, Bradley and Cooper's response is more erotic and closer to Winckelmann's (and Pater's) sensual reading
of the art of sculpture.[52] Bradley and Cooper may be interested in the abstrac-
tion that is "Eternal Womanhood," but they saw the beauty of the statue of
Ilaria as a sexual beauty, and Bradley's reaction was sexual. In fact, Bradley acts
here as receiver, transmitter, and agent of homoerotic agalmatophilia, a para-
philia discussed by Richard von Krafft-Ebing in his *Psychophathia Sexualis* that
involves sexual attraction to a statue or other similar figurative object (one of
the cases mentioned is that of a gardener who had fallen in love with the Venus
de Milo).[53] When Bradley finally got to see the Capitoline Venus in Rome, she
wrote to Cooper that

> Most happily her garments are beside her, not on her, and the
> lovely form from throat to foot is unmutilated and unshrouded,
> the dimpled back—the real beauty of the waist is only seen in
> the back—made me long again and again for the attendant Scott

> or Blythe to turn the statue for me; and all the circling beauty of
> the loins Kept me in lingering adoration; but for the bosom heave
> Milo's Venus is to me unrivalled.[54]

These letters show that the female form encouraged a shared, intimate language of same-sex eroticism between Bradley and Cooper.

But alongside this sexual reaction, it is significant that Bradley and Cooper were keener to use male statues to brand their decadence, a recurrent theme in their work, setting up a tension between the sexual response to the female form and the sexual and intellectual identification with the male form. For, as we saw in "To Apollo—The Conqueror," in her sexual fantasy Apollo makes of Cooper a mother of poems.[55] This letter about the Venus Capitolini ends with the following comment: "I saw a bust of Julian the Apostate: Capital beard. His hair was Knotted under his chin. . . . Your own Marcus, My Love, I will try to get for you!"[56] The Roman emperors and philosophers, Julian the Apostate (the last pagan emperor, who fought to keep the Roman Empire pagan) and the Stoic Marcus Aurelius were heroes of Edith Cooper.[57] In Roman times, they were often compared (it is understood that Julian the Apostate grew a beard in homage to Marcus Aurelius—the would-be hero of Walter Pater's *Marius the Epicurean* [1885]). Pagans, Epicureans, with generations in between, Marcus Aurelius and Julian the Apostate represented the kind of intergenerational aesthetic lives Bradley and Cooper aspired to live and the aesthetic writers they wanted to become. Indeed, Bradley sent Cooper as a gift to England a cast of Marcus Aurelius. Cooper called it the "glorious gift of my own Marcus," one of her "greatest" treasures.[58]

As we have seen, writing to each other about sculptures had important outcomes: the unification or articulation of their approaches to beauty, to the male and female form; the unveiling of desire and sexuality through a haptic experience of the aesthetic; the trialing of writing formats through sculptural language; and, furthermore, as seen in the following letter, the structuring of writing from individual thoughts or ideas to the actual production of poems that could be recast before the final "casting." In short, sculpture became a metaphor for composition, decomposition, and recomposition, with the poem conceived as a piece of sculpture.

One of the most important letters exchanged during this trip allows us to see how they are composing together when apart and how white sculptural thought is embedded in their poetic imagination. "It would have made your heart ache to be in the Pantheon yesterday and see the empty niches, where Athene, and all the glorious ring of Zeus once stood. If there is such a thing as dry weeping, I experienced it then." Perplexed by the juxtaposition of the Christian and the pagan, she provocatively asks, "Is that dark figure on the Cross, a great Prometheus, who[se] suffering brought good to men, while we, the great gods, lazy in the sunshine of Olympus, mingling[.]"[59] *"There, Persian, are the blocks: chip!"* (my emphasis).[60] Again, a day later Bradley writes:

> I have seen *the fair Greek lips with wh. you have been dowered,* and
> the Laöcoon of course but it is Antinous to which I turn, to wh
> I prayed to be taken again, after the hurrying attendant led us
> away. I think, P.P. that the Antinous we worshipped in "art's
> early days" at the Bath Museum is a copy of the Antinous of the
> Capitol, the statue to which one turns gracefully from the Faun
> of Praxiteles. . . . *"For we also are His offspring."* . . . I must get a
> bronze of him, or a cast, and if the Master does not repent soon,
> we will have our young Greek hero instead!![61] [italics mine]

Subtly referring to "To Apollo—The Conqueror" and identifying herself and her coauthor as the offspring of Antinous, Bradley nudged her fellow into writing. And Cooper obliged by transposing Bradley's sculptural thoughts into poetry. She composed the sonnet sequence "The Pantheon at Vespers," which she sent to Bradley in Rome. The poem presents sculpture as the realm of their poetic imaginary. Even Bradley and Cooper appear represented as statues, as "Karyatides" bearing the weight of Antiquity:

VI

This is our temple still! The cross may frown,
Like an ill-look upon our niches, bare
Of images; but every brain must there
In white thought sculpture them, and cast it down
With memory, and its stark form with crown
Of thorny rays. We are the Karyatides
Bearing Antiquity, whose power abides[.]
Built as a way to man's beginning, brown
With passing of the years. We have the age
Of mountains; and though shrouded, at our base
Men realize our greatness, vast, unseen,
And turn from the new mound—their heritage[.]
Let the black cross retain its recent place,
Our rule is here even as it hath been!

"These [are] the sonnets wh. were sent to you at Venice—my dearest," writes Cooper. *"Remember they are but your living blocks!"* (my emphasis).[62] Soon after this letter, Bradley intimates she is writing *Callirrhoë*, Michael Field's first white sculpture, a marbled book.[63] This letter and Cooper's poem demonstrate how the language of sculpture was instrumental in finding methodologies for writing in collaboration, offering the poets numerous ways of thinking about joint poetic composition. As they saw it, whether by casting or by chiseling, their task as poets was to unlock from inside every "living block" the idea for a poem, working the chisel to give the poem shape and form.

"Life Plastic," or the Potter Michael Field

We have seen how in the early 1880s, the poets used the art of sculpture in their search for models of authorship to construct decadent lyrics founded upon a sculptural vision of poetry. When the women finally became "Michael Field," sculpture was already the foundational art of their decadent poetics. "Some of the scenes of our plays are like mosaic-work," Cooper would write to Robert Browning in 1884.[64] They would use sculpture regularly for the purpose of characterization and for their book art, which is the topic of the final section of this chapter. Thus, for example, in *Callirrhoë*, the Dionysian priest Machon is described by Callirrhoë as "the statue of a human form," "a god/ Hardened against his suppliants."[65] Lucrecia, in *Brutus Ultor*, is quite literally characterized as a statue:

> she does not sleep,
> But stays awake most happy; and the moon
> Lies right across her; though her eyes are wide,
> I scarce should dare to go to her again.
> She's like a statue.

After she is defiled, Brutus shows her corpse: "Here is her statue," he exclaims, uncovering her dead body.[66] Sculpture becomes central to the plot and characterization of *The Father's Tragedy*. In April 1885, as they are finessing the moment in the play when King Robert III realizes that unwittingly he has allowed his brother, the Duke of Albany, to starve his son, David the Duke of Rothsay, to death, Cooper dreams about his marble tomb:

> I find I have not made my vision clear. This is what I dreamt. In
> the monastery-aisle I saw the tomb—and on the tomb the figure
> in its marble-stillness, with the beautiful round lines of youth
> (cheek and chin) clear in the moonlight and the blank page of the
> brow glistening white. . . . I *never saw the body*—only the statue
> after life's fitful fever sleeping well. I only felt how the body was
> contradicting this simulation.[67]

Cooper would not give up her vision and rewrote the whole section in light of this dream. The new lines would appear almost verbatim in the finished play, as she would link the statue with the blank page of the whitest white:

> Within the monast'ry
> Of far Lindores I saw the straight cold tomb
> And the straight marble statue (figure) [*sic*]—the round lines
> Of slumb'ring Youth chasten'd by Death's grave stamp,
> The brow a blank page of the whitest peace.[68]

Many examples can be found of characters imagined as statues in their dramas, but perhaps the most significant is the character of Mary, Queen of Scots. For the writing of *The Tragic Mary* (1890), Bradley and Cooper would often go to Westminster Abbey to consult her effigy and check if their play matched her marbled face: "I saw again Queen Mary's effigy," writes Bradley, "the figure lying white before God. Are we doing wrong to the noble brows?"[69] As they would write in "Effigies," in sculpture "there is no trace of those qualities which are, as it were, the accidents of the universal End," because they are "endowed" "with the wholeness and serenity of art."[70] And through their serene beauty, Michael Field could shape and cast the characters of their plays.

In the midst of Michael Field's fame in the 1880s, Bradley and Cooper saw sculpture as the "primal creative instinct" of their poetics. After visiting a pottery in Cranham in 1887, Bradley "made" Cooper "grow solemn over the Potter's wheel."[71] In a letter marked "private" to Cooper, Bradley writes that she is thinking of writing another play, "The Potter's Wheel," a dramatic play to accompany the earlier drama *The Cup of Water*, which was based on a poem by Rossetti of that title. Bradley writes, "'The Cup of Water' gets down to the well-springs of the heart—so 'The Potter's Wheel' should touch the primal *Creative instincts of man*—the laying of his *hands to the clay*—his plastic power—the discipline of art—the fellowship it opens with God" (Bradley's emphasis). She continues thus: "The very heart of Michael ought to be in it and it should be full of the deep emotions behind labour and thought." Bradley's new idea again has echoes of the story of Pliny the Elder: "A love-story there must be in it—but it must tell of the *artist's* passions and desires—deeper holier than the lover's—untouched by time" (Bradley's emphasis). She tells Cooper, "[T]hink what the spinning-wheel was to the Greeks—and the Potter's Wheel has never been adequately touched." Bradley concludes the letter urging her to "[l]ove him the Young Potter-*poet—and idealist*" (her emphasis).[72]

The play was never written, but Bradley returned by herself to see the potter's wheel. "The brown clay—taken in its aimless lumpdom, moulded, hollowed, turned, *touched*—the hand inexorable tender, the artist's throughout:—beholding

I shuddered at predestination!" (her emphasis). She identified her art directly
with that of the potter, linking the modeling of clay to their own poetic history
of seven years of joint toil, first as the Leighs and now as "Michael Field": "Yet
not the clay, but the potter has cause to complain; 7 long years Must he toil, ere
with a thumb-pat he can curve a spout. Humble dairy-bowls we may be, and yet
have Much to be grateful for: we are the fruit of skilled labour, over us Creative
Art has lingered, curiously wrought by the Master Craftsman." She added, "The
spinning-wheel teaches of life, the potter's wheel of destiny. . . . We all bear the
art-mark enough."[73] The poetic drama became instead the sonnet "Life Plastic."
Written by Bradley in 1895 and subtitled "The Potter," it would be published in
1908 in *Wild Honey*. Melancholic and full of questioning, the autobiographical
poem speaks metaphorically of Michael Field as a plastic artist whose creativity
comes from plunging her hands in clay:

> In my despair, my idle hands are cast,
> Are plunged into the clay: they grip, they hold,
> I feel them chafing on a moistened line;
> Unconsciously my warmth is in the cold.
> O Life, I am the Potter, and at last
> The secret of my loneliness is mine.[74]

Marble Books: Taxidermy for Decadence in White

We have seen that Bradley and Cooper's sculptural poetics encompassed all aspects of their work, from theories of poetic composition to plot and characterization. In this final section, we see that it also included the concept of the book.
It is no coincidence that Michael Field would call their first book, the jointly
published poetic dramas *Callirrhoë. Fair Rosamund*, a "white book."[75] Their choice
of binding material for this first collaboration as Michael Field, white parchment, which gave the book a hard, stony feel, was a clear indication of the type
of art object they wanted their books to be. A comment made in a private letter
aids our terms of discussion. Fearing the intrusion of Cooper's mother into their
writing, Bradley wrote to her sternly: "Tell Muddie, she cannot be admitted into
the workshop. Only into the room where the perfect statues are *exhibited*" (Bradley's emphasis).[76] As plastic artists, they conceptualized their books as white
statues, and from 1884 to 1890 all their books except one were bound in white
leather. The exception was *Brutus Ultor* (1886). Due to the democratic nature of
its plot, the poets chose to publish it as a pamphlet: it was thus bound as a small
paper-covered booklet, costing nine pence.[77] But they had one copy bound in
white, which at the death of Cooper's mother was buried with her.[78]

Figure 3.5. *Callirrhoë. Fair Rosamund* (1884); *Canute the Great. The Cup of Water* (1887); *Long Ago* (1889). Ana Parejo Vadillo, *Marble Books I* (2017).

The poets were influenced by book experiments carried out by Pre-Raphaelite artists including Dante Gabriel Rossetti and, particularly, the Kelmscott Press of William Morris. They led the revival of printing and book production at the fin de siècle. One of its outcomes was the explosion of marble books, books bound in white, principally in vellum, which made them look like Medieval or Renaissance books. Now and then, these white bookworks looked strangely antique and modern, their formal construction exposing the book as an art object, a sculptural icon of the author's modernity. Marble books made the book feel sculpted, a 3-D block on which the writing appeared as if it were bas-relief.

During the latter part of the nineteenth century, white books came mostly in three different materials: cloth, paper, and leather. The first type of material, cloth, was made out of cotton, which was a cheap material but created fragile books. The second was leather, which was the base material for two types of binding: parchment (untanned animal skin of any type: sheep, goat, pig) and, particularly, vellum. As book historians explain, writing on skin and preserving books in skin had been common since the fifth century BC, when parchment, which originated in the Hellenic city of Pergamon, replaced the highly priced papyrus to become the main material for the preservation of documents.[79]

In part, this history explains why parchment became again so common at the end of the nineteenth century: though parchment was more expensive than cloth, it was still cheap and made decadent books look antique. Vellum, which was made mostly from calfskin (the best being uterine vellum), was the

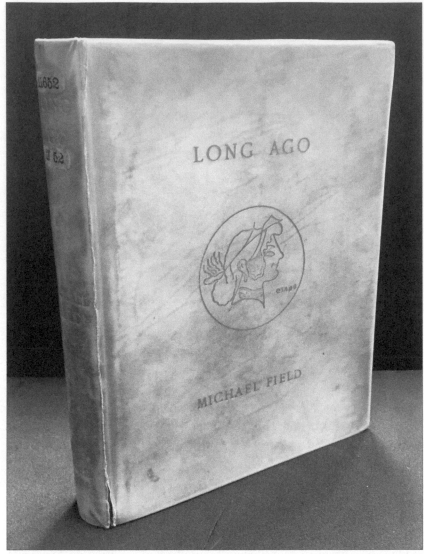

Figure 3.6. *Long Ago* (1889). Full vellum with decorations in gold. Ana Parejo Vadillo, *Marble Books II* (2017).

most expensive of all materials. Of higher quality, it was the preferred choice for unique, exquisite fin-de-siècle deluxe editions. Once finished, to the eye and the hand, it was also the closest to marble for its translucent, shiny look and hard feel. Carefully designed by distinguished artists, with limited print runs, vellum books were made to look unique, to stand out. They were created as artworks, at times shown at exhibitions, and carefully arranged and showcased in the private libraries of artists, writers, and collectors—though their physical beauty often transformed them into art objects more to be seen or touched than to be read. Usually, these vellum books were designed in such a minimalist manner that they indeed looked like white blocks of marble.

Finally, the third most common type of material was Japanese vellum, the base material of which was paper. Easier to work with, it was a cheaper version of animal vellum and was frequently used for decadent books; Japanese vellum, for example, was the preferred material of the publisher Leonard Smithers. The Bibelot series of the Mosher Press, which reprinted many decadent books, always produced shorter print runs on Japanese vellum. Books in Japanese vellum were similarly produced for an exclusive—yet cheaper—market of book connoisseurs, though often artists and writers combined vellum and handmade Japanese vellum paper to produce outstanding art.

White parchment—being cheaper than vellum—was the material Michael Field would start using for the binding of their first three books: *Callirrhoë. Fair Rosamund* (1884); *The Father's Tragedy. William Rufus. Loyalty or Love?* (1885); and *Canute the Great. The Cup of Water* (1887). It is easy to see that this whiteness, with its antique allure, must have been very attractive to Michael Field, allowing them to produce a unified marmoreal aesthetic. The books look today like aged statues. And just like John Gibson's beautiful *Tinted Venus* (1851–56), Michael Field's "statues" were also "tinted." The top edges were in gold; titles and the author's name came in gold or in red—the latter color symbolic of life in Michael Field's poetics. The decorated engravings in the bindings of *Callirrhoë. Fair Rosamund* and *The Father's Tragedy. William Rufus. Loyalty or Love?* were modeled on the Italian and French Renaissance. Their motifs echo Venetian and French bindings, particularly those of Jean Grolier (1479–1565). The "blackberry block"—flower and fruit—symbolic of Michael Field's united life, which as noted earlier had been designed by Cooper's father and is discussed in the context of queerness in Thomas's chapter in this book, appeared first in *Brutus Ultor* (1886) to become the sculptural motif engraved on the covers of *Canute the Great. The Cup of Water*; *Long Ago*; and *The Tragic Mary*. This engraving would continue to be used until the Bacchic staff was chosen, in 1893, for *Underneath the Bough*.

As Michael Field's fame increased, so did the quality of their bindings. Precious, and of higher aesthetic quality, were *Long Ago* (1889) and *The Tragic Mary* (1890), both bound in vellum by the book artist Joseph Zaehnsdorf. Inspired by H. T. Wharton's *Sappho: A Memoir and Translation* (1885), in *Long Ago* Michael Field recreated and reassembled Sappho's lyric fragments that had been recently recovered among the "Fayum papyri in the possession of the Archduke Rénier."[80] In terms of its binding, *Long Ago* (the "white volume," as they called it) followed

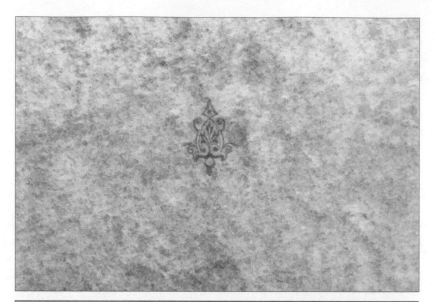

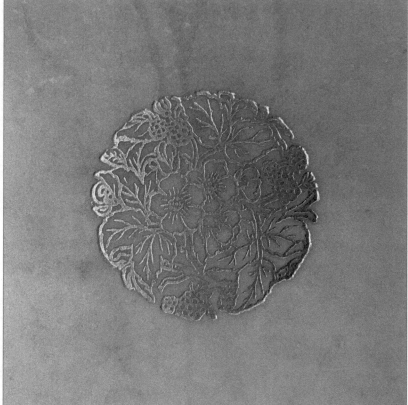

Figure 3.7. Woodcuts for *Callirrhoë* and *Long Ago* (back cover).

aesthetically the look of Wharton's *Sappho*, also bound in vellum.[81] They were punctilious about the cover, taking advice from Alexander Stuart Murray, the keeper of Greek and Roman Antiquities at the British Museum. At the Private View of the Royal Academy in May 1889, Murray showed them two statues of Sappho, one difficult to identify and the other a "beautiful nude figure of a girl with a lyre which he called an Egyptian Sappho." The latter was Edward Onslow Ford's *The Singer*.[82] After much deliberation and research, and helped by Murray, they decided to engrave an archaic head of Sappho found in a nearly contemporary vase.[83]

Figure 3.8. Illustration for front cover of Michael Field's *Long Ago* (1889), plate III in Jean De Witte, *Antiquitées Conservées a L'Hôtel Lambert* (Paris: G. Chamerot, 1886), 33.

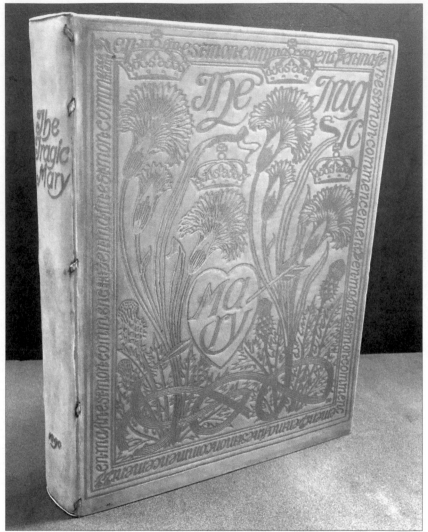

Figure 3.9. Selwyn Image's copy of *The Tragic Mary* held at the British Library. Ana Parejo Vadillo, *Marble Books III*.

Designed by Selwyn Image, the vellum extravagance of *The Tragic Mary* (1890) is simply exquisite. For its design, Michael Field gave Image very particular details. He "set down every suggestive point," they wrote in their diary, and "made a special note as to the Carnation as the Stuart Flower. . . . As we were parting he suggested (by prearrangement we divine) that we should look in on Herbert Horne & see his fine collection of contemporary wood-cuts from Mantegna & Raphael."[84] Perhaps because of the success of *Long Ago*, the book was published with two different bindings, one on brown paper—for connoisseurs but cheap—and sixty copies in very costly vellum, bound by Zaehnsdorf, some of which were given to fellow aesthetes and decadents (Oscar Wilde, Walter Pater, Robert Browning, Pen Browning, Selwyn Image, and Arthur Symons, among others). Wilde called it the second most beautiful book of the nineteenth century. But its combination of Renaissance aesthetics and Art Nouveau style did not quite make sufficient sales.[85]

To conclude then, this chapter endeavors to theorize Michael Field's sculptural poetics in the marble period, from their early fascination with statues to the very design of their own marble books. Sculpture, I have argued, created their poetry, and they shaped their poetry into sculpture. After so much whiteness, it is perhaps not surprising that they rejected in 1894 the "incurable jaundice" of the *Yellow Book*.[86] But this chapter finishes with a final white sculptural thought: that these books are also, as it were, statues of the poet Michael Field. For Bradley and Cooper were bound by the very flesh of their books' marmoreal skin.

Notes

1. The Elder Pliny, *Chapters on the History of Art*, translated by K. Jex-Blake, with commentary and historical introduction by E. Sellers and additional notes contributed by Dr. Heinrich Ludwig Urlichs (New York: Macmillan, 1896), 175.

2. Clara Erskine Clément, *Women in the Fine Arts: From the Seventeenth Century B. C., to the Twentieth Century* (Boston and New York: Houghton, Miffin, 1905), 200.

3. Deborah Tarn Steiner, *Images in Mind: Statues in Archaic and Classical Greek Literature and Thought* (Princeton, NJ: Princeton University Press, 2002), 3.

4. Michael Field, *Callirrhoë. Fair Rosamund* (London: George Bell & Sons, 1884).

5. Michael Field, *Sight and Song* (London: Elkin Mathews and John Lane, 1892). See Ana Parejo Vadillo, "*Sight and Song*: Transparent Translations and a Manifesto for the Observer," *Victorian Poetry* 38, no. 1 (2000): 15–34, and her *Women Poets and Urban Aestheticism* (Houndmills, Basingstoke: Palgrave Macmillan, 2005), 154–95; Jill R. Ehnenn, "Looking Strategically: Feminist and Queer Aesthetics in Michael Field's *Sight and Song*," *Victorian Poetry* 43, no.1 (2005): 109–54; Julia F. Saville, "The Poetic Imaging of Michael Field," in *The Fin-de-Siècle Poem*, ed. Joseph Bristow (Athens: Ohio University Press, 2005), 178–206; Hilary Fraser, "A Visual Field: Michael Field and the Gaze," *Victorian Literature and Culture* 34, no. 2 (2006): 553–71; Linda K. Hughes, "Michael Field (Katharine Bradley and Edith Cooper) and Significant Form," in *The Oxford Handbook of Victorian Poetry*, ed. Matthew Bevis (Oxford: Oxford University Press, 2013), 563–79.

6. My study of Michael Field as book artists has been influenced by Garrett Stewart, *Bookwork: Medium to Object to Concept to Art* (Chicago: University of Chicago Press, 2011).

7. Michael Field, "Effigies," *Art Review* 1, no. 3 (March 1890): 49–50. Though published under the pseudonym "Michael Field," the essay is the work of Edith Cooper. For an examination of this piece, see Catherine Maxwell, "Michael Field, Death, and the Effigy," *Word & Image* 34, no. 1 (2018): 31–39.

8. Private collectors, however, may have bound their copies in white vellum.

9. Michael Field, "Works and Days," BL Add MS 46776, fols. 29v–30r (November 1868) [K.B.]. (Transcriptions from manuscript sources are my own.)

10. Michael Field, "Works and Days," BL Add MS 46776, fol. 30v (November 1868) [K.B.].

11. Auguste Rodin, "Pierre et marbre," *Paris Journal*, January 1, 1912, quoted in Celeste Farge, Bénédicte Garnier, and Ian Jenkins, *Rodin and the Art of Ancient Greece* (London: Thames and Hudson, 2018), 90.

12. Michael Field, "Works and Days," BL Add MS 46776, fols. 30v–31r (November 1868) [K.B.].

13. Michael Field, *The Fowl and the Pussycat: Love Letters of Michael Field, 1876–1909*, ed. Sharon Bickle (Charlottesville: University of Virginia Press, 2008), 31 (K.B. to E.C, September 9, 1880).

14. Field, 11 (K.B. to E.C., n.d., ca. summer 1880).

15. See Martha Vicinus, "The Adolescent Boy: Fin de Siècle Femme Fatale?" *Journal of the History of Sexuality* 5, no. 1 (July 1994): 103.

16. Stefano Evangelista, *British Aestheticism and Ancient Greece: Hellenism, Reception, Gods in Exile* (Houndsmill: Palgrave Macmillan, 2009), 93–95. The poem was first published in Michael Field, *Uncertain Rain: Sundry Spells of Michael Field*, chosen and annotated by Ivor C. Treby (Bury St. Edmunds, UK: De Blackland Press, 2002), 58–59.

17. Field, *The Fowl*, 28, 156 n.4 (K.B. to E.C., September 9, 1880; E.C. to K.B., October 1895).

18. Field, *Uncertain Rain*, 58–59.

19. Field, *The Fowl*, 28 (K.B. to E.C., September 9, 1880).

20. Field, 78 (K.B. to E.C., 14 September 1882).

21. Field, 155–56n4 (E.C. to K.B., n.d., ca. October 1885).

22. Field, 155 (E.C. to K.B., n.d., ca. October 1885).

23. See Euripides, *Selected Fragmentary Plays: 1, Telephus, Cretans, Stheneboea, Bellerophon, Cresphontes, Erectheus, Phaethon, Wise Melanippe, Captive Melanippe* (Warminster: Aris and Phillips, 2009); "Arran and Isla Leigh," *Bellerophôn* (London: C. Kegan Paul, 1881), 1–127.

24. Field, *The Fowl*, 9 (K.B. to E.C., n.d., ca. September 1880).

25. Johann Joachim Winckelmann, *History of the Art of Antiquity*, intro. Alex Potts (Los Angeles: Getty Publications, 2006), 28–30.

26. See, for example, his description of the *Apollo Belvedere* in *The History of the Ancient Art*, vol. 3, trans. G. Henry Lodge (Boston: James R. Osgood, 1873), 312–14, n.478–79.

27. The relief is in the Palazzo Spada alla the Rogola in Rome; Winckelmann, *History of the Art of Antiquity*, 81.

28. David J. Getsy, ed., *Sculpture and the Pursuit of a Modern Ideal in Britain, c. 1880–1930* (Aldershot, UK: Ashgate, 2004). Bradley and Cooper would become good friends of Robert Browning's son, Pen Browning, visiting him in Italy. In 1892, Bradley and Cooper visited the studio of Edward Onslow Ford to see his "Shelley Memorial."

See Michael Field, "Works and Days," BL Add MS 46780, fols. 67–68 (April 2, 1892) [E.C.].

29. See Ana Parejo Vadillo, "Walter Pater and Michael Field: The Correspondence, with Other Unpublished Manuscript Materials," *Pater Newsletter* 65 (Spring 2014), 46. Walter Pater's "The Beginning of Greek Sculpture" appeared in the *Fortnightly Review* in February and March 1880; "The Marbles of Aegina" also appeared in the *Fortnightly Review* in April 1880. Both were reprinted in Walter Pater, *Greek Studies*, ed. C. L. Shadwell (London: Macmillan, 1895). The reason for Cooper's intense study is that she was working on "Effigies," published a year later in 1890. In those two essays, Pater questions the role of the museum in experiencing sculpture, the freedom to roam, and the positioning of the object in the eye of the beholder. This is at the heart of Cooper's "Effigies," in which she walks figuratively around Westminster Abbey to experience sculpture as a living art.

30. We cannot forget that in 1873, Cooper would have been eleven years old.

31. Symons's "Rodin" was published much later, in 1902, and reprinted in Arthur Symons, *Studies in Seven Arts* (London: Archibald Constable, 1906), 3–30. See Michael Field, "Works and Days," BL Add MS 46778 fol. 134v (June 13, 1890) [E.C.].

32. See Michael Field, "Works and Days," BL Add MS 46778 fol. 135r (June 14, 1890) [E.C.].

33. Symons, "Rodin," 3.

34. Field, *The Fowl*, 9 (K.B. to E.C., n.d., ca. spring 1880).

35. Field, 10–11 (K.B. to E.C., n.d., ca. summer 1880).

36. For a history of the interpretation of Bellerophon and the Chimaera in this bas-relief, see A. H. Smith, *A Catalogue of the Sculpture in the Department of Greek and Roman Antiquities*, vol. 2 (London: William Clowes, 1900), 54.

37. Field, *The Fowl*, 10 (K.B. to E.C., n.d., ca. summer 1880).

38. Field, 11 (K.B. to E.C., n.d., ca. summer 1880).

39. Arran and Isla Leigh, *Bellerophôn*, 96.

40. Arran and Isla Leigh, 106.

41. Arran and Isla Leigh, 104–5.

42. Arran and Isla Leigh, 119.

43. Field, *The Fowl*, 15 (K.B. to E.C., August 21, 1880).

44. Robert Browning, *Dramatic Idylls: Second Series* (London: Smith, Elder, 1880), 137–47.

45. Browning, 137.

46. See Vicky Greenaway, "Robert Browning: SCULPTOR & Poet," *19: Interdisciplinary Studies in the Long Nineteenth Century* 22 (2016) DOI: http://doi.org/10.16995/ntn.759.

47. Field, *The Fowl*, 15 (K.B. to E.C., August 21, 1880).

48. Arran and Isla Leigh, *Bellerophôn*, 159.

49. Field, *The Fowl*, 19 (E.C. to K.B., August 24, 1880).

50. Field, 20 (K.B. to E.C., August 26, 1880).

51. See John Ruskin, "Three Colours of Pre-Raphaelitism," in *The Works of John Ruskin*, vol. 34, ed. E. T. Cook and Alexander Wedderburn (London: George Allen, 1908), 171–72.

52. See Lene Østermark-Johansen, *Walter Pater and the Language of Sculpture* (Farnham, Surrey: Ashgate, 2011), 95.

53. Richard von Krafft-Ebing, *Psychophathia Sexualis* (London: F. J. Robman, 1894), 396.

54. Field, *The Fowl*, 24 (K.B. to E.C., September 7, 1880).

55. For a discussion of Michael Field and the male muse in the context of their complex relationship to Bernard Berenson, see Sarah Parker, *The Lesbian Muse and Poetic Identity, 1889–1930* (London: Pickering and Chatto, 2013), 43–71.

56. Field, *The Fowl*, 24 (K.B. to E.C., September 7, 1880).

57. Field, *Binary Star*, 84.

58. Field, *The Fowl*, 45 (E.C. to K.B., n.d., ca. September 1880).

59. Field, 26 (K.B. to E.C., September 8, 1880).

60. Field, 27 (K.B. to E.C., September 8, 1880).

61. Field, 31 (K.B. to E.C., September 9, 1880).

62. Field, 45 (E.C. to K.B., 15 September 1880).

63. Field, 46 (K.B. to E.C., n.d., late September 1881).

64. Edith Cooper to Robert Browning, May 30, 1884, in Michael Field, *Michael Field, the Poet: Published and Manuscript Materials*, ed. Marion Thain and Ana Parejo Vadillo (Peterborough, Ontario: Broadview, 2009), 310.

65. Field, *Callirrhoë*, 117.

66. Michael Field, *Brutus Ultor* (London: George Bell & Sons, 1886), 25, 36.

67. Field, *The Fowl*, 118–19 (April 4, 1885).

68. Field, 119 (April 4, 1885). The sculptural dream is transposed verbatim into the final version in the play: "Of far Lindores I saw the straight cold tomb, / And the straight form—all the round lines of youth, / The full serenity of cheek and chin / Cut clearer in the moonlight's marble mould; / The brow a blank page of the whitest peace" (Michael Field, *Father's Tragedy*, 100).

69. Michael Field, "Works and Days," BL Add MS 46778 fol. 33r (May 7, 1890) [K.B.].

70. Field, "Effigies," 49.

71. Field, *Binary Star*, 106.

72. Field, *The Fowl*, 192–93 passim (K.B. to E.C., August 8, 1887).

73. Field, 194 passim (K.B. to E.C., August 8, 1887).

74. Michael Field, *Wild Honey from Various Thyme* (London: T. Fisher Unwin, 1908), 121.

75. Field, *The Fowl*, 128.

76. Field, 65.

77. See Emma Donoghue, *We Are Michael Field* (Bath: Absolute Press, 1998), 32.

78. "Her right hand on her beautiful white copy of <u>Brutus Ultor</u> (the most beloved play)." See Michael Field, "Works and Days," BL Add MS 46777 fol. 102r (April 18, 1886) [E.C.].

79. The classic bookbinding text of this period is Joseph Zaehnsdorf, *The Art of Bookbinding* (London: George Bell & Sons, 1880). He was the preferred bookbinder of Bradley and Cooper in the late 1880s and early 1890s.

80. Henry Thornton Wharton, *Sappho: Memoir, Text, Selected Renderings and a Literal Translation* (London: David Stott, 1885).

81. Michael Field, "Works and Days," BL Add MS 46778 fol. 78 (May 23, 1890) [E.C.].

82. A. S. Murray, keeper of Greek and Roman Antiquities at the British Museum from 1886 to 1904, was a good friend of Bradley and Cooper, often advising the women on all matters of sculptures at the British Museum. Michael Field, "Works and Days," BL Add MS 46777 f. 64r (May 9, 1889) [K.B.]. Molly Youngkin incorrectly suggests that the Egyptian Sappho "was likely the bas-relief of Sappho and Alcaeus pictured in Victor Duruy's *History of Greece and of the Greek People* (1892)." See Molly Youngkin, "[W]e Had Never Chosen a Byzantine subject . . . or One from Alexandria': Emancipation Through Desire and the Eastern Limits of Beauty in Michael Field's Verse Dramas," in *British Women Writers and the Reception of Ancient Egypt, 1840–1910: Imperialist Representations of Egyptian Women* (Houndmills, Basingstoke: Palgrave, 2016), 112. It was Edward Onslow Ford's *The Singer*. See *The Exhibition of the Royal Academy of Arts, The One Hundred and Twenty-First, 1889* (London: Royal Academy of Arts, 1889) and Henry Blackburn, ed., *Academy Notes* (London: Chatto and Windus, 1889), 97.

83. Michael Field writes that the vase was the property of Prince Czartorysky (*Long Ago*, cix). The illustration appears in Jean de Witte, *Description des antiquités conservées a L'Hôtel Lambert* (Paris: G. Chamerot, 1886), 33, plate III.

84. Michel Field, "Works and Days," BL Add MS 46778 fol. 19v (March 5, 1890) [E.C.]

85. For more on this play and the book, see Ana Parejo Vadillo, "Another Renaissance: The Decadent Poetic Drama of A. C. Swinburne and Michael Field," in *Decadent Poetics: Literature and Form at the British Fin de Siècle*, ed. Jason Hall and Alex Murray (Basingstoke, UK: Palgrave Macmillan, 2013), 13.

86. Michael Field, "Works and Days" (April 17, 1894) [E.C.], quoted in Thain and Vadillo, *Michael Field, the Poet*, 261.

FOUR

Sister Arts

Michael Field and Mary Costelloe

SARAH PARKER

In the sleepy depths of the lanes Mrs C spoke of the freedom that
is breaking round womanhood—she spoke of things new, while
the old oaks nodded. . . . I told her I should never fight for any
freedom that to gain /which\ would perturb my art. I have only so
much energy—if the god demands it—the cause of womanhood
must go hang!

—Michael Field, "Works and Days" (May 27, 1892)

THIS EPISODE RECOUNTED BY EDITH COOPER HAS FREQUENTLY
been used to demonstrate Michael Field's resistance to "the cause of womanhood." Unlike other poets of the era, such as Alice Meynell and Constance
Naden, Bradley and Cooper lacked interest in the suffrage movement and
preferred to avoid "the Woman Question." They were more likely to associate themselves with male aesthetes than with politically motivated New
Women. Indeed, their relationships with other women, including Cooper's

mother Emma Harris Cooper (Bradley's sister), can be described as ambivalent at best, with Cooper writing that the "Mother One" "did not understand my need of freedom, she bound & overawed me."[1] However, despite this ambivalence, women often played important roles in Bradley and Cooper's lives and careers—influences that have been overlooked by critics who tend to adhere to the construction of "Michael Field" as a male dandy.[2] This chapter addresses this by attending to Bradley and Cooper's important friendship with the critic and art historian Mary Costelloe Berenson (1864–1944), the "Mrs C" mentioned in the passage above. This evolving relationship lasted twenty-three years, until Bradley's death in 1914.

Born in Philadelphia to a well-respected Quaker family, Mary Whitall Smith studied at Smith College and later the Harvard Annex, specializing in philosophy and psychology (she attended the Concord School of Philosophy in 1883 and was deeply affected by a lecture delivered by William James).[3] In 1885, she married the barrister Frank Costelloe, moving to England to raise their daughters. Mary was actively involved in suffrage as the president of the Westminster, Chelsea, and Guildford Women's Liberal Associations; in an interview, the *Women's Penny Paper* described her as "always engaged in promoting by every means in her power the welfare of her sex."[4] She gave several speeches during the late 1880s and 1890s on Walt Whitman (a poet she admired intensely and befriended as a young woman), women's rights, and worker's rights.[5] In the summer of 1890, Mary Costelloe embarked on an affair with the art critic Bernard Berenson. She left her husband (and daughters) in summer 1891 and henceforward dedicated herself to the study of Italian Renaissance art. The couple collaborated on studies that were published under Berenson's name, such as *The Venetian Painters of the Renaissance* (1894). Costelloe is one of several nineteenth-century female art historians whose work, previously overlooked, has recently come to prominence through the scholarship of Hilary Fraser, Meaghan Clarke, and others.[6]

Bradley and Cooper first met Costelloe on February 27, 1891, and shortly after joined her and Berenson on their tour of German art galleries during the summer of that year. In this chapter, I concentrate on the creative ferment that resulted from this trip and the subsequent trip to Paris in 1892, expressed in poems found in *Sight and Song* (1892) and *Underneath the Bough* (1893). The first part of my chapter focuses on the development of *Sight and Song* alongside Costelloe's art historical writings. Although they were writing different genres, I ask, Does Costelloe's work in art criticism share affinities with Michael Field's work in lyric? Reading Costelloe's writing alongside Bradley and Cooper's reveals that they were engaged in a shared project of art historical investigation, one that placed tactile values, female spectatorship, and collaboration at the center, rather than the margins, of aesthetic response.

The second part of the chapter looks at Bradley and Cooper's poems about or inspired by Costelloe. As I have observed elsewhere of Bernard Berenson, Mary Costelloe starts as someone who taught Bradley and Cooper to look at art but eventually came to function as an object of contemplation herself.[7] Through analyzing Costelloe's perceptive abilities, Bradley and Cooper sought to attain their own visual authority. This endeavor resulted in poems such as "I Have Found Her Power," in which Michael Field fantasize about "stealing" Mary's gaze. This shift as their friendship developed means that the collaborative project of sharing the gaze with others (Berenson and Costelloe) increasingly breaks down into a battle over who is doing the looking and who is being objectified (Berenson, for example, responded to his own objectification by judging whether Cooper's face "would paint well").[8] Ultimately, the gendered dynamic of subject/object persists and troubles this collaborative quartet. My conclusion suggests that although Costelloe played an important role in developing their response to art, Bradley and Cooper's ambivalence toward her, combined with the unequal gender relations underlying art history (demonstrated by the fact that Costelloe cowrote Berenson's books but did not receive credit for them), has led to this key influence being overlooked. Bradley and Cooper were more indebted to Costelloe than we realize; my chapter seeks to put her firmly back in the frame.

The "Immortal 4": *Sight and Song* and Collaborative Pairings

Bradley and Cooper set off on their first major European gallery trip on June 5, 1890. Cooper was finally free to travel with Bradley abroad following her mother's death in 1889. They first encountered Bernard Berenson on June 10, 1890, in Room VII of the Louvre, the space dedicated to "Early Italian pictures." They were instantly enamored with this passionate young art historian. The women returned to England toward the end of July 1890, invigorated by experiencing Renaissance masterpieces firsthand, armed with notes and charged with new creative energy. They began drafting the ekphrastic poems that became *Sight and Song*; some were written about paintings in the Louvre, such as *La Gioconda* and *L'Indifférent*, others in Italy where they traveled later (such as the poems treating the Botticellis in the Accademia and Uffizi).

In previous discussions of this phase of Michael Field's development, scholars have emphasized Berenson's pivotal influence in a triangular dynamic with Bradley and Cooper.[9] I want to instead propose that this phase involved four writers operating as a mutually inspiring *quartet*—but that Costelloe's role has been overlooked in favor of emphasizing a triad with Berenson. Seven months after returning in February 1891, Bradley records their first meeting with Costelloe: "On <u>Friday</u> we went to lunch at the house of his [Berenson's] hostess, Mrs Costelloe. She is a comely young creature, fresh after much experience of London Society."[10] The group went to visit the National Gallery, where Bradley observed a striking alteration in Berenson's attitude:

> On Bernard a great change has fallen. Last summer there was no doubt in him, no fear! He was a piece of pure, unflawed paganism. Now he wants to make others enjoy. <u>He is thinking of taking to journalism</u>—perhaps writing on Dosso Dossi—& those artists who have given him such intense pleasure. . . . He feels powers of joy developing within him, fresh powers of sympathy and appreciation. He has suffered horrible pain from enjoying alone. . . . This will be good, if he does not popularise. If he could record his responses to pictures, what they waken in him & suggest it would be well.[11]

Bradley is surprised at Berenson's urge to educate others to "enjoy" Renaissance art by writing journalistic pieces. This shift in attitude may be attributed to Costelloe's influence. Costelloe and Berenson had spent the winter of 1890 viewing art together in Florence and Rome (in the company of Costelloe's husband), and Costelloe was already receiving Morellian tuition from Berenson. As she explains in her 1894 essay "The New and the Old Art Criticism," Giovanni Morelli "was the first art critic who went to work with the aid of photographs to study Italian art in a really scientific way," through close, even forensic attention to idiosyncratic use of color, light, and the formation of particular details such as ears and hands.[12] Berenson had received tuition from Morelli and was eager to pass on his knowledge; Costelloe became "the one person in the world" he "desired most to educate."[13] Thus, he became accustomed to having a regular, enthusiastic pupil with whom he could share his ideas on art; he was no longer experiencing art alone. More than that, the couple began to collaborate on writing down these ideas, with Costelloe playing a pivotal role. As Berenson's critics acknowledge, some of his most important studies, such as *The Venetian Painters of the Renaissance* (1894) were coauthored by Costelloe. As Costelloe explained to her father Robert Pearsall Smith in a letter of 1893, since the summer of 1891 she had been working on a study of Venetian painting, in addition to a volume on the Italian paintings at Hampton Court. She offered this study to the publisher George Putnam,

> along with the badly arranged Hampton Court material. He said he liked it, and if it could be combined with something

less cumbrous and of more general interest than the Hampton
Court stuff, then he would print it. As I was not in possession
of sufficient knowledge to do anything else with it, I gave it to
Berenson and advised him to make lists of all the genuine works of
Venetian painters. This he did, and I submitted it to Mr Putnam
last summer and he accepted it at once.[14]

But as Costelloe goes on to explain, the volume, despite being largely her
work, with Berenson adding the list of painters included as an appendix, was
eventually published solely under Berenson's name:

> My idea of course was to have both names because I thought
> and I still think that the best way to answer scandal is to tell the
> exact truth as openly as possible, namely that we have been doing
> serious and scholarly work together. Mr Putnam wanted both
> names, but mother opposed it so decidedly that I yielded the point
> and asked Mr Putman to leave out my name.[15]

Hence, Costelloe, though publicly unacknowledged, was the coauthor of *Ve-*
netian Painters and continued to be crucial to Berenson's writing career. As she
later reflected in her memoirs, "Perhaps I was, after all, wrong, as sometimes,
even now I am charged with having been, to try to turn this creature, so rarely
gifted . . . into the 'worker.'"[16] But while she was criticized (mostly by Berenson himself) for turning his pure aesthetic enjoyment toward commerce and
criticism, she reassured herself that "my baleful . . . influence modified his life,
and gave him a secondary 'conscience' about work, and especially about writing
that has never ceased to harass him."[17]

Therefore, as Bradley and Cooper were engaged in drafting poems for *Sight*
and Song in the summer and autumn of 1891, Berenson and Costelloe were collaborating on the two volumes that would become *The Venetian Painters of the Re-*
naissance and *Guide to the Italian Pictures at Hampton Court: With Short Studies of the*
Artists (both published in 1894). As Berenson wrote to Bradley, "I have been at
work on an article on the Venetian School—the introduction to my Hampton
Crt. Book. I, or rather <u>we</u> are now re-writing it."[18] As Hilary Fraser has observed,
Bradley and Cooper were clearly inspired to meet a couple whose collaboration mirrored their own. Both couples "responded to the tactile, physiological,
and psychological qualities of paintings together, as lovers, and together tried to
translate their intensely felt experiences into words."[19] Bradley and Cooper were
aware that Berenson was greatly assisted by Costelloe when writing his aesthetic theories. For example, in 1895, Cooper lamented that Berenson could not

articulate his ideas in writing: "How I grieve that B. is as incapable as Socrates of writing his thoughts. . . . His great effects as an artist are as fugative [*sic*] as an actor's or singer's—they pass living from his lips, and have no further life of their own."[20]

Berenson had earlier attempted to persuade Cooper to write for him also: "He allowed all his disappointment to escape that I have not given up my life & followed him—the St. John as he used to call me beside St. Luke—Mary! He wants me to have a fine, expressive prose style to perpetuate his thoughts with the sensuous charm they need to be characteristic & that he cannot give them in writing."[21] Although Cooper did not succumb to such pressure, from the earliest stages of their friendship Berenson relied on Bradley and Cooper to revise his essays, such as that on Correggio, drafted in September 1891. As he wrote on behalf of both himself and Costelloe, "We are sorry that the article took so long. Even now it is coming to you in a raw state. It would be awfully good of you if you would give it a little cooking. It would be highly appreciated if as you read the article you would make such corrections in English as seem desirable to you."[22] Cooper replied with a "suggestion or two in pencil, where it seemed to me that the English required to be sharper or the fall of the sentence more gracious" and suggestions of journals where Berenson could place his work.[23]

My point here is not to suggest that Berenson took advantage of either Costelloe or Bradley and Cooper but rather to emphasize that Bradley and Cooper's collaborative dynamic as Michael Field mirrored Berenson and Costelloe's working relationship. Costelloe and Berenson's model of collaborative viewing certainly further fueled Bradley and Cooper's desire to record their own artistic impressions in their diary and in collaborative poems. In February 1892, Cooper drafted the preface to the volume, asserting that "the effort to see things from their own centre, by suppressing the habitual centralisation of the visible in ourselves, is a process by which we eliminate our idiosyncrasies and obtain an impression clearer, less passive, more intimate."[24] This statement is strikingly close to Berenson's pronouncement in June 1892 regarding their collaborative partnerships, recounted by Cooper: "Before the picture he & Mary leave us to go on to the Louvre: Bernhard has been speaking of their companionship & ours—he leaves us with the profound remark: 'It takes two to be impersonal; otherwise one is solitary.'"[25] As Ana Parejo Vadillo has observed, Michael Field unseated the Paterian model of the singular viewer, focusing instead on a collaborative gaze.[26] They perceived how such a collaboration could function through observing Berenson as he progressed from "enjoying alone" in 1890 to a dynamic collaboration with Costelloe.

But this configuration is more than just two couples with mutual interests; the gaze that functions here in fact involves *four* pairs of eyes, the magical observer that Bradley described as the "immortal 4, Faun, Our Lady of Prose, & that Cloud that moves together."[27] This dynamic is key to the development of Michael Field's intersubjective gaze. This configuration moves beyond one person looking at another or even two people joining together to gaze as one at a work of art. Within the latter collaboration, the subject-object binary is to some extent reconfigured but not entirely disrupted (as I have argued elsewhere, Bradley and Cooper often collaborate in objectifying another figure, such as Berenson or Whym Chow). By looking at *and with* another couple, possibilities for desire and identification multiply. This looking leads to an intense crossing of gazes. The effects of this may be seen in Michael Field's poem "Correggio's Saint Sebastian," in which, as Fraser has observed, there are multiple "erotically charged look[s]" being exchanged by figures within and without the painting; the reader is "in their own visual triangle . . . made party to the triangulated desiring gaze of Sebastian, the Madonna and the Christ child."[28] But one could argue that rather than a triangle, it is in fact a quartet at work here: the reader looks on at Sebastian, the Madonna, and the Christ child looking at each other. However, both these interpretations overlook the central figure of St. Gimignano, who looks directly at the viewer and points toward the exchange of maternal and saintly gazes. The painting is in fact *full* of looks, with at least twenty distinguishable figures, including a gathered host of putti looking down at the Christ child. This entangled nexus of multiple gazes is emblematic of my overall point here: that Bradley and Cooper's relationship with Berenson and Costelloe led to an ever-more-complex engagement with the look, with the potential to break down subject/object binaries entirely.

Bradley and Cooper turned as frequently to Costelloe as they did to Berenson for assistance with their volume *Sight and Song*. For example, in April 1892, Costelloe offered advice regarding Lorenzo di Credi at the Uffizi and Giorgione's Shepherd: "[T]he crown the angel holds is a crown of olive leaves. The description of the 'shepherd' comes in at the Catalogue part."[29] Bradley frequently asked Costelloe questions about the paintings featured in *Sight and Song*; for example, in a letter dated February 2, 1892, she wrote, "Can you tell me whether Giorgione's Venus is a noontide picture? It seems to M.F. it is; but out on seeming! 'the male conscience'—exclusion of fancy & all sentiment not as truly of the picture as the drop of honey oozing from a plum—that is our aim."[30] There is a certain irony here, as Bradley and Cooper have to seek the help of another woman in order to attain the (singular) male conscience (we may also recall Costelloe's functioning as a "secondary conscience" in Berenson that improved his writing but remained concealed in the authorship of his works). In the same letter, they refer to Mary as a "Botanist" who will be able to identify trees and plants in pictures. This was a mutually supportive relationship, as Bradley and Cooper helped Costelloe with her own art historical writings. For example, in the same letter, Bradley responds to critical writings sent by Costelloe: "Thank you so much for the papers & the literary criticism. I do not think you can understand how we desire you should excel in literature. You know how often the notes to a book may be of quite rare value. Think what it would be to make perfect guide books."[31] She goes on to give advice on how Costelloe should structure the artists' biographies, cautioning her not to assume knowledge on the part of the reader: "I should quietly state what were the religious, & political influences of the painter's youth. & what the character of the scenary [sic] in wh. he lived. . . . I should never say 'of course such an[d] such a person bears trace of Giorgione's influence'—such a remark makes the poor student hot with shame & angry at his ignorance—tell the poor novice who were the artist's masters, & give the names of his most receptive & sensitive pupils."[32]

For the most part, Costelloe (and Berenson) followed this advice in both *Venetian Painters* and the Hampton Court volume; studies of individual artists tend to concentrate on their masters, their influences, their ideal of beauty, characteristic subject matter, and how their work developed throughout their career. Bradley particularly admired Costelloe's attention to color and texture: "'With stuffs that tickle the eye & yet rest it' is a phrase in the Bonifazio paper—that gives one the very artist. You can give the artists . . . by their way of taking pleasure, whether they liked the feel of the stuff, as well as its hue, & how it seemed to them the nicest folds sh[oul]d. fall."[33] This emphasis on texture anticipates the tactile values that Berenson late expounded: "I must have the illusion of being able to touch a figure, I must have the illusion of varying muscular sensations inside my palm and fingers corresponding to the various projections of this figure, before I shall take it for granted as real, and let it affect me lastingly."[34] Alison Brown explains that in developing these theories, both Costelloe and Berenson responded to "impressionism and the discovery of photography" and "new intellectual stimuli: the evolutionary psychology of thinkers like William James (post-Darwin and Freud), and the German philosophers Hegel and especially Nietzsche."[35] Indeed, Costelloe was taught by William James at the Harvard Annex, he was a family friend, and she frequently consulted his works, including *The Principles of Psychology* (1890) and *Pragmatism* (1907), in order to develop her theories of art.[36]

Costelloe and Berenson's art historical writings and Michael Field's *Sight and Song* reference a number of the same paintings by Antonello da Messina,

Bartolommeo Veneto, Carlo Crivelli, Giorgione, and others. But how exactly does this mutual influence operate? Does Costelloe's work in art criticism share affinities with Michael Field's work in lyric? In the work of all three women, we can identify an emphasis on tactility and light and a striving to reject subjectivity in favor of objectivity (in the words of Michael Field, "what the lines and colours of certain chosen pictures sing in themselves") through accurately recording impressions.[37] This, somewhat paradoxically, throws the emphasis back onto the individual's perception and the physical circumstances of their particular viewing experience. I will demonstrate this mutual influence with an example, focusing on Costelloe's discussion of Giorgione's *Head of a Shepherd* in the Hampton Court volume and Michael Field's poem about the same painting in *Sight and Song*. All three women went to look at the painting on June 8, 1891, in the company of "little Ray, Bernie & Miss Hall."[38] In Cooper's diary description, she emphasizes Giorgione's use of light, lending the shepherd's flesh an ethereal golden glow:

> One glance was enough to enchant. "Time had run back &
> fetched the Age of Gold"—it glowed before us on the brow &
> chest of Giorgione's young shepherd. The beautiful oval face
> ripened by the sun into colour no wheat-field could show, the
> hair about it so very blonde that the shadows are just green, is
> thrown out from a background of dense blue; the brown hand
> closes over a flute. . . . There are no lines to the face, the colour of
> the skin & the light of the sun coming from above on it suggest
> all the solidity of outline form.[39]

By December that year, Bradley and Cooper had drafted the poem that would eventually be published in *Sight and Song*. This poem contains a number of phrases that, as with other poems in the volume, closely echo Cooper's original diary descriptions (for example, lines 49–50 of the poem: "Ah, Golden Age, time has run back / And fetched you for our eyes to greet," echoing Cooper's immediate Miltonian reaction to the painting in the diary).[40] However, the finished poem also strikingly echoes Costelloe's description of Giorgione's painting in the Hampton Court volume:

> [Giorgione] has left no picture more in harmony with this feeling
> than the Shepherd's Head. The face is so *radiantly* beautiful, that
> even retouching and blackening have not been able to hide the fine
> *oval*, the exquisite proportions, the lovely brow, the *warm eyes, the
> sweet mouth*, the soft waving hair, and the easy poise of the head. . . .
> [T]he mere quality of his colour was extraordinarily different from

anything that had gone before. It may be said, almost literally, that the chief colour on his palette was sunlight.[41]

Compare the above with the first stanza of Michael Field's poem, in which matching phrases are italicized:

> A *radiant, oval face:* the hair
> About the cheeks so blond in hue
> It shades to greenness here and there
> Against the ground of densest blue
> A cloak flax-grey, a shirt of white,
> That yellow spots of sunshine fleck;
> The face aglow with southern light,
> Deep, golden sunbrown on the neck;
> *Warm eyes, sweet mouth* of the softest lips:
> Yea, though he is not playing,
> His hand a flute Pandean grips,
> Across one hole a finger laying.[42]

As we can see, Michael Field's poem and Costelloe's art historical description are intimately related. From the echoing of exact phrases ("warm eyes," "sweet mouth") to close resemblances ("the lovely brow" and "waving hair" of Costelloe, the "wide forehead" and "curls" of Michael Field) through the general emphasis of sunlight and the subtlety of Giorgione's line (Costelloe emphasizes the "subtlety and refinement as Giorgione's, such flow of line," while Michael Field write of "the line / Of cheek and chin is only made / By modulation, perfect, fine"), these two texts if placed alongside one another are strikingly similar. This is not surprising when we consider that all four viewed the painting together and likely discussed its effects as a group. In addition to this, these impressions of the shepherd were written on a particularly Giorgionesque day. Following their visit to Hampton Court, their party spent time together in idyllic natural surroundings: "We sat in community under a yew tree by the pond. Little Ray brought us heaps of new-mown grass to smell, rode on B's foot for a kiss, & plucked the green tips of yew, wh[ich] she gave us with the air of Perdita in miniature."[43] When we compare to this to Costelloe's description of Giorgione "making the beholder feel refreshed and soothed, as if actually reclining on the grass in the shade of the trees, with his mind free to muse on what delights it most," we can see that Costelloe's employment of the "tactile imagination" in her criticism arose not only from her and Berenson's philosophical interest in the work of William James but also from the circumstances in which the Giorgione painting was viewed.[44] This physically situated response to art, attentive to the effects of one's surroundings, can be seen in Costelloe's other writings, such as "The March of Ancona," which combines a discussion of Lotto, Perugino, and Crivelli with travel writing elements, drawing attention to the old towns, palaces, and churches in which paintings can be found and the "wonderful hills and valleys" of the landscape.[45] Both Costelloe's and Michael Field's writings merge objectivity (what "pictures sing in themselves") with situated impressions; attention to the specifics of the painting combine with physical sensations, the weather, the mood of a particular gallery, features of the surrounding landscape, and the interpersonal relationships of the gallery attendees. In a similar way, this idyllic June day infuses the response of "the immortal four" to Giorgione's painting, glowing beneath the surface of their writings just as light pervades the shepherd's flesh.

"I Have Found Her Power": Michael Field's Poems about Mary Costelloe

Spurred on by the success of their experiment so far, Bradley and Cooper traveled to Germany in August 1891. Their itinerary was dictated by Berenson: "[W]e seek out many of the pictures on Bernard's list, and enjoy the first thrilling shock of their colour & conception."[46] During this time they viewed Antonello da Messina's *Saint Sebastian* and *The Sleeping Venus* by Giorgione, resulting in further poems for *Sight and Song*. Unfortunately, during this trip Cooper fell seriously ill with scarlet fever. Berenson and Costelloe visited her in the hospital, bringing gifts such as a peach, pink roses, and a "little white cotton jacket with black & red spots."[47] The art critics continued to offer intellectual support, discussing Dosso Dossi, and Costelloe later mailed them Berenson's notes on Frankfurt pictures. This support during Cooper's convalescence led to a deeper bond between the poets and the art critics. This intimacy is shown in Bradley's two short lyrics inspired by Costelloe, "I Have Found Her Power" and "Irises," later published in *Underneath the Bough* (1893). These poems reveal a fascination with Mary's magnetism that echoes Bradley and Cooper's poems about Berenson himself, such as "I Live in the World for His Sake," also published in *Underneath the Bough*.

"I Have Found Her Power" fantasizes about co-opting the subject's gaze. The poem has enigmatic connections to Costelloe. It is drafted below a diary entry for April 29, 1892. As Bradley recounts, she and Cooper visited the National Gallery, and while Cooper "studies Salvodo's weird, & Whistler-like Magdalen," Bradley composes a poem: "I sing Julie's blue eyes. As one smells a flower possessing its fragrance, so she gave me the blue colour of her eyes."[48] The poem, drafted under the title "Julie's Eyes" is eventually published as "I Have Found Her Power" in *Underneath the Bough*:

I have found her power!
From her roving eyes
　　Just a gift of blue
　　That away she threw
As a girl may throw a flower.
　　I am weary of glances;
　　This blue enhances
My life: I have found her power.[49]

Although the subject remains unidentified (Ivor Treby's catalogue does not identify "Julie"), I propose that Costelloe is a lingering presence in this poem. At the time of its drafting, she was in nearly constant attendance at the National Gallery, and Bradley and Cooper frequently fixate on the blueness of her eyes. For example, on May 21, 1892, Cooper recounts Costelloe's joy at the publication of *Sight and Song:* "I wait before Crivelli's Madonna in Ecstasy (Nat. Gal.) & Sim brings Mrs Costelloe to me. . . . So very blue her eyes— such self-reliant freshness in her face. Sight & Song she has bought & there & then sits down rejoicing to tell us of her favourite poems. She really greets the book."[50] A few days later, Cooper refers to Costelloe as a "certain blue eyed Morellian."[51] The emphasis on blue eyes and intense glances reflects Bradley and Cooper's fascination with Costelloe's potent blue gaze and her ability to penetrate art that they certainly coveted. This poem is about a woman who gains power through looking. It is also about the ability to steal that power— or at least to appropriate it for one's own purposes. The "roving" glance is a "gift" that is thrown like a flower—a love token, caught by the (ambiguously gendered) speaker, although it is not necessarily intended for them. Moreover, it is significantly a glance, not a gaze. According to the art historian Norman Bryson, a "division separates the activity of the gaze, prolonged, contemplative, yet regarding the field with a certain aloofness and disengagement—from that of a glance, a furtive or sideways look—carrying messages of hostility, collusion, rebellion and lust."[52] In contrast to the detachment of the gaze, the glance "proposes desire, proposes the body, in the *durée* of its practical activity."[53] Fraser links this to Michael Field's "La Gioconda," whose "side-long, implicating eyes" subvert the gaze of the painting's (implicitly male) viewer.[54] But in "I Have Found Her Power," the speaker is "weary of glances" and wishes for steadier eye contact from this blue, life-enhancing gaze. They desire to still and freeze the momentary, fleeting glance and to *feed* on it. In this sense, the poem recalls "I Live in the World for His Sake," which appears in the same book, *Underneath the Bough:*

I live in the world for his sake,
For the eyes that sleep and wake,
I live in the world for his eyes:
Earth's kingdoms may pass away,
I heed not these things of clay,
But I live, I love, I pray
From the light of his eyes.[55]

Inspired by a portrait of Berenson, this short lyric is an attempt by Bradley and Cooper "to sing what his eyes are to us—all the joy we have in him—to make a portrait."[56] As I have argued elsewhere, this poem fantasizes about usurping Berenson's objectifying, authoritative gaze.[57] "I Have Found Her Power" can be read alongside this, as can other poems in *Underneath the Bough* that meditate on the gaze and the glance and the relationship between subject and object.[58] In both cases, the consummate gazer becomes the viewed (and desired) object. As Robert P. Fletcher argues, this volume encourages "the critical practice of finding the story . . . in a sequence of love poems."[59] The poems within *Underneath the Bough* not only merge hetero- and homoerotic desire but also simultaneously complicate the positions of subject and object within and between the poems.

These poems represent Bradley and Cooper's attempts to analyze the perceptive abilities of those consummate viewers, Costelloe and Berenson, and in doing so attain visual authority for themselves. It is no coincidence that "I Live in the World for His Sake" is inspired by Berenson's static *portrait.* "I Have Found Her Power" is also mediated by a painting: Salvodo's *Mary Magdalene* (ca. 1535–40). Bradley and Cooper are, in this sense, translating real people into semi-ekphrastic poems. Salvodo's painting shows a hooded Magdalene, her knees hugged to her chest within folds of gray drapery, waiting at the entrance to Jesus's tomb. She glances directly at the viewer, her head tilted inquisitively to the left. Cooper composed her description of the painting while Bradley was writing "I Have Found Her Power":

The water & sky are worthy in intention of Whistler—they form a true Nocturn: they are modern. The whole picture is a harmony in grey & blue. The vague agony of the hours before sunrise deepens the world & deepens the eyes of Mary with thoughts that grow & then wait—as the most momentous thoughts always do. . . . [T]he eyes are watchful, are meditative; the fine brows have a prescient tranquillity.[60]

This emphasis on the blue harmonies and the "watchful" gaze of the Magdalene also infuses Bradley's poem. Indeed, if divested of its biblical context, the look of Salvodo's Magdalene could be read as flirtatious, coyly glancing at the viewer with a slight smile playing on her lips. I therefore suggest that "I Have Found Her Power" is haunted by *two* Marys—in this poem, Costelloe's active, "self-reliant" glances merge with the painting's watchful gaze. This poem, composed in the National Gallery, captures the response of two women (Bradley and Cooper) looking at a woman (Costelloe) looking at a painting of a woman (Salvodo's Magdalene), causing the boundaries between painting/object and viewer/s to blur. As critics (including Jill Ehnenn, Thain, Fraser, and Saville) observe, several poems in *Sight and Song* recognize the agency of the female subject within the painting, whether Leda, Venus, La Gioconda, or the mysterious subject of Bartolomeo Veneto's portrait. As Brooke S. Cameron explains, the volume "carves out a space for the feminist gaze that is attentive to and enjoys the feminine object, who in turn looks back and asserts her agency."[61] My claim is that Michael Field are able to enact and recognize the assertive female gaze in part due to their friendship with Costelloe, a woman for whom looking was a profession.

"I Have Found Her Power" anticipates a significant shift in Bradley and Cooper's relationship with Costelloe. During the spring of 1892, their friendship intensified. On May 27, Costelloe came to visit the women in Reigate, and they took care to display "the same stone-irises & yellow composite flowers in the Vases as when she & B. came last year."[62] After a walk through the lanes (and the conversation about womanhood cited at the start of this chapter), Costelloe "lay on the Morris couch—Sim [Bradley] & I beside her."[63] In this intimate setting, Costelloe confided,

> She has always been & is totally without the sense of sin—she
> recognises <u>errors</u> in her life, some so sweet she would not have
> them undone. She is a necessitarian: she would not like anyone
> to be different to what they are, she would never blame them—if
> Ray were to murder atrociously, her mother would love her as
> passionately as now. While she was speaking so, she lay back, her
> cheeks flushed, her eyes glorified by passion, her hands in her
> lustreless auburn hair . . . much—a dreadful so much was revealed
> in her aspect—A tragic double meaning gave the spark like glint
> to her expression & obstinate energy to her manner.[64]

This description is noticeably ambivalent—on the one hand, Cooper appears exhilarated by Costelloe's "necessitarian" attitude, noting her "flushed" cheeks and "eyes glorified by passion" (one can feel the proximity between the women in this description, as Cooper studies Costelloe at close range). Costelloe's pose here is suggestively orgasmic, lying back with her hands in her hair, unconsciously embodying the "sweet sins" of which she speaks. But Cooper is also disturbed by Costelloe's ethical (and physical) abandon: "a dreadful so much was revealed in her aspect."

In addition to hinting at her extramarital affair with Berenson, the "double-meaning" could also relate to Costelloe's awareness of Bradley and Cooper's own transgressive lesbian relationship. Bradley later referred to this intimate moment in a letter to Costelloe following Oscar Wilde's imprisonment: "Mary, you once said that nothing, not murder, or any crime could make you love any one you love less. Then, my hair rose; but at present I am in doubt."[65] This suggests that Bradley understood that Costelloe would accept other sins (in addition to murder), such as homosexuality, in her friends as well as her daughter. Entwined on the Morris couch, the women recognize—and to some extent embody—each other's sexual transgressions, though these remain unspoken. These ambivalent feelings of attraction and repulsion infuse the poem "Irises," written by Bradley on the day of Costelloe's visit:

> In a vase of gold
> And scarlet, how cold
> The flicker of wrinkled grays
> In this iris-sheaf; my eyes fill with wonder
> At the tossed, moist light, at the withered scales under
> And among the uncertain sprays:
>
> The wavings of white
> On the cloudy light,
> And the finger-marks of pearl;
> The facets of crystal, the golden feather,
> The way that the petals fold over together,
> The way that the buds unfurl!
>
> Of the gray iris for Mrs Costelloe[66]

This poem offers a close-up, impressionistic picture of the gray iris, described in a painterly manner with emphasis on light, texture, and color harmonies. As Fraser notes, "word-painting" or "blocking-in" was one of the ekphrastic methodologies employed in *Sight and Song*; details were applied in layers to the poems.[67] One can observe this painterly method too in the "finger-marks of pearl" and "facets of crystal"—touches of light and shade that resemble impressionistic brushstrokes. This poetic "still life" reflects all three women's interest in impressionist painting (seen in Cooper's earlier emphasis on the Whistlerian aesthetics of Salvodo's painting). Indeed, it is tempting to liken this poem to Vincent Van Gogh's *Bouquet d'Iris* (1890), exhibited in Brussels in February 1891, in which the artist sought through "vigorous brushwork" to extract "the savage beauty of the flowers, densely packed into an earthenware vase."[68] The color contrast that Van Gogh sought through the bright yellow vase and background is replicated in Bradley's poem, where the vase of gold and scarlet contrasts with the gray flowers.

But in Bradley's poem, the flowers are delicate and fragile: their petals are "wrinkled grays," their "uncertain sprays" waver in the Giorgionesque "moist light." As with other flower poems by Michael Field, these flowers are redolent of feminine sexuality—but in contrast to the confident eroticism of "Unbosoming," in which the iris's vermillion seeds rapturously "burst the sides of the silver scrip," in "Irises" the flowers are cold, they flicker, are wrinkled, withered, uncertain, and scaly.[69] These associations suggest doubt or wavering on the part of the speaker. In this poem dedicated to Costelloe, Bradley's, as well as Cooper's, ambivalent feelings toward her sexualized "confession" find metaphorical expression. The gray iris, symbolic of Costelloe, is a complex flower, multifaceted like crystal, partially shrouded in a sheaf. The unfurling of the buds echoes Costelloe's unfurling on the couch in confession. The speaker can only observe, with wonder and uncertainty, the blooming of these ambiguous flowers (gray itself is an interesting color, suggestive of liminality—Costelloe's ambiguous marital state perhaps—as well as a Whistlerian hue). A similar feeling of uncertain awe is mentioned a month later, in June 1892, when Bradley and Cooper stayed with Costelloe at her brother's flat in Paris:

> Mary shows me the studio under our vine-tree—a painter lives
> with his mistress—a grisette. We seem to live in the air of a
> French novel; there is a strangeness in us—an awe that is not
> sacred. Then she speaks to us of life, of the dissolution of family
> bonds, of the divorce she hopes to get, by residence in America.
> With her soft voice ... Oh it is like the delicious sweep of the
> scythe, mowing down what is ripe for destruction![70]

Once again, Costelloe's candor exhilarates Bradley and Cooper, but her iconoclastic attitude also provokes unholy awe in Michael Field. Such feelings become entangled with the gray irises that clearly held ritualistic associations with Berenson and Costelloe (Bradley and Cooper often celebrated their most important friendships through flowers, as Catherine Maxwell discusses in her chapter in this volume). In "Irises," Michael Field render these flowers aesthetic, by applying the artistic, impressionistic methods they had developed in writing *Sight and Song.* Thus these two short lyrics, "I Have Found Her Power" and "Irises," provide a subtle link between the ekphrastic project of *Sight and Song* and the ambiguous lyric sequence that is *Underneath the Bough.* Costelloe's role in both has been subsumed and disguised, as Bradley and Cooper struggle to process their ambivalence toward this forward-thinking woman. "I Have Found Her Power" expresses their wish to co-opt Costelloe's powerful gaze, while in "Irises," contemplation of Costelloe (mediated through the flower imagery) leads to awe and uncertainty. Both poems use the language of painting—specifically the portrait and the impressionistic still life—to capture and to understand this iconoclastic female art historian.

Paris 1892, and After

If this poem suggests Bradley and Cooper's ambivalence regarding Costelloe and her illicit relationship with Berenson, the situation only worsened during the 1892 Paris trip. In these close quarters, Bradley and Cooper became increasingly disillusioned when they realized that Costelloe and Berenson were essentially using them as a cover for their affair:

> Probably knowing that as Michael & Field we are inseparable
> companions they have counted on long absences from our
> company & refreshing recontres at breakfast, afternoon-tea & at
> night. Yet such a hope on their part is unfair; for we were induced
> to visit Paris on the ~~understanding~~ /condition\ that we should
> receive guidance to an understanding of recent art & Morellian
> help in the Louvre.[71]

The friendship eroded further as Cooper's dramatized passion for Berenson intensified and she began to reconfigure Costelloe as a love rival. In a scene that epitomizes the tensions between all four writers, Cooper, Costelloe, and Berenson ended up sharing a bed one morning:

> He greets me "O Field, how picturesque you look." Then he
> begins, sitting by my bedside. But Mary will not let us have him to
> ourselves & she totters in to lie again by me, like a drift of snow. I
> stoop to kiss her—half to teaze [*sic*] him! With a flash of envy that
> ends . . . in a smile he says "For once in his life he would like to be
> a girl."[72]

Though seemingly envious, Berenson manages to turn the situation to his advantage by reasserting his authoritative gaze, assessing the relative beauties of the two women:

> Sim has the misfortune to remark as she looks at Mary & me,
> how she would like these two faces painted—He answered
> "Field would paint well; but Mary has far too much beauty to
> be painted." He then makes us the text of a discourse on the dif-
> ference between nice picturesqueness & real beauty ... my heart
> blanches a little at the personal comparison he draws. It is impossi-
> ble I should have an hour of pleasantness with him.[73]

During this trip, Cooper shifts from being a viewer of art to being assessed and objectified herself. Rather than receiving Morellian tuition as promised, she becomes its subject: "I am with Bernard. He again says I am looking very well, my hat throws delicate green onto my face. Again I feel the same cyni- cal wrath, especially as the tints of the hat are only demonstrating Bernard's method on my face. I am but a living example of what the New Salon can show in paint."[74] For her part, Bradley seemed to relish sparring intellectually with Berenson and to feel affection for Costelloe, as she wrote on New Year's Eve, 1892: "Most of our friends are further from us than last year—at least none of our bonds have deepened, with the exception that I have grown to love Mary more."[75]

But the "break" was finalized in November 1895, when Costelloe appar- ently insulted Michael Field's latest verse drama, *Attila, My Attila!*: "Mary writes about our work as if she <u>must</u> /just\ as unsympathetic people write to children about their games. . . . These two have never <u>done</u> anything but discouraged persistently, methodically."[76] As Joseph Bristow shows (in his chapter in this volume), Costelloe was increasingly exasperated by "the Mikes," especially during their visit to Florence in 1895, in which they proved particularly demanding houseguests. In her letters to Berenson and her mother, Costelloe vents her private feelings about Bradley and Cooper, regarding them as mis- guided, overly sensitive, and as suffering a deluded sense of their genius. Still, she continued to remain in regular contact with both women up until their deaths, despite frequent temporary "rifts," usually provoked by Costelloe's seeming callousness (for example, Bradley and Cooper took offense to Costel- loe's response to the death of their dog Whym Chow in 1906, suggesting that they take a holiday).

Costelloe's consistent presence in Bradley and Cooper's lives is attested to by the fact that she indirectly features in several later poems, including "Eros of the Summits" (1901), "Chalices" (1901), "Sweet, my abode is by the running brooks" (1903, written about Costelloe's cottage where Bradley and Cooper stayed but addressed to Charles Ricketts), and the comical:

There was a fine woman named Mary
Who never of pleasure was charry—
                She drank all her fill
                Yet never did ill
This child of Renaissance, blessed Mary.[77]

Costelloe was indeed a "child of the Renaissance" whose influence on Michael Field deserves to be recognized. Bradley and Cooper were complicit in upholding the "Doctrine" as the ultimate force in their burgeoning aesthetic inspiration during 1891, but their interactions with Costelloe reveal that they were more indebted to another woman than they cared to admit. Further investigation of Bradley and Cooper's relationships with other significant women, such as Vernon Lee, Maud Cruttwell, and Alice Trusted, may build a more accurate picture of their interactions and female literary networks. This chapter has endeavored to show that through tracing Costelloe's influence on *Sight and Song, Underneath the Bough*, and Michael Field's life writing, we can begin to understand the complexity and centrality of Bradley and Cooper's relationship with this pioneering female art historian. Looking at pictures with Berenson and Costelloe enabled Michael Field to see beyond the subject/object binary and to forge a truly collaborative gaze. While Berenson inspired their work, to see a woman engaged at the cutting edge of art historical research spurred Bradley and Cooper in their own radical experiments with looking. As they sought to attain both visual and poetic authority, Costelloe's presence in their work and life writing remains ambivalent, partly because it was at odds with their enduring dedication to the model of the singular male genius and partly also because Costelloe's sexual transgressions were troublingly close to their own sexual dissidence. By uncovering the mutual influence of "the immortal 4" on each other's work, we can begin to appreciate the complexity of Michael Field's engagement with art and their relationships with women.

Notes

The chapter epigraph is from Michael Field, "Works and Days," BL Add MS 46780, fols. 99r–v (May 27, 1892) [E.C.]. Slashes indicate text inserted into the diaries by Bradley or Cooper.

    1. Michael Field, "Works and Days," BL Add MS 46780, fol. 13r (January 12, 1892) [E.C.].

    2. For example, Julia F. Saville claims that Bradley and Cooper's journal entries for the early 1890s are "filled with references to eminent male literati . . . rarely are women mentioned, and when they are it is usually as hostesses of literary gatherings or social mediators of literary men" ("The Poetic Imaging of Michael Field," in *The Fin-de-Siècle Poem: English Literary Culture and the 1890s*, ed. Joseph Bristow [Athens: Ohio University

Press, 2005], 198). As I show in this chapter, this is in fact not the case: Mary Costelloe serves as just one example of the important role of women in Bradley and Cooper's life and work. Though they do to some extent play down this influence in their diaries, women certainly feature more significantly in "Works and Days" than Saville's statement suggests.

3. I refer to Mary as "Costelloe" in order to distinguish her from Berenson (whom she married in 1900, later than the period I will be discussing). This is also the name that Bradley and Cooper knew her by.

4. "Mrs. Costelloe," *The Women's Penny Paper* 3, no. 112 (December 13, 1890): 113–14.

5. Along with other American women of this period, Costelloe found Whitman's ideas about personal freedom and democracy intensely inspiring for building a discourse of women's rights. See Sherry Ceniza, *Walt Whitman and Nineteenth-Century Women Reformers* (Tuscaloosa: University of Alabama Press, 1998), 1–2.

6. As further evidence of this resurgence, in the process of preparing this chapter for publication, a special issue of *Visual Resources: An International Journal on Images and Their Uses* on "Women's Expertise and the Culture of Connoisseurship" has been published, edited by Meaghan Clarke and Francesco Ventrella (vol. 33, no. 1-2, 2017).

7. Sarah Parker, *The Lesbian Muse and Poetic Identity, 1889–1930* (London: Pickering and Chatto, 2013), 56–70.

8. Michael Field, "Works and Days," BL Add MS 46780, fol. 157v (July 7, 1892) [E.C.].

9. See Martha Vicinus, "Sister Souls: Bernard Berenson and Michael Field," *Nineteenth-Century Literature* 60, No. 3 (2005): 326–54; and Parker, *The Lesbian Muse*, 56–70.

10. Michael Field, "Works and Days," BL Add MS 46779, fol. 19r (February 27, 1891) [K.B.].

11. Michael Field, "Works and Days," BL Add MS 46779, fols. 19r–20r (February 27, 1891) [K.B.].

12. Mary Whitall Costelloe, "The New and the Old Art Criticism," *Nineteenth Century* (May 1894): 834. For more on Morelli's scientific methods, see Carlo Ginzburg and Anna Davin, "Morelli, Freud and Sherlock Holmes: Clues and Scientific Method," *History Workshop* 9 (Spring 1980): 5–36.

13. Hutchins Hapgood to Costelloe, January 1926, quoted in Ernest Samuels, *Bernard Berenson: The Making of a Connoisseur* (Cambridge, MA: Harvard University Press, 1979), 171.

14. Costelloe to Robert Pearsall Smith, November 24, 1893, in *Mary Berenson: A Self-Portrait from Her Diaries and Letters*, ed. Barbara Strachey and Jayne Samuels (New York: W. W. Norton, 1983), 54–55.

15. Strachey and Samuels, *Mary Berenson*, 54–55.

16. Mary Costelloe Berenson, *Life of Berenson* (MS), I Tatti Version, 17.

17. Costelloe Berenson, 28.

18. Berenson to Bradley, BL Add MS 45855 (April 17, 1892).

19. Hilary Fraser, "A Visual Field: Michael Field and the Gaze," *Victorian Literature and Culture* 34, no. 2 (2006): 557.

20. Michael Field, "Works and Days," BL Add MS 46783, fol. 68v (ca. April 30, 1895) [E.C.].

21. Michael Field, "Works and Days," BL Add MS. 46782, fol. 93r (July 16, 1894) [E.C.].

22. Berenson to Bradley, BL Add MS 45855 (September 28, 1891).

23. Cooper to Berenson, ca. October 1891, quoted in *Michael Field, the Poet: Published and Manuscript Materials*, ed. Marion Thain and Ana Parejo Vadillo (Peterborough, Ontario: Broadview, 2009), 315. Berenson's article was eventually published as "Some Comments on Correggio in Connection with His Pictures in Dresden," *Knight Errant* 1, no. 3 (October 1892): 73–85.

24. Michael Field, "Works and Days," BL Add MS 46780, fol. 47r (February 14, 1892) [E.C.].

25. Remarks reported in "Works and Days," BL Add MS 46780, fol. 118r (June 24, 1892) [E.C.]. Since *Sight and Song* was published in May 1892, Berenson is actually repeating Cooper's preface back to her here. "Bernhard" was the original spelling of his name, which he altered to "Bernard" in 1914.

26. Ana Parejo Vadillo, "*Sight and Song*: Transparent Translations and a Manifesto for the Observer," *Victorian Poetry* 38, no. 1 (2000): 15–34.

27. Bradley to Costelloe, n.d. (ca. 1894), quoted in Thain and Vadillo, *Michael Field, the Poet*, 329.

28. Hilary Fraser, *Women Writing Art History in the Nineteenth Century: Looking Like a Woman* (Cambridge: Cambridge University Press, 2014), 86.

29. Costelloe to Bradley, BL Add MS 45855 (April 17, 1892).

30. Bradley to Costelloe, February 2, 1892, quoted in Thain and Vadillo, *Michael Field, the Poet*, 326–27.

31. Thain and Vadillo, *Michael Field, the Poet*, 327. By the literary criticism, Bradley means the review of Joris-Karl Huysmans's *À rebours*. Vadillo and Thain attribute this piece to Berenson, but Bradley's response suggests it was authored by Costelloe: "The criticism on *A Rebours* is far better than any of the work on the painters. One feels brought into contact with the book" (328). The essay is written in Costelloe's hand but signed as "Doctrine on *A Rebours*"; perhaps it is another of their truly collaborative productions.

32. Thain and Vadillo, *Michael Field, the Poet*, 328.

33. Thain and Vadillo, 328. The quoted sentence is from Mary Logan [Costelloe], *Guide to the Italian Pictures at Hampton Court: With Short Studies of the Artists* (Kyrle Pamphlets No. 2, 1894), 54.

34. Bernard Berenson, *The Florentine Painters of the Renaissance* (New York: G. P. Putnam's Sons, 1896), 4–5.

35. Alison Brown, "Bernard Berenson and 'Tactile Values' in Florence," *Berenson & Harvard* (online exhibition), accessed July 15, 2016, http://berenson.itatti.harvard.edu/berenson/items/show/3021.

36. See Tiffany L. Johnston, "Mary Whitall Smith at the Harvard Annex," *Berenson & Harvard* (online exhibition), http://berenson.itatti.harvard.edu/berenson/items/show/3030, accessed July 15, 2016.

37. Michael Field, "Works and Days," BL Add MS 46780, fol. 47r (February 14, 1892) [E.C.].

38. Michael Field, "Works and Days," BL Add MS 46779, fol. 49r (June 8, 1891) [E.C.]. "Little Ray" is Ray Pearsall Conn Costelloe (later Strachey), Mary's daughter from her marriage to Frank Costelloe. She later became a prominent suffragist and politician. I have not been able to identify "Miss Hall."

39. Michael Field, "Works and Days," BL Add MS 46779, fol. 49v (June 8, 1891) [E.C.].

40. Cooper writes "Time had run back & fetched the Age of Gold," alluding to Milton's *On the Morning of Christ's Nativity* (1629): "Works and Days," BL Add MS 46779, fol. 49v (June 8, 1891) [E.C.].

41. Mary Logan [Costelloe], *Hampton Court*, 13 (my italics).

42. Michael Field, *Sight and Song* (London: Elkin Mathews and John Lane, 1892), 65–66 (my italics).

43. Michael Field, "Works and Days," BL Add MS 46779, fol. 51v (June 8, 1891) [E.C.].

44. Mary Logan [Costelloe], *Hampton Court*, 14.

45. MW [Costelloe], "The March of Ancona," *Woman's Herald* 7, no. 213 (November 1892): 7–8. Costelloe's sensory imagination was indeed strong that her one of her final publications was *A Vicarious Trip to the Barbary Coast* (London: Constable, 1938), in which she imagined herself in this location, using the letters of Berenson and his secretary-lover, Nicky Mariano.

46. Michael Field, "Works and Days," BL Add MS 46779, fol. 69r (August 10, 1891) [E.C.].

47. Michael Field, "Works and Days," BL Add MS 46779, fols. 98r–99r (August 30, 1891) [E.C.].

48. Michael Field, "Works and Days," BL Add MS 46780, fol. 78r (April 29, 1892) [K.B.].

49. Michael Field, *Underneath the Bough* (London: George Bell and Sons, 1893), 120, and in *Underneath the Bough* (Portland, ME: Thomas B. Mosher, 1898), 89.

50. Michael Field, "Works and Days," BL Add. MS. 46780, fol. 90v (May 21, 1892) [E.C.].

51. Michael Field, "Works and Days," BL Add. MS. 46780, fol. 95r (June 1892) [E.C.].

52. Norman Bryson, *Vision and Painting: The Logic of the Gaze* (London: Macmillan, 1983), 94.

53. Bryson, *Vision and Painting*, 122.

54. Michael Field, *Sight and Song*, 8. See Fraser, "A Visual Field," 555.

55. 1893 edition of *Underneath the Bough* [hereafter *UTB*], 88 (Fourth Book); 1898 edition, 91 (Fifth Book).

56. Michael Field, "Works and Days," BL Add MS 46780, fol. 137r (October 2, 1892) [K.B.].

57. See Sarah Parker, *The Lesbian Muse*, 56–70.

58. Such as "O Love, Remember That Your Eyes" (*UTB* 1893, 56–57). Another poem, entitled "We Meet, I Cannot Look Up, I Hear" is published above "I Have Found Her Power" in both editions of *Underneath the Bough*. This poem describes an encounter with George Meredith and describes "his eyes. / Oh to greet such skies—The delicate,

violet, thunder gray, / Behind, a spirit at mortal play! / Who cares the fog should roll away?" (*UTB*, 1893, 120).

59. Robert P. Fletcher, "'I Leave a Page Half-Writ': Narrative Discoherence in Michael Field's *Underneath the Bough*," in *Women's Poetry, Late Romantic to Late Victorian: Gender and Genre, 1830–1900*, ed. Isobel Armstrong and Virginia Blain (Basingstoke, UK: Macmillan, 1999), 165.

60. Michael Field, "Works and Days," BL Add MS 46780, fol. 80r (April 29, 1892) [EC]. These notes were presumably intended to form the basis for a potential ekphrastic poem to be included in a projected second volume.

61. Brooke S. Cameron, "The Pleasures of Looking and the Feminine Gaze in Michael Field's *Sight and Song*," *Victorian Poetry* 51, no. 2 (Summer 2013): 160.

62. Michael Field, "Works and Days," BL Add MS 46780, fol. 99r (May 27, 1892) [E.C.].

63. Michael Field, "Works and Days," BL Add MS 46780, fol. 99v (May 27, 1892) [E.C.].

64. Michael Field, "Works and Days," BL Add MS 46780, fol. 99v (May 27, 1892) [E.C.]. The ellipses are included in the original diary entry.

65. Bradley to Costelloe, n.d. (ca. 1895), Berenson Papers, Biblioteca Berenson, Harvard Center for Italian Renaissance Studies, Villa I Tatti. This letter was kindly shared with me by Ilaria Della Monica.

66. Michael Field, "Works and Days," BL Add MS 46780, fol. 91r (May 21, 1892) [K.B.]. The poem appears under the May 21 entry but is dated "27 May" by Bradley. *UTB* 1893, 107–8; *UTB* 1898, 90.

67. Fraser, "A Visual Field," 560.

68. Metropolitan Museum of Art, "Vincent Van Gogh Departs the Asylum with Irises and Roses," Newsweek.com, May 30, 2015, http://www.newsweek.com/vincent-departs-asylum-irises-and-roses-337131, accessed March 5, 2019.

69. "Unbosoming," *UTB* 1893, 77–78; *UTB* 1898, 84.

70. Michael Field, "Works and Days," BL Add MS 46780, fol. 108v (June 21, 1892) [E.C.].

71. Michael Field, "Works and Days," BL Add MS 46780, fols. 114v–115r (June 22, 1892) [E.C.].

72. Michael Field, "Works and Days," BL Add MS 46780, fol. 157v (July 7, 1892) [E.C.].

73. Michael Field, "Works and Days," BL Add MS 46780, fol. 157v (July 7, 1892) [E.C.].

74. Michael Field, "Works and Days," BL Add MS 46780, fol. 107v (June 20, 1892) [E.C.].

75. Michael Field, "Works and Days," BL Add MS 46780, fol. 162v (December 31, 1892) [K.B.].

76. Michael Field, "Works and Days," BL Add MS 46784, fol. 14v (November 7, 1895) [E.C.].

77. Michael Field, "Works and Days," BL Add MS 46793, fol. 183v (December 1904) [E.C.].

FIVE

Michael Field's "Unwomanly Audacities"

Attila, My Attila!, Sexual Modernity, and the London Stage

JOSEPH BRISTOW

Of course we are learning much from frequent attendance at the theatres—we knew nothing of the contemporary stage except some few Ibsen plays; we have learnt much from rehearsal & from the untiring instruction of our stage-manager & we ~~have~~ learnt most of all on Oct. 27. It was like a Day of Judgment, all we had done seen from the other end—a really horrible experience.

—Michael Field, Letter to William Archer (December 1893)

We trust to see <u>Honoria</u> on the boards—<u>Somewhere</u>.

—Michael Field, "Works and Days" (December 31, 1894)

IN LATE 1894 AND EARLY 1895, KATHARINE BRADLEY AND EDITH Cooper devoted formidable amounts of energy to drafting *Attila, My Attila!*— the eleventh blank-verse drama that they published under the name of Michael Field. This was the work that they believed (at least for several months before

Elkin Mathews published it) would once and for all place them among a rising generation of playwrights whose daring dramas were transforming the London stage. This heavily wrought historical play about Justa Grata Honoria—whose desperate plight appears in Edward Gibbon's *Decline and Fall of the Roman Empire* (1776–88)—features a plot crammed with controversial incidents that promised, from the very first scene, to startle a fin-de-siècle theater audience. Yet, as I show in this chapter, this particular verse-drama, on which they staked such high hopes, fared even worse than *A Question of Memory*, their bold play about a traumatic episode from the Hungarian revolution of 1848. Attacked on all sides, *A Question of Memory* endured a single poorly reviewed performance in October 1893.

Before venturing any further into Bradley and Cooper's desire to rise above the difficulties that beset *A Question of Memory*, it is useful to begin with the extraordinary ambition and scope of *Attila, My Attila!* whose title comes from the pounding refrain in George Meredith's poem, "The Nuptials of Attila," which appeared to great acclaim in 1879. As my account of the frenetic action should explain, Michael Field's tumultuous drama—which is filled with scenes of sexual violence and political insubordination—concentrates attention on the potential of women's eroticism to overturn imperial rule. For some time, Bradley and Cooper earnestly believed that the startling plot of their Roman verse drama would move by leaps and bounds beyond their failed attempt at impressing the theater world and that they should rank alongside leading playwrights of the day. But, as they began to realize, the immense effort that they dedicated to *Attila, My Attila!* had been radically misplaced—at least as far as trying to establish their position as acknowledged writers who could level with the likes of Oscar Wilde and Arthur Wing Pinero.

Act I of this Roman tragedy, whose title Bradley and Cooper frequently recorded in "Works and Days" as *Honoria*, is set in the western Roman capitol Ravenna. Immediately, we learn from the senior chamberlain Satyrus that the Roman princess, who has just turned sixteen, is disobeying instructions to stay in her rooms until she has been "summoned by her mother to receive / The state's congratulations on her birthday."[1] Honoria has no conception of the birthday gift that her mother—the widowed Galla Placidia, Empress of the West—is about to bestow upon her. Placidia has decided that she will elevate her daughter to the imposing title of Augusta. Placidia, however, is granting this title with the strictest of caveats. She prepares the way by informing Honoria that in future the only friendship that her daughter shall enjoy is hers: "From to-day / You will be my companion" (10). The implication is clear. Placidia wishes to prevent the young woman from marrying. Honoria shrieks with horror at the thought of such a segregated existence. In response, the unforgiving mother reproves Honoria, whose outburst evokes for Placidia the grievous memory of her late husband, whose effeminacy she clearly despised: "do not shriek like that—your father's habit, / But very vulgar" (10). Offended, Honoria asks Placidia, "If he did not please you, / Why did you choose my father?" (10). The ensuing dialogue makes it plain that Placidia believes she had no choice in the matter: "I have lived / As women must to please my family" (10). Yet Honoria, who refuses to comply, immediately challenges her mother. She declares that Placidia was rumored to have "had lovers" when she "was taken prisoner by the Goths / In girlhood" (10). Having made this point, Honoria defiantly announces, "I want to be a captive and have lovers, / Two at a time, and freely choose at last / The great, barbaric fellow as you chose" (10–11).

Honoria's lines herald what becomes, in the latter half of this drama, her mutinous desire for the fading Roman Empire's archenemy Attila the Hun. In the meantime, however, the first act maintains the focus on Placidia's vengeful scheme to eliminate her daughter's marital prospects. Once she confers with her cynical son, Emperor Valentinian III, Placidia's treacherous reasoning becomes clear:

> I live,
> As you must, for the glory of our house,
> The Theodosian House: Honoria too
> Must live for it. Think of the great example
> Her cousin gives her in Byzantium!
> Pulcheria, the Augusta, keeps herself
> A virgin that her brother may continue
> Sole emperor in the East, as in the West
> It is my will you should be sole Augustus.
> A son-in-law shall never share your throne[.]
> (13)

Valentinian is equally heartless toward the potential threat that he would face if his older sister selected a husband. "I will," he ominously observes, "take care she does not spoil my life" (14). On this basis, should Honoria not follow this stipulation, fail to preserve her virginity, and bear any child that threatens the male imperial bloodline, she might as well be dead.

Yet there is worse to come. At this early stage, the plot hurtles toward a fresh crisis. The moment she learns that she must follow Pulcheria's dreaded example, Honoria expresses outrage. "It is fate to love," she exclaims without shame. "You cannot alter that" (21). Undefeated, Honoria remains true to her word by starting a clandestine affair with Eugenius. The sexual excitement between them grows intense. He confesses to experiencing uncontrollable eroticism: "A madness in my heart to spread this fire / Across your cheeks, your breast, to hold your lips / Thus helpless to my pleasure" (29). As one might predict, once we reach Act II Placidia hears rumors from Satyrus that Honoria is "with child" (45). Eugenius, agonized by guilt, confesses that he is the father. Horrified that her daughter could yield to "a caitiff-slave" (48), Placidia threatens to take Eugenius's life. Honoria, though, does not capitulate entirely: "I am not sorry," she emphatically tells Placidia. "I am glad I meet you as a woman, / I meet you as a mother" (52). In every respect, she refuses to admit that her actions amount to "sin, when nothing but the purest impulse / Of nature called" (52). Eugenius, for his part, also asserts his right to express his passion: "deeper far / Than any treason is the truth I *loved*" (52). Still, even if Placidia succeeds in sparing Eugenius's life, it proves impossible for love to conquer all. No matter how much Honoria determines to emancipate her desires, she remains at the mercy of an imperial regime that does its utmost to control her mind and body.

Honoria's anguished predicament deteriorates even further in the third act. There we discover the demoralized Augusta, now thirty years of age, imprisoned and loveless. Having lost her child to the murderous Placidia, she exists under lock and key as an exile in the eastern capitol Byzantium, where she suffers the unwelcome desires of Pulcheria, a figure masquerading as a nun, whose lesbian yearning for her cousin becomes immediately apparent. ("You know I am intensely fond of her," Pulcheria confides to Satyrus. "I do believe you love her," he replies. "As my life," she insists [59].) In an attempt to extricate herself from this situation, Honoria employs Satyrus as a go-between in order to engage in secret communications with Attila the Hun, parting with a ring as a token of her engagement. "I have decreed," she tells Satyrus, "His passion shall be drawn across the borders / To me" (65). Honoria's hope is that her rebellious actions will usurp Theodosius, who has complied with Placidia's demand to deny her everything she wants in life: "I desire," she says, "Nothing but retribution on them all" (66). Time and again, she exults in the thought of her prospective husband: "Attila, / My Attila!" (65). Yet in Byzantium the only yearning that she arouses comes in the form of Pulcheria's advances: "I love you," she says to Honoria, "with the passion / The heathen give to those who bring them life" (80). Even though it is clear that Honoria cannot reciprocate (Pulcheria, we read in the stage directions, *tries to embrace her and is repulsed* [80]), there is no question that this is for its time an especially unapologetic depiction of female homosexuality. In this insufferable predicament, once Honoria's subterfuge to betroth Attila is discovered, it leads to Satyrus's execution and her banishment from Theodosius's court.

By Act IV, we witness the rebellious Honoria returned to Ravenna. Here Placidia has inaugurated a new plot in order to stymie her daughter's unruly passion for the Hun. At this juncture, the empress releases Eugenius from jail, with a view to forcing him to marry Honoria: "We must," Placidia states, "either / By Christian marriage put her beyond reach / Of [Attila's] unlawful claim, or give his lust / And avarice their victim" (93). Once again, Honoria remains steadfast: "I am," she insists, "the bride / Of Attila whatever you may do" (99). But, then, when Placidia and Valentinian appear more indomitable than ever in subjugating Honoria to their will, the recalcitrant protagonist resolves that she might as well make a mockery of the imposed marriage ceremony by cursing everyone around them, "with the storms, / Nature's own incantations, devilry / That heaven itself unlooses" (100). Just at the point, however, where she *"takes Eugenius's hand, and, laughing a low, wild laugh, goes up the altar"* (101), the drama endures another sudden shift, which on this occasion manages to destroy Honoria's will. The assembled court learns from the Roman emissary Anthemius that "Attila is dead" (102). In a graphic speech, Anthemius recalls that Attila perished after his public rape of his bride Ildico on a "nuptial couch, / Piled high above the throne" (105). Anthemius reveals that Attila's men discovered in the morning that the Burgundian princess Ildico avenged the rapist, leaving him "prostrate in a mass / Of frozen blood!" (106). With these words ringing in her ears, the powerless Honoria *"throws up her arms, shrieking the name"* of Ildico, whom she proclaims is the only "sister" she has ever known, and then *"falls a senseless heap on the ground"* (107). Eugenius, whose life has been spared, tries to touch Honoria. But Placidia, who has the last word, forbids him. "Take her to her cell," she observes of her mortified daughter. "She must be hidden" (107).

For several months, Michael Field believed that Honoria's drastic story, which marked their second concerted attempt at staging their drama in the West End, would at last confirm their preeminence "on the boards."[2] Their faith in this project, however, arose in the face of the considerable ground they had lost with *A Question of Memory*, which had also consumed their energies. For several weeks before *A Question of Memory* premiered, Bradley and Cooper had attended the rehearsals of this fervent drama, which depicts a harrowing episode about the national hero Ferencz Renyi during the nationalist convulsions of 1848. They were convinced, as coordinator of the Independent Theatre Society (ITS) J. T. Grein initially was, that their rendition of Renyi's remarkable story—one whose "Spirit of Freedom" their contemporaries such as E. Nesbit had also celebrated—would succeed as a distinctly modern work.[3] In telling the tale of the silence Renyi maintained when Austrian forces threatened to kill the women closest to him if he failed to disclose the whereabouts of his revolutionary comrades, *A Question of Memory* was unquestionably steeped in vibrant political realism. Besides, the play proved altogether more up to date in style than the dramas they had previously published, since on this occasion they had written the work not in blank verse but entirely in prose. Scarcely anyone, however, had a good word to say about Michael Field's stagecraft.

In the discussion that follows, I consider how Bradley and Cooper's determination to succeed with *Attila, My Attila!* throws into relief several significant aspects of their professional practice. The first is the somewhat stubborn terms on which they were prepared to accept or reject the abundant amounts of criticism that friends, reviewers, and literary figures gave them about their aptitude in producing modern drama. Here I begin by exploring several of the difficulties that engulfed the staging of *A Question of Memory*. Thereafter I turn to their dismay at the reception of their stouthearted play, especially the sharp comments from William Archer, a recognized authority on Ibsen and a leading voice against theater censorship. At the same time, however, Bradley and Cooper declared their willingness to learn from their mistakes by attending many different plays in the West End, including several works sponsored through Grein's society. Their preparedness to engage with harsh criticism, though, had mixed results. Even if they promptly decided to reconstruct *A Question of Memory* pretty much from scratch (they made the dialogue more naturalistic and dispensed with the original fourth and final act), they did so mainly to satisfy themselves, though they left a copy of the typescript with the actress Elizabeth Robins, who had made her mark in London with commended performances in Ibsen's controversial works. In the end, as their creation of *Attila, My Attila!* shows, the coauthors decided that their greatest talents lay with the passionate blank verse that they had been composing devotedly for years. Their resolve to do this, in many respects, marked a pivotal moment in Michael Field's career. From this point onward, the coauthors largely withdrew from the public world of theater, though they did so in a dauntless spirit that spurred them on to write many more—increasingly ambitious—verse plays that placed the liberated expression of women's desires at the center of epochal change.

"[A] Touch of <u>Malice</u> . . . in your Method of Retort":
A Question of Memory and Its Critics

Michael Field was not mistaken when they initially perceived that *A Question of Memory* would raise their literary profile. On January 9, 1893, Cooper observed, "Grein has expressed a wish to become acquainted with our plays."[4] This was certainly a welcome overture, since it occurred when Bradley and Cooper harbored resentment at their marginal status in literary London. "We are," Cooper declared two weeks later, "desperately alone in this world that shuns us. What can it be? <u>Stephania</u> cannot be responsible for it all. We are boycotted in the papers, by the men ([Walter] Pater, [George] Meredith, [Richard Holt] Hutton) to whom we have sent our books, & by even literary society. It is mysterious."[5] As Bradley and Cooper realized, *Stephania: A Trialogue* (1892)—a work that concentrates on the sexual resourcefulness of the tenth-century widow of Crescentius who vows to avenge Otho the Great, the murderer of her husband— attracted comparatively few critical notices. ("The book might be a <u>deader</u>," they feared.[6]) The most substantial of the reviews—Lionel Johnson's in the *Academy*—appeared somewhat belatedly and was not exactly complimentary. Although he acknowledged that there was "positive dramatic genius" in their previous verse plays, Johnson concluded that this "trialogue" (he termed it "an unhappy form") proved "elusive and unsatisfactory," since the work for three voices succeeded "less in presenting characters and scenes, than in suggesting dramatic thoughts and possibilities."[7] To Johnson's mind, Stephania's "act of revenge does not bear thinking upon," since she remains "a perverse and well-nigh frantic figure."[8] The outcome, he believed, was a mediocre drama from such a "fascinating and powerful a poet" as Michael Field: "confused and monotonous, vague and perplexing, partly from its very subject."[9]

With such adverse criticisms in mind, Michael Field took Grein's theatrical venture very seriously. As we can see from their journals, they had become avid theatergoers. They reflected at length on the inspiring production of Ibsen's *Ghosts*, which they watched on January 26 that year. The same was true of their detailed responses to Ibsen's *The Master Builder*, which played at the Trafalgar Square Theatre on February 21, 1893. Cooper relished the performance: "Miss Robins's Hilda is Modernity itself in skirts—they are blue, short supple to motion."[10] Clearly, this was just the kind of theatrical company that Michael Field wanted to keep, and the prognostications were promising. Grein, who maintained a commitment to discovering fresh, homegrown talent to complement his productions of advanced European plays, accepted *A Question of Memory* on August 4, 1893, and several weeks later in the *Daily Chronicle* he revealed that he had good reason for welcoming Michael Field into his well-regarded society: "If you must know," Grein said to an interviewer, "'Michael Field' stands for two ladies—Miss Bradley and Miss Cooper." He expressed considerable admiration for their dramas:

> I may say that I had originally intended bringing out a poetical drama by "Michael Field" called "William Rufus," but on studying the possibilities of staging it, I found the difficulties in the way were great, such an enormous amount of male talent being

required—there being no heroines in the piece—that I despaired of getting the actors required in the beginning of the autumn season, and therefore finally decided to let it alone until later. But just as I was writing to this effect to the two ladies a letter from them was crossing mine which brought me the welcome news that they had completed a prose play dealing with a very stirring incident of the Hungarian revolution of 1848. I immediately asked for the play itself, and when I got it I saw it was well worthy of the writers from whom it came, and I accepted it.[11]

As Grein's comments show, he certainly desired to support plays that offered strong parts for actresses. His allusion to Michael Field as "two ladies," however, characterizes them in far more genteel terms than they wished to be perceived, since—as they make clear about their time attending the rehearsals—they were highly conscious of their gender presentation: "black coffee & cigarettes have made us ourselves . . . not the nervous quarrelsome females we were fast feigning to be."[12]

Despite Grein's enthusiasm, the production ran into numerous wrangles with the stage manager Herman de Lange and several members of the cast. In "Works and Days," Bradley and Cooper inserted an unpromising note beneath an obituary clipped from the *Pall Mall Gazette* in 1886 about Renyi, whose traumatic experience occasioned their play: "News of the cast," they observed on September 23, 1893, "most dispiriting."[13] As Jan Macdonald has remarked, Bradley and Cooper kept making suggestions for several leading actors—including Johnston Forbes-Robertson, Elizabeth Robins, Herbert Waring, and Janet Achurch—who might be cast, only to discover that these individuals were either too expensive for the low-budget ITS or already booked for other productions. In Macdonald's view, the troublesome "casting negotiations" remain instructive because "they demonstrate both the aims of the ITS management as regards assembling a company, and the difficulties it faced in achieving them."[14] To make matters worse, de Lange—who created a furor when he tried to reorganize one of the major scenes—expressed intolerance toward some of the actresses: "The jabbering women," Cooper records him saying to her, "never think of anything but themselves; they have no sense of art."[15] (He was exceptionally rude about some of the male actors, too. "The man will ruin the play," he said of Acton Bond, who took the leading role of Renyi.[16])

The upshot was that the production, after much tampering from de Lange, drifted away from the original script, which adopts a dauntless approach to sensitive topics such as political betrayal and sexual dissidence during the turmoil of 1848. In her searching analysis of the four-act version of *A Question of Memory*, Jill R. Ehnenn points to the fact that Michael Field conceived the drama as a complex psychological inquiry into the ways in which "male hysteria is a function of the repressed femininity of men."[17] This idea is central to Renyi, who in Michael Field's adaptation of his well-known story suffers a terrifying breakdown when General Haynau, on behalf of the Austrian authorities, shoots the hero's mother, sister, and bride-to-be. In Bradley and Cooper's version, Renyi finds himself too mentally unable to disclose that his insurgent compatriots have assembled in the Jablonkar Defile. From the outset, the play symptomizes Renyi's sensitivity and vulnerability through his close identification with the feminine. As his friend Stanislaus tells him, in the opening scene, "It amazes me. Ferencz, the patriot, stroking the ribbons of his sister's silk gown."[18] Very soon, we learn that Ferencz abhors "real war and bloodshed" (4). Far better, he thinks, are "women's clothes": "The soft scent, the crumpled folds, every dint of their printing! (6). This is the first sign that throughout this drama, the lines of sexual and political identification are awry. No sooner have we witnessed the pleasure he takes in such feminine softness than we learn that his sister Fina is attracted to an Austrian officer named Mansfelt. Not long after, Fina—who is preparing a lesson for her schoolchildren—expresses frustration with the gendered division of labor that structures her world: "Mother, why did you not make me a man? Then I too could have gone to war" (8).

By this point, we can grasp the contradictions that lie at the center of the play's intricate action. In every respect, the characters remain dissatisfied with the sexual and political roles that Hungarian culture—at a time of acute crisis—has assigned them. And as if this were not enough, it becomes plain that all of the romantic ties in the drama are mismatched. Ferencz's passion for his fiancée Thekla is not reciprocated, just as Stanislaus's desire for Thekla's older sister Elizabeth remains hopeless. In Act III, where Haynau is about to shoot Fina, Thekla, and Ferenz's mother off scene, the stage directions indicate that Ferencz expresses himself "wildly, with a hysterical laugh" (36). His speech becomes rambling: "I have seen people die . . . hearing it, hearing it, mother's death!" (36). When Haynau presses him to recall the mountain gorge where Janos's men are based, Ferencz cannot recollect it at all: "My memory is roving about among rocks" (38), he says, while screaming to the general to spare Thekla.

How, then, does the play resolve this terrible crisis? Act IV presents Stanislaus, Ferencz, and Elizabeth together, attempting to rebuild their lives, after the Austrians have murdered not only the three women but also all of the men hiding in the defile. Stanislaus admits that he betrayed his comrades: "They are all butchered now, not one of them is left" (44). Indignant, the patriotic Elizabeth is at first horrified to learn that Stanislaus believes that his action has spared her life. "No woman," she says, "was ever so dishonored as I am" (45). But she rapidly comes around to the view that both she and Stanislaus must concentrate on caring for Ferencz, who is slowly but surely recovering his memory. ("*Dianthus caryophyllus,*" he cries, bizarrely, after snatching a sheaf of carnations. "Good heavens, I can remember *that,*" he adds [44].) The final scene presents a tableau where Stanislaus holds Ferencz's hand and Elizabeth wipes his brow. This triadic relationship is implicitly superior to the failed sexual intimacies and botched political loyalties that have led to such sorrow, death, and destruction.

This summary of *A Question of Memory* certainly points to its conceptual and emotional ambition, although it also raises questions about the ways that such a fraught drama might translate to the stage. In a thoughtful review, the *Theatre* acknowledged that the extreme situations Michael Field devised, in order to create a dramatic success, demanded "the greatest tragic acting."[19] "What Mdme. [Sarah] Bernhardt and Mr. [Henry] Irving and Mr. [Johnston] Forbes Robertson could do with" the most tragic scene in the drama, the journal remarked, "would probably pass the limit of human endurance"; the "actors," however, "were, as a body, unequal to their task."[20] Meanwhile, other observers identified shortcomings in the writing itself. In the *Speaker*—one of the more liberal journals of the time—A. B. Walkley found the drama so inadvisably drafted as to appear "absolutely without significance."[21] He heartlessly characterized *A Question of Memory* as the naive handiwork of a "theatrical tyro": "A couple of ladies, who know nothing of the practical requirements of the theatre, who stand outside the current of dramatic evolution, have attempted to write a play: that is all."[22] Equally discouraging was the commentary in the *Pall Mall Gazette,* which expressed intolerance toward Michael Field's depiction of a "Hungary of nervous, of neurose shadows, fantastically introspective—an Austria officered by phrasemongering nonentities."[23] As far as this reviewer could see, such neurotic psychology was "all that the Iliad of 1848" had "suggested to Michael Field."[24]

By far the greatest blow, however, was the one that Archer dealt in the *World.* In dismay, Michael Field took careful note of his wearied response to their writing: "a merciless attack on our archaic style."[25] But even more dispiriting were Archer's observations about what was supposed to have been the high point in the lamentable production; he made, Bradley and Cooper observe, "the admission that the Shooting-Scene, if it had been as well-written as it is finely conceived, would have been one of the most moving in English Drama."[26] His comments clearly mattered more than those of any other critic, since the co-authors promptly sent him their quickly rewritten version of the scene where Renyi's memory disintegrates:

We send you our Third Act, /now the final Act of the Play\
revised with the most conscientious determination to avoid false
writing. We ask you, have we avoided it, where does it still lurk, are
there any more writhed images to blot, is the "dramatic" impulse
unretarded? . . . Your own words are the appeal we make to you &
we are certain you will aid us.[27]

Archer, however, did not take entirely kindly to Bradley and Cooper's plea for
guidance. "I cannot," he responded, "but be touched by the way in which you
accept what I fear was a very ungentle criticism, but I cannot help suspecting a
touch of <u>malice</u> (in the French sense) in your method of retort. It is one thing to
say . . . 'This scene is not right' & quite another thing to put it right."[28]

By accusing Bradley and Cooper of mischief, Archer—who had the grace
to make generous opinions on their fresh draft—intimated that they were
perhaps reacting in a style that aimed more to exploit his expertise than respect his insights. In return, the joint dramatists reassured him that they had
no such intent. Michael Field declared that their desire was simply to learn how
to write in a style that reflected their passion for the present-day culture that
they had come to appreciate: "[W]e have grown to love what for shortness I
must call <u>modernity</u>."[29] At the same time, Archer evidently embodied for them
a modern spirit that they found intimidating, especially when he snubbed them
at the Shakespeare Reading Society's performance of *Measure for Measure* two
weeks after *A Question of Memory* played at the Opera Comique. At the very moment when Oscar Wilde (who had taken a box at *A Question of Memory*) pointed
Archer out to them and John Todhunter (whose *Black Cat* appeared later in
Grein's season) uttered Archer's name, his and Cooper's eyes met momentarily:
"It was," she says, "a most modern encounter, 'frightfully thrilling'": "His eyes are
like doors into a lethal chamber, but they certainly are capable of expressing
Ibsenism in real life."[30] Such phrasing, which is tinged with knowing irony, intimates that perhaps the dramatic excitement that Bradley and Cooper experienced in London's theatrical world lay as much in the personalities attending
modern productions as in the performances themselves. Archer, however, hardly
felt the same. In December 1893, he begged Michael Field not to "mention that
any portion of" the revised draft had been through his hands.[31] One senses
that, for him, any public association with the coauthors might involve needless
embarrassment.

In any case, Bradley and Cooper, as these brushes with prominent theater
people show, had their own reservations about modern theater, which we can also
see in their responses to the works of their most feted dramatic contemporaries

in England. Recent plays by such successful dramatists as Pinero failed to inspire them. Certainly, they found his *Second Mrs. Tanqueray* (1893)—the well-received "problem play" about a cruelly treated "woman with a past" that they saw on November 18 that year—to be "full of tragic situations," but the clueless husband struck them "as a model on which the emotions are hung lifelessly."[32] They were equally lukewarm about the much-applauded Wilde, who had expressed his encouragement to Michael Field over the years. (Wilde, who, as we have seen, attended *A Question of Memory*, was kind enough to tell them that he thought the "third act . . . quite admirable."[33]) On January 6, 1895, less than a week after it opened, Bradley and Cooper went to the Theatre Royal, Haymarket, to see Wilde's third society comedy, *An Ideal Husband*. In "Works and Days," Bradley makes some incisive observations about this epigrammatic play that unfolds the sexual and political intrigues of the English upper crust: "Brilliant comments brought to life by puppets, yet Oscar in this play has got down a little deeper into human nature."[34] "He exposes," she continues, "the folly of the woman who worships her husband, but he does not make her loveable," a feature that Bradley regards as a fault.[35] "Even women with principles," she notes, "may have charms."[36] At this juncture, it is clear that Bradley and Cooper had little interest in emulating the modernity that Wilde's comedy embodied. They had other plans in mind. Earlier that day, Bradley had visited a literary agent, to whom she entrusted the manuscript of *Attila, My Attila!* with a view to finding both a prestigious publisher and a producer for this recently completed play in pentameter. Very quickly, however, as I reveal below, they realized that this was the first of several missteps in their efforts to put what they thought was the contemporaneousness of Honoria's blank-verse drama onto the London stage.

"We Have Not Made Yes": *Attila, My Attila!*

"Works and Days" reveals that the enormous amount of energy invested by Michael Field in *Attila, My Attila!* proved both exhausting and exhilarating. Cooper records the "weeks of revision, cutting, ceaseless copying, feverish nights, fiery days in which the power of walking had ceased under the storm of excitement."[37] "We read it over in the train," she notes as they traveled from their home in Reigate to London, "& find it good."[38] The purpose of their journey was to offer their draft to the well-regarded agent A. P. Watt. Yet the meeting, as Cooper recalled, did not proceed in their best interests. Once they entered Watt's office, Michael Field unhesitatingly ventured their late friend Robert Browning's name "as a recommendation to Smith, Elder," the somewhat staid company whose establishment reputation contrasted with that of their most recent publisher Elkin Mathews.[39] As it turned out, Watt promised to speak with Smith, Elder, even though he did not "care to have relations with the acting world."[40] "We must not," Cooper notes in words that appear to echo Watt's sentiments, "send our M.S. to [the French tragedienne] Sarah Bernhardt . . . till we have published & secured our acting rights."[41] As Cooper promptly conceded, the reluctant Watt's willingness to oblige with Smith, Elder was likely to prove unproductive. Furthermore, they learned that Watt had "no wish to treat with Ibsen's English publisher," William Heinemann.[42]

With great resolve, Michael Field renewed their pursuit to find a home for their play by sending their manuscript themselves to Heinemann. By late April, while they were enjoying the hospitality of Bernard Berenson and Mary Costelloe in Fiesole near Florence, they received a letter from Ibsen's English publisher declining the drama. It was, as Cooper observed, "the second absolute refusal."[43] By the middle of May, Ernest Bell, with whom they had published five volumes between 1884 and 1890, also declined Michael Field's newest tragedy. It was not until July 19, 1895, that Bradley signed a contract with Mathews, on terms that were not exactly advantageous. Even though the coauthors kept the copyright and acting rights, Mathews was "to take all profits."[44] By August, they were correcting the revises, though any further discussion of a stage production had by that time dropped out of the picture. They were also sensing that they might have deluded themselves about the value they had once staked on this drama: "We read of Honoria & are terrified at the fatal little thing."[45] The work struck them as "just like the other side of the moon, barren with the very fatalness of fate."[46]

As their journal entries reveal, at this time Michael Field's apprehensiveness about the success of *Attila, My Attila!* is also evident in the somewhat overreaching "Preface" that they drafted for their volume. Their comments open with a statement about their chosen genre: "Tragedy is the conflict of man with the indifference of nature" (v). Yet once they have provided examples of this antagonism (they mention Prometheus contesting Zeus, Satan battling Jehovah, Lear withstanding Cordelia, and, in a modern example, Hedda Gabler standing up to her motherhood), they describe their leading figure simply as "Little Honoria" (vi). Without a doubt, the epithet seeks to arouse sympathy for one who suffers such extreme wrongdoing, but it still proves difficult to see how Honoria's desire to "give freedom to her womanhood by unwomanly audacities" (vi) might rank with these other well-known characters' imposing struggles. Subsequently, Michael Field tries to account for Honoria's "importunate desire *to be herself*" through the expression of her eroticism as "a tragedy of tragedies" (vi). In phrasing indicating that Bradley and Cooper recognized something might be amiss in their conception of Honoria's predicament, they claim that she was "urged by nature, and yet outrage[d] her [i.e., nature] through obedience" (vi). The moment they have identified this contradiction, they claim that their protagonist's "tragedy of tragedies" is "one not remote": "for Honoria is the *New Woman* of the fifth century" (vi). Such wording constitutes an arresting extension of Sarah Grand's earliest formulation of the "new woman," which had appeared in the *North American Review* the previous year. In her influential article, Grand observes that the "new woman" has recently "proclaimed for herself what was wrong with Home-is-the-Woman's-Sphere, and prescribed the remedy," which in her view entails a sexual revolution, not just for women but for both of the sexes, given "the death of manliness" and the "ever more effeminate" nature of men.[47]

The strain in the "Preface" becomes even more noticeable toward the end. In the final sentences, we discover that "who shall read [Honoria's] story" will learn the truth of her plight from two famous lines in the prologue to *Pyramus and Thisbe*, the amusing play within a play that draws Shakespeare's *Midsummer Night's Dream* to an end: "This man, with lanthorn, dog, and bush of thorn, / Presenteth Moonshine" (vi). Shakespeare's words, of course, remind us that theater involves magical illusions, many of which—if we suspend disbelief—can appear somewhat crude and mechanical. Then again, the implication that Honoria's tragedy generates the humor that we find in the concluding act of Shakespeare's comedy assuredly gives one pause. The "Preface" attempts to explain this unexpected move from tragedy to comedy through the assertion that their "play presents Irony" (vi). By any account, this description proves hard to construe, since it remains unclear whether *Attila, My Attila!* is supposed to undercut the tragic form that places Honoria's sexuality in opposition to the harsh political forces that entrammel her.

By October that year, Mathews had managed to produce the edition well ahead of schedule, since the title page records the publication date as 1896. On receiving their first two copies, Bradley and Cooper looked admiringly on the finely printed and bound volume: "On the breakfast table we find <u>Attila, My Attila!</u>—2 vols. sent as the above label [from Elkin Mathews, Vigo St., London, W., 26/10/95] shows post-haste. Folkard [the printer] has been gallant."[48] At once, Michael Field followed their habitual practice of reading their drama aloud. Yet, as they made their way through all four acts, the experience of uttering each and every line swerved from inspirational satisfaction to structural disappointment:

> Michael & I read the play aloud—each an act by turns. It takes 2 full hours. We greatly enjoy the way it advances on its own velocity—the test of true dramatic life: we are satisfied with the characterisation, except perhaps in the case of Placidia, & the

style demands the voice & gesture as the rhythms of some kind
of music implores the first to dance. So far, so good. But ..."the
hungry we have sent empty away" [cf. Luke 1:53]. The Curtain goes
down on <u>No</u>, not on <u>Yes</u>. Nietzsche says Raphael said <u>Yes</u>, Raphael
made <u>Yes</u>—We have not made Yes in <u>Attila, My Attila!</u>[49]

Mindful of Friedrich Nietzsche's *The Birth of Tragedy* (they thought it "the only
prose statement of the Dionysiac attitude toward Life that exists"), Bradley and
Cooper concluded that they had not produced the dazzling "illusion of an illusion" that the German philosopher found in Raphael's *Transfiguration*.[50] As far as
they could tell, the ending of *Attila, My Attila!* rang hollow, despite the immense
amount of refining and revising that they had brought to Honoria's inconsolable
life story. What, then, had gone wrong?

Perhaps the best way of responding to this inquiry is to look first at their
main sources and then the connections that they wished to make between these
materials. As the coauthors acknowledge in the "Preface," Gibbon treats the
young Augusta's plight "with great sympathy" (vi). He explains in fairly explicit
terms how Placidia and Valentinian denied the sixteen-year-old daughter of
empire the pleasures of conjugal love:

> The sister of Valentinian was educated in the palace of Ravenna;
> and as her marriage might be productive of some danger to the
> state, she was raised, by the title of *Augusta*, above the hopes of
> the most presumptuous subject. But the fair Honoria had no
> sooner attained the sixteenth year of her age, than she detested
> the importunate greatness which must for ever exclude her
> from the comforts of honourable love: in the midst of vain and
> unsatisfactory pomp, Honoria sighed, yielded to the impulse
> of nature, and threw herself into the arms of her chamberlain
> Eugenius. Her guilt and shame (such is the absurd language
> of imperious man) were soon betrayed by the appearances of
> pregnancy: but the disgrace of the royal family was published
> to the world by the imprudence of the empress Placidia; who
> dismissed her daughter, after a strict and shameful confinement, to
> a remote exile at Constantinople.[51]

Gibbon proceeds to comment on the cruelty of consigning Honoria to a life of
celibacy among the sisters of Theodosius in the Eastern Empire. His profound
sense that her natural desires had been repressed through "twelve or fourteen
years" of imposed monasticism makes it perfectly understandable that Honoria
should "embrace a strange and desperate resolution."[52] After months of isolation,

Honoria "offered to deliver herself into the arms of a Barbarian" whose troops had gathered on the banks of the Danube.[53] As Gibbon recalls, it was well known that the polygamous Attila had "professed himself the lover and champion of the princess Honoria."[54] Through her eunuch, as Michael Field shows in their play, Honoria sought to secure her marriage to the Hun by pledging a ring. Gibbon proceeds to observe that once consular officers had foiled her plot, Honoria was banished to her home city of Ravenna, where—as he remarks— she was forced into a marriage with "some obscure and nominal husband" before being "immured in a perpetual prison."[55] In *The Decline and Fall*, Honoria's history stops there.

Michael Field blended this section of Gibbon's chronicle with a later episode that records Attila's sexual assault of the Burgundian princess Ildico, whose horror of forced union with this marauder proved terrifying:

> Yet, in the mean while, Attila relieved his tender anxiety, by adding a beautiful maid, whose name was Ildico, to the list of his innumerable wives. Their marriage was celebrated with barbaric pomp and festivity, at his wooden palace beyond the Danube; and the monarch, oppressed with wine and sleep, retired at a late hour from the banquet to the nuptial bed. His attendants continued to respect his pleasures, or his repose, the greatest part of the ensuing day, till the unusual silence alarmed their fears and suspicions; and, after attempting to awaken Attila by loud and repeated cries, they at length broke into the royal apartment. They found the trembling bride sitting by the bedside, hiding her face with her veil, and lamenting her own danger, as well as the death of the king, who had expired during the night. An artery had suddenly burst: and as Attila lay in a supine posture he was suffocated by a torrent of blood, which, instead of finding a passage through the nostrils, regurgitated into the lungs and stomach.[56]

Most commentators assume that Ildico murdered Attila because of his unwanted sexual advances. As Act IV shows, Michael Field reports this incident at the moment when Honoria believes the time has come for her to be added to the Hun's list of wives. The point of this conclusion is to emphasize the fact that the anguished Honoria, who tries to take her sexual and political destiny into her own hands, is tragically defeated by another—equally tormented—woman who brought an end to sexual abuse through homicide.

Michael Field's account of Ildico's murderous act took its cue from Meredith's "Nuptials of Attila," which was the longest work in *Ballads and Poems of Tragic Life*

(1887). The *Pall Mall Gazette* was hardly alone in deeming this poem the "finest" in Meredith's volume: "Its movement is magnificent."[57] Composed in jolting trochaic meter, the four-beat catalectic lines record the voice of an officer in Attila's camp who urges his commander to rape Ildico, not least because it is an act that needs to be done quickly, lest it become a distraction from urgent military maneuvering:

> Eye and have, my Attila!
> Fair in her wide robe was she:
> Where the robe and vest divide,
> Fair she seemed surpassingly:
> Soft, yet vivid as the stream
> Danube rolls in the moonbeam
> Through rock-barriers: but she smiled
> Never, she sat cold as salt:
> Open-mouthed as a young child
> Wondering with a mind at fault.
> Make the bed for Attila![58]

As the thumping prosody insists, the officer who summons Attila to fix his gaze upon Ildico and possess her without any further ado is also aware that the beautiful young woman is petrified by her uninvited lover. In this finely crafted poem, the repeated phrase "Attila, my Attila" begins to resonate jarringly. Each time the line recurs, we begin to understand that the intimacy it expresses combines two conflicting emotions. At the same instant, it points to the male homosocial desire that Attila's men have toward his rapacious sexuality, just as it evokes the fearful thoughts that Ildico harbors once she realizes that she must comply with the Hun's sexual advances.

Repeatedly, Meredith's poem intimates that Attila's hunger to invade Rome works in tandem with his erotic desire to subjugate any woman he wants. By the end, Ildico's decision to plunge a dagger into Attila's chest strikes his men as so unbelievable that they remain confused, unable to agree that they should punish her:

> Could a little fist as big
> As the southern summer fig,
> Push a dagger's point to pierce
> Ribs like those? Who else! They glared
> Each at each. Suspicion fierce
> Many a black remembrance bared.

Attila, my Attila!
Death, who dares deny her guilt!
Death, who says his blood she spilt!
Traitor he, who stands between!
Swift to hell, who harms the Queen![59]

In "The Nuptials of Attila," Ildico escapes, while the Hun's armies disperse into chaos as the narrator once more declares, with fierce irony, "Make the bed for Attila." Ultimately, we learn that the "Empire built of scorn / Agonized, dissolved and sank."[60] Such phrasing indicates that in avenging her rape, Ildico toppled a ferocious patriarchy. Hers is perhaps one of the best-known "unwomanly audacities" in the later phases of Roman history.

In their play about "the *New Woman* of the fifth century," Michael Field shifted the focus from condemning Attila's predatory sexual appetite to affirming Honoria's yearning for intimacy. To be sure, the overall trajectory of *Attila, My Attila!* is to expose Honoria's desire as circumstantially misplaced. Yet what the play refuses to deny is the naturalness of her wish to "have lovers." At the same time, Bradley and Cooper gradually recognized that the conflicted path they chose for Honoria's tragedy did not necessarily lead to the capitalized "Irony" they wanted to extract from their execution of her story. In spite of her will to triumph, Honoria's discovery that Attila has died at Ildico's hands rests on the fact that the man she desired was a rapist. This is the revelation that devastates her. As we have already seen, in the concluding act the Roman consul Anthemius recalls the dreadful spectacle of witnessing Attila sexually abuse the scared Burgundian princess: "As the girl passed, a shudder followed her; / Although the host of warriors roared and stamped / Acclaimingly, they knew she had been forced" (106). What remains crucial to note is that these lines intensify the assault recorded in Meredith's "Nuptials of Attila" by having a political commentator recount the horrors of witnessing a brutal rape that the Hun's rowdy officers relished.

If Bradley and Cooper were to some degree dissatisfied with Honoria's desolation once she hears Anthemius's terrifying report, they did not anticipate that their critics would be hostile about a drama that appeared to have failed even more decisively than *A Question of Memory*. As usual, they unpicked the reviews that steadily flowed from a stream of periodicals. Especially galling was the commentary they read in the *Daily Chronicle*. The reviewer immediately attacked the sexual politics of the play as a symptom of the coauthors' ingenuousness: "For it is in effect an excursus against chastity, obviously written by the most harmless and well-behaved of ladies."[61] But, worse still, this reviewer feared that the two witless "ladies" hardly understood the message they wished to extract from Honoria's history: "There have been rash critics who have said that Ibsen himself is irony, and that he is laughing all the while at Ibsenism. Michael Field may be not at all the apologist of the women who conceived, at thirty, a *crise passionelle* for the pig-eyed, flat-nosed Hun, but may be using the follies of Honoria as a warning to the revolted daughters of another decadence."[62] Through such mockery, this sneering contributor wished to make it plain that the female coauthors—whose status as spinsters had circulated for some time in the press—were the last individuals who could claim authority when writing about women's sexuality. Cooper, who at first mistakenly assumed that the review must have come from Richard Le Gallienne's pen, records her exasperation:

> I open the <u>Daily Chronicle</u> at breakfast & find the article "The New Woman—or the Old" (obviously by R. L. G./no—he did not write it\). He states of Attila that it is "an excusing against chastity, obviously written by the most harmless and well-balanced of ladies ... etc. through a column of wilful misunderstanding, insult & ignorance."[63]

The *Chronicle's* merciless comments, as Cooper undoubtedly could see, epitomize a style of masculine condescension that *Attila, My Attila!* goes out of its way to critique.

Although other critics found aspects of the dramatic situation admirable, they took pains to observe what they deemed to be clumsy or inapposite rhetoric. Here, writing in the *Academy*, is the classicist E. D. A. Morshead, who was obviously impressed by Michael Field's earlier volumes:

> Admirers of Michael Field's work will not find here many of the imaginative touches that adorned "Canute the Great" [1887], nor of the depth of feeling that made *Long Ago* [1889] nearly achieve, in places, some part of its daring ambition. But yet, in spite of harsh modernisms—Honoria (p. 12) calls Valentinian "Val," and her lover Eugenius (p. 100) actually says, "I do this for your sake and ... damn your mother!"—in spite, I say, of things like this, which belong to that modern conception of the New Woman which haunts the writer, there is a subtle skill in the presentment of Honoria not unworthy of Michael Field.[64]

There was not much letup in these tirades. Naturally, Bradley and Cooper were cheered to read a short review in the *Scotsman* that gave "warm praise and welcome."[65] But several months later, it was clear that the onslaught from the London press refused to settle down. In the *Athenæum*, even though the reviewer thought Michael Field had "produced a play with much genuine power, and one on which the Independent Theatre might cast its eyes," such glowing praise sounded somewhat tongue in cheek once the commentary turned to mocking the coauthors' dramatic language:

> We do not know whether to laugh or be shocked when the living
> Eugenius addresses to Satyrus, the eunuch, such a John Bullish
> curse as "Damn your eyes!" We protest against such nonsense as
>
>> There is a stormy pout upon her lip—
>> Her father's pout.
>
> Our author is fond of pouts.
>
> Moreover, for this critic such undignified dialogue looked just
> as absurd as the deplorable stage directions following the final
> revelation that "Attila is dead!": "*Honoria turns her back on the priest
> and Eugenius, the marriage having been consummated*" (103). This
> unkind commentator could not resist chuckling at Michael Field's
> inopportune choice of words, which to his mind suggested that a
> sexual act had taken place "*coram populo.*"[66]

Michael Field's phrasing, as Cooper admitted, was indeed "an unhappy slip," though it was one identified by a man she dismissed as "ill-bred and nothing worse."[67]

Such hostility, however, was nothing compared to the volleys of criticism that Bradley and Cooper endured from their closest companions. In late November 1895, Meredith—whom they had recently befriended and who had made encouraging noises about their earlier volumes—hardly minced his words:

> Now bear with me, I have little praise for the line or the characters
> of your *Attila*. If you had irony in *aim* you should not have made
> a drama. You could of course produce keenest irony through the
> clashes of your personae. But poor Honoria is hardly a subject for
> it. Perhaps you meant the reflecting of grim light on the sex-mania
> current. That would be satire, quite enough to kill your poetry.
> Will you come and hear more? I have not time to write a criticism.
> It seems to me that your present failure comes of the design to do
> too much. Your naturally splendid dramatic line sinks under the
> burden of a satire and stage constrictions.[68]

Meredith, at Bradley and Cooper's bidding, went so far as to restate many of these criticisms when he welcomed the dramatists into his home at nearby

Box Hill, in early December 1895. "I am afraid," he gingerly told them, "you are abashed by what I have written."[69] They took careful note of his each and every observation. But once they reflected at length on Meredith's exacting criticisms, they remained unconvinced that his insights had much validity. His belief, for example, that the joint dramatists had mistakenly left Honoria "quite un-protected" through failing to present Placidia as "an exquisite character" (pre-sumably, as a model of motherhood) was wholly unreasonable to them.[70] "We have," Cooper protests in "Works and Days," "<u>suggested</u> all the protection that Meredith elaborately weaves," before trenchantly observing that "he is incapable of the chronometrical alertness necessary to the playwright"—a heedlessness to timing that in her view relates to his inability to "prepare for /the\ action" in his novels.[71]

Bradley and Cooper's resistance to Meredith's advice, however, hardly bore comparison with their retaliation against their much more established friends, Berenson and Costelloe, the unmarried couple in whose company they had spent five weeks during April and May of 1895.[72] Cooper's long entries about this intense period of conversations with their hosts—as well as with the Italian Re-naissance scholar Maud Cruttwell, the aesthetic theorist Vernon Lee, and other companions at Villa Rosa, Villa Kraus, and Il Palmerino—have become well known to students of this noted expatriate circle. The reason is that these sec-tions of "Works and Days" provide some of most revealing evidence of Cooper's unrequited passion for Berenson, the gifted art historian whom she and Bradley nicknamed "the Doctrine" after they started taking instruction from him in 1890. Martha Vicinus has traced the complicated emotional investment that Cooper, in particular, developed through her contact with this brilliant young intellec-tual: "For Cooper," Vicinus writes, "Berenson's delicate perceptions and finely tuned sensibility mirrored her own."[73] Cooper's journal entries do not hold back on the rapture she experienced in his presence: "I have touched moments with him that made the universe <u>gold</u>."[74] In all likelihood, Costelloe perceived this obsessiveness. She certainly found these somewhat intrusive friends a source of irritation. In a letter to her mother, Costelloe breathes a sigh of relief that the "Mikes"—as she calls them—have finally departed for Padua:

> The Mikes went away last night, and Maud and I began to breathe
> freely again—literally and metaphorically. Their dread of *draughts*
> has condemned us to close stuffy rooms, and the monstrous
> delusions about themselves in which they have condemned us to
> the worst stuffiness of hypocrisy. . . . They think they are a Great
> Poet—unappreciated at present, but certain to be famous and
> adored in the next generation—and they think their souls are

united and that it is good for them to be together. As a matter
of fact, the utter mistake of both these theories is "obvious to the
meanest intelligence."[75]

From this perspective, Bradley and Cooper appear almost unhealthy in their
habits, outlooks, and talents, not to say their intimacy.

Costelloe never expressed such forthright remarks to Bradley and Cooper
directly. Instead, she made solicitous inquiries about their forthcoming book:
"[W]e are looking for our copy, & you may be sure that [we] shall read it with
seriousness & write about it fully."[76] But, as it turned out, Costelloe demonstrated an almost willful lack of tact when the time came to offer her and Berenson's opinions. "I begged him," Costelloe said on behalf of her partner, "to write
to you his ideas about it very fully, but I fear he will not do so. . . . [H]e says
you would not care to hear what he <u>really</u> thinks."[77] Cooper, who long feared
that their hosts harbored antipathy toward Michael Field's poetry and drama,
had already reflected on the ways in which Berenson and Costelloe adopted a
patronizing stance toward herself and Bradley:

> Mary [Costelloe] writes about our work almost as if she <u>must</u>,
> /just\ as unsympathetic people write to children about their
> games—it is most depressing. And if she mentions our work
> even I am struck with a momentary paralysis, a sort of desperate
> obstinacy—a rigid fist. These two have never <u>done</u> anything but
> discouraged, persistently, methodically.[78]

On November 29, 1895, after they received a letter from Costelloe that
they found to be "full of jeers," Bradley lost patience and made this blunt reply:
"[B]ecause of your lack of sympathy our friendship closes."[79] As a result, relations between all four parties—if not entirely estranged—were much more
tempered than before, although Bradley and Costelloe still managed to maintain a regular correspondence, since (as Vicinus notes) "over three hundred
letters survive."[80] And Cooper, too, exchanged what Costelloe called "very
beautiful and touching" items of correspondence with Berenson before her
death in 1913.[81]

By all accounts, *Attila, My Attila!* could not have turned out to be a more discouraging affair. It is little wonder that many years afterward, the artist Charles
Ricketts—who did so much to support the publication of their work, especially
with the printing and design of the beautifully produced Roman trilogy from
the Vale Press (1898–1903)—thought Honoria's tragedy was Michael Field's
"weakest book"; he noted, too, that its lack of success damaged their friendship
with Meredith, whom they clearly hoped would respond sympathetically to a

work that took some of the leads from his stirring 1879 poem.[82] Still, it is worth recognizing that in spite of the unsparing criticism they received from different quarters, Bradley and Cooper sustained unswerving faith in their dramatic skills for the next nineteen years. They went on to publish in their lifetimes no fewer than thirteen additional verse dramas, whose powerful voices they understood would never be animated on stage. Moreover, these later plays, from *Borgia* (1905) onward, appeared without the name of Michael Field on the title page. In theory, these largely blank-verse writings—whose energetic range encompasses biblical, classical, Ethiopian, Irish, and Renaissance history—exist in authorless suspension. By this time, their readership, too, had narrowed considerably, since Bradley and Cooper no longer moved in the London literary circles where they once believed they should have had their rightful place.

It would therefore be unreasonable to conclude that *Attila, My Attila!* was the misjudged play that marked the decline of their career. On analysis, Bradley and Cooper's uninhibited verse play about Honoria's terrible plight draws into focus the fact that much of their writing was insistently out of sync with their epoch, both behind and ahead of a modern theatrical world that in the long run would never embrace them. Their 1895 tragedy, which marks certain sexual and political advances on their dramas from the 1880s, is at once formally rooted in Shakespeare's era ("1590 is second nature to us," they told Archer) and topically at the forefront of the fin de siècle (they could not, for instance, abide the influential *Athenæum's* suggestion that women "cannot approach the fires of Eros").[83] This double temporality, which is at once antiquated and avant-garde, prompts a positive reassessment of the striking idea that Honoria was "a *New Woman* of the fifth century," one whose yearnings were inspired by nothing less than her "unwomanly audacities." With these points in mind, it is surely worth remembering what Mary Sturgeon said almost one hundred years ago, in what remains the most detailed published account of these dramas to date. Whether Bradley and Cooper are depicting "the fierce chastity of an Irish Deirdre," "the subtlety of a Lucrezia Borgia," the "proud singleness of a Mariamne," or even "the wrongheadedness of a little princess whose instincts have been perverted through frustration," one point is unmistakable.[84] The sexual courageousness of *Attila, My Attila!*—no matter how much it fell short of its aims—reminds us still of how the legacy of Michael Field "has greatly enriched the world's knowledge of womanhood."[85]

Notes

Epigraphs: Michael Field, draft of letter to William Archer, early December 1893, "Works and Days," BL Add MS 46781, fol. 98v [E.C.]; Michael Field, December 31, 1894, "Works and Days," BL Add MS 46782, fol. 144v [E.C.].

1. Michael Field, *Attila, My Attila! A Play* (London: Elkin Mathews, 1896), 6; subsequent page references appear in parentheses in the main text.

2. Michael Field, "Works and Days," BL Add MS 46782, fol. 98v (December 31, 1894) [E.C.].

3. E. Nesbit, "The Ballad of Ferencz Renyi," *Longman's Magazine* 9 (1886–87): 603.

4. Michael Field, "Works and Days," BL Add MS 46781, fol. 3v (January 9, 1893) [E.C.].

5. Michael Field, "Works and Days," BL Add MS 46781, fol. 7r (January 26, 1893) [E.C.].

6. Michael Field, "Works and Days," BL Add MS 46781, fol. 6v (January 26, 1893) [E.C.].

7. Lionel Johnson, "Review of Michael Field, *Stephania: A Trialogue*," *Academy* (April 22, 1893): 342.

8. Johnson, 342.

9. Johnson, 343.

10. Michael Field, "Works and Days," BL Add MS 46781, fol. 18v (February 24, 1893) [E.C.].

11. "The New Program of the Independent Theatre: An Interview with Mr. J. T. Grein," *Daily Chronicle*, August 23, 1893, clipping pasted into Michael Field, "Works and Days," BL Add MS 46781, 54v (August 23, 1893).

12. Michael Field, "Works and Days," BL Add MS 46781, fol. 73r (October 13, 1893) [K.B.].

13. Michael Field, "Works and Days," BL Add MS 46781, fol. 71v (September 26, 1893) [K.B.].

14. Jan Macdonald, "'Disillusioned Bards and Despised Bohemians': Michael Field's *A Question of Memory* at the Independent Theatre Society," *Theatre Notebook* 31, no. 2 (1977): 24.

15. Michael Field, "Works and Days," BL Add MS 46781, fol. 77v (October 22, 1893) [E.C.].

16. Michael Field, "Works and Days," BL Add MS 46781, fol. 86r (ca. October 26, 1893) [E.C.].

17. Jill R. Ehnenn, *Women's Literary Collaboration, Queerness, and Late-Victorian Culture* (Aldershot, UK: Ashgate, 2008), 117.

18. Michael Field, *A Question of Memory: A Play in Four Acts Produced at the Independent Theatre, London, on Friday, October the 27th, 1893* (London: Elkin Mathews and John Lane, 1893), 3; subsequent page references appear in parentheses in the main text.

19. "A Question of Memory," *Theatre* (December 1, 1893): 341.

20. "A Question of Memory," 342.

21. A. B. Walkley, "The Drama," *Speaker* (November 4, 1893): 494.

22. Walkley, 494.

23. "The Theatre," *Pall Mall Gazette* (October 28, 1893): 3.

24. "The Theatre," 3.

25. Michael Field, "Works and Days," BL Add MS 46781, fol. 90v (November 1, 1893) [E.C.].

26. Michael Field, "Works and Days," BL Add MS 46781, fol. 90v (November 1, 1893) [E.C.]

27. Michael Field, "Works and Days," BL Add MS 46781, fol. 91r (November 1, 1893) [E.C.]. The version of the play that Michael Field sent to Archer is presumably the one that appeared posthumously in *Deirdre; A Question of Memory; and Raz Byzance* (London: Poetry Bookshop, 1918), 89–129.

28. Michael Field, "Works and Days," BL Add MS 46781, fol. 92r (November 7, 1893) [E.C.].

29. Michael Field, "Works and Days," BL Add MS 46781 fol. 92v (November 7, 1893) [E.C.].

30. Michael Field, "Works and Days," BL Add MS 46781 fol. 92v (November 9, 1893) [E.C.].

31. Michael Field, "Works and Days," BL Add MS 46781, fol. 100r (December 11, 1893) [E.C.].

32. Michael Field, "Works and Days," BL Add MS 46781, fol. 93r (November 18, 1893) [E.C.].

33. Oscar Wilde, "To Michael Field," [late October 1893?], in *The Complete Letters of Oscar Wilde*, ed. Merlin Holland and Rupert Hart-Davis (London: Fourth Estate, 2000), 574. In his letter, Wilde passes on the address of his American agent, Elisabeth Marbury.

34. Michael Field, "Works and Days," BL Add MS 46783, fol. 4r (January 6, 1895) [K.B.].

35. Michael Field, "Works and Days," BL Add MS 46783, fols. 4r–4v (January 6, 1895) [K.B.].

36. Michael Field, "Works and Days," BL Add MS 46783 fol. 4v (January 6, 1895) [K.B.]. Michael Field had found more to praise in Wilde's first society comedy, *Lady Windermere's Fan*, in 1892; although they found it "monstrously unnatural," Bradley and Cooper enjoyed "the conversation of the men," which was "so cynical, brilliant, modern, repulsive" (Michael Field, "Works and Days," BL Add MS 46780 fol. 59r [March 6, 1892] [E.C.]). Then again, when they visited his home, they were very critical of his self-presentation: "There is no charm in his elephantine body stuffed into his clothes"; and they despised him when he appeared condescending: "When he shows himself as a snob he is disgustingly repulsive" (Michael Field, "Works and Days," BL Add MS 46780 fol. 97v [May 25, 1892] [E.C.].

37. Michael Field, "Works and Days," BL Add MS 46783, fol. 25v (February 28, 1895) [E.C.].

38. Michael Field, "Works and Days," BL Add MS 46783, fol. 25v (February 28, 1895) [E.C.].

39. Michael Field, "Works and Days," BL Add MS 46783, fol. 26r (February 28, 1895) [E.C.].

40. Michael Field, "Works and Days," BL Add MS 46783, fol. 25v (February 28, 1895) [E.C.].

41. Michael Field, "Works and Days," BL Add MS 46783, fol. 25v (February 28, 1895) [E.C.].

42. Michael Field, "Works and Days," BL Add MS 46783, fol. 25v (February 28, 1895) [E.C.].

43. Michael Field, "Works and Days," BL Add MS 46783, fol. 60v (April 1895) [E.C.].

44. Michael Field, "Works and Days," BL Add MS 46783, fol. 124r (July 28, 1895) [K.B.].

45. Michael Field, "Works and Days," BL Add MS 46783, fol. 125r (July 28, 1895) [E.C.].

46. Michael Field, "Works and Days," BL Add MS 46783, fol. 125r (July 28, 1895) [E.C.].

47. Sarah Grand, "The New Aspect of the Woman Question," *North American Review* 158 (1894): 271, 275.

48. Michael Field, "Works and Days," BL Add MS 46784, fol. 10r (October 27, 1895) [E.C.].

49. Michael Field, "Works and Days," BL Add MS 46784, fol. 10r (October 27, 1895) [E.C.].

50. Michael Field, "Works and Days," BL Add MS 46784, fol. 24r (November 26, 1895) [E.C.]. In section 4 of *The Birth of Tragedy*, Nietzsche speaks of "the value of dreams" as opposed to that of empirical reality; he claims that the dream is "*a mere appearance of mere appearance*" and is thus "a still higher appeasement of the primordial desire for mere appearance." His discussion proceeds to the ways in which Raphael's *Transfiguration* "has represented for us this demotion of appearance to the level of appearance" (*The Birth of Tragedy and The Case of Wagner*, trans. Walter Kaufmann [New York: Vintage, 1967], 45). Michael Field had been reading Nietzsche's *Geburt der Tragödie* (1872) in the original German. On the broader impact of Nietzsche's thought on Michel Field's subsequent dramas, see Ana Parejo Vadillo, "'This Hot-House of Decadent Chronicle': Michael Field, Nietzsche and the Dance of Modern Poetic Drama," *Women: A Cultural Review* 26, no. 3 (2016): 195–220.

51. Edward Gibbon, *The History of the Decline and Fall of the Roman Empire*, ed. H. H. Milman, 6 vols. (London: John Murray, 1846), 3:262–63.

52. Gibbon, 263.

53. Gibbon, 263.

54. Gibbon, 262.

55. Gibbon, 263.

56. Gibbon, 280.

57. "Mr. George Meredith's New Poems," *Pall Mall Gazette* (May 26, 1887): 5. Bradley and Cooper's friend John Miller Gray commented similarly in the *Academy*; he found Meredith's poem to be "informed by a strange, fierce intensity, and with touches of a weird and ghastly terror" (June 11, 1887: 406).

58. George Meredith, "The Nuptials of Attila," in *Ballads and Poems of Tragic Life* (London: Macmillan, 1887), 75. The poem had first appeared in the *New Quarterly Magazine* 11 (1879): 47–62.

59. Meredith, "The Nuptials of Attila," 96–97.

60. Meredith, 100.

61. "The New Women—and the Old," *Daily Chronicle* (November 20, 1895): 5.

62. "The New Women—and the Old," 5.

63. Michael Field, "Works and Days," BL Add MS 46784, fol. 20v (November 20, 1895) [E.C.].

64. E. D. A. Morshead, "Review of *Attila, My Attila! A Play*," *Academy* (January 25, 1896): 71.

65. Michael Field, "Works and Days," BL Add MS 46784, fol. 20v (November 20, 1895) [E.C.].

66. "Recent Plays," *Athenæum* (April 11, 1896): 487.

67. Michael Field, "Works and Days," BL Add MS 46785, fol. 55r (April 11, 1896) [E.C.].

68. Meredith, "To Michael Field," November 28, 1895, in *The Letters of George Meredith*, ed. C. L. Cline, 3 vols. (Oxford: Clarendon Press, 1970), 3: 1214.

69. Michael Field, "Works and Days," BL Add MS 46784, fol. 34v (December 2, 1895) [E.C.].

70. Michael Field, "Works and Days," BL Add MS 46784, fol. 34v (December 2, 1895) [E.C.].

71. Michael Field, "Works and Days," BL Add MS 46784, fol. 35r (December 2, 1895) [E.C.].

72. For more on Bradley and Cooper's relationship with this couple, see Sarah Parker's chapter in this volume.

73. Martha Vicinus, "'Sister Souls': Bernard Berenson and Michael Field (Katharine Bradley and Edith Cooper)," *Nineteenth-Century Literature* 60 (2005): 331. For a different reading of this relationship, see Sarah Parker, *The Lesbian Muse and Poetic Identity, 1889–1930* (London: Routledge, 2015), 43–71.

74. Michael Field, "Works and Days," BL Add MS 46784, fol. 54v (December 31, 1895) [E.C.].

75. Mary Costelloe, "To Hannah Whithall Smith," May 15, 1895, in *Mary Berenson: A Self-Portrait from Her Letters & Diaries*, ed. Barbara Strachey and Jayne Samuels (London: Victor Gollancz, 1983), 64.

76. Michael Field, "Works and Days," BL Add MS 46784, fol. 14r (November 7, 1895) [E.C.].

77. Michael Field, "Works and Days," BL Add MS 46784, fol.19r (November 19, 1895) [E.C.].

78. Michael Field, "Works and Days," BL Add MS 46784, fol. 14r (November 7, 1895) [E.C.].

79. Michael Field, "Works and Days," BL Add MS 46784, fols. 26v–27r (November 29, 1895) [K.B.].

80. Vicinus, "Sister Souls," 346. Friction between the friends remained. Three months before Bradley died, Costelloe was troubled to learn that Bradley and Cooper "kept intimate journals and put down everything B. B. said and did. . . . B. B. is furious at being treated as manuscript for a minor minimist poet" ("To Alys Russell," June 19, 1914, in Strachey and Samuels, *Mary Berenson*, 197).

81. Costelloe, diary entry, January 27, 1937, in Strachey and Samuels, *Mary Berenson*, 300.

82. Charles Ricketts, *Michael Field*, ed. Paul Delaney (Edinburgh: Tragara Press, 1976), 3. Ricketts's comments were prepared in the early 1920s for Mary Sturgeon's pioneering monograph on Michael Field.

83. Michael Field, "Works and Days," BL Add MS 46781, fol. 91r (November 1, 1893) [E.C.], and BL Add MS 46783, fol. 151r (September 10, 1895) [E.C.]. Michael Field's criticism of the *Athenæum* relates to a review of Dollie Radford, *Songs and Other Verses*, and Ernest Radford, *Old and New*, in which the critic speaks of "modern woman's striving after the experiences she had not had and the sensations she could never render," before going on to praise Dollie Radford's evocation of "a sentimental experience, known to every woman, probably, and to many men." This critic also observes, "Women being less naturally and less strongly erotic than men, no woman will ever achieve any very considerable success in this very experimental branch of literature" (September 21, 1895: 37).

84. Mary Sturgeon, *Michael Field* (London: Harrap, 1922), 243. Sturgeon is alluding to *Borgia: A Historical Play* (London: A. H. Bullen, 1905); *Deirdre* (published posthumously, with *Raz Byzance* and the revised *Question of Memory*, in 1918); *Queen Mariamne* (London: Sidgwick and Jackson, 1908), and *Attila, My Attila!* The most comprehensive account of Michael Field's verse dramas is Joan Evelyn Biederstedt, "The Poetic Plays of Michael Field," unpublished doctoral dissertation, Loyola University Chicago, 1963.

85. Sturgeon, *Michael Field*, 243.

SIX

Michael Field's Fragrant Imagination

CATHERINE MAXWELL

PERFUME WAS A CONSTANT PRESENCE IN THE LIVES OF
Katharine Bradley and Edith Cooper, an expression of their personalities and
their love for each other.[1] Writing to the twenty-year-old Edith in September
1882, Katharine Bradley signs off, "And so my sweet Sea Lavendar [sic], Farewell.
Thou are not a savour to me like the saints; but a *fragrance*. Some are born so. I
think of you more as scent than colour."[2] And in March 1914, four months after
Cooper's death from cancer, Bradley notes sadly that "The fragrance of Henry
seems fainter in Paragon."[3]

Establishing the importance of perfume to both women, this chapter examines its key role in some poems of the 1890s produced by Katharine Bradley
with reference to the influential and complementary diary entries produced by
Edith Cooper and Bradley herself. During this period, the women's growing interest in scent and scented plants merges with the expression of their love. Love
is the emotion that most often inspires Bradley's poems, and her use of perfume
in her poetry is shown as inextricable from the way that she expresses love and
affection for those dearest to her. Moreover, fragrance is closely identified with
poetic creativity itself, and the second part of this chapter focuses on one particular flower cherished by Michael Field, showing how its fragrance, combined
with some other distinctive notes, could be said to represent a signature scent
for the Fieldian imagination.

"Again the Aroma!": Savoring the Scent of Love

Both Bradley and Cooper seem to have been remarkably sensitive to fragrance, and both loved flowers. Their friend, the artist Charles Ricketts, remarked of Edith Cooper that "Her passion for flowers was without comparison greater than that of any person I have met."[4] Cooper writes beautifully about flowers in the women's shared diary, where her sensitivity to color and texture is matched by her appreciation of fragrance. Finding the "most delicate primroses" in March 1894, she recorded that "we smell the breath of their softness."[5] The following year she enjoys "a great sheaf of chrysanthemums, filling the air with the cordiality of their scent, & the eyes with the confluence of their splendid hues dreaming as one dreams of colour."[6] She also takes pleasure in other vegetal scents, noting, for example, how bracken is "full of that intimate, vigorous odour that seems to come from the very body of the earth."[7] Gathering hops with Bradley and her sister Amy in September 1890, she writes, "We picked for ½ an hour. The scent is stimulating, with a wonderful richness under the bitter suggestion with wh: it meets you. We plunged our hands into the pale harvest, as soft as curds—delicious and astringent."[8]

Katharine Bradley also relishes the nuances of plant aroma, as seen in her short lyric "Apollo's Triumph" (1894) about the nymph Daphne who escaped Apollo's advances by being changed into a laurel tree. The poem, Bradley later notes, was "[w]ritten in full perfume of the daphne—the deep pink daphne with its honey, and the laurel-spurge with its emphatic, arresting perfume."[9] In this witty revisionist lyric, Daphne, regretting her rejection of Apollo, solicits him through her lovely fragrance:

> She fled from love, her suit was granted,
> Daphne was changed into a laurel-tree.
> But after, with so keen a zest she panted
> To yield her sweets, and, in despair,
> Cast such engrossing odours through the air,
> Apollo, breathing them, had all he wanted.[10]

Perfume—not only a seduction and delight but also the essence of a thing, person, or experience—recurs repeatedly in Bradley's verse. A more prolific poet than Cooper—and the author of many of the best poems that appear under the name "Michael Field"—she is also responsible for the preponderance of "scented verse."[11] Although not one of her more polished compositions, the unpublished poem "On Opening a Box of Flowers from the Riviera," from December 1894, is a lively occasional piece that celebrates her intense sensory pleasure in the fragrance, color, and texture of flowers sent from Italy. Following a first line that doubles as an aside—"From Bordighera: I am glad"—the poem continues:

> Open! What fragrance meets the nose—
> Spices and pepper in a dose,
> Overcome by the heaps of rose;
>
> Eucalyptus, in silky sheen
> Of flowers and scimitar leaf, between
> Wedges of violets; acacia-green
>
> Of saffron-feather, and, under these,
> Stuffed in as ballast, what you please,
> Rainy-scarlet anemones;
>
> And in the corners what treasure-trove—
> Anthers and pollen, silver-mauve,
> With bloody spots of carnation-clove.
>
> Again the aroma! Crush the pad
> Of fern on the flowers; they drive me mad![12]

The intoxication of scent produces something akin to pagan rapture or maenadic madness. Bradley and Cooper, passionate about ancient Greek myth and religion, loved to imagine themselves as Dionysus' entranced female followers, but they also saw themselves as worshippers of Aphrodite, goddess of love.

Bradley's "An Invitation," from *Underneath the Bough* (1893), features an aromatic plant that becomes an emblem of the couple's love. Written in January 1891, the poem imagines the poets' study at Durdans, their Reigate home, where they would move in March of that year. Enticing the "Lady" (Cooper) with a description of this room and images of their shared life together, the speaker (Bradley) tells her:

> There are myrtles in a row;
> Lady, when the flower's in blow,
> Kisses passing to and fro,
>   From our smelling
> Think, what lovely dreams will grow![13]

This, the last poem in the collection's "Third Book of Songs," acts as prelude to "Our Myrtle is in Flower," the opening poem of "The Fourth Book of Songs," composed August 7, 1891. The all-important myrtle of both poems has its basis in reality, as borne out when the artists Charles Ricketts and Charles Shannon first visited them in May 1894. Cooper recorded that "they compare the actual study with the study as described in <u>Underneath the Bough</u>. 'You have real myrtles' exclaims Ricketts—'Shannon, you see the myrtles.'"[14] As predicted in "An Invitation," the shared smelling of myrtle inspires the lovelier, more potent dream of the later poem:

> Our myrtle is in flower;
> 　　Behold Love's power!
> The glorious stamens' crowded force unfurled,
> 　　Cirque beyond cirque
> At breathing, bee-like, and harmonious work:
> The rose-patched petals backward curled,
> 　　Falling away
> To let fecundity have perfect play.
>
> 　O flower, dear to the eyes
> 　　Of Aphrodite, rise
> As she at once to bare, audacious bliss;
> 　　And bid us near
> Your prodigal, delicious hemisphere,
> Where thousand kisses breed the kiss
> 　　That fills the room
> With languor of an acid, dark perfume![15]

In the women's diary, the poem follows an entry by Cooper dated July 29: "The first bloom on our myrtles—a perfect little hemisphere of stamens, close, white, with an acid fragrance. And the tiny curled petals, blotted with crimson beneath, fall away before the expansive freedom of love."[16] Central to the poem is the praise of myrtle (*Myrtus communis*), an evergreen shrub with sweetly scented white blossoms and aromatic leaves, sacred to Aphrodite. In his six-volume poem, the *Fasti*, the Roman poet Ovid describes Venus-Aphrodite shielding her nakedness with myrtle, but Bradley's goddess glories in her "bare, audacious bliss."[17] (Four years previously, Bradley had been rather disapproving of Botticelli's depiction of a "shy, recoiling girl-form" in *The Birth of Venus*, intimating her preference for "the Greek Venus, joyous & unabashed.")[18]

Geoffrey Grigson writes that "For the Greeks, in a frank way, these scented leaves and stems indicated love, and its pleasures, in mutuality."[19] It has also been said that the myrtle was dedicated to Aphrodite because the shape of its leaves resembles the female pudenda; indeed, the ancient Greek word for myrtle (*murtos*) can signify "pudenda," thus helping confirm the plant's reputation as an aphrodisiac.[20] Bradley, a competent Greek scholar, may have been aware of this possible connotation, although the poem has its own intense erotic charge without it. For here it is the flower—its five white petals surrounding a half sphere of multiple radiating stamens—that captures the speakers' gaze and, by implication, becomes the symbol of their love and an invitation to further intimacy.

Open to the pollinating activity of the bee, the fertilized flowers eventually result in the blackish-blue myrtle berries, considered an aphrodisiac in Roman times and still used in Mediterranean cooking and mirto liqueur. (Bradley will refer explicitly to "The myrtle berry's black" in her unpublished sonnet "Bits of Things" and "Thy myrtle with its Erebus-black fruit" in her sonnet "To the Winter Aphrodite.")[21] The berries taste something like juniper and rosemary with an initial aroma of pine, and when fresh they have a bitter tannic aftertaste. Although in her diary entry Cooper refers to the scent of the white myrtle flowers as "acid," Bradley's addition of the word "dark" makes one think of the black myrtle berries. The scent of myrtle flowers is delicate and sweet, with a faint camphoraceous note that is much stronger in the leaves, where it combines with an orange citrus note and a touch of nutmeg. Thus it could conceivably be the fragrance of the astringent berries that is alluded to in the "acid, dark perfume" of the poem's final line.[22] The "delicious hemisphere" of the flower, whose alluring scent represents a "thousand kisses" to its admirers and the pollinating bee, metamorphoses or is "bred" into the aromatic berry, whose "kiss" or scent "fills the room / With languor of an acid, dark perfume!" Yet also implied by the natural rhythm of that sequence is a possible languorous human kiss and love scene. Another reading might be that the flower's fragrant kisses directly prelude and provoke the more sensual scent of human intimacy. Either way, there is a shift in the poem from the garden outside to the scented "languor" of the room inside and from the flower's inviting receptivity to the bee through to consummation or ripeness.

Bradley may have been aware of the popular etymology that connects the ancient Greek words for myrtle (*murtos*) and perfume or scented oil (*muron*), a link possibly suggesting that the scent of Aphrodite's plant with its arousing properties is an archetypal perfume that plays an essential role in human experience.[23] Moreover, in the poem, the subtle parallels between myrtle and the love shared by the speakers also imply that the "perfume" or "essence" of their love is distilled from the authentic flower or fruit of Aphrodite. In October 1904, in a little two-line poem addressed "To Michael from Field," Cooper would write to Bradley, "You shall find the lover's wreath of myrtle / Deathless as the poet's wreath of bay."[24] Recognizing that in antiquity, "The myrtle was the symbol of lovers and their poets," both women claim it as the symbol of lovers who *are* poets and who understand love as central to their poetry.[25]

"Rose-Leaves from the Rose of Your Imagination"

At the back of the women's diary for 1898, Edith Cooper copied out under the heading "Poetry: Smell" an extract from *The Omen*, a gothic novel by the Scottish novelist John Galt (1779–1839) containing this observation: "I have sometimes thought that the faculty of the poet was liveliest in his smell, for no other revels so luxuriously in the reveries and ruminations of the aromatic summer, nor finds in the perfume of leaves & flowers such delicious reminiscences of wisdom & beauty."[26] The perfumed leaves and flowers providing Bradley and Cooper with the most "delicious reminiscences of wisdom & beauty" were undoubtedly those of the rose, and from early on Cooper treasured Bradley's "fine thoughts . . . as rose-leaves from the rose of your imagination."[27]

Roses and rose leaves are a fitting symbol for the Michael Fieldian imagination because of their special significance for both women. In an exquisite passage copied by Bradley into their joint diary "Works and Days," Cooper describes their trip in May 1888 to see Lawrence Alma-Tadema's masterpiece, *The Roses of Heliogabalus*:

> Ah, how I have been kindled by no picture save <u>The Roses of Heliogabalus</u>, Tadema's <u>chef-d'oeuvre</u> in the Academy. On Monday last Sim and I did battle with the fair & polished crowd that nearly removed all air from one's lungs with heat & gentle but firm pressure at Burlington House. Suddenly we were faced by "a rain & ruin of roses"—a red-rose picture with flakes of cream petals. It has a divine power of endowing the mind with fragrance, & with that delicate transporting joy that roses alone can give. The sweetness, the muffling softness, the unutterable pink—ah, it is a picture that makes one's heart-blood leap delightedly.[28]

Here Cooper's own vibrant imagination supplies the fragrance suggested by the painted pink blossoms, and in the following June her imagination enters into the thoughts of the rose itself when she says, "The fragrance of a red rose is like rain as the flower imagines it (or as that has passed into the imagination of the flower.)"[29] For Bradley, Tadema's painting induces "a fervour to crown the rose with praise," making her recollect a saying by Philostratus: "Sappho loves the Rose & always crowns it with some praise, likening beautiful maidens to it; she likens it also to the arms of the Graces, when she describes their elbows bare."[30] This results in Lyric 58 in *Long Ago* (1889), which opens, "What are these roses like? Oh, they are rare, / So balmy pink / I will not shrink / Them to the Graces to compare."[31] Another artwork, a drawing by Leonardo in the Venetian Accademia seen the following year, inspires a poem in *Sight and Song* (1892), in which

Bradley depicts Leonardo's rose "Mystic, shining on the tufted bowers / [That] burns its incense to the summer hours."[32]

Roses recur repeatedly in the pages of *Underneath the Bough* (1893), but Bradley and Cooper's use of the rose is no poetic commonplace: it arises out of a deep love and knowledge of the flower. There are many references throughout "Works and Days" to specific kinds of roses, such as the white moss rose, the sweetbriar or eglantine rose, and named types such as Banksiae, Malmaison, Maréchal Niel, and Marie Van Houtte. In November 1893, two years after moving into their Reigate home, Durdans, Bradley writes to the art historian John Miller Gray: "Oh but, did I tell you of the excitement of our rose garden? Two hundred rose-bushes my brother has bought—so come in June, & it will be 'roses, roses all the way.'"[33] By "brother," Bradley means her brother-in-law, James Cooper, who was a keen amateur gardener. By the following summer the new roses were happily bedded in. On July 3, Cooper reports how she and Bradley return from a brief trip to town:

> Father is working in the garden. We go out to him, & the roses swell up to our eyes like blood from the veins, blood from the arteries of summer, dark & carmine, used & adolescent, glowing in the noon. I have never seen such a sight before—every bush had a dozen or more roses on it, & the sweet-pea hedge took up their colours and cried them out with an airy insolence—as if in a popular song.[34]

In June she had enthused, "Our chief balm is the presence on our desk of Marshall Niel roses, with snow-green shadows on their warmest yellow petals & a breath coming from their heart that lulls like sinking into a velvet couch."[35] Apart from Maréchal Niel, the diaries reveal that the rose garden included the light-pink tea rose Souvenir d'un Ami and the first hybrid tea La France, both heavily fragrant. Bradley writes on June 4, 1894, "Among the <u>Sensations de Durdans</u> just now is the joy of seeing the new tea roses come out. Michael is beginning to have a bowl on his desk always, & the tumbling-over of their leaves almost drives him mad. What miracles!" She adds: "One must see the light through not on them, & how they understand labyrinths. One would never find one's way out of the heart of a rose."[36]

The heart of the rose that seems to have most entranced Bradley is the one she explores in "The Grand Mogul," a poem dated July 11, 1894, composed a month after that diary entry and included only in the revised American edition of *Underneath the Bough*, published by Thomas B. Mosher in 1898.[37] The poem is there untitled, although all the drafts and typescripts use the title "The Grand

Mogul." Many readers, including the critic Chris White, who has written about it on more than one occasion, have encountered this poem either through A. J. A. Symons's *An Anthology of "Nineties" Verse* (1928), where it is titled after its first line, "Your Rose is Dead," or in subsequent anthologies that also give the poem this title.[38] Noting the original title, Ivor Treby includes the poem as "The Grand Mogul" in his annotated Michael Field collection *Uncertain Rain* (2002), but he writes, "Since no rose called 'The Grand Mogul' has proved traceable . . . this may be another apposite coinage of Michael's."[39]

But there *is* a Grand Mogul rose, which at the time Bradley wrote her poem was relatively new. In the 1888 edition of his authoritative work *The Rose Garden in Two Divisions*, the Victorian rose expert William Paul lists Grand Mogul, a rose supplied by his own company, among the hybrid perpetuals, a group he describes as "fine roses, quite hardy, and very sweet."[40] He indicates that Grand Mogul was introduced between 1876 and 1886 and notes its origins as "a seedling from A. K. Williams, producing flowers of a deep brilliant crimson, shaded with scarlet and black; in dull weather and in Summer the flowers are darker, approaching to maroon. They are large, full, of symmetrical shape, and produced in great profusion; the foliage is large and massive." He also adds that the rose won a "First-Class Certificate from the Royal Horticultural Society," a detail surely attractive to anyone planning a new rose garden in the early 1890s.[41] The color-illustrated version of his book (10th ed., 1903) also includes an artist's impression of the rose, which on the left-hand margin bears the attribution "J. L. Goffart, Brussels."[42]

That Bradley is describing a particular rose, one whose colors are true to the description provided by Paul—"deep brilliant crimson, shaded with scarlet and black"—and one most likely growing in her own garden, does make a difference to the way we read the poem:

> Your *rose is dead,*
>   They said,
> The *Grand Mogul*—for so her splendour
> Exceeded, masterful, it seemed her due
> By dominant male titles to commend her:
>   But I, her lover, knew
> That myriad-coloured blackness, wrought with fire,
> Was woman to the rage of my desire.
>   My rose was dead? She lay
> Against the sulphur, lemon and blush-gray
> Of younger blooms, transformed, morose,
> Her shrivelling petals, gathered round her close,

And where before
Coils twisted thickest at her core
A round, black hollow: it had come to pass
Hints of tobacco, leather, brass,
Confounded, gave her texture and her colour.
I watched her, as I watched her, growing duller,
   Majestic in recession
   From flesh to mould.
My rose is dead—I echo the confession,
  And they pass to pluck another;
While I drawn on to vague, prodigious pleasure,
   Fondle my treasure.
O sweet, let death prevail
Upon you, as your nervous outlines thicken
And totter, as your crimsons stale,
I feel fresh rhythms quicken,
Fresh music follows you. Corrupt, grow old,
Drop inwardly to ashes, smother
Your burning spices, and entoil
My senses till you sink a clod of fragrant soil.[43]

In the late spring and summer of 1894, Bradley and Cooper hosted two visits by their new friends, Charles Shannon and Charles Ricketts, whom they had first met in January and whom Bradley would describe the following year as "very much like us . . . tingling with pleasure at sight of exquisite flowers or fruit."[44] The first visit of May 22 was a success, with Cooper recording the painters' pleasure in the garden: "Every herb is examined with eyes that discover quality in the leaves. . . . Ricketts knows a great deal about flowers."[45] However, with regard to the second visit of July 9, the women felt they had failed to please their guests' fastidious tastes, with Cooper lamenting, "Our flowers went wrong—we got too many kinds in the room—we lost the tact of decoration: . . . & when we went into the damp garden sweet-peas were found to be 'violent' & roses, we felt, were silently dubbed 'fat'—although La France, with her outer pyramids of silver & her inner core of fresh pink won Ricketts' attention."[46] Bradley's lyric, dated just two days after this visit, features the speaker in the company of a group viewing her roses. This coincidence suggests that the speaker's response to the comment "Your rose is dead" may have been triggered by a similar disparaging comment passed by one of the women's exacting guests.[47]

My reading then is different from that of Chris White, who disregards the specificity of the rose to argue that "the text pursues a celebration of a woman who has been loved for a very long time, and whose aged appearance has made no difference to the love, even when compared to younger, more perfect, alive blooms."[48] Clearly the rose is both feminized and eroticized—though not, as I would see it, to provide a primary allegory of enduring love for an aging beloved. The name "Grand Mogul" is a term coined by Europeans for the ruler of the Mughal Empire, a domain that extended over large parts of the Indian subcontinent during the early sixteenth to the early eighteenth centuries when the empire was at its peak, with Mughal rule continuing after that in a diminished way till the mid-nineteenth century. "Grand Mogul" is an appropriate name for a fragrant rose because, according to legend, attar of roses, or rose essential oil, was supposedly discovered during the Mughal rule in India, a discovery popularly attributed to Nur Jehan, wife of Emperor Jahangir (1569–1627; ruled 1605–27) but recounted by him as being the work of her mother, Asmat Begum, who skimmed off and preserved the strongly scented froth that formed on rosewater.[49] Amina Okada comments, "Of all the fragrances, rosewater and rose essence . . . were the most closely associated with the refined way of life upheld at the Mogul court, where an elegant and civilised custom involved sprinkling the hands and clothes of guests with rosewater to welcome them."[50] Given the "dominant male title" of "Grand Mogul" as commendation of her "splendour," this commanding bloom, in an elegant implied "sub rosa" pun, is to her knowing owner and lover emphatically female—"woman to the rage of my desire." It is a masquerade that parallels Bradley and Cooper's own claim to poetic power under the male title "Michael Field," with White herself noting how the poem's opening signals "the mixed gender identity that is shared by the name of Michael Field."[51]

For me this extraordinary lyric is about the romantic poetic imagination, or the moment of poetic inspiration as Bradley sees it, something that is strongest and most characteristically itself at the very moment when it is about to die, embracing death or the "dying fall" as the very nature of lyric itself. In another exquisite pun, the rose is "morose," a dead or dying rose, but in dying also "more rose," more itself, strangely more of a rose than it has ever been. Bradley's poem is clearly in dialogue with Blake's "The Sick Rose," another lyric that apostrophizes the flower. A traditional interpretation sees Blake's rose as feminized beauty destroyed by the phallic and masculine evil of "the invisible worm," although, as Elizabeth Langland points out, twentieth-century male critics have perpetuated misogynist readings that see the rose as deceptive and blamed for her own sickness.[52]

In contrast, for Bradley's speaker, there is no blame for the rose, only love, and admiration is undimmed in celebration of a demise that is "Majestic in recession." The dying but still potent rose is a decadent variant of other key nineteenth-century tropes of triumphant deaths, like those lyric swans and nightingales that sing most sweetly in their dying throes. It is a daring fin-de-siècle revision of Shelley's image of poetry as the perfect rose in his "Defence," where he declares poetry "the perfect and consummate surface and bloom of things; it is as the odour and colour of the rose to the texture of the elements which compose it, as the form and splendour of unfaded beauty to the secrets of anatomy and corruption."[53] In Bradley's lyric, the unsparing willed anatomy of the disintegrating rose endorses decay and corruption, as the beloved poetic image pushed to crisis dissolves to induce a fresh new lyricism: "as your crimsons stale, / I feel fresh rhythms quicken, / Fresh music follows you." Moreover, words and phrases like "wrought with fire," "ashes," and "burning" hint at a possible ghostly resurrection, the specter of a rose, that famous Renaissance wonder, the "re-individualling of an incinerated plant," or the rose that the alchemist Paracelsus boasted he could raise from its ashes.[54] Indeed, fresh generation is implied by the "fragrant soil," which, unlike dust, suggests a growing medium enriched for the next flowering cycle.

Yet those shriveled falling petals, what Cooper calls "the rose-leaves of your imagination," would still hold fragrance. As the aromatherapist Julia Lawless observes, "Rose petals have a very tenacious scent which actually increases when they are kept (just as rose oil improves with age) which is why they form the basis for many pot pourri recipes."[55] The poem produces another ghost in the guise of perfume that lives on after the rose itself has expired, or as Cooper writes in another lyric, "The roses wither and die, / But their fragrance is not dead."[56] In Bradley's lyric, as the petals shrivel and fall, they expose the heart or "core" of the rose, "A round, black hollow," suggestive of female sexuality but also more generally a figure of the poetic or imaginative unconscious where images coalesce or decompose.

Interestingly, just as we encounter the feminine core of the poem, a tantalizing aroma of masculinity appears in the "hints" of "tobacco, leather, brass," said to give the dead rose "her texture and her colour." Yet the word "hints" irresistibly suggests the idea of fragrance; indeed, "texture" and "colour," though keyed to visual impression, are words that might well be used by a perfumer. Karen Gilbert, advising the perfume student how to build up an olfactory vocabulary, writes, "Think on different levels. Consider whether the fragrance recalls a color, texture, or weight?"[57] The perfumer Jean-Claude Ellena, recording his desire to express the "tactile aspect" of a particular perfume, observes, "A perfume never speaks to one sense alone, but offers itself to all the senses," and the poetic speaker urges the Grand Mogul rose to "entoil" or entangle "[her] senses."[58]

The trio "tobacco, leather, brass" is an unusual one to find in a lyric by a Victorian woman; Chadwyck-Healey's poetry database reveals no other use of the word "tobacco" by a woman poet in the period 1880–1900.[59] Such odorous "hints" seem to anticipate twentieth-century perfumes, where it is not uncommon to encounter masculine "leather," "tobacco," or metallic notes combined with florals such as rose—rose oil being the most common floral ingredient in modern perfume.[60] Early influential tobacco and leather perfumes such Tabac Blond (1919), Habanita (1921), Cuir de Russie (1924), and Bandit (1944)—the last three containing rose—are daring perfumes, specifically designed for the twentieth-century emancipated woman who smoked.[61] Some later rose perfumes are also said to have a metallic aspect because certain essential oils and synthetic molecules used to create a rose fragrance, such as rose attar, geranium oil, palmarosa oil, rose oxide, and geraniol, have metallic notes. And, indeed, botanical roses themselves offer a huge range of notes, often varying with temperature and time of day and reminiscent of many fruits, spices, and what the horticultural historian Jennifer Potter calls "sundry substances," including moss, damp earth, musk, rancid butter, face powder, and Russian leather.[62] Bradley and Cooper were clearly aware of such variety; in "Festa," a later poem in *Wild Honey from Various Thyme* (1908), written by Bradley on July 15, 1900, the speaker portrays her beloved "with me in the bloom of roses," laughingly trying to identify the notes of different rose scents with descriptions such as "A cedar-coffer, a miasma dense / With suck of honey."[63]

Although "The Grand Mogul" anticipates the avant-garde leather and tobacco-rose perfumes to come, it also evokes scents nearer at hand that could be combined with rose. The leather note in perfume is actually an old one dating from the Renaissance, when perfume was applied to gloves and other items of leather apparel to disguise the unpleasant smell of the tanning process. This eventually evolved into the perfume "Peau d'espagne," or "Spanish leather," a unisex handkerchief and sachet perfume popular in the late nineteenth and early twentieth centuries that contains leather notes, spices, and florals, including rose. It seems less surprising that tobacco appears in this poem when one recalls that Bradley and Cooper were respectively the daughter and granddaughter of Charles Bradley, a Birmingham tobacconist and snuff manufacturer who died when Bradley was two but whose money effectively financed their independent lifestyle and writing career. Tobacco might be considered a subtle aromatic reminiscence of the absent enabling father who infiltrates the poem alongside the poetic fathers of Blake and Shelley. Moreover, both women were smokers, with Bradley in particular daring to smoke in male company. Smoking was another olfactory pleasure for them, with Bradley recording how, as presents on Easter Day 1904, "We give each other, not eggs,—fine cigarettes & liquid ambergris."[64]

As Penny Tinkler points out, smoking among middle- and upper-class women in the period 1880 to 1920 can be regarded as "a gendered statement of modernity" and "a sign of gender rebellion," although a concession to femininity might be made in the form of ladies' cigarettes: "very dainty in appearance," which gave off "the sweet odours of violets and roses."[65] From the Regency period, snuff, finely ground tobacco for inhalation, had been scented with essential oils, with rose a popular note in varieties such as Macouba.[66] Brass—a metal that gives off a distinct smell in contact with human skin—was used during the nineteenth century for the buttons on men's uniforms, but also for snuff boxes, cigarette cases and holders, and perfume bottles and stoppers, becoming an additional element in the olfactory experience. Thus, if the Grand Mogul rose forges an identity of masculine command and authority fused with an underlying feminine desire, pleasure, and imaginative inspiration, this is echoed in a ghostly smell-signature, an emancipated fragrance of rose with masculine notes of tobacco, leather, brass—a sort of "essence of Michael Field" that is left lingering at the poem's close.

Notes

1. For more on Michael Field's theory of fragrance, see the much longer chapter, "Michael Field's Fragrant Imagination," in my monograph, *Scents and Sensibility: Perfume in Victorian Literary Culture*, 201–39 (Oxford: Oxford University Press, 2017), from which this current chapter derives.

2. *The Fowl and the Pussycat: Love Letters of Michael Field 1876–1909*, ed. Sharon Bickle (Charlottesville: University of Virginia Press, 2008), 93.

3. Michael Field, "Works and Days," BL Add MS 46804A, fol. 21r (March 21, 1914) [K.B.].

4. Charles Ricketts, "Michael Field," in *Letters from Charles Ricketts to "Michael Field,"* ed. J. G. Paul Delaney (Edinburgh: Tregara, 1981), 1–8 (at 7).

5. Michael Field, "Works and Days," BL Add MS 46782, fol. 19r (March 22, 1894) [E.C.].

6. Michael Field, "Works and Days," BL Add MS 46784, fols. 23r–v (November 21, 1895) [E.C.].

7. Michael Field, "Works and Days," BL Add MS 46782, fol. 84v (July 6, 1894) [E.C.].

8. Michael Field, "Works and Days," BL Add MS 46778, fol. 114r (September 13, 1890) [E.C.].

9. The poem, "Apollo's Triumph" (dated April 29, 1894), appears in various draft forms in Michael Field, "Works and Days," BL Add MS 46782, fols. 38v–39r [K.B], with an entry on fol. 39r about the daphne scent. For Bradley's note on the poem as cited, see typescript MS, Bodleian Library, Oxford, MS Eng. poet. d. 65, fol. 10. The poem was

published in the American edition of *Underneath the Bough* (Portland, ME: Thomas B. Mosher, 1898), 79.

10. Michael Field, *Underneath the Bough* (1898), 79.

11. For a discussion of the debate over division/unity in Michael Field's work, see Marion Thain, *Michael Field: Poetry, Aestheticism and the Fin de Siècle* (Cambridge: Cambridge University Press, 2007), 100–101. Exploration of Michael Field's archive reveals that Bradley contributed far more poems than Cooper, including many of those that are most celebrated. For me, Cooper's strengths lie in her prose, often displayed to best advantage in "Works and Days." For a further discussion of her prose, see my "Michael Field, Death, and the Effigy," *Word & Image* 34, no. 1 (2018): 31–39.

12. "On Opening a Box of Flowers from the Riviera," transcribed from Bodleian typescript, MS Eng. poet. d. 65, fol. 40. Some slight variations from the original composition found in Michael Field, "Works and Days," BL Add MS 46782, fol. 142r (December 21, 1894) [K.B.].

13. Michael Field, *Underneath the Bough* (London: George Bell & Sons, 1893), 80.

14. Michael Field, "Works and Days," BL Add MS 46782, fol. 45v (May 22, 1894) [E.C.].

15. Michael Field, *Underneath the Bough* (1893), 87.

16. Michael Field, "Works and Days," BL Add MS 46782, fol. 61r (July 29, 1891) [E.C.]. The poem is on fol. 61v.

17. Ovid, *Fasti* 4:141–44.

18. Michael Field, "Works and Days," BL Add MS 46778, fol. 64v (Summer 1890) [K.B.].

19. Geoffrey Grigson, *The Goddess of Love: The Birth, Triumph, Death and Return of Aphrodite* (London: Constable, 1976), 195.

20. Malcolm Stuart, *Encyclopedia of Herbs and Herbalism* (London: Orbis, 1979), 27; Jeremy Tanner, *The Invention of Art History in Ancient Greece: Religion, Society and Artistic Rationalisation* (Cambridge: Cambridge University Press, 2006), 48.

21. "Bits of Things," composed January 1895, first published in *Music and Silence: The Gamut of Michael Field*, ed. Ivor C. Treby (Bury St. Edmunds, UK: De Blackland, 2000), 102; "To the Winter Aphrodite" (composed 1901), in Michael Field, *Wild Honey from Various Thyme* (London: T. Fisher Unwin, 1908), 23.

22. *Piesse's Art of Perfumery and the Methods of Obtaining the Odours of Plants, the Growth and General Flower Farm System of Raising Fragrant Herbs*, ed. Charles H. Piesse, 5th ed. (London: Presse and Lubin, 1891), states that "Myrtle-flower water is sold in France under the name of eau d'ange" and also that "A very fragrant otto may be procured by distilling the leaves of the common myrtle" (159).

23. See Pierre Chantraine, *Dictionnaire étymologique de la langue grecque: Histoire des mots* (Paris: Librarie Klincksiek, 2009), 696. A link with myrrh (*murra*) is also suggested.

24. Dated October 27, 1904, and included as a manuscript illustration in Ivor C. Treby, *The Michael Field Catalogue: A Book of Lists* (Bury St. Edmunds, UK: De Blackland, 1998), 125. Cooper possibly recalls James Thomson's "The Lover's myrtle and the Poet's bay," line 1513 from his book *The Seasons* (London: W. Lewis, 1819), 126.

25. *The Natural History of Pompeii*, ed. Wihelmina Feemster Jashemski and Frederick G. Meyer (Cambridge: Cambridge University Press, 2002), 130.

26. Michael Field, "Works and Days," BL Add MS 46787, fol. 145v (1898) [E.C.]; extract taken from John Galt, *The Omen* (Blackwood: Edinburgh, 1825), 119.

27. Cooper to Bradley (September 1880), *The Fowl and the Pussycat*, 37.

28. Michael Field, "Works and Days," BL Add MS 46777, fol. 5r (May 9, 1888) [E.C.].

29. Michael Field, "Works and Days," BL Add MS 46777, fol. 76v (June 1889) [E.C.].

30. Michael Field, "Works and Days," BL Add MS 46777, fol. 4r [K.B.].

31. Michael Field, *Long Ago* (London: G. Bell & Sons, 1889), 105.

32. Michael Field, "Drawing of Roses and Violets," in *Sight and Song* (London: Elkin Mathews and John Lane, 1892), 5. Draft in Michael Field, "Works and Days," BL Add MS 46778, fols. 80v–81v (August 1890) [K.B.].

33. Bradley to John Miller Gray, Add MS 45854, fols. 195r–v (November 1893).

34. Michael Field, "Works and Days," BL Add MS 46782, fol. 84r (July 3, 1894) [E.C.].

35. Michael Field, "Works and Days," BL Add MS 46782, fol. 52r (June 1, 1894) [E.C.].

36. Michael Field, "Works and Days," BL Add MS 46782, fol. 52r (June 4, 1894) [K.B.].

37. Michael Field, *Underneath the Bough* (1898), 85–86. I use this edition for the text below.

38. *An Anthology of "Nineties" Verse*, ed. A. J. A. Symons (London: Elkin Mathews & Marot, 1928), 55–56. See most recently, *Victorian Women Poets: An Anthology*, ed. Angela Leighton and Margaret Reynolds (Oxford: Blackwell, 1995), 503–4.

39. Ivor Treby on "The Grand Mogul," *Uncertain Rain: Sundry Spells of Michael Field*, ed. Ivor Treby (Bury St. Edmunds: De Blackland Press, 2002), 121.

40. William Paul FLS, *The Rose Garden in Two Divisions*, 9th ed. (London: Kent & Co., 1888), 260.

41. Paul, *The Rose Garden*, 187, 272.

42. Color plate in William Paul, *The Rose Garden in Two Divisions: Illustrated with Twenty-one Coloured Plates and Numerous Engravings in the Text*, 10th ed. (London: Simpkin, Marshall & Co., 1903), opposite page 55. There is apparently a color-illustrated version of the 9th edition, but I have not been able to trace a copy.

43. Michael Field, "The Grand Mogul," in *Underneath the Bough* (1898), 85–86.

44. Michael Field, "Works and Days," BL Add MS 46783, fol. 127v (August 8, 1895) [K.B.].

45. Michael Field, "Works and Days," BL Add MS 46782, fol. 46v (May 22, 1894) [E.C.].

46. Michael Field, "Works and Days," BL Add MS 46782, fol. 85v (July 9, 1894) [E.C.].

47. For MS drafts annotated "Wednesday 11 July," see Michael Field, "Works and Days," BL Add MS 46782, fol. 78v, 79r, 81v [K.B.].

48. The same sentence occurs in identical passages in Chris White, "The Tiresian Poet: Michael Field," in *Victorian Women Poets: A Critical Reader*, ed. Angela Leighton (Oxford: Blackwell, 1996), 148–61 (at 159), and "Flesh and Roses: Michael Field's Metaphors of Pleasure," *Women's Writing* 3, no.1 (1996): 47–62 (at 57). White's analysis

in an earlier essay is hampered by the fact that she reproduces only the first eleven lines under the mistaken belief that these constitute the whole poem. See "The One Woman (in Virgin Haunts of Poesie): Michael Field's Sapphic Symbolism," in *Volcanoes and Pearl Divers: Essays in Lesbian Feminist Studies*, ed. Suzanne Raitt (London: Only Women Press, 1995), 74–102 (at 98–99).

49. Amina Okada, "India and Perfume in the Mughal Period, Sixteenth to Nineteenth Centuries," in *Perfume: A Global History*, 172–73 (at 172). See also Jennifer Potter, *The Rose: A True History* (London: Atlantic Books 2010), 348. Potter nominates Geronimo Rossi of Ravenna as the first to develop a technique for separating rose oil from rosewater as "described in a European source dated 1574" (348).

50. Okada, "India and Perfume," 172.

51. White, "The Tiresian Poet," 158; "Flesh and Roses," 57.

52. Elizabeth Langland, "Blake's Feminist Revision of Literary Tradition in 'The Sick Rose,'" in *Critical Paths: Blake and The Argument of Method*, ed. Dan Miller, Mark Bracher, and Donald Ault (Durham, NC, and London: Duke University Press, 1987), 225–43.

53. Percy Bysshe Shelley, "A Defence of Poetry," *Shelley's Poetry and Prose*, ed. Donald H. Reiman and Sharon B. Power (New York: W. W. Norton, 1977), 503.

54. Dr. Henry Power to Sir Thomas Browne, February 10, 1868, in *Works of Sir Thomas Browne*, vi, 280. Quoted in Walter Pater, "Sir Thomas Browne," *Appreciations* (London: Macmillan, 1910), 151.

55. Julia Lawless, *Rose Oil: The New Guide to Nature's Most Precious Perfume and Traditional Remedy* (London: HarperCollins, 1995), 80.

56. "The roses wither and die," *Underneath the Bough* (1893), 117–18. Cooper echoes Shelley's "Rose leaves, when the rose is dead / Are heaped for the beloved's bed." See "To——," *Shelley's Poetry and Prose*, 442.

57. Karen Gilbert, *Perfume: The Art and Craft of Fragrance* (London: Cico Books, 2013), 60.

58. Jean-Claude Ellena, *The Diary of a Nose: A Year in the Life of a Parfumeur*, tr. Adriana Hunter (London: Particular Books, 2012), 136.

59. This is, of course, a very partial mode of assessment, and it should be said that "The Grand Mogul" itself does not appear in the database.

60. See Lawless, *Rose Oil*, 81.

61. Barbara Herman, *Scent and Subversion: Decoding a Century of Provocative Perfume* (Guilford, CT: Lyons Press, 2013), 29, 33, 37, 79.

62. Potter, *The Rose*, 338.

63. Michael Field, "Festa," in *Wild Honey*, 176.

64. Michael Field, "Works and Days," BL Add MS 46793, fol. 68r (Easter Day [April 3] 1904) [K.B.].

65. Penny Tinkler, "Sapphic Smokers and English Modernities," in *Sapphic Modernisms: Sexuality, Women and National Culture*, ed. Laura Doan and Jane Garrity (Basingstoke, UK: Palgrave Macmillan, 2006), 75–90 (at 79); Tinkler, *Smoke Signals: Women, Smoking and Visual Culture* (Oxford: Berg, 2006), 21.

66. John Arlott, *The Snuff Shop* (London: Michael Joseph, 1974), 34.

SEVEN

"Profane Travelers"

Michael Field, Cornwall, and Modern Tourism

ALEX MURRAY

KATHARINE BRADLEY AND EDITH COOPER WERE INVETERATE
travelers, making regular tours of the Continent and taking trips all over the
British Isles. They were not alone: the fin de siècle saw an exponential rise in
the tourist industry, both domestic and European. Bradley and Cooper had a
troubled relationship to this industry: on the one hand, they had to use its infrastructure to facilitate their own travel; on the other, they found their fellow
travelers, the trains, hotels, and tourist sites of the well-traveled routes of the
culture industry profane and vulgar. This chapter explores these tensions and
the various strategies that the two women used to transform their own experience into a form of Bacchic and spiritual travel. As they struggled to reconcile
themselves to the modern world of tourism, they began repopulating the landscapes around them with a spiritual life that was anathema to the cheap, showy
world of late-Victorian travel. The chapter begins by charting their increasingly
hostile relationship to the tourist industry that developed over the course of the
1890s as they entered their most intensely "Bacchic" phase, as captured in their
prose sketches "For That Moment Only" (1893–95) and their journal "Works
and Days" (particularly the mid- to late 1890s). The second part examines in
detail one of their own holidays (of May 1896)—at St. Mawgan in Cornwall—
where they transformed their own travel into spiritual pilgrimage and Bacchic
revelry, culminating in the verse drama *Noontide Branches* (1899).[1] In that play,

they explore the problematic tensions between the profane and the spiritual that would dominate the rest of their lives, making their own travel a form of self-reflexive pilgrimage.

Michael Field and Modern Tourism

"We were a party of profane travelers." So begins Michael Field's prose sketch "The Lady Moon" (1893), in which the narrator, observing her fellow passenger in a carriage, declares, "[W]e all thought we had done with religion."[2] The young, anonymous man with whom she shares the carriage joyously announces the appearance of "the Lady Moon"; his rapture, his exaltation in the presence of nature and the landscape of the Adriatic Coast forces the narrator into a recantation: "[N]o, we had not yet done with religion."[3] When this sketch was written, most likely in spring 1893, Michael Field had not yet "done with religion." They were, however, entering the height of their "Bacchic" period and may have suspected instead that they were "done" with the Christian Church as they embraced the Dionysiac. It is in this sense that Michael Field were "profane" travelers, transforming the very mundane late-Victorian experience of travel into Bacchic revelry. Yet there is another sense in which Michael Field were profane: as they followed the well-worn paths of cultural tourism, were they not themselves buying into the tawdry, profane world of Cook tours and Baedeker and Murray guidebooks?

Michael Field's anxiety about being tourists was common in the late nineteenth century. As James Buzard so persuasively argued in *The Beaten Track: European Tourism and the Ways to 'Culture,' 1800–1918* (1993), tourism and antitourism had been trapped in a symbiotic relationship since the Romantics. The desire to distinguish one's own adventurous travel from everyone else's mundane tourism was a staple of nineteenth-century literature. As Buzard explains, "Snobbish 'anti-tourism,' an element of modern tourism from the start, has offered an important, even exemplary way of regarding one's own cultural experiences as authentic and unique, setting them against a backdrop of always assumed tourist vulgarity, repetition and ignorance."[4] More often than not, Buzard argues, women in the nineteenth century were supposed to be the most passive of tourists: their role was to "demurely interest themselves in sightseeing while they await deliverance by a husband or father."[5] While Buzard's model here is predominantly mid-Victorian travel, by the fin de siècle women aesthetes were rejecting the role of passive consumers of the tourist industry. For instance, Vernon Lee, in her book, *The Sentimental Traveller* (1908), declared that the modern manifestations of travel—"*trains de luxe*, motors, and Cook's hotels"—were of "all modes of life the most sacrilegious, to the Genius Loci," that deep reverence for the spirit of place that was so essential to Lee's aestheticism.[6] Bradley and Cooper were, like Lee, consciously trying to distance themselves from this commercial world of organized tourism, and as Hilary Fraser has made clear, we should resist the narrative—perpetuated by Bernard Berenson and other male art critics of the period—that women such as Cooper and Bradley were unable to strike out on their own.[7] Bradley and Cooper, as I hope to demonstrate, interrogated these codified practices so obviously associated with Berenson, attempting, at key moments, to forge a truly Bacchic travel that turned away from museums and galleries toward landscapes and those inhabiting them.

The trip the two women made to Paris and Italy in the of summer 1890 is arguably their most well known and documented. The relatively conventional itinerary of that trip would be transformed into the dynamic ekphrasis of *Sight and Song* (1892), in which the static location of each painting is juxtaposed with the movement and vitality of their poetic revision. Indeed, as the volume of "Works and Days" that documents that trip makes clear, the practical, tawdry world of tourism, the hotels and pensiones, the carriages and trains was to be stubbornly ignored. Their vocation as aesthetes meant that art had to be quarantined, sequestered from the mundanity of tourism; at the very end of the 1890 volume of their diaries, secreted away from the proper stuff of art and literature, is a list of presents they purchased and hotels they stayed in on their holiday.[8] Despite their desire to elevate the aesthetic, there was for one reader a sneaking suspicion that *Sight and Song* had failed to achieve poetic transformation and remained, sadly, in the quotidian world of the tourist. W. B. Yeats, reviewing the collection for the *Bookman*, lamented that the two women had only managed to produce "something of an age of text-books" and that was "in no wise given over to that unprincipled daughter of whim and desire we call imagination." Toward the end of the review, Yeats revised his own categorization: these poems were not "text-books," perhaps after the manner of Ruskin or Berenson, but a "simply unmitigated guide-book."[9] On their next continental sojourn, perhaps still smarting from Yeats's barb, Bradley and Cooper began to develop a different means of engaging with the modern tourist industry.

On their return to France and Italy in April and May 1893, the two women exhibited a profound ambivalence over their position as tourists. The first diary entry after they cross from Dover to Calais sets an iconoclastic and corybantic tone: their coach hits a pedestrian in Paris, and Cooper transforms this mundane accident into a pagan sacrifice: "[H]is sooty head, his sooty blouse, his whole figure hopping under the horse's legs, in Bacchic elation."[10] This man—we presume an industrial worker of some description from the excess of soot—is an innocent victim, an arbitrary oblation given up in the worship of a greater power.

While Cooper and Bradley provide an account of the 1893 trip in "Works and Days," two tiny surviving notebooks in Cooper's hand reveal the tensions between the touristic and the aesthetic. The first is a prosaic record of their travels, providing little more than a collection of places visited, drives taken, and so on. A representative entry reads, "April 23rd Mr Shakespeare's birthday. We see the capella Pazzi & some of the frescos at S. Croce Accademia. Primavera. Some Peruginos. Breakfast at restaurant with cigarettes. Uffizi—Venus, Calumy, Leonardo. Doctrine delicious."[11] The accompanying notebook, recording their impressions of the artworks they saw, reveals the discriminating aesthete at work, revisiting some of the paintings they had transcribed into verse in *Sight and Song* (1892), such as an elaborate note on the composition of Botticelli's *Birth of Venus* at the Uffizi.[12] A third notebook in Bradley's hand also provides an account of the trip, mixing the mundane with art criticism, yet there emerges the world-weary tone of the traveler. On their return to Paris at the end of May, she writes the following:

Saturday morning

> We all start together in gayest spirits on the top of an omnibus to
> the new Salon. I could catch at every branch of every tree as I pass
> it & pluck the leaves off it in the gladness of my heart. But—the
> new salon is not a famous show—everything is a little less than last
> year, & some of the greatest artists are at Chicago at their best.[13]

If the two women were to find inspiration on that 1893 trip, it came from nature rather than from museums and monuments. In the prose sketch "A Traveler's Tale," set on an "April day in Tuscany," the women (the sketch is in Bradley's hand) witness a dramatic rainstorm after weeks of drought. The essence of the Bacchanal is revealed in this moment, as the grape vines on the surrounding hills dance, buffeted by wind and rain, "thousands of little vines in Bacchic elation." Watching them, "one forgot all that poets have said, or sculptors cut in honour of fauns and satyrs."[14] In sketch after sketch in "For That Moment Only," they encounter Bacchic nature, even real-life fauns and satyrs in the landscape around them. In "A Faun" they eroticize a sleeping young man they voyeuristically observe near a waterfall opposite the temple they had gone to visit in Tivoli. The real, living faun is a shock to them, who have only accessed the pagan world through art and literature: "We think of a Faun as marble; we rarely imagine them in all their weird gracefulness of flesh & blood, vivid with the health of pleasurable existence." The marble faun here seemingly alludes to the numerous marble statues of fauns they may have seen on their European travels (such as the Barberini Faun at the Glyptothek in Munich), but also to Nathaniel Hawthorne's novel *The Marble Faun* (1860), in which one of the Italian characters is said to resemble the faun of Praxiteles. This aesthetic mediation is no preparation for their encounter with the young man, "a creature the earth had formed." "Scarcely human," he is wholly at odds with the prosaic world of the tourist. After he has awoken, they leave the woods. "In half an hour we were drinking lemon squash at a Casino, to the accompaniment of an Italian band; & a little later we mounted the steam-train & were jolted across the Campagna to Rome in the chill of sunset. 'Oh poor Faun, poor Faun, poor Faun!'"[15] That the living, breathing faun has to live in the world of tawdry bands and Casinos is too much to take.[16]

With the continent increasingly tainted by the specter of organized tourism that plagues the poor faun—if it was all a "little less than last year"—then Michael Field increasingly undertook to become Bacchic tourists of the British Isles, traveling overseas with far less regularity in the late 1890s. From Scotland to Cornwall, they would find landscapes that resonated with their interest in the literary and the pagan. However, the places they visited in England or Scotland were not free from tourism. On Box Hill in Surrey, the two women were part of a female party picnicking in the woods. This rather conventional outing was transformed by a young woman in their party whose dancing was so memorably captured in one of their prose croquis. "A Maenad" is one of the most erotic and sensual works they ever penned, as the young woman hitched "up her skirt 'round her black pantaloons, pulled off her shoes, and in her black stockings began to dance a hornpipe on the grass."[17] The description of the girl and her dance is prolonged, tender, and voluptuous. However, the beautiful young maenad's dance is disrupted:

> It was one of those sights that are sacred to half the world of
> mortals; & when a couple of tourists broke on the solitude our
> maenad fled into the box-grove. The men looked at the remaining
> trio; they saw feet only covered with stockings, shoes among the
> beech-roots, while scattered over cloaks and hats were branches of
> box & branches of sweet-briar. The tourists lowered their eyes and
> passed the group rigidly. How much of the spirit of Pentheus lived
> in the breast of those two Cockneys. How we longed to tear them
> to pieces![18]

In Euripides's *The Bacchae*, Pentheus, the king of Thebes, attempts to ban the worship of Dionysus; on entering the forest to confront the god of intoxication, he is attacked and torn limb from limb by the Bacchanal.[19] Michael Field then imagine themselves as maenads in a Bacchic chorus, symbolically tearing tourists and tourism itself to pieces.

One of Cooper and Bradley's favorite holiday destinations was Scotland: they traveled to the Borders and Edinburgh on numerous occasions. Chief among the attractions of this region were the echoes of Scott, Wordsworth, and Burns that they heard reverberating around its landscapes. Yet these journeys were compromised by their proximity to the emerging literary tourism industry, for which the Borders was fertile ground. Literary tourism began, according to Nicola J. Watson, in the eighteenth century, growing steadily throughout the nineteenth, before the turn of the twentieth century "brought the development of full-blown 'literary geography' and the concomitant invention of the literary 'land' or 'country.'"[20] Michael Field were then writing at the point at which literary tourism was reaching cultural saturation and a new generation of guides, travel narratives, and organized tours encouraged ever more tourists to descend on Wordsworth's Lake District, Dickens's London, the Brontës's Haworth, or Shakespeare's Stratford-upon-Avon. Particularly striking, Watson notes, was this development of literary geographies in which whole landscapes could be annexed under the sign of a single literary author, overlaying fictionalized landscapes onto a real, lived environment: "This wholesale geographical naturalization of fiction designedly dramatizes the nation to itself and to outsiders, by setting up affective relations within whole quarters of the map of Great Britain."[21] While many associated with decadence and aestheticism found literary tourism anathema to their elitist views, William Sharpe—who was to produce his own decadent-inspired landscape writing of the Outer Hebrides under the nom de plume Fiona Macleod—embraced it. He compiled in *Literary Geographies* (1905) a series of his sketches of famous literary regions. The collection was far from academic, as the foreword announced, "The present volume aims at nothing more than to be a readable companion in times of leisure for those who are in sympathy with the author's choice of writers and localities; and if they share his own pleasure in wandering through these 'literary lands' he on his part will be well content."[22] If there was a literary industry increasingly "content" with providing nothing more than a "readable" companion to literary ramblers, it underscored the increasingly homogenous nature of literary landscape writing in the period.

Arguably the most overdetermined of all literary landscapes in the British Isles was the southeast of Scotland: Scott country. There was, by the 1890s, already a large tourist industry based on Sir Walter Scott; no less than Thomas Cook, father of the package tour, would declare that Scott had given "a sentiment to Scotland as a tourist destination."[23] Travelers armed with *The Lady of the*

Lake would visit Loch Katrine, others Scott's home Abbotsford. Ann Rigney has described Abbotsford as "something of a nineteenth-century Graceland."[24] Andrea Zemgulys notes that literary tourism's investment in the domestic "enhanced" rather than "compromised" the image of male writers, particularly amongst female tourists.[25] For the new generation of literary tourists, the quotidian lives of writers, particularly in their childhood and formative years, had begun to take on all the allure of Romance; a new genre of affective literary geographies was produced for the aspiring literary tourist to consume at home narratives that described the immersive experiences they then hoped to replicate in situ. For instance, in Marion Harland's *Where Ghosts Walk: The Haunts of Familiar Characters in History and Literature* (1898), a visit to Robert Burns's birthplace is both guide and memoir: "We gasp involuntarily as the civil custodian tells the story of the solitary window, and points out that there was no outer door to the 'but.'"[26] The reader here is twice removed from the literary text with Harland's experience of visiting the site of Burns's birth, at some significant remove from Burns's poetry: the work itself recedes into the background as the cult of authorship and the commodification of place predominate.

The modern literary tourist, reading such guides and then descending on the Borders, was to cause Bradley and Cooper no little annoyance. The two women took numerous trips to southern Scotland, where they were, in many respects, diligent and conventional literary tourists, visiting Carlyle's house in Ecclefechan in 1894—first opened to tourists in 1881—as well as making a pilgrimage to Robert Burns's grave in 1895. Their account of their trip to Carlyle's birthplace is striking in its sentimentality, similar to Harland's account of visiting Burns's birthplace. Carlyle's birthplace "has great charm—two little white houses round a central archway, with blackened posts & lintels in white-washed frontage. . . . [N]ow we stand in the chamber where Carlyle first breathed."[27] There is, as so often in the work of Michael Field, a movement from the sentimental, conventional language of Victorian literature to an irreverent dismissal of such conventions, and their travel writings are no exception.

In August and September 1895, Cooper and Bradley went to stay with Mrs. Miller-Morrison, a poet who had also written a study of Browning's *Sordello*, at Morrison House in Ruthwell, before moving on to stay at the Crook Inn in Tweedsmuir farther to the east. The Crook Inn is one of the oldest inns in Scotland and is reportedly the place where Burns penned "Willie Wastle's Wife."[28] The valley in which the inn sits is remote and the landscape treeless and bleak. For Cooper and Bradley, these were "perfect conditions for overwrought poets. Crook Inn & its valley are characteristic of all we enjoy most on earth when we seek a holiday."[29] During their time there, they began to pen descriptions of the landscape that were to be used in a projected revised edition of *The Tragic Mary* (1890). From Crook Inn they then traveled some fifteen miles west to the Gordon Arms in Yarrow Valley, another inn with great literary heritage, having been frequented by Hogg, Scott, and Burns. On this trip they also took in a number of sites on what was already a well-established Sir Walter Scott tourist route, yet they were unwilling to allow themselves to be classed with the lowly literary tourist. Cooper, writing of their visit to Tibbie Shiels' Inn, complained, "[T]he whole place is alive with tourists, who consider a holiday the excuse for any relaxation of discipline, who peep at the portraits of great men with a smirk & get wrong about everything."[30] This is in striking contrast to the visit the two women made to the same inn exactly a year earlier. On this visit, they frame themselves as classic tourists:

> We rush to Tibbie Shiels' for tea, & have there a quarter of an
> hour's enjoyment. Scott & Wilson knew what they were about
> . . . a visitor's book in the window where I write confidently
> <u>Michael Field, Surrey, England</u>, knowing we have the night to
> inscribe ourselves, two beds in niches of the parlour, a nice young
> fox-hound & a red, red, flower of creeper round the porch—
> that's Tibbie Shiels.'[31]

The desire to "inscribe" themselves in a space that has been carefully curated for tourists suggests that the two women simultaneously conform and disrupt its conventions by writing the name "Michael Field" in the guest book, indulging in the romance of the scene, yet performing that indulgence as the poet rather than as individuals. Yet at the same time, they were trying to distance themselves from the tourists who visited Scott country. In one of the prose pieces in "For That Moment Only" set in the Scottish Borders, the narrator complains of being made to sit "behind the coachman, a commonplace tourist on each side of me."[32] A year earlier, on a similar trip to St. Mary's Loch, Cooper complains, "The coach is full of violent, ill-bred people."[33] The paradox I have outlined so far, of both conforming to and resisting the controlled and proscribed world of tourism, was, I suggest, to lead the two women to develop an alternative mode of engaging both with the places they visited and those places' relationship to literary history. In doing so, they developed a peculiarly Bacchic mode of tourism as they holidayed in remote northern Cornwall.

Bacchic Tourism in St. Mawgan

If Bradley and Cooper had become increasingly frustrated with the tourist industry that was ruining their favorite haunts in Italy and Scotland, they were determined to find their own means of becoming "profane" travelers, of turning the mundane activity of domestic travel into a form of Bacchic worship. "Bacchic" is, in "Works and Days," and in Cooper and Bradley's letters, one of their most overused words. As Stefano Evangelista has noted, the terms "aesthetic" and "Bacchic" became "almost synonymous" for them.[34] Yet, as for so many other writers in the period, aestheticism was far more than a literary, artistic, or even cultural pursuit. Michael Field thoroughly domesticated both the aesthetic and the Bacchic, transforming quotidian spaces into altars of Dionysiac worship. Yet at the same time, they were aware of the potential for the Bacchic to lose its adversarial force. Reflecting on Berenson's increasingly dull and domestic life, they wrote, "Imagine Bacchus with the poker of the hearth in his hand instead of the thyrsus! Curse the thought! Curse it bitterly!"[35] Berenson, often named "the faun" in "Works and Days," had become a symbol of domesticity now that he had entered into a relatively conventional relationship with Mary Costelloe; to find the truly Bacchic, they had to leave the world of urban culture behind and engage in their own unique form of queer travel.

If the Scottish Borders were already well-established sites of literary and cultural pilgrimage, Cornwall was yet to become so heavily codified. The great texts of Cornwall's tourist industry—Daphne Du Maurier's novels, Winston Graham's Poldark series—were some years off, although Tintagel had already become something of a site of worship for those inspired by Tennyson's *Idylls of the King* (1859–85). Yet for the most part, Cornwall's role in the late-Victorian cultural imaginary was as a primitive, undeveloped cultural other. In 1851, Wilkie Collins feared that with the coming of the railway, something of the county's "pleasant primitive" quality was destined to be lost.[36] By 1867 the Great Western Railway had been connected to Penzance, and Cornwall began to develop the tourist infrastructure that would transform the region into an iconic holiday destination. Yet in their trip of May 1896, Michael Field didn't venture to the more popular tourist destinations of Falmouth, Penzance, or St. Ives.

Bradley and Cooper stayed at Dartmouth in Devon before traveling farther west to spend almost a month in St. Mawgan, a small village that lies on the banks of the River Menalhyl, some two and a half miles from the Atlantic Coast. Like most of north Cornwall, the area was largely agricultural in this period, and the village had little more than an inn—the Falcon—and a general store. The two traveled there ostensibly to visit Katharine Bradley's Bristol friend Alice Trusted, a devout Catholic who was now attached to the Lanherne Convent, where an order of Carmelite sisters had been based since 1794. Trusted was, arguably, as important a spiritual influence on their lives as the *pères frères* John Gray and Vincent McNabb. During the 1890s, both

Bradley and Cooper exchanged numerous letters with her on a variety of literary, artistic, and spiritual matters, occasionally counseling her against what they perceived to be the life-denying creed she had entered into. In 1894 Bradley wrote,

> I am not a Roman Catholic myself—I think any one may see from
> my works how much, under some aspects, I admire the Roman
> Church. May her banner over you be love & may you while on
> earth know the restfulness of being among Christ's faithful people.
> Do not feel that we are shut out from anything you can experience.
> We are with the nun in her cell, as with the pagan at the Dionysius'
> feast—wherever there is worship, & faith, & tremulous joy there
> surely it is easy for the poet to be.[37]

Eighteen months later the two women, writing as Michael Field, were themselves attempting to combine the religious adoration of the nuns of Lanherne Convent with the Dionysiac festival of the forest, turning north Cornwall into a very Fieldian landscape. This visit to Cornwall and the spiritual questions it raised has been wholly absent from scholarship on Michael Field. Their journey witnessed an acceleration of Bradley's interest in the Roman Catholic faith, and their subsequent attempt to negotiate the Christian and the Hellenic set the model for the dramatic reinvention of their literary personae that followed their conversion in 1907.

On this trip, they were to turn the quotidian agricultural lives of the fields into a landscape throbbing with Hellenic vitality and to fuse that vitalism with the Roman Catholic faith of the convent at Lanherne. In the entries for "Works and Days" in this period, we can clearly see the spiritual split that was developing between the two women, as Cooper Hellenizes while Bradley Christianizes their experience (the two would in later years switch positions, Cooper far more willing to convert). In one of the most memorable passages in their journal, they describe stalking a local ploughboy whom they spy in the fields. The young man pays little attention to them until Bradley asks him endless questions about how to get back to St. Mawgan "while we gaze." Cooper describes him thus:

> I have seen many handsomer faces—nothing so sculptural in its
> mould—the chin and mouth are those of a youth in the Elgin
> frieze. The nose is strong with delicate nostrils, the eyes are the
> brown of a wood-stream—deep set with a droop of the lid; the
> brow furrowed, not with care, but a charming seen-frown, the
> hair all tendrils & drift & play fullness under the cap.... When I
> question in silver tones behind him "We shall not be lost, you are

quite sure?" he turns, throwing his left hand on his mare's back &
we see before us the flower of the Panathenaic procession.

He is like a closed chestnut-bud—full of force, unlightened by
actual spring as yet—youth half-slumbering, with those vague touches
of down on the Greek chin, with the candid slowness of the eyes. If
Pylades had been a plough boy it was so he would have looked.[38]

The sculptural beauty of the young man is clear, and as Cooper sexualizes
him she also homosexualizes him—if he is Pylades, who is his Orestes? While
Cooper has captured the young man's youthful vitality, she has paradoxically
petrified it, turning him into an ancient marble sculpture in the process of sexu-
alizing him; a process that, as Sarah Parker has argued, was an important feature
of the work of "Michael Field."[39] As outlined above, they had become suspicious
of the cold and abstract quality of the Hellenic as they accessed it through art
and sculpture, yet so many of their models and analogies came from the inani-
mate world of museums. The relationship between viewer and sculpture was, all
too often in aestheticism, one of subordinated eroticism; as Pater had remarked
of the Panathenatic frieze in his essay on Winckelmann, "that line of youths
on horseback, with their level glances, their proud, patient lips, their chastened
reins, their whole bodies in exquisite service."[40] Like Pater, they too imagine the
male body presented for their pleasure, serving their own individualism while
denying the agency of the young farmworker.

Yet the process of reimagining the landscape as one of Bacchic revelry is
far from a complete picture. As "Works and Days" made clear, Cooper was attempting to Hellenize the landscape, while Bradley was increasingly drawn to
the spiritual power of the Roman Catholic faith she found there. This division
was one that would lie at the heart of the literary project that emerged from that
trip, a verse drama that attempted to reconcile the Hellenic and the Christian.
Yet at this point, their record of the trip makes clear their differing approach.
Take for instance their visit to the orchard attached to Lanherne Convent.
Cooper describes it as follows:

> This is the forsaken garden of the ancient mansion, banned to
> the nuns, unenjoyed & disappearing. In the midst one apple tree
> stands, radiant, convincing one of desire, appealing with all its
> whites & roses & ripe stain, and tremulous shadows, as Tintoret's
> Angel of the Temptation appeals to natural lust. The bees enjoy
> profoundly in their every movement & hum—petal after petal
> steals down the air & a few of the buds are mantled in such red
> crimson that one acclaims them as if they triumphed.[41]

Cooper here uses the reference to Tintoretto's *The Temptation of Adam* (1551–52) to frame the orchard as a veritable Garden of Eden. The life-denying creed of the Carmelite sisters has kept these women away from temptation but also from the throbbing vitality of nature, figured here with the bees, which as Marion Thain has noted are such a key symbol for Michael Field.[42] "Lust" is as natural as nature itself, but it remains in the Catholic faith "unenjoyed." Cooper frames her own union with Bradley as a moment in which desire and landscape join together in exquisite harmony, describing a visit to Mawgan Porth Beach as follows:

> The sea resembles the breast of a peacock—traversing half a mile of sand we reach the white waves. Then Mick & I paddle—I have never paddled before. We take hands and spring about or sink our feet in the warm sand till an insinuating coldness has its way & the brine hardens us. One never knows the spirit of frolic till one is in company with the waves—they have more contagiousness than childhood wh[ich] rarely makes us as itself. Mick & I were just two waves at our dance on the shore.[43]

The sea is both aestheticized as the beautiful plumage of the peacock—reminiscent of Whistler—and the source of the simplest physical pleasure. In its presence, the two can achieve unity with one another but also with the land-scape itself, their desire naturalized in the eternal movement of the waves and, by inference, the tide, and with it the lunar cycle.

While Cooper was embedding their union in the landscape of Mawgan Porth, Bradley was turning to Catholicism, reading Cardinal Newman's *Meditations and Devotions*—"a book in exquisite tone with the vale of Lanherne," copying out large passages into "Works and Days," declaring that "these passages have become part of the sun and quiet of Mawgan." It is not coincidental that the first pages of Newman's *Meditations* are devoted to the month of May; he explains that it is the month of both joy and promise, a month dedicated to the Blessed Virgin: "It is because the blossoms are upon the trees and the flowers are in the gardens. It is because the days have got long, and the sun rises early and sets late. For such gladness and joyousness of external Nature is a fit attendant on our devotion to her who is the Mystical Rose and the House of Gold."[44] Where they had been deifying nature in a wholly pagan manner earlier in their trip at Dartmouth, their time at St. Mawgan recalled for Bradley in particular that Christian theology is often in as great accordance with the cycles of nature. This strange fusion between the pagan and the Christian persists—they sit in "alder shadows" by the river and alternate between reading Newman and *Lycidas*,

Bradley declaring that "only prose and verse of high distinction can be read at St. Mawgan in Pydar. Newman is the voice of its atmosphere."[45]

Their final day (a Sunday) sees them attend High Mass. Cooper has a terrible time—the holy water strikes her between the eyes, and listening to the mass she is "plunged into deep seas of ignorance, cannot follow or am averse from what I can." Repulsed by the Church, Cooper again turns to the revivifying sea: down at the Porth, "Michael and I dip hands in the ocean & ask that we may lie salted until brine & be same & great in all we do as it is. We watch the waves rush up the little stream, watch them change its current into themselves & it is changed."[46] While Cooper was still clearly opposed to the Catholic Church, Bradley had undergone something of a spiritual awakening, writing two months later to Trusted, "I want Benediction: it seems as if worship had gone out of my life," and declaring that "S. Mawgan is rapidly becoming the dearest place to me in all my dear England—except Glastonbury."[47] Bradley recalled this brief engagement with the Catholic Church some eleven years later, when, following her conversion, she wrote again to Alice Trusted, "[Y]ou took me to Benediction at S. Mawgan's. I shall always remember how you taught me what to do in the sanctuary & brought me in to breathe the sweetness there."[48] On their way home they visit Glastonbury, where Cooper, in the ruins of St. Edgar's Chapel at the site of Glastonbury Abbey, dedicates "The Masque," "asking for summer dreams."[49] It is fitting that Cooper sits in the ruins of a medieval monastery that had been ransacked in the Reformation and its abbot (Richard Whiting) hung on Glastonbury Tor, and that she prays to a god, whether Christian or pagan, for the success of a play that is an attempt to rewrite their travel experience as both Bacchic revelry and a form of mystical devotion.

"The Spirit That Is Life": *Noontide Branches*

On returning to Reigate, the two women set about composing their masque. As Cooper relates in "Works and Days," it is filled with the spirit of the places they have been: "I begin the masque—the prologue of Artemis . . . it is just holding to the pen—Devon and Cornwall and the Spirit that is life write." "The Masque grows as a watered plant—joyous magic is at our call." "The Masque grows as the roses—there is no effort in any word of it we write. Dartmouth, St Mawgan . . . all I have felt for Bernhard & feel make it grow of its nature."[50] At the end of January 1895, Cooper, after the severing letter was written to Berenson, confesses that she cannot yet write of how it has affected her: "[[I]t must come out some day in a drama."[51] It seems that *Noontide Branches* was the drama (along, arguably, with *World at Auction* [1898]) in which they would, however obliquely, explore the sense of betrayal both women, particularly Cooper, felt after their break from Berenson. It is also a text that signals the beginning of their departure from the sort of Hellenic-inspired aestheticism they had shared with Berenson and the increasing pull of Roman Catholicism.

Noontide Branches is short—one act, some forty-five pages or 1100 lines—and the poets had intended at first for it to be published in The Pageant, edited by J. W. Gleeson White and Charles Hazelwood Shannon, in which they had previously published another short drama, "Equal Love," in the second volume.[52] Yet Shannon wasn't convinced that a third volume would go ahead unless they could convince George Meredith to support and contribute to it. Meredith did not, and the drama went unpublished until 1899 when it was printed in Oxford. The delay in publication was a result of their desire to have the play printed by the Oxford don and part-time printer Henry Daniel, who was well known in literary circles for his antiquated methods and for using the Fell type, long since out of fashion. Daniel was notoriously slow, and when Michael Field convinced him to print their masque they made him guarantee that it would be published before the century was out. It was duly published in October 1899, and they were delighted with the results—it arrived just after the wedding of Amy Cooper and John Ryan on September 25: "How much more of life this is than the wedding—splendid, little Amy, if you ever read this—but how good it is to find one's happy moments in vials stored by mindful and admiring angels."[53]

On publication they sent the third copy of the drama to Alice Trusted as a memento of their time in St. Mawgan and asked her whether or not "worldly books" can enter the convent. If so they would like to send a copy to the Reverend Mother, "as the references to her convent and the addresses to Our Lady might be of interest."[54] They also sent a copy to George Meredith, who had some years earlier been deeply critical of their verse drama Attila, My Attila! (1895), of which he wrote in a letter, "If you had irony in aim you should not have made a drama."[55] But he was full of praise for Noontide Branches, writing to them "[Y]our noble stand for pure poetic literature will have its reward, but evidently you will have to wait."[56] Posterity has not been kind to Noontide Branches (or indeed to any of their verse dramas), with literary critics seemingly concurring with Charles Ricketts, who, on the publication of the play, declared, "The masque is a mistaken form no modern ought to be allowed to use—like tapestry it is wrong as a means of expressing a story, or true human qualities . . . it is one of art's failures."[57] Despite Ricketts's damning assessment of their little masque, it is, I hope to demonstrate, a work that attempts to translate the quotidian experience of travel into a dynamic commingling of the Christian with the pagan, transforming the tidal valley around St. Mawgan into a landscape of both desire and prayer.

The play is prefaced by an epigraph (in Greek) from Antiphilus of Byzantium that sets the tone: nature, the forest, can provide a refuge from that which lies without; the forest with its "closer roofing than tiles" protects pigeons and crickets, and Antiphilus asks that the same protection be extended to him. In one of the manuscript notebooks, Bradley translates the end of the epigraph as follows: "O noontide branches, protect me likewise who lie beneath your tresses, fleeing from the sun's rays."[58] The play explores this theme of the forest and nature as protection and security, most notably by giving the forest over to the stewardship of supernatural nymphs and satyrs.

Noontide Branches was originally conceived as a masque, loosely modeled on Milton's *Comus* (first performed in 1634) and suffused with pagan personae from the Virgilian pastoral. Bradley and Cooper had taken Ricketts and Shannon's Vale Press edition of Milton's *Early Poems* with them to the West Country and read to Alice Trusted the lines of Comus's opening speech: "We that are of purer fire / Imitate the Starry Quire," commenting that "they are full of Milton's complete magic—complete because every word directs vision unerringly to its aim. These lines give the life that wakes all through the night, defying sleep as no others have done."[59] The influence of *Comus*, more accurately known as *A Mask Presented at Ludlow Castle*, is clear, although how exactly Michael Field intended their masque to be read in the light of Milton's is ambiguous. The masque was a popular dramatic form in early modern England, and Milton followed Ben Jonson, Thomas Carew, and Inigo Jones, who successfully staged a number of masques in the court of Queen Anne. Yet Milton's *Comus* was far more moralistic and religious than the typical Jonsonian masque. The story is straightforward: a young woman and her two brothers are lost in a forest and the brothers leave their sister while they seek help. While waiting she is found by Comus, a Greek god of festivities and the son of Bacchus, who is determined to seduce her. She, a chaste virgin, resists, but Comus takes her to his palace where he is in the process of drugging her, when, assisted by a benevolent Attendant Spirit, her two brothers come to rescue her. In the final scene, the three are reunited with their parents in Ludlow. Milton's masque clearly venerates the chastity of the young lady, a chastity that is seemingly at odds with the Bacchic eroticism of much of Michael Field's work. Their own masque is an attempt to return feminine sexuality, a Bacchic sexuality, to the pastoral landscape of the West of England, but also to the Christian Church, in the play seemingly set in a pre-Reformation moment.

The locale of the play would seem, on the surface, to be immaterial, yet the stage directions make it clear that the play is set in "*A Woodland by a tidal river in the West of England*," and the opening speech by Artemis Dictynna, goddess of the hunt, implores her: "Cold sisterhood, / Whose vows are mine, rouse up the hern and rook / With bugle-blast that scales the thin-leaved elms, / Those dainty wands engarlanded and high / Above our Cornish haunt" (9–13).[60] A tidal river in Cornwall then becomes the location for a struggle between the pagan world of nymphs and satyrs and early Christian belief. The play revolves around two central characters: Ervan, a young man (in an earlier draft, he is more specifically a "Knight of the West Country")[61] who is in love with Lysithoë, one of the nymphs; and Genifer (in the working notes called Morwenna, after the sixth-century Cornish saint), the young woman who seemingly owns the land around the tidal river. Artemis commands her nymphs to "stablish / our right to hunt the forest as of yore," to challenge a "stranger" who "bought the countryside as mortals buy" (15–18). Genifer is disinclined toward the worship of Artemis, who likens her materialistic possession to the "Christian maids among these holy vales / Where convents hide their loneliness" (21–23). Property is then likened to the suppression of female freedom and sexuality, and defeating Genifer will see the triumph of Artemis's own "mystic ownership" of the forest. While we may expect the triumph of a pagan idea of free use, the play instead sees Ervan turning away from the beauty of Lysithoë and from the animistic world she represents; he tells Genifer,

> If these woods
> Are dear it is—at last I understand—
> It is that you, sole lady of this land
> Within the precincts of this shadowed creek
> Have drawn me to your heart.
>
> (958–63)

It is then feminine ownership and virtue that win out here, not puritanical chastity. In the notes they made in "Works and Days" on their initial ideas for the play, Bradley made it clear that Genifer was not meant to symbolize the puritanical chastity of "the Lady" in Milton's *Comus*: "She is virginal, free—no nun of chastity—love then w[oul]d be fetters."[62]

Noontide Branches then symbolizes the fusion of the Christian and of property with the pagan and stewardship. Genifer draws Ervan's attention to the music of a procession of "country maidens met to praise / Our lady of the Summer" (1003–4). The songs variously sung by the children and their mothers blend the forest deity Artemis with the Virgin Mary repeatedly. Many critics, including Ruth Vanita, have observed that the conversion of Michael Field "occasions a shift from Sapphic to Marian imagery, but the content does not alter substantially."[63] What we see in *Noontide Branches*, and consistently in "Works and Days," is that their Bacchic paganism is at no point in outright opposition to Christian theology, and their conversion might mark an intensification of their use of Catholic imagery but not its beginning. The chorus of children sings, seemingly to Artemis, "Ave, most fair / Queen of our bowers / Queen of the woodlands, and the white-thorn air," before this sylvan figure becomes Marian: "To thee we shout / As Children shouted on thy Son's highway, / And round his ass did throng" (1014–16; 1028–30). In Matthew 21:5, Jesus, it is prophesied, will come "sitting upon an ass." In the play the mothers, watching the procession of children from the chapel gate, sing praise to "Dear Mother": "When thy Belovéd being gone, / Even from thy rest, His tomb, / Thou did'st live on" (1067–69), before concluding their song:

> We bless
> Our sons, we watch them forth,
>   Not to return; and from the little path
> Hasting to thy green altar in the vale,
>   Where we can see
> The Babe for ever on thy breast,
> We say the prayers of thy sweet rosary,
>   Turn to our homes and rest.
>
>   (1073–80)

The Marian devotion is combined here with the pagan "green altar in the vale," the people of this small community having taken Christian ceremony and transplanted it into their environment. In the play the final act of transformation from pagan to Christian comes when Ervan confesses to Genifer that he has killed the satyr Dryaspis and worries that he has left "all this Sylvan folk without a god." She tells him to "be comforted" and explains how Christ brought forth the "plagued and sorrowful" "at dawn to threshold of his mother's door / Who, first embracing Him, took, for his sake, / These strangers to her heart" (1100–1103). The figure of the Blessed Virgin has embraced the lost sylvan nymphs and satyrs of the forest. The ending of *Noontide Branches* is deeply ambivalent. In Katharine Bradley's notebook draft, the play ends with Genifer observing the community leaving the church and Ervan announcing, "we instead will pass up to its altar-steps to wed."[64] This conventional ending sees Genifer drawn into a union with Ervan and he drawn from the world of the nymphs to the world of Christianity. In the published ending, we see the two lovers on the threshold, their approaching union narrated by Ervan. His final speech sees him render her silent:

And if I draw you now down to the boat,
It is that I may cross to yonder chapel
Where the good priest still lingers, wed you fast,
And by all hard, inextricable ties
Knit you my own. It is too perilous
To guard the treasure of so great a love
Till by your vows you have confirmed it mine,
O Genifer, for ever. You are dumb!

(1118–25)

Genifer's reply, and the final line of the play, is the most perplexing of submissions: "We travel where speech has no power: I come" (1126). The marriage of Genifer and Ervan is seemingly figured as an act of silencing, in which the young woman sacrifices freedom in crossing the threshold into the church. Yet there is another means of reading these final lines: Cooper and Bradley have, like Genifer, taken part in a radical form of travel that has seen them arrive in the cloistered and quiet vale of Lanherne. Members of the Carmelite Order, while not undertaking a vow of silence, are forbidden to speak from evening vespers until the completion of lauds the following morning. Silence here is part of female community and empowerment. And it is important to note that for Genifer, both she and Ervan travel to a place beyond speech, he having turned his back on the Bacchic world of the sylvan forest. If we recall that the play was meant to be a working through of their strained relationship with Berenson, we can then understand a little more the politics of having the two central characters turn their backs on the fauns of the forest. Berenson's Bacchic worldview had come to seem to the two women increasingly self-interested and hollow. In this play, they considered the politics of profanation in its manifold terms: "profane" originally meant literally "before the temple," designating things or persons that lie *outside the sacred space of the temple* and are therefore unholy or unclean. What Michael Field attempt to do in this play is to interrogate the boundaries between the sacred and the profane; to be a "profane traveler" is to explore these interstitial spaces.

Attempting to isolate a consistent cultural politics in the work of Edith Cooper and Katharine Bradley, writing as Michael Field, is a fraught enterprise: they remain notoriously erratic in their responses to people, places, and works of art. Their experience as tourists is an apposite case in point, as they attempted to negotiate what they perceived as a vulgar cultural institution while trying to remake it for their own ends. As they profaned the world of late-Victorian travel, they put it toward a new use, transforming the places they visited into vital and spiritual landscapes. Their revision of north Cornwall in *Noontide Branches* stands as testament to their practice as profane travelers who elevated a quotidian and highly codified modern experience into a Bacchic and Marian drama.

Notes

1. Michael Field, *Noontide Branches: A Small Sylvan Drama* (Oxford: Henry Daniel, 1899).

2. Michael Field, "The Lady Moon," in "For That Moment Only," Ms. Eng. Misc. d. 976, Bodleian Library, Oxford. Transcriptions from manuscript materials are all mine.

3. Michael Field, "The Lady Moon."

4. James Buzard, *The Beaten Track: European Tourism and the Ways to 'Culture,' 1800–1918* (Oxford: Clarendon Press, 1993), 5.

5. Buzard, 152.

6. Vernon Lee, *The Sentimental Traveller: Notes on Places* (London: John Lane, 1908), 4.

7. Hilary Fraser, *Women Writing Art History in the Nineteenth Century: Looking Like a Woman* (Cambridge: Cambridge University Press, 2014).

8. Michael Field, "Works and Days," BL Add MS 46778, fols. 145r–146r (1890) [K.B./E.C.].

9. W. B. Yeats, "*Sight and Song*" [1892], rpt. in *The Collected Works of W. B. Yeats*, vol. 9: *Early Articles and Reviews*, ed. John P. Fraye and Madeline Marchaterre (New York: Scribner, 2004), 167–69.

10. Michael Field, "Works and Days," BL Add MS 46781, fol. 40r (April 17, 1893) [E.C.].

11. Michael Field, Ms. Eng. Misc. g. 16, Bodleian Library, Oxford.

12. Michael Field, Ms. Eng. Misc. g. 17, Bodleian Library, Oxford.

13. Michael Field, Ms. Eng. Misc. e. 341, Bodleian Library, Oxford.

14. Michael Field, "A Traveler's Tale," in "For That Moment Only," Ms. Eng. Misc. d. 976, Bodleian Library, Oxford.

15. Michael Field, "A Faun," in "For That Moment Only," Ms. Eng. Misc. d. 976, Bodleian Library, Oxford.

16. Bradley and Cooper's complex use of the faun as a symbol has been explored in Martha Vicinus, "Faun Love: Michael Field and Bernard Berenson," *Women's History Review* 18, no. 5 (2009): 753–64.

17. Michael Field, "A Maenad," in "For That Moment Only," Ms. Eng. Misc. d. 976, Bodleian Library, Oxford, fols. 15–16.

18. Michael Field, "A Maenad."

19. Euripides, *Bacchae and Other Plays*, trans. and ed. James Morwood (Oxford: Oxford University Press, 2008), 78–79.

20. Nicola J. Watson, *The Literary Tourist: Readers and Places in Romantic and Victorian Britain* (Basingstoke, UK: Palgrave Macmillan, 2006), 11.

21. Watson, 170.

22. William Sharp, *Literary Geographies* (London: Pall Mall Publications, 1905), vi.

23. Thomas Cook, as quoted in Ann Rigney, *The Afterlives of Walter Scott: Memory on the Move* (Oxford: Oxford University Press, 2012), 135.

24. Rigney, *Afterlives of Walter Scott*, 152.

25. Andrea Zemgulys, *Modernism and the Locations of Literary Heritage* (Cambridge: Cambirdge University Press, 2008), 26. Alexis Easley offers a cognate exploration of the gendered nature of celebrity culture during the period in her *Literary Celebrity, Gender, and Victorian Authorship, 1850–1914* (Newark: University of Delaware Press, 2011).

26. Marion Harland, *Where Ghosts Walk: The Haunts of Familiar Characters in History and Literature* (New York: G. P. Putnam's, 1898), 21.

27. Michael Field, "Works and Days," BL Add MS 46782, fol. 122v (September 10, 1894) [E.C.].

28. Michael Field, "Works and Days," BL Add MS 46783, fols. 131r–142r (August–September 1895) [K.B./E.C.].

29. Michael Field, "Works and Days," BL Add MS 46783, fols. 141r–v (September 8, 1895) [K.B.].

30. Michael Field, "Works and Days," BL Add MS 46783, fol. 150r (September 10, 1895) [E.C.].

31. Michael Field, "Works and Days," BL Add MS 46782, fol. 118v (September 8, 1894) [E.C.].

32. Michael Field, "Incongruity," in "For That Moment Only," Ms. Eng. Misc. d. 976, Bodleian Library, Oxford.

33. Michael Field, "Works and Days," BL Add MS 46782, fol. 116v (September 7, 1894) [E.C.].

34. Stefano Evangelista, *British Aestheticism and Ancient Greece: Hellenism, Reception, Gods in Exile* (Basingstoke, UK: Palgrave Macmilllan, 2009), 121.

35. Michael Field, "Works and Days," BL Add MS 46784, fol. 4v (October 19, 1895) [E.C.].

36. Wilkie Collins, *Rambles beyond Railways; or, Notes in Cornwall Taken A-Foot* (London: Richard Bentley, 1852), 3.

37. Katharine Bradley to Edith Cooper, Alice Trusted Collection, BL Add MS 84073 (November 20, 1894).

38. Michael Field, "Works and Days," BL Add MS 46785, fols. 66r–v (May 5, 1896) [E.C.].

39. Sarah Parker, *The Lesbian Muse and Poetic Identity, 1889–1930* (London: Pickering and Chatto, 2013), 43–70.

40. Walter Pater, *The Renaissance: Studies in Art and Poetry* [1893], ed. Donald Hill (Berkeley: University of California Press, 1980), 174.

41. Michael Field, "Works and Days," BL Add MS 46785, fols. 69r–70v (May 3, 1896) [E.C.].

42. Marion Thain, *Michael Field: Poetry, Aestheticism and the Fin de Siècle* (Cambridge: Cambridge University Press, 2007), 130–67.

43. Michael Field, "Works and Days," BL Add MS 46785, fol. 74v (May 14, 1896) [E.C.].

44. John Henry (Cardinal) Newman, *Meditations and Devotions* (London: Longmans, Green & Co., 1893), 1.

45. Michael Field, "Works and Days," BL Add MS 46785, fol. 86r (May 17, 1896) [K.B.].

46. Michael Field, "Works and Days," BL Add MS 46785, fol. 85r (May 17, 1896) [E.C.].

47. Katharine Bradley to Alice Trusted, Alice Trusted Collection, BL Add MS 84073 (June 15, 1896).

48. Katharine Bradley to Alice Trusted, Alice Trusted Collection, BL Add MS 84075 (June/July 1907).

49. Michael Field, "Works and Days," BL Add MS 46785, fol. 89r (May 21, 1896) [E.C.].

50. Michael Field, "Works and Days," BL Add MS 46785, fol. 92r (June 7, 1896) [E.C.].

51. Michael Field, "Works and Days," BL Add MS 46783, fol. 13v (January 28, 1895) [E.C.].

52. Michael Field, "Equal Love," in *The Pageant* II (London: Henry and Co., 1897): 189–228.

53. Michael Field, "Works and Days," BL Add MS 46788, fol. 105r (October 3, 1899) [K.B.].

54. Katharine Bradley to Alice Trusted, Alice Trusted Papers, BL Add MS 84074 (October 3, 1899).

55. George Meredith, "To Michael Field, November 28, 1895," in *The Letters of George Meredith*, ed. C. L. Cline, vol. 3 (Oxford: Oxford University Press, 1970), 1214.

56. George Meredith, "To Michael Field, November 16, 1899," in *Letters of George Meredith*, 1341.

57. Charles Ricketts to Michael Field, "Works and Days," BL Add MS 46788, fol.106r (October 8, 1899) [E.C.].

58. Michael Field, Mss. Eng. Poet. e. 83, Bodleian Library, Oxford [K.B.].

59. Michael Field, "Works and Days," BL Add MS 46785, fol. 70r (May 16, 1896) [E.C.].

60. Michael Field, *Noontide Branches*. This and all subsequent quotations are given with line numbers parenthetically.

61. Michael Field, Mss. Eng. Poet. e. 83, Bodleian Library, Oxford.

62. Michael Field, "Works and Days," BL Add MS 46785, fol. 98r (June 27, 1896) [K.B.].

63. Ruth Vanita, *Sappho and the Virgin Mary: Same-Sex Love and the English Literary Imagination* (New York: Columbia University Press, 1996), 133.

64. Michael Field, Mss. Eng. Poet. e. 83, Bodleian Library, Oxford [K.B.].

EIGHT

"Thy Body Maketh a Solemn Song"

Desire and Disability in Michael Field's "Catholic Poems"

JILL R. EHNENN

"HE DETESTS RELIGIOUS POETRY . . . AND HE BREAKS INTO A
frenzy about the psalms, Verlaine's 'Catholic work,' and *Poems of Adoration*. He
[would] not know I had written it. [He says] there is nothing in it like me."[1] Thus,
with unfiltered bitterness, writes Edith Cooper on May 8, 1912, after a visit from
Michael Field's close friend and fellow aesthete, Charles Ricketts. Indeed, in listening both to students and fellow literary scholars, I have observed that for many
readers first encountering Michael Field's Catholic poems, their response is much
the same as Ricketts's. Readers tend not to like the Catholic poems, and their
negativity is often articulated in a tone of disappointment, exasperation, and even
betrayal. At least on a surface reading, *Poems of Adoration* (1912), written largely by
Cooper, and *Mystic Trees* (1913), written largely by her longtime coauthor and life
partner, Katharine Bradley, seem to lack many of the elements—sexy sapphics,
playful fauns, witty commentary on art, love poems filled with longing—that
have long drawn literary critics and other readers to Michael Field's earlier verse.
Their Catholic poems do not seem to touch modern readers in the way that the
devotional verse of Christina Rossetti or Gerard Manley Hopkins continues to
do. Perhaps it should not be a surprise that *Poems of Adoration* and *Mystic Trees*
have remained relatively unstudied compared to other Michael Field texts.[2]

This chapter begins by asserting that Michael Field's devotional verses
should not, in fact, be so quickly categorized as anomalies. Here, I build upon

the observations of Hilary Fraser and Marion Thain, who each argue that *Poems of Adoration* and *Mystic Trees* possess many elements also found in Michael Field's earlier poetry—that they represent a shift, rather than a radical departure, from Michael Field's other writing. My work in this chapter considers *Poems of Adoration* and *Mystic Trees* in the context of Michael Field's other revisionary experiments in genre and form, such as *Long Ago* (1889), which creatively engages the traditions of Sapphic verse; the innovative picture-poems of *Sight and Song* (1892); *Underneath the Bough* (1893), which draws upon Renaissance songbooks; and two verse collections that experiment with elegy: the "Longer Allegiance" cycle from *Wild Honey* (1908) and *Whym Chow, Flame of Love* (1914). Beyond defense or apologia, however, my aim in this chapter is to advance three claims.

First, through close readings of selected verse from *Poems of Adoration* and *Mystic Trees*, I demonstrate how Michael Field sought to become *Catholic* poets by appropriating the formal, including metric, conventions of devotional poetics while also maintaining many of the queer characteristics of their earlier work; in terms of meter, these queer characteristics manifest themselves in shifting, ambiguous metrics that resonate with today's thinking about queer temporality. Second, by drawing upon recent insights from disability studies,[3] as well as my own previous claims that characterize Michael Field's ongoing revisionary projects as possessing qualities we today call both queer and feminist,[4] I argue that Michael Field's Catholic verses articulate spiritual and homoerotic love and desire specifically in the context of being, seeing, and desiring an embodied (female) subject in pain. Third and throughout, my approach to *Poems of Adoration* and *Mystic Trees* is *not* to categorize them as postconversion texts posited against preconversion texts. Instead, I argue here that a more useful and interesting shift can be observed among the poems before and after Cooper's diagnosis of bowel cancer in February 1911.

Becoming "Catholic," Remaining "Michael Field"

Studies of *Poems of Adoration* and *Mystic Trees* do not fail to note that, unlike Michael Field's other work, the coauthors were quite frank about the fact that Cooper wrote most of *Poems of Adoration* and Bradley wrote most of *Mystic Trees*.[5] Therefore, some foundational remarks on the authorship and organization of these two volumes perhaps are warranted before proceeding. First, as critics have often argued, Michael Field's claims to likeness, joint authorship, and shared subjectivity were always to a certain extent strategic and, by early critics, over-emphasized and romanticized.[6] Bradley and Cooper wrote in separate rooms and then edited one another's work, sometimes delegating to each other responsibility for different characters or scenes. This process was not radically altered for these two devotional collections. Primary sources make clear that the books were written individually, yet Bradley and Cooper edited and ordered them collaboratively, and each felt more than a small degree of joint responsibility for both. For instance, on March 8, 1913, Cooper wrote to Father John Gray about "Bradley's" book: "I am getting anxious about 'Mystic Trees'—for lately there has been reconsiderence of my malady and much pain; and I always grow yearning and desirous for the work to be over."[7] Although Cooper is ill and technically not the author of *Mystic Trees*, "the work" belongs to Michael Field and thus is a matter demanding Cooper's attention as well as Bradley's.

As with all their books of verse, the poems in each of the two Catholic collections are not ordered by date of composition, and the organizational structure of each volume is complex. *Poems of Adoration* is a series of verse meditations on the embodied experience of celebrating several of the Catholic sacraments, including devotional reflection in anticipation of Mass, contemplation of saints and religious doctrines after receiving the Eucharist, and meditations after receiving last rites. As for *Mystic Trees*, its first two divisions ("Hyssop" and "Cedar") correspond to the volume's epigraph—one that designates the Virgin Mary and Christ as the two mystic trees:

Hic Virgo Puerpera,	This Virgin mother
Hic Crux salutifera:	This saving Cross:
Ambo ligna mystica	Both mystic trees
Haec hyssopus humilis	This humble hyssop
Illa cedrus nobilis	The noble cedar
Utraque vivifica.	Both quicken [revive].[8]

Notably, a sequential reading of the people and trees alluded to in the epigraph (Virgin, Cross; hyssop, cedar) misleadingly suggests that "Hyssop" (an aromatic plant used for various medicinal purposes) will be a section dedicated to Mary and that "Cedar" (as in the wood of the cross) will be about Christ. Only when meticulous readers work through the volume do they gradually realize that the identity of the mystic trees is foreshadowed in the chiasmatic relation between the epigraph's lines 1–2 and 4–5. The first section of *Mystic Trees*, "Hyssop," is not about the Virgin Mary; instead, "Hyssop" presents a roughly chronological biography of Christ, calling to mind Christ's saving grace via Psalm 51: "Thou shalt purge me with hyssop and I shall be clean." The "Cedar" section then provides a similarly chronological account of the Virgin Mary's life and especially resonates with her contemplations of Christ on the wooden cross. After "Cedar," the third section of *Mystic Trees* is titled "Sward," which means a stretch of grassy turf. "Sward" is, with some exception, a collection of verses contemplating nature, various saints' lives, and other devotional topics inspiring the pleasant sensation of religious solace, perhaps like walking on grass. The poems in the brief, final section, "A Little While," illustrate that the faithful devotee of the two mystic trees (presumably the ailing Cooper) will, like Christ and Mary themselves, vanquish Death.

The poems composed prior to Cooper's cancer diagnosis can firmly be described as efforts and experiments in how to be devotional poets, writing about Catholic topics. Typical of Bradley and Cooper's obsessive tendencies when working on new subjects, especially historical events and people, in *Poems of Adoration* and *Mystic Trees* we observe the coauthors attempting to master a genre by meticulously depicting events (sacraments) and characters: Christ, the Virgin Mary, and Mary Magdalene in both collections; St. John the Divine, St. Clement, and Simeon among others in *Poems of Adoration*; and Joachim and Anna, St. Agnes, and Fr. Vincent McNabb among others in *Mystic Trees*. In the remainder of this section, I examine how Michael Field experiment with Catholic topics within and against nineteenth-century prescriptions about devotional poetics but also alongside various formal and stylistic techniques familiar to readers of their earlier queer, feminist, aesthetic work. As the second half of this study shows, it is not until Cooper's cancer diagnosis in 1911 that we see Michael Field's devotional verse shifting from the worship of Catholic figures to identifying with them—a shift in relationship and orientation nuanced by the poets' personal experiences with disability, illness, and pain.[9]

Victorian devotional verse, according to F. Elizabeth Gray, often portrays one's struggle with oneself through tropes of confession, petition, praise, and meditation. From early nineteenth-century verse collections (such as John Keble's extraordinarily popular *The Christian Year* [1827]), through to the end of the century, Tractarian poetics emphasized feeling and perception, favoring characteristics such as poetic orthodoxy, correctness, and a concept called "Reserve," which can be defined as proper reverence for sacred matters that involved suggestion yet restraint in representing religious knowledge and the mysteries of faith.[10] As Gray observes, "appropriate subject matter, according to Keble, was to be found in the moral lessons taught by Nature (through the process Keble called Analogy) and in the emotional responses of the religious and sincere heart."[11] Perhaps rather surprisingly, there does not appear to be evidence in Britain of a nineteenth-century (Roman) Catholic poetics that differs significantly from Anglo-Catholic, Tractarian poetics. As Kirstie Blair writes, "Anglo-Catholicism and Roman Catholicism may have had significant theological and doctrinal differences, but on the general question of forms they were united."[12] Devotional styles differ significantly, of course (Hopkins from Rossetti, Field from Patmore, etc.), but these differences are due to individual temperament rather than to a generalized poetic sensibility informed by theology.[13] Thus Tractarian instruction for how to create Anglo-Catholic devotional verse is also apropos to nineteenth-century (Roman) Catholics writing devotional verse.[14] Indeed, many characteristics of Tractarian devotional poetry, especially depicting nature for the greater purpose of Keble's "Analogy," can be found in Michael Field's exercises in writing Catholic verse.

For instance, in "Thou Comest Down to Die" composed in 1910, human spiritual joy finds its analogue in the beauty and spontaneity of natural animal actions:

> Each day another girds
> And binds Thee to the Wood.
> I sing as singing birds,
> The glory of Thy mood.[15]

Similarly, "O Lovely Host," also composed in 1910, draws a comparison between Christ and the desert rose:

> I
> O lovely Host
> Thou art the Rose
> That on us from the desert glows!
>
> II
> Thou art the Flower
> Beloved so
> Beyond all other flowers that blow.[16]

Such worshipful interaction with the natural world and finding spiritual/philosophical insight in the environment is not, as we know, new to Michael Field. For example, the images and allusions in "A Cette Heure Où J'ecris," [At this time where I write] create an apt example of analogy in a manner that also resonates with well-known themes from their earlier work:

> On the other side the road
> Facing this our little parlour, glowed
> Over by a murderous sun,
> Is a hedge of holly deep, stone-dun:
> And this hedge is as a leathern targe
> Reared between us, and the open, large
> Fields of mustered sunshine on the plain[17]

Here, in the first half of a modified sonnet composed in 1911, we see a struggle wherein a stalwart neighborhood holly bush protects a domestic space—Bradley and Cooper's "little parlour"—from the "murderous sun." Using a typically Michaelian archaism, the hedge is described as a leather "targe" or target, but it also "rears up" like a horse in battle against the troops "mustered" on the other side and ready to attack. As the second half of this modified Italian sonnet concludes, the stakes become higher as the battle between the natural elements calls to mind for the Michaels the ongoing battle between the Trinity and the Devil:

> Holy Trinity, against the strain
> Of the Devil, and his demon spite
> Twinkling on the fainted anchorite,
> Thou the holy Office dost provide—
> Buckler of impenetrable hide:
> Faithful in its shadow we abide,
> And of God, our God, are sanctified.[18]

In this poem's second half, the archaism of the "targe" continues its work. The holly hedge is shown to be both holy and holey, as it performs the sacred labor of protecting the "fainted anchorite" (presumably Cooper) from the demonic efforts of the "spite[ful]" sun, which the chinks in the hedge reduce to mere "twinkling." The word "anchorite" also has the effect of rendering the embowered, modern, aesthetic space of the Field's parlor now a different kind of enclosure: one for abiding faithfully in the shadows, perhaps more prayerfully and less pridefully than before. Notably, by the poem's end the solitary anchorite has become the familiar doubled "we" of Michael Field. Meanwhile, the hedge's stone-dun "Buckler of impenetrable hide" calls to mind a more modest and retiring version, for these two holy virgins, of how Arnold's "Sea of Faith / . . . at the full, and round earth's shore / Lay like the folds of a bright girdle furled" in "Dover Beach."[19] This buckler is more enduring, however, than Arnold's girdle; and thus their observations about the holly bush that shields their home from the sun becomes a meditation on how, for Bradley and Cooper (if not for Arnold), God protects the faithful from all evil. Granted, in Michael Field's oeuvre they frequently represent themselves as sanctified, set apart, such as the oath to dwell "Indifferent to heaven and hell" in "It Was Deep April" and how "The Poet" is "a work of some strange passion / Life has conceived apart from Times harsh drill // . . . / Holy and foolish, ever set apart."[20] Yet, here in "A Cette Heure Où J'ecris," what motivates Michael Field's quiet seclusion is not the world's disapproval but their faith: "of God, our God, we are sanctified."[21] Each of the above examples is typical of devotional verse that sets forth a poetic meditation on a natural scene.

The point for Tractarian doctrine, as described by Joshua King, is that analogies to spiritual mysteries can be glimpsed everywhere in the world. In other words, in devotional verse, literary deployment of metaphor and simile takes on added weight, just as Nature, by analogy, teaches the Christian with an open heart.

In addition to the depiction of nature in the service of analogy, Keble praised the effect of metrically composed language, which functions as a mode of reserve by "regulating, and thereby mitigating, the expression of feeling."[22] He advocated that meter could provide some clue to "guide [poets] amid a thousand paths to take the right, and this clue, as everyone can see, scansion and measure, simply in themselves, are well able to supply."[23] Like for Bradley and Cooper, who over the years frequently described their creative ideas as "coming to them" as if from outside themselves, for Keble, "poets do not choose metrical form, they are 'naturally' directed to it; but since nature is a form of divinity, the ultimate arbiter of form is always God's will."[24] In keeping with tenets of Anglo-Catholic poetics, much of Michael Field's devotional verse features metrical virtuosity that reinforces their theological engagement with the natural world and their newly discovered religious thoughts and feelings.

Take for example, the 1908 "Fregit" (He broke) from *Poems of Adoration*, where Christ breaking the Host is brought to mind by observing familiar phenomena like picking fresh blooms, dropping a vase, and the strike of lightning, which are conveyed in "Fregit" through these natural images and also via meter:

> On the night of dedication
> Of Thyself as our oblation
> Christ, Belovèd, Thou didst take
> In Thy very hands and break. . . .
> O Christ there is a hiss of doom
> When new-glowing flowers are snapt in bloom
> When shivered, as a little thunder cloud
> A vase splits on the floor its brilliance loud;
> Or lightning strikes a willow-tree with a gash
> Cloven for death in a resounded crash.[25]

Here, the trochaic tetrameter's regularity in the first four lines conveys the inevitability of Christ's sacrifice, while the catalexis of lines 3 and 4 portends that something momentous is about to occur. In contrast, the jawbreaking extra syllables of the next lines combine with the alliterative emphasis of the "snap," "shiver," "split," and "strike" of each of the broken items. These breakages, as the poem unfolds and returns to trochaic tetrameter catalectic, call to mind both Judas's break of trust and Christ's (symbolic and real) broken body:

> Thou, betrayed, Thyself did break
> Thy own body for our sake:
> Thy own body Thou didst take
> In Thy holy hands—and break.[26]

Meanwhile, where meter, aural sensation, and vibrant imagery convey how shocking it can be even when relatively common things break, the final four lines' repetition of "Thy's" and "Thou's" emphasize the divine mystery and tremendous self-sacrifice of Christ's breaking of transubstantiated bread and His subsequent Passion.

In addition to analogy and strict attention of meter, Victorian devotional poetry is also characterized by paradox and contradictory positions; and, of course, much has been made of Michael Field's aesthetic use of paradox throughout their career, beginning with the paradox of their dual identity and their logos of the early bramble-bough and the later pagan/Christian thyrsus interlaced with rings. In 1886, Cooper emphasizes paradox in explaining to Robert Browning how Bradley composed a poem about "the bramble-bough the emblem of our united life:

> My poet-bride, sweet songmate do I doom
> Thy youth to age's dull society?
> On the same bramble-bough the pale-cheeked bloom
> Fondling by purple berry loves to lie;
> Fed by one September sunshine, there is room
> For fruit and flower in living unity.

> When we adopted this as our symbol [Cooper writes to
> Browning], my father carved the berried and flowery sprays over
> our mantelshelf and we have them on our study-chair also.[27]

As I have previously discussed, the bramble-bough symbol transforms Bradley and Cooper's age difference into an aesthetic woodcarving that comes to adorn both their home and several of their publications.[28] The bramble-bough's bloom and berry grow on the same vine, under the same sun. In this brief poem, it is the aesthetic contrast and paradoxical coexistence of the "pale-cheeked bloom" and "purple berry" that justify the song mates' intellectual, emotional, and erotic attraction to one another. The similarly paradoxical "Stream and Pool" from the American version of *Underneath the Bough* (1898) likewise advances an erotics of difference-within-union:

> Mine is the eddying foam and the broken current
> Thine the serene-flowing tide, the unscattered rhythm

Light touches me on the surface with glints of sunshine
Dives in thy bosom, disclosing a mystic river
. . .
What is my song but the tumult of chafing forces
What is thy silence, Beloved, but enchanted music?[29]

Here Michael Field portrays the play of light upon a river, exploring impossible, paradoxical questions: Is there a real difference between foam and current? Where does the glint of light end and the water begin?[30]

Marion Thain finds comparable contradictions and paradoxes in Michael Field's religious poetry: "the fluidity of a poetic identity that interlaces past and present, as well as self and lover, to create a personal mythology."[31] As Hilary Fraser also observes, aesthetic paradox, especially of Christian and pagan intertextuality, provides just one of many continuities between the Catholic poems and Michael Field's earlier work. For example, the aforementioned "Thou Comest Down to Die" (1910) from *Mystic Trees* juxtaposes Christ with a classical figure:

> How beautiful Thy feet
> Even as Hermes' are
> That Thou shouldst run so fleet
> To Golgotha![32]

"White Passion-Flower," from *Mystic Trees*, first composed in 1909, provides another striking devotional experiment in aesthetic paradox. Here an all-white passionflower inspires the speaker's meditation on the absence and presence of color, which leads to contemplation of Christ's Passion:

> I
> White exceeding is the passion-flower,
> When it rayeth and extendeth white.
> Where is the purple thorn,
> Or the robe that He hath worn?
> Where are the Wounds? From the waxen flower
> The virulence is drawn, the power.
>
> II
> Dark exceeding is the passion-flower,
> When it rayeth and extendeth, dark,
> The passion intricate
> Of a God in man's debate:
> We beheld the Wounds, the Blood is red,
> And the dark Blood gathers round His head.

III
Lovely, waxen flower, I am content
With your whiteness of the firmament:
Even as in the Host
The Precious Blood is lost,
On your unblooded disk I see
How the Lord is dying on Calvary.[33]

In this poem, the speaker admires the white cultivar while simultaneously think-ing of the more common species with the purple ring and the religious symbols generally associated with it. Paradoxically, although the contrast between white and purple is great, and although light and dark generally symbolize quite differ-ent things in literature, here both the white (present) and purple (absent) flowers create the same effect: they "rayeth and extendeth," touching the devout heart and inviting the religious mind to contemplate Christ's wounds at the moment of His death. The white passionflower seems to help the speaker apprehend that, seen or unseen, Christ is always present, always sacrificing, always dying for the faithful believer. As the third stanza moves from the white flower to the white altar host, the paradoxical play of a string of absences and presences intensifies: the poem's flower becomes the Host; for Catholics, Christ is present in the Host as bread becomes body; in the holy Body of the Host there is no blood ("The Precious Blood is lost"), yet at the same time the Host serves to remind the faith-ful how "the Precious Blood [was] lost" for their sake (Do this in remembrance of me). And finally, as the last lines of the poem return to the pure white of both the flower and the Host, the poem's overarching message is reiterated: the body of Christ need not be present in order to experience his Presence, just as the speaker claims, "on your unblooded disk I see / How the Lord is dying on Calvary."

Adoration of the crucified Christ, of course, is an enduring and often eroticized feature of devotional poetry, and many critics have made similar argu-ments about the homoerotics of *Sight and Song*'s representations of St. Sebastian, especially in the context of the many homoerotically inclined men in Michael Field's circle of aesthetes.[34] Such observations take on a particularly lesbian con-notation in "A Crucifix," an ekphrastic poem written in 1909 about a crucifix that Bradley gave to Cooper:

I
Thee such loveliness adorns
On Thy Cross, O my Desire—
As a lily Thou art among thorns,
As a rose lies back against his briar.

II

Thou art as a fair, green shoot,
That along the wall doth run;
Thou art as a welcoming open fruit,
Stretched forth to the glory of the sun.

III

Thou art still as one in sleep,
As the blood that Thou dost shed;
Thou art as a precious coral-reef
That scarce lifteth himself from his bed.

IV

Thy limbs are so fine, so long,
'Mid the cords and nails that bind,
Thy body maketh a solemn song,
As a stream in a gorge confined.[35]

Devotional and homoerotic desire become intertwined in this poem, with contrasting images in the first stanza that perhaps recall the earlier Michaelian bramble-bough. Reclining floral images give way to the more vulvular conceit of the "welcoming opening fruit" in the second stanza; meanwhile, the movement of the second stanza contrasts the stillness of the first and third. Cooper's willowy form seems to haunt Bradley's admiration of Christ's feminine limbs, "so fine, so long" in the final stanza, especially as the speaker declares that "Thy body maketh a solemn song" in the streaming and feminine genital gorge—a speaker, one remembers, who often referred to her fellow poet-lover as her song mate.

But let us return to Michael Field's prowess with metrics, for there is much more to say about the queer sounds of this song, or poem, confined in the gorge. As in their earlier verse queering ekphrasis and elegy, in this devotional poem (among others) we see how innovative Michael Field's experimentations with form can be. Just as Bradley and Cooper eagerly sought to learn Catholic ritual while also arguing with their confessors and bending the rules,[36] we see in "A Crucifix" how Michael Field eschew Keble's prescription about divinely inspired strict meter. As talented metrists, they indubitably attend to their metrics in *Poems of Adoration* and *Mystic Trees*; but in "A Crucifix," instead of self-constraint and reserve, they employ restless, shifting, and downright ambiguous verse forms. Are the first two seven-syllable lines of each stanza primarily trochaic? Or are they mixed anapests and iambs? If trochees, the mood is heavier and plodding and emphasizes each stanza's initial Thee, Thous, and Thys (lines 1, 5,

9, and 13) and thereby the person (Christ/Cooper) who is the object of the gaze. If anapests and iambs, the mood is much lighter, emphasizing the particular aesthetic and/or sensual embodied qualities that the speaker finds worthy of adoration and thereby privileging the natural, feminine imagery of the fair green shoot and the stream in the gorge over the blood, cord, and nails.

Trochaic reading of the first two lines of each stanza (stress in bold):	Iambic reading of the first two lines of each stanza (stress in bold):
Thee such **love** li **ness** a **dorns**	Thee **such** love li **ness** a **dorns**
On Thy **Cross**, **O** my De **sire**—	On Thy **Cross**, **O** my De **sire**—
	(lines 1–2)
Thou art **as** a **fair**, **green shoot**,	Thou **art** as a **fair**, green **shoot**,
That a **long** the **wall** doth **run**;	That a **long** the **wall** doth **run**;
	(lines 5–6)
Thou art **still** as **one** in **sleep**,	Thou **art** still as **one** in **sleep**,
As the **blood** that **Thou** dost **shed**;	As the **blood** that **Thou** dost **shed**;
	(lines 9–10)
Thy limbs **are** so **fine**, so **long**,	Thy **limbs** are so **fine**, so **long**,
'Mid the **cords** and **nails** that **bind**,	'Mid the **cords** and **nails** that **bind**,
	(lines 13–14)

Either way, the last two lines of stanzas one and three necessitate a certain awkwardness and inventiveness in reading aloud their beautiful natural images that so strikingly contrast the lines about the cross and blood that they follow. It is very difficult to pin down the meter of "As a lily Thou art among thorns, / As a rose lies back against his briar" (lines 3–4) and "Thou art as a precious coral-reef / That scarce lifteth himself from his bed" (lines 11–12). It is only the last two lines of stanzas two and four—the ones most suggestive of lesbian erotics—that most easily and unambiguously trip off the tongue in this poem inspired by a gift from one song mate to another.

> Thou **art** as a **wel** com ing **o** pen **fruit**,
> Stretched **forth** to the **glo** ry of the **sun**. (lines 7–8)

> Thy **bo** dy **ma** keth a **so** lemn **song**,
> As a **stream** in a **gorge** con **fined**. (lines 15–16)

The metrical shifts and pauses and ambiguities in these verses reveal the homoeroticism otherwise concealed within; they also provide yet another way to think about what Kate Thomas terms "Michael Field's queer temporalities."

In addition to her arguments about their intergenerational relationship, their obsession with historical figures, and the fact that they believed they have always been and always will be "out of time," the asymptotic wobble in the metrics of Michael Field's Catholic poems offers another example of "that queer sense of being out of sync."[37]

In sum, in this section I have argued that the devotional poems written before 1911 illustrate Bradley and Cooper's formal efforts to become Catholic poets not only in their choice of subject matter but also in their use of analogy, paradox, particular emphasis on the crucified body of Christ, and attention to meter. Yet, in deploying the formal characteristics of devotional poetics, Michael Field's religious verse also reveals their long-standing poetic engagement with nature and aestheticism, homoeroticism and queer temporality. As the next section shows, the poets' task of becoming-Catholic becomes markedly more complicated when their negotiations of nature, art, and religion, body, spirit, and time also become negotiations with disabled embodiment and pain.

Desiring Disability

Although Cooper, much more so than hearty Bradley, was no stranger to illness and in fact had often been ill over their years together, her diagnosis of bowel cancer in early February 1911 brought many changes to their intersubjective relationship, as well as their relationship to the physical body, to spirituality, and to writing. A phenomenological approach provides an apt lens for analyzing these changes, especially the work of Sara Ahmed, who, following Merleau-Ponty, locates subjectivity not in the mind but in the body as it is oriented in space. Phenomenology helps us recognize that experience is the embodied engagement of subjects with their world and also helps us understand subjectivity as located in the body, as it is oriented to other subjects and objects in the world.[38] As Nirmala Erevelles asserts, "[T]he phenomenological argument—that the body is not just an objective, exterior, institutionalized body . . . but is rather a living, animated, experiencing body . . . is especially useful in the representation of the embodied experiences of people diagnosed with cancer."[39] Michael Field's life writing and poetry in their final years depicts a new kind of intimate boundary crossing for the poet-lovers, a relational corporeality focused upon Cooper's body—always the beloved subject of Bradley's gaze, always luminous and frail, but now increasingly a conduit for theological considerations, now struggling to walk to church, and ultimately confined to writing in bed. The shifting role of Cooper's body provides an example of how "all bodies are in a constant state of renewal and adjustment in changing physical and environmental contexts, making the body intensely aware, not just of its be-ing but also of its becoming-in-the-world."[40] These ideas, combined with Ahmed's assertions about the importance of bodily orientation, guide the work of the remainder of this chapter. In this section I explore how their devotional verse and related diaries and letters demonstrate how Bradley and Cooper shift from being embodied queer subjects oriented toward "becoming Catholic" to being embodied queer subjects in physical pain and emotional distress, oriented toward both God and Cooper's chronic and ultimately fatal illness.

In *Fictions of Affliction: Physical Disability in Victorian Culture* (2004), Martha Stoddard Holmes identifies, in the nineteenth century, a melodramatic mode of representing disability; one popular trope is the ailing woman whose physical weakness begets increased spiritual insight, such as *Jane Eyre*'s Helen Burns on her deathbed. To a certain extent, this mode characterizes many of the journal and epistolary representations of Cooper as she suffers the ravages of her cancer. But the Catholic poems composed during and after 1911 differ from this melodramatic mode. In the devotional poetry from Cooper's cancer years, Michael Field's engagement with disability blends those homoerotic elements so familiar to readers of their earlier works with qualities that, "out of time," anticipate current discussions in disability studies about desiring disability and queer, crip futures.[41]

In their critiques of both compulsory heterosexuality and compulsory able-bodiedness, Robert McRuer, Abby Wilkerson, and Alison Kafer each contemplate the place of queerness and disability in thinking about the future, and, contra seeing queerness and disability as "no future," posit a crip futurity where queerness and disability are seen as valuable, integral, and desirable.[42] Contrary to the medical/individual model, where disability is a problem to be solved, and also contrary to the social model, where disability "is seen less as an objective fact of the body or mind than a product of social relation," Kafer posits a "hybrid political/relational mode of disability that does not erase the lived realities of impairment, and that acknowledges how disability is not experienced in isolation; but in and through relationships."[43] This model is quite useful for considering Michael Field's devotional poetry after 1911, in which one can observe their shift from largely technical experiments about Christian figures and themes to much more personal identification with Christ and Mary.

After the initial grief and shock of the news of her cancer, Cooper writes in "Works and Days" and also to Father John Gray: "Fiat, voluntas tua [Thy will be done]."[44] At this time, both Bradley and Cooper can be seen to identify, through their Catholic verse, with Christ, who through His Passion also said those words. Although Cooper's pain is certainly a problem and they both pray for its respite, and although they both want to prolong her life because they don't wish to part, neither desires a miraculous "cure" for Cooper; neither wishes for her to return to a normate body. Instead, Cooper perceives her suffering as martyrdom and as a way to become closer to God. Identifying with the suffering Christ and other suffering male saints is a way to aestheticize her pain and to do so within a homoerotic context. Take, for example, Cooper's erotic, embodied praise of the "Holy Cross" written in 1912 and published in *Poems of Adoration*:

> Mysterious sway of mortal blood,
> That urges me upon Thy wood!—
> O Holy Cross, but I must tell
> My love; how all my forces dwell
> Upon Thee and around Thee day and night!
> I love the Feet upon thy beam,
> As a wild lover loves his dream;
> My eyes can only fix upon that sight.
>
> O Tree, my arms are strong and sore
> To clasp Thee, as when we adore
> The body of our dearest in our arms!
> Each pang I suffer hath for aim
> Thy wood—its comfort is the same—
> A taint, an odour from inveterate balms.
>
> My clasp is filled, my sight receives
> The compass of its power; pain grieves
> About each sense but as a languid hum:
> And, out of weariness, at length,
> My day rejoices in its strength,
> My night that innocence of strife is come.[45]

Here, with passion that eschews the doctrine of Reserve, the speaker both beholds and *is* the suffering body. As the speaker worships the crucifix, identifies with Christ's pain, imagines embracing the body of Christ-the-lover, and aspires to share His fate, multiple senses are activated: there is a comforting aroma of "inveterate balms," and the "languid hum" of constant physical pain paradoxically blurs the boundary between touch and sound. Although vision is mentioned, the poem does not dwell clearly on what is seen, which reiterates Cooper's physical and spiritual identification with the suffering Christ but also reflects the practical reality that while in an close embrace it is difficult to see "The body of our dearest in our arms."

In contrast to "Holy Cross" is Bradley's much more insistently visual 1913 "The Captain Jewel" from *Mystic Trees*. According to "Works and Days," these two are companion pieces:[46]

> We love Thy ruddy Wounds,
> We love them pout by pout:
> It is as when the stars come out,
> One after one—
> We are
> As watchers for the Morning Star.
>
> The jewels of Thy Feet,
> The jewels of Thy Hands!...
> Lo, a Centurion stands,
> Openeth Thy Side: Water and Blood there beat
> In fountain sweet:
> Our Master-jewel now we dote upon![47]

Here, in a more strongly erotic and aestheticized conceit of pouting wounds as jewels, Bradley, who writes often of watching Cooper's body in pain, also compares this act of looking to watching for the Morning Star or Venus, goddess of Love. In both "Holy Cross" and "Captain Jewel," the disabled, eroticized Christ is passionately desired, not in spite of but because of his physical state, both in his own right and as a stand-in for Cooper.[48] In both of these examples, Michael Field creates a kind of queer disability poetics that uses their embodied experience with cancer to identify with Christ and love Him more deeply, while it also uses Christianity to articulate their love and desire for one another—for "loving...wounds."

Both Cooper and Bradley also write Annunciation poems in which they identify with the Virgin Mary, who famously agreed to bear the burden thrust upon her. As Ruth Vanita and others have observed, Michael Field's praise of Sapphic beauty easily shifts to Marian praise in their devotional verse. Thus, consider the first stanza of Cooper's 1911 "Hour of Need":

> O Mother of my Lord,
> Beautiful Mary, aid!
> He, whom thy will adored,
> When thy body was afraid,
> Is coming in my flesh to dwell—
> Pray for me, Mary...and white Gabriel![49]

Here, embodied fear is acknowledged for both Mary and the speaker (Cooper) who identifies with Mary. Christ simultaneously inhabits Mary's body as the child, the speaker's body as the Eucharist, and Cooper's body as God's will (in this case, cancer). Once again, Mary (and by extension, Cooper) adores "thy will"—in other words, desires her embodiment. She does not wish to escape, deny, or minimize it.

A similar if more pathos-filled poem is Bradley's "Pondering," composed in 1913:

> I see a Garden, my little son,
> Thou art praying there God's will be done:
> The ground is wet
> With bloody sweat . . .
> Yea, and fulfilled His Will shall be
> In Thee and me!
>
> Thou art bound, art bleeding in a hall . . .
> There is wrath at my breast . . . The scourges fall;
> And the swimming eyes of Thine agony
> Have no part in me.
> Lo, Thine hour is come!
> My Bud, my Rose, I am distant, dumb!
>
> Belovèd, I can see a road;
> They spur Thee along it as with a goad;
> I hear Thy Voice "Ye must not weep" . . .
> Babe, Babe, but my sobs will break Thy sleep!
>
> To a Cross Thou art nailed by cruel men—
> But I see myself and beside Thee then,
> At the foot of that Cross—and it is His Will!
> My little One, we will both lie still,
> In one peace together, loving His Will![50]

A meditation on Mary and Christ as well as a vision of impending suffering and death apropos to Cooper's illness, "Pondering" is another example among many in these poems of how Michael Field indulges in creative asynchrony, making the here and now congruent with the historical there and then. "Pondering" also portrays what Kafer describes as crip time, or those strange temporalities peculiar to how disability orients one to time. Thinking about waiting, anticipatory time, Kafer points out how queer and crip time trouble the future in refusing (like Mary and Christ, like Bradley and Cooper) to privilege longevity at all cost. In the opening stanza, the speaker (Mary/Bradley) sees her boy's imminent death on the cross and echoes Christ's/Cooper's *Fiat, voluntas tua:* "fulfilled His will shall be / In Thee and Me." In the second and third stanzas, Mary/Bradley acknowledges Christ's/Edith's physical pain and her own intense emotional suffering; but in the final stanza, we see the speaker not merely accepting their lot but "loving" God's will.

In February 1911, motivated by realities of Cooper's illness, Bradley and Cooper decide to take vows to become Dominican Sisters of the Penance, to "have new nuptials of love within the Church."[51] This act brings new weight to their devotional writings' standard trope of Christ as Bridegroom. On December 31, 1911, Cooper writes, "We are here together, hoping together to take the Vow that gives us wholly to our Bridegroom Christ, hoping to love each other in Him . . . and beloved Michael, growing so patient, showing me such loveable fruits out of the pain, bitterer than mine she has to bear."[52] Looking forward to the rings that will join them—and in language that recalls the Trinity that she and Bradley formed with Whym Chow—Cooper writes, "We shall be in Thee together and not alone—forever Thine and Thy Twain in thee."[53] In this queer marriage, Christ as Bridegroom, like Whym Chow, becomes another erotic proxy for Michael Field.[54] Thus, in this future-oriented journal entry, Cooper records how she and her beloved approach a new threshold in their relationship. The account provides a sense of Bradley's awareness of Cooper's suffering body but also Cooper's awareness of Bradley's pain, which she deems more severe than her own. Both experience pain in their own way, but through their love for one another and for Christ they articulate desire for their new life together, not in a spirit of resignation but actively embracing "Thy will be done."

Less than six months later, Charles Ricketts would state how alienated he felt by Michael Field's religious verse and would voice the scathing critique with which I opened this chapter. Yet, as I hope I have demonstrated, with its aesthetic pouts, wounds, jewels, and flowers; with paradox and asynchrony; with experimental approaches to form; and animated by both masculine and feminine homoerotic tropes, *Poems of Adoration* and *Mystic Trees* are *very much* like Michael Field's earlier poems—like the poems Charles Ricketts prefers over the Catholic verse he claims that he does not recognize. Explorations in how and why one might desire disability—both Christ's and one's own—these devotional poems expand our understanding of what it meant for Bradley and Cooper to become Catholic poets while remaining Michael Field.

Notes

Many thanks to Joe Bristow, Kim Q. Hall, Nathan K. Hensley, Martha Stoddard Holmes, Linda K. Hughes, Sarah Parker, and Ana Parejo Vadillo, who each provided useful feedback at different stages of this project's development.

1. Michael Field, "Works and Days," BL Add MS 46802, fol. 48 (May 8, 1912) [E.C.].

2. Hilary Fraser's "The Religious Poetry of Michael Field," in *Athena's Shuttle: Myth Religion Ideology from Romanticism to Modernism*, ed. Franco Marucci and Emma Sdegno (Milan: Cisalpino, 2000), 127–42, and Marion Thain's *'Michael Field': Poetry, Aestheticism and the Fin de Siècle* (Cambridge: Cambridge University Press, 2007) have long provided the most extensive existing treatment of *Mystic Trees* and *Poems of Adoration*, with Leire Barerra-Medrano's "'St. Theresa, I Call on You to Help'" in this volume making another valuable recent contribution. Many Michael Field scholars mention biographical aspects of the coauthors' Catholic conversion, but most literary analyses of Michael Field's Catholic writing tend to focus more on selections from *Whym Chow, Flame of Love* and the posthumous collection, *The Wattlefold*, than upon the two collections that are the subject of my chapter here. See Sarah Kersh's chapter, "Betwixt Us Two" in this collection; Ruth Vanita, *Sappho and the Virgin Mary: Same-Sex Love and the English Literary Imagination* (New York: Columbia University Press, 1996); Frederick S. Roden, *Same-Sex Desire in Victorian Religious Culture* (Basingstoke, UK: Palgrave, 2003); Camille Cauti, "Michael Field's Pagan Catholicism," in *Michael Field and Their World*, ed. Margaret D. Stetz and Cheryl A. Wilson (High Wycombe, UK: Rivendale Press, 2007), 181–89; and Maria LaMonaca, *Masked Atheism: Catholicism and the Victorian Secular Home* (Columbus: Ohio State University Press, 2008).

3. Cf. Robert McRuer and Abby Wilkerson's "Introduction" to "Desiring Disability, Queer Theory Meets Disability Studies," special issue, *GLQ* 9.1–2 (2003): 1–23; Alison Kafer, *Feminist, Queer, Crip* (Bloomington: Indiana University Press, 2013).

4. See Jill R. Ehnenn, *Women's Literary Collaboration, Queerness, and Late-Victorian Culture* (Aldershot, UK: Ashgate, 2008), especially chapter 2, "Sight and Song."

5. In *The Michael Field Catalogue: A Book of Lists* (London: De Blackland, 1998), Ivor Treby conjectures that Bradley's contributions to *Poems of Adoration* may include the following: "The Blessed Sacrament," composed September 1908; "The Blessed Sacrament," composed July 1910; "Marcinus against Trees," composed April 1912; "The Flower Fadeth," composed March 1908; and "Recognition," composed 1908. He also asserts that Cooper's contributions to *Mystic Trees* are "The Homage of Death," composed in January 1911; "Qui Renovat Juventutem Meam," composed in September, 1912; and "Moss," composed in 1913.

6. See, among others, Yopie Prins, "Sappho Doubled: Michael Field," *Yale Journal of Criticism* 8, no. 1 (1995): 165–86; Virginia Blain, "'Michael Field, the Two-Headed Nightingale': Lesbian Text as Palimpsest," *Women's History Review* 5, no. 2 (1996): 239–57; and Jill R. Ehnenn, "'Our Brains Struck Fire Each from Each': Disidentification, Difference, and Desire in the Collaborative Aesthetics of Michael Field," in *Economies of Desire at the Victorian Fin de Siècle: Libidinal Lives*, ed. Jane Ford, Kim Edwards Keates, and Patricia Pulham (New York: Routledge, 2015), 180–203.

7. Edith Cooper to John Gray, National Library of Scotland, Dept. 372 #16, fol. 7, 8 (March 8, 1913).

8. Michael Field, *Mystic Trees* (London: Eveleigh Nash, 1913), no page number (translation author's own).

9. While illness narratives, including cancer narratives, have long been a staple of literary disability studies, some theorists within critical disability studies today fiercely debate what constitutes a disability, including to what extent illnesses like cancer should be considered a disability. Strong proponents of the social model argue there is a difference between a disease and an impairment (which may result in a non-normate body yet a perfectly healthy one); such thinking might also invite making a distinction between the lived experience of the "healthy vs. unhealthy" disabled, chronic vs. acute illnesses, and so on. On the other hand, critics of the social model would deem such thinking to depend too much on the concept of diagnosis and to erase the lived realities of pain irrespective of the social politics of built environment. In referring in this chapter to Cooper's cancer as a disability, I align my thinking with Alison Kafer in *Feminist, Queer, Crip*, whose work is self-described as a "friendly departure" from the social model and seeks to "pluralize the way we understand bodily instability" while still critiquing the "social exclusions based on and social meanings attributed to impairment" (7). I find Kafer's focus on lived experience, including the experiences of pain, social and political relationships, and thinking of the future, to be particularly helpful for addressing subjects whose historically contingent concepts of identity, embodiment, diagnosis, cure, and so on may be different from ours today. For varied thinking on these debates, see, among many others, Susan Wendell, "Unhealthy Disabled, Treating Chronic Illnesses as Disabilities," *Hypatia* 16, no. 4 (2001): 17–33; Tom Shakespeare, "The Social Model of Disability," *Research in Social Science and Disability* 2 (2002): 9–28; Emilia Nielsen, "Chronically Ill, Critically Crip?: Poetry, Poetics and Dissonant Disabilities," *Disability Studies Quarterly* 36, no. 4 (2016), n.p.; and Nirmala Erevelles, "Introduction," in *Disability and Difference in Global Contexts: Enabling a Transformative Body Politic* (Basingstoke, UK: Palgrave, 2011), 1–23.

10. Emma Mason, "Christina Rossetti and the Doctrine of Reserve," *Journal of Victorian Culture* 7, no. 2 (2002): 196.

11. F. Elizabeth Gray, "Syren Strains: Victorian Women's Devotional Poetry and John Keble's *The Christian Year*," *Victorian Poetry* 44, no. 1 (2006): 62.

12. Kirstie Blair, *Form and Faith in Victorian Poetry and Religion* (Oxford: Oxford University Press, 2012), 199.

13. For a different interpretation, see Leire Barrera-Medrano's chapter in this volume, in which she traces Michael Field's debt to Spanish mystic theology.

14. Many thanks to Michael Hurley and Joshua King for their advice on this topic.

15. Field, *Mystic Trees*, 44 (lines 9–12).

16. Field, 45 (lines 1–6).

17. Field, 139 (lines 1–7).

18. Field, 139 (lines 8–14).

19. Matthew Arnold, "Dover Beach," in *English Victorian Poetry: An Anthology*, ed. Paul Negri (Mineola, NY: Dover Thrift, 1999), 114–15 (lines 22–23).

20. Michael Field, *Underneath the Bough* (London: George Bell and Sons, 1893), 79 (lines 15–16); *Wild Honey from Various Thyme* (London: T. Fisher Unwin, 1908), 58 (lines 9–10, 13).

21. Michael Field, *Mystic Trees*, 139 (line 14).

22. Keble quoted in Blair, *Form and Faith*, 37.

23. John Keble, *Lectures on Poetry, 1832–1841*, vol. 1 (Oxford: Clarendon Press, 1912), 22.

24. Blair, *Form and Faith*, 39.

25. Michael Field, *Poems of Adoration* (Edinburgh: Sands & Co., 1912), 6 (lines 1–10).

26. Field, 6 (lines 23–26).

27. Michael Field [E.C.] to Robert Browning, BL Add MS 46866, fol. 43v, (1886).

28. See Ehnenn, "Our Brains," 192. Kate Thomas and Ana Parejo Vadillo also write about the bramble-bough, specifically the bramble-bough carving, in the "Vegetable Love" and "Sculpture, Poetics, Marble Books" chapters in this volume.

29. Michael Field, *Underneath the Bough* (Portland, ME: T. Mosher, 1898), 53.

30. For an expanded discussion of these two poems in the context of erotic difference, see Ehnenn, "Our Brains," 192–93.

31. Marion Thain, "'Damnable Aestheticism' and the Turn to Rome: John Gray, Michael Field, and a Poetics of Conversion," in *The Fin-de-Siècle Poem: English Literary Culture and the 1890s*, ed. Joseph Bristow (Ohio: Ohio University Press, 2005), 332.

32. Field, *Mystic Trees*, 44 (lines 5–8).

33. Field, 43.

34. Cf. Ehnenn, *Women's Literary Collaboration*, 92–96; Martha Vicinus, "The Adolescent Boy: Fin de Siècle Femme Fatale?" *Journal of the History of Sexuality* 5, no. 1 (1994): 90–114; and Richard Kaye, "Saint Sebastian and the Victorian Discourse of Decadence," *Victorian Literature and Culture* 27 (1999): 269–303.

35. Field, *Mystic Trees*, 36.

36. Here I am thinking particularly of how Bradley and Cooper continued to hold fast to their private beliefs about Whym Chow and what Frederick Roden terms their "lesbian Trinitarianism."

37. Kate Thomas, "What Time We Kiss: Michael Field's Queer Temporalities," *GLQ* 13, no. 2–3 (2007): 330.

38. Cf. Sara Ahmed, *Queer Phenomenology* (Durham, NC: Duke University Press, 2010).

39. Erevelles, *Disability and Difference*, 8.

40. Erevelles, 36.

41. Here I use "crip" as a reclamatory term that refers to non-normate bodies and identities. Crip theory is influenced by queer theory's critique of the naturalization and normalization of bodies and encourages a troubling of the boundaries that establish given ontologies. Accordingly, a crip reading will be critical of how medical models define and stigmatize disability.

42. For foundational arguments about heternormative time and the idea that queer theory instead should approach time from the perspective of "no future," see Lee Edelman, *No Future: Queer Theory and the Death Drive* (Durham, NC: Duke University

Press, 2004); J. Jack Halberstam, *In a Queer Time and Place* (New York: New York University Press, 2005); and *The Queer Art of Failure* (Durham, NC: Duke University Press, 2011). For recent queer critiques of the antifuturity movement, see, in addition to Alison Kafer's work, Kim Q. Hall's "No Failure: Climate Change, Radical Hope, and Queer Crip Feminist Eco-Futures," *Radical Philosophy Review* 17 (2014): 203–25; and Kate Thomas's "Vegetable Love" in this volume.

43. Kafer, *Feminist, Queer, Crip*, 6, 8.

44. Michael Field, "Works and Days," BL Add MS 46801, fol. 21v (February 6, 1911) [E.C.]; Edith Cooper to John Gray, National Library of Scotland, Dept. 372#16, fol. 2 (February 1911).

45. Field, *Poems of Adoration*, 31.

46. "A sense of the old Michaelian life comes on us. The little black leather strap, that is to bind our Catholic book 'Adoration' and 'Mystic Trees' together, arrives . . . at night we read from the enchained books dual poems on the same subjects" (Michael Field, "Works and Days," BL Add MS 46803, fol. 39r (May 6, 1913) [E.C.]). The companion poems are then listed in pairs in the diary (*PoA: Poems of Adoration; MT: Mystic Trees*): Cooper's "Real Presence" (1912 *PoA*) and Bradley's [blank]; Cooper's "Virgo Potens" (1910, *PoA*) and Bradley's "Midsummer Night's Dream" (1913, *MT*); Cooper's "Columba Mea" (1911 *PoA*) and Bradley's "Nondum errant abyssi" (1913 *MT*); Cooper's "Purgatory" (1907 *PoA*) and Bradley's "In Die Obitus" (1908 *MT*); Cooper's "Holy Cross" (1912 *PoA*) and Bradley's "Captain Jewel" (1913 *MT*); Cooper's "Qui Renovat Jevuntitem Meam" (1912 *MT*) and Bradley's "Gather Gather" ("The Blessed Sacrament I) (1908 *PoA*); and Cooper's "To Notre Dame de Boulonge" (Pax Vobiscum) (1910 *PoA*) and Bradley's "Praises" (1908 *MT*).

47. Field, *Mystic Trees*, 28.

48. For foundational insights about the disabled Christ from a disability studies perspective, see Nancy Eiesland, *The Disabled God: Toward a Liberatory Theology of Disability* (Nashville: Abingdon Press, 1994).

49. Field, *Poems of Adoration*, 103 (lines 1–6).

50. Field, *Mystic Trees*, 65. Ellipses in original.

51. Michal Field, "Works and Days," BL Add MS 46801, fol. 26v (February 9, 1911) [E.C.].

52. Michael Field, "Works and Days," BL Add MS 46801, fol. 161r (December 31, 1911) [E.C.].

53. Michael Field, "Works and Days," BL Add MS 46801, fol. 166r (December 31, 1911) [E.C.].

54. Among others, cf. Ehnenn, "'Dragging at Memory's Fetter': Michael Field's Personal Elegies, Victorian Mourning, and the Problem of Whym Chow," *Michaelian* 1 (2009); and Roden (*Same-Sex Desire*, 2002) on Whym Chow as erotic proxy between Bradley and Cooper.

NINE

"St. Theresa, I Call on You to Help"

Michael Field and Spanish Mysticism

Leire Barrera-Medrano

"SUPPOSING GOD WISHES ME TO LEAVE ALL THESE HOLY ACTIVE
Dominicans, & to find my rest at Wincanton <u>Convent</u>. St. Theresa, I call on
you to help."[1] Katharine Bradley wrote these words on September 16, 1914, in
the final page of the diary that she had shared for almost thirty years with Edith
Cooper. Cooper had passed away nine months prior to this entry, on December
13, 1913, and Bradley would die ten days later, on September 26, 1914. Bradley's
allusion to this Carmelite convent and, more importantly, her exhortation to the
Spanish Carmelite mystic St. Teresa in her final days, should not be overlooked.
These words illustrate her religious devotion to the Spanish female saint and
serve as the starting point for this chapter, allowing me to reconstruct a crucially
Spanish mystic presence in Michael Field's later work.

In 1922 Mary Sturgeon already noted how, after Michael Field's Catholic
conversion in 1907, their minds were "possessed by the exaltation of the mystic."[2]
Bradley's chosen title for *Mystic Trees* (1913) clearly defined the mystical inclinations of the two women. Michael Field's poetry appeared in the first *Oxford
Book of English Mystical Verse*, published in 1916. Yet critics have not examined
Michael Field's relation to mystical theology in depth. If we are to take the Catholic poetry of Michael Field seriously, exploring their understanding of Catholic theology is of primary importance. As Mark Knight and Emma Mason
put it, recognizing the unique contribution of Catholic theology to literary and

cultural developments in the late nineteenth century "does not entail privileging theology as the only cultural determinant. . . . It does, however, insist on acknowledging a religious element that has sometimes been ignored."[3] For Knight and Mason, "even if theology is understood as non-essential, as it is for Ellis Hanson, it can still provide a primary category for thinking about the writing of late nineteenth-century writers."[4] In her chapter in this volume, Jill R. Ehnenn highlights the importance of Tractarian devotional poetry for Michael Field's Catholic verse. This chapter unveils Michael Field's engagement with their primary source of mystical theology—Spanish mysticism—with the aim of enabling a better understanding of the integrity and richness of their Catholic poetry. Michael Field's underexplored relationship to Spanish mysticism serves as a prominent example of the ways in which theological writing contributes to and to some extent determines artistic form and content.

The new millennium has seen scholars such as Marion Thain (2000, 2007), Frederick S. Roden (2002), and Thain and Ana Parejo Vadillo (2009) challenge the assertion that Michael Field's Catholic verse—namely *Poems of Adoration* (1912), *Mystic Trees* (1913), *Whym Chow: Flame of Love* (1914), and *The Wattlefold* (1930)—is inherently less valuable than their previous work. For Roden, Michael Field's late work demonstrates "not the triviality of Decadent Christianity . . . but its rich space for imaginative, and in fact spiritual, satisfaction."[5] Thain emphasizes the dialectic between religion and sexuality, which "produces a dynamic as exhilarating as that found in their earlier work."[6] It is in the construction of this distinctive dialectic between sensuality and spirituality, alongside excess and intensity of expression, that Spanish mystic poetry plays a central role for Michael Field. The fervent, religious eroticism of Spanish mysticism, this chapter contends, provides a way of taking Michael Field's turn to Catholicism seriously without simply reading it as repressive and inherently less interesting than their previous life.

Before analyzing Michael Field's engagement with Spanish mystic poetry in depth, it is necessary to outline briefly the importance and main features of this religious and literary tradition. The significance of the Spanish mystic school that flourished in the sixteenth century is, indeed, twofold—both religious and literary. This movement included some of the most important leaders in Christian mystical theology and in the early modern Catholic Reformation, namely St. Teresa of Ávila (1515–82) and St. John of the Cross (1542–91). Both saints are also regarded as the two most important figures of the Spanish mystic movement. Coinciding with the Counter-Reformation, St. Teresa and St. John were united in their desire to drastically reform their monastic order, the Carmelites, and to train its members in mystical prayer through a renewal of primitive communal discipline and individual spiritual direction. Indeed, much of the newly emerging mysticism in staunchly Catholic Spain during the sixteenth century presented, as Ursula King puts it, "a dramatic break with the spiritual tradition of the early Church and the Middle Ages [and was] marked by a mixture of activity, austerity and ceaseless striving."[7] In a similar vein, Julia Kristeva describes the Spanish mysticism of the Counter-Reformation as "the supernatural excess, the fervid amorous transports, the ever more bizarre extremes that enacted the risks of subjective freedom."[8] These nonconformist mystical movements attracted the attention of the Spanish Inquisition, which judged some of their methods as unorthodox and dangerous.

Alongside this transgressive spiritual dimension, the literary works of the mystics catalyzed the golden age of Spanish literature. Their literary importance lies in their attempts to transcend the boundaries of language and liberate previously untapped resources of expression. The writings of the Spanish mystics dramatize a search for God rooted in passion and desire rather than in duty and medieval legalism. Edgar Allison Peers singles out a combination of distinct features that gave Spanish mystic literature an unmistakable individuality: "It is concrete, practical, personal, experiential, active."[9] One striking attribute of their writing is also the use of an intense, passionate language of love, drawn largely from the courtly love tradition of the *cancioneros* or Spanish chansonniers. In real life the mystics aspired, like the poets of the *cancioneros*, to a perfect love purified by suffering. Their poetry is courtly, but it is also extremely erotic, with allusions to "encounters" and the "rending of the veil." These were well-established concepts in sixteenth-century Spain, signifying "sexual intercourse" and the "breaking of the hymen."[10] Spanish mystic poetry establishes, then, a perfect poetic analogy between profane and sacred love and, indeed at times, same-sex desire: an enabling analogy for the formerly pagan and newly Catholic lesbian poets Bradley and Cooper.

In particular, an awareness of Michael Field's association with the female figure of St. Teresa is crucial in order to broaden understanding of the relationships between aestheticism, decadence, modernism, Catholicism, and female homosexuality, as her work offers explicit readings of same-sex desire. The relationship between decadence and Catholicism, especially its connection to same-sex desire, has been the object of increasing interest since Ellis Hanson's pivotal *Decadence and Catholicism* (1997). Frederick S. Roden suggests in *Same-Sex Desire in Victorian Religious Culture* (2002) that Cooper and Bradley can be placed at the beginning of a continuum of modern lesbian Catholicism, an assertion to which, I would add, St. Teresa proves instrumental. It is not a coincidence that Vita Sackville-West, lover of Virginia Woolf, and

Gertrude Stein would place St. Teresa in "the gallery of twentieth-century lesbian icons."[11]

This chapter focuses on the importance of Spanish mystic doctrine—first that of St. John and then that of St. Teresa—for Michael Field's personal life and in their work, by analyzing allusions to the mystics in their correspondence and joint diary in the period 1907–14. I also illustrate how the traditional Spanish mystic diction and verse form are also present in Michael Field's poetry of conversion, particularly in *Poems of Adoration* and *Mystic Trees*. The latter was almost entirely written by Bradley and the former mainly by Cooper, which testifies, as Thain and Parejo Vadillo note, "the greater distance between the two women that religion established." At the same time, however, these two volumes together "form the major collaborative work of the period: they were designed as counterparts, which would form a complete whole."[12] The presence of Spanish mysticism seems to be more evident in Bradley's *Mystic Trees*, but it is also distinctly noticeable in Cooper's *Poems of Adoration*. The letters examined here were all written by Bradley, but she claimed to write also in the name of Cooper. There seems thus to be a clear unity in their understanding and absorption of Spanish mysticism, which was translated differently into written form.

The chapter pays particular attention to six works by St. John and St. Teresa of special relevance to Michael Field. These works have, however, passed relatively unnoticed. Michael Field's direct allusion to St. John's *The Living Flame of Love* (1585–87) in *Whym Chow: Flame of Love*, and its significance, have already been noted by scholars.[13] Yet other works of St. John that are referred to throughout Michael Field's later poems have been hardly acknowledged—particularly the *Spiritual Canticle* (1578–84), the *Ascent of Mount Carmel* (1579–85), and *The Dark Night* (1582–85). Nor have the numerous references to St. Teresa's poems and prose works—*Life* (1562–65), *The Way to Perfection* (1566–67), and *The Interior Castle* (1577)—been properly considered.

"Sensually and Spiritually:" St. John of the Cross

Michael Field decided to enter the Roman Catholic Church in 1907 in response to a series of events, such as Cooper's frequent illnesses, but mainly due to the death of their beloved dog Whym Chow in 1906, which prompted a spiritual crisis. One of the crucial dilemmas they faced after their conversion was how to reconcile their art with their Catholic life. In entries by Cooper in Michael Field's mutual diary, there are passages of conversations with Father Vincent MacNabb, Bradley's confessor, which reflect these difficulties: "What is a dramatic poet to do, who, receiving Christ corporeally each day, must needs deal with sinners and become, as Matthew Arnold says 'what we sing,'" recorded Cooper.[14]

The priest's answer pointed toward a clear path, mysticism: "The poets are the mystics—they lead the way to revelation—. . . The Church welcomes poets. Heaven is full of song. But there will always be the delicate question with you, what you must bear for your art, as Christ bore sin, and what must be rejected in your material."[15] The answer to this "delicate question" came through the figure of John Gray (1866–1934) and, I propose, through Spanish mysticism.

Gray, one of the main representatives of the decadent poetry of the nineties, had become a Catholic priest in 1901. For most of his life he was also involved romantically with the poet and theorist of homosexuality André Raffalovich (1864–1934), who had converted in 1896. After Michael Field's conversion, Gray became a close friend and confessor and helped them to cope with their transition from fin-de-siècle poets to Catholic converts.[16] As Thain claims, "in providing them with his own most comforting elements of doctrine, he gave Bradley and Cooper the theological tools . . . to accomplish their own reconciliation of their perverse, pagan poetic past (and their desire for each other) with their newly found Catholic faith."[17] When Gray became Michael Field's confessor, they were indeed actively seeking role models, as the following words that Bradley wrote to Gray in the spring of 1907 testify:

> & there are no frankly Christian poets? . . .
> I fear Oscar is right—the real Catholic poet is Verlaine?
>
> ———————————
>
> And might there be a fresh poetry—interpreting, <u>painting</u> the great mystery . . . ?[18]

John Gray, then, gave the women some answers: he encouraged Michael Field to ardently read St. Teresa—and St. John the Cross, his most esteemed biblical figure and one of the most homoerotic of Catholic writers. With time, St. John's work would prove to be as important to Field as it had been to Gray: "How I thank God for you—first of all that you made me a Catholic, & then the good <u>method</u>—St. John of the Cross. When, & how did you first draw him into my life? How bitter he was to me! Choose 'the most afflictive way' . . .—I need him."[19] It seems almost impossible to avoid drawing parallels between these two Spanish mystics and their "English counterparts." Indeed, the two most important figures of Spanish mysticism forged a close friendship and partnership, which is echoed by that between John Gray and Michael Field. St. Teresa acted as a mentor figure to St. John, while the reverse was true in the case of Field-Gray. All of them were Catholic poets, yet they were outcasts and rebels in search of new forms of expression—and just as the homosexuals and former decadents Gray and Field had been condemned,

St. Teresa and St. John were persecuted by the Inquisition for their unusual approach to religion.

The correspondence between Gray and Bradley (Bradley claimed to write also in name of Cooper) after 1907 reveals the importance of St. John first for the former and then for the latter. Even before Gray had encouraged her reading of St. John, Bradley had revealed her preference for the Spanish religious school. In an undated but circa 1907 letter, Bradley wrote to Gray: "I plunged myself into the Spanish school—when in Ireland—the Spiritual Exercises of St Ignatius of Loyola ... the Lover in St Ignatius! The Lover that gives him genius! My soul leans back against these sentences!"[20] The letter thus stresses one of the main features of Spanish mysticism treasured by Bradley: the intensity used to describe Love. The title of the book that Michael Field would publish a few years after writing these words, *Mystic Trees*, was Bradley's homage to the Spanish school. Already in 1911, Cooper indicated the title's source: "The great joy is that our Lady has given Michael a title for her Catholic Poems from an old Spanish hymn Mystic Trees.... Not only is this a title: it is an incentive."[21]

Through John Gray, Michael Field's affections moved from St. Ignatius of Loyola (1491–1556), considered the first great Spanish mystic, toward the next generation of Spanish mysticism, St. John of the Cross. In October 1908, Gray encouraged Bradley to read St. John more fervently, whom he loved "very much with a firm persuasion that I should now be in hell but for him."[22] In November 1908 he lent Bradley the first volume of the 1864 *Complete Works of St. John of the Cross* translated by David Lewis. This work contained St. John's two-part work *Ascent of Mount Carmel* (1579–85) and *The Dark Night* (1582–85), which comment on and explain his poem "The Dark Night of the Soul" (1578–81). Bradley's response to this volume was decidedly effusive: "Then of S. John of the Cross! Oh that I could read him with quiet heart! I send you 2 or 3 lines of translation or thought-reading ... Father, what St John says about the substitution of Hope for Memory is vital to me—I cannot speak of the new life I am getting from St John."[23]

That translation or "thought-reading" that she referred to was the short poem entitled "Aridity," which she added to her letter to Gray and which she would later include in *Mystic Trees*. The poem reads as follows:

> O Soul, canst thou not understand
>   thou art not left alone,
>   as a dog to howl and moan
> His master's absence; thou art as a book
>   Left in a room that He forsook,
>   a book of His dear choice,—

> that, quiet, waiteth for His Hand,
> that, quiet, waiteth for His eye,
> that, quiet, waiteth for His voice.[24]

Bradley rewrites here some of the ideas of St. John's poem "The Dark Night of the Soul." This poem narrates the journey of the soul from its bodily home to its union with God. The journey is called the "Dark Night" because darkness represents the hardships the soul suffers in detachment from the world and in reaching the light of its union with the Creator. St. John wrote a treatise (*The Dark Night*) commenting on the poem, in which he explains that the dark night of the senses consists of an "aridity" of the sensual appetite by which the soul is purified of desires. In the text, St. John explains that "nothing remains in that aridity and detachment but an anxious desire to serve God. . . . [W]hen the natural desires are lulled to sleep in our sensual nature by persistent aridities, when the senses and the interior powers of the soul cease to be active . . . then the liberty of the spirit is unassailable by these enemies and the house remains calm and tranquil."[25]

St. John of the Cross's concept of "aridity" thus helped Bradley not only to address Whym Chow's death in 1906 but also her own mundane and bodily concerns and losses—the "passions of the soul"—such as Cooper's various illnesses and eventual cancer (diagnosed in 1911) and her necessary celibacy as a result of their conversion.[26] Cooper would also find refuge in the dark night metaphor to alleviate the intense pain she was suffering due to her illness. In "Holy Cross," she wrote:

> pain grieves
> About each sense but as a languid hum:
>
> . . .
>
> My day rejoices in its strength,
> My night that innocence of strife is come.[27]

Above all, the "dark night" offered Michael Field a necessary metaphor of spiritual yet earthly love: "Then St. John of the Cross speaks to me—'the difference is that in the next world they are purified by fire, & here, purified & enlightened by love.' I am happy . . . on the green pastures now I have found St. John of the Cross."[28] Bradley was quoting here an extract of *The Dark Night*, in which St. John refers to "the dark night of loving fire," which "purifies in the darkness."[29] St. John's emphasis that love on earth is necessary to clean one's soul enabled Michael Field to reframe their "indecent" relationship.

The Ascent of Mount Carmel (1579–85), also based on St. John's poem "Dark Night of the Soul" and included in the volume lent by Gray, became equally crucial to Michael Field's conversion. This long treatise is structured around the idea of a spiritual ascent that can be undertaken only after purgation. In this volume, Field found further mystical ways to purge their pagan past, as it details the earthly and spiritual privations that the soul undergoes in search of union with God. As had happened with John Gray previously, St. John was finally, with this volume, "steadily quieting" Michael Field: "[A]t last I am learning to take the slow ways of God with gratitude & to have faith."[30] The most important doctrine extracted from that work came from a chapter in Book Two, which Bradley copied in the first page of Michael Field's 1911 diary (with two sentences underlined):

> Christ annihilated himself at the Cross:
> Therefore it is that the Psalmist saith of Him,
> "I am brought to nothing, & I knew not."
> ... This consisteth ...
> in the living death
> of the cross, sensually & spiritually,
> outwardly & inwardly.[31]

In this extract, St. John stresses how detached and unencumbered must be the soul of those who will walk in eternal life. Awareness of the senses is equally necessary in illuminating the soul as is acceptance of pain and grief. As a result, with this book, Bradley finally "became quiet"; in other words, St. John's doctrine provided her with solace.[32] This notion only intensified as Michael Field continued to read other works by St. John. After her revelatory experience with the *Dark Night of the Soul* and *Ascent of Mount Carmel*, Bradley asked Gray for translations of St. John's *Spiritual Canticle* (1578–84), writing "It is life to have access to the Spiritual Canticle."[33] "[It] is my first experience of a book in the ~~Catholic~~ (o forgive!) Church," she joked.[34] The sensual symbolism and imagery of this book so attracted Field that they emulated it in some of their verse. In "Words of the Bridegroom," Cooper writes,

> Fragrance to Me of lily-fields;
> How shall ye keep the whiteness of your vow?
> My Virgins, My white Brides, I whisper how:
> Of Virgin flesh, a Virgin God,
> Incarnate among men I trod.[35]

In this poem, Cooper draws on almost the same linguistic resources as St. John of the Cross in his *Spiritual Canticle*, but she remodels them to fit her own interests. In *Spiritual Canticle*, St. John attempts to explain the mystical process that follows the soul until it reaches its union with God through the Song of Songs' allegory: the search for the bridegroom (Christ) by the bride (the human soul). Cooper reinterprets this heterosexual allegory, transforming it into a poem of female same-sex desire. Portrayed as a merely human love, these verses would have been perceived as perverse, but, sanctified to divine virginal uses, they serve their Godly purpose.

Michael Field also borrowed St. John's imagery from his last work, *Living Flame of Love* (1585–87). In *Whym Chow: Flame of Love* (published in 1914 but composed around 1907), Michael Field echoes St. John's work, which describes the state of the soul emerging from the dark night. To convey this complex state, St. John appropriates the conventional courtly love language of flames of love, wounding, and suffering as a living death. It is the Holy Spirit that acts as a purgatorial flame in the soul. To Bradley and Cooper, their beloved dog Whym Chow represented the flame that reciprocates love fully, and the wound was the longing for ever-greater union. As Thain has convincingly argued, St. John's *Living Flame of Love* allowed Field to understand the loss of the dog as a necessary sacrifice, which brought them nearer to God.[36]

St. John's doctrine of the growth of the soul, his direct and intense diction, and his rich symbolism and imagery thus helped Michael Field to develop their new spirituality. Likewise, St. John's versification was also a formally enabling— and experimental—influence on Michael Field's poetry. In "Fregit," for instance, Cooper gives a personal interpretation of a Spanish verse form popularized by St. John (and St. Teresa): the *glosa*. This form consists of two parts: the first, a few lines that set the theme for the entire poem, while the second is a gloss on or explanation of the text (my emphasis):

> On the night of dedication
> Of Thyself as our oblation,
> *Christ, Belovèd, Thou didst take*
> *In Thy very hands and break.* . . .
>
> . . .
>
> Broken before him, as his sin's award.
> *These were broken; Thou didst break.* . . .
>
> . . .
>
> Thy own Body for our sake:
> *Thy own Body Thou didst take*
> *In Thy holy hands—and break.*[37]

With this *glosa*, the poet, like the mystic, becomes a popular exegete of the Eucharistic notion of the "breaking of the bread," the "fregit" of Christ's body.

In spite of this and a few other examples from *Poems of Adoration*, the Michael Field volume that better reproduces the Spanish mystic verse form is Bradley's *Mystic Trees*. Spanish mystic poetry tends to condense emotion into brief forms, generally using short lines and stanzas, and these simple yet impassioned statements are also a constant in *Mystic Trees*. Bradley also uses a brief poetic form favored by St. John in several of her poems: the five-line stanza, which is very rare in English poetry and is used in Spanish poetics to express deep emotions. "Annunciation Silence" and "Caput tuum ut carmelus," for instance, both contain reinterpretations of the *quintilla*—that is, a stanza of five lines that has nine or fewer syllables (a loose equivalent of the English iambic pentameter), in which there may not be more than two rhymes or two consecutive rhymes, and the stanza may not end with a couplet. By using this brief, intense verse form, Bradley's poems display an equally concise and profound sentiment. If St. John of the Cross's doctrine had become a crucial point of reference in Michael Field's new Catholic life, his distinctive diction, imagery, and verse forms opened up new poetic paths of experimentation.

"O My Desire": St. Teresa

We have seen so far how St. John became Michael Field and John Gray's shared saint, a Catholic and decadent symbol of their poetic friendship: "I have just been commemorating St. John of the Cross. What prayers for the dear Father! How indeed he was meant for us—our Saint," wrote Bradley to Gray.[38] The female figure of St. Teresa, however, seems to have been kept almost exclusively for Michael Field. St. Teresa does not appear as often as St. John in their correspondence with John Gray. Yet the fact that Bradley exhorted St. Teresa, and not St. John, in her last hours, testifies to the crucial role played by the female saint. St. John's metaphor of the dark night allowed Michael Field, as well as former decadent Gray, to purge their past sins and gave them a decadent frame for understanding their new Catholic life. St. Teresa's language of female ecstasy also served to explicate their new faith, but more importantly it invigorated their religious poetry.

It is through St. Teresa, I argue, that Michael Field were able to free themselves from their mentor, John Gray, and create a new religious, female-centered verse. The necessary "quietness" that Field found through St. John to comprehend their newly converted status burst into fullness through St. Teresa. "As you would imagine S. Theresa absolutely is what I should <u>Love</u> to have been—orthodox, full of 'fire'—blest with visions," wrote Bradley to Gray, after requesting volumes of works of the female saint.[39] If John Gray identified himself with the homoerotic figure St. John, Michael Field identified with St.

Teresa, the ecstatic woman saint. In 1907, Bradley wrote to Gray mentioning the *Life of St. Teresa* (1562–65) that the poet-priest had lent her.[40] In likely allusion to that book, Bradley wrote again to Gray on September 15, 1907: "Such delight I have in S. Teresa. I was about in my haste to apologise for cutting some of the leaves with a hair pin."[41] Bradley seems to be embodying here Teresa's ecstasy by making a playful analogy between the piercing of the book by her pin and St. Teresa's piercing by an angel's dart:

> In his hands I saw a great golden spear, and at the end of the iron
> tip I seemed to see a point of fire. With this he seemed to pierce
> my heart several times so that it penetrated to my entrails. When
> he drew it out, I thought he was drawing them out with it and he
> left me completely afire with a great love for God. The pain was
> so sharp that it made me utter several moans; and so excessive was
> the sweetness caused me by this intense pain that one can never
> wish to lose it.[42]

In this game of saintly self-identifications, Bradley's reference to the pin resembles Gray's correlation between a "brown" volume by St. John and the "brown" curtains of his bedchamber. On January 20, 1908, Gray wrote to Michael Field how he "used to lie in bed, having at the time a brown eiderdown & brown curtains reading a brown book—works of St. John of the Cross."[43] As Thain notes, St. John seems, in this quotation, "to be blended into the embracing environment of the bedchamber, enabling him to be equated with sensuous protection as well as being the means by which Gray is made exposed and vulnerable."[44] Similarly, St. Teresa's piercing serves Bradley as a dual tool to explore sensual and religious feelings. Thain has shown how Bradley and Cooper learned from their male mentors, such as John Gray, about the erotic potential of the stigmata (particularly Christ's wounds) for reconciling earthly and transcendent desires: "[T]he use of Christ's body and his wounds as an erotic interface between Gray and his religion no doubt influenced Michael Field's work, but Bradley and Cooper concentrate particularly on the 'hands' of Christ in order to imagine . . . a specifically female sexuality."[45]

The clearest wound that Michael Field uses to express their own desire, I would add, is St. Teresa's wounding of the heart. In "Prophet," included in *Poems of Adoration*, we find the line, "How a sword shall pierce her heart alone," a clear allusion to a female wounded heart.[46] Less directly, but just as revealingly, in "Viaticum" Cooper also replicates St. Teresa's description of her ecstasy. The poem opens with these two lines, "O Heart, that burns within / Illuminated, hot!" and closes

> With Him who died for me,
>
> . . .
>
> Is felt by me as Fire;
> Who is my way and all
> My wayfaring's Desire.[47]

For Thain and Parejo Vadillo, poems such as "Viaticum" show "how religious fervour can translate wholly convincingly into poetic effusion for Cooper."[48] This poetic effusion is successfully achieved through St. Teresa's language of female ecstasy, which speaks of fire and sweet desire.[49] In relation to this discursive intertwining of religion and sexuality, Joy Dixon, in the introduction to a special issue on the subject in the *Victorian Review* (2011), has explicated the ways in which recent studies have rejected repressive theories of late Victorian religion "in favour of an emphasis on the complex ways in which sexuality is produced discursively."[50] Michael Field's understanding of and engagement with St. Teresa represents a prime example of the fruitful ways in which religion, and Catholicism in particular, served to express rather than repress female sexuality.

St. Teresa's *Transverberation* (the piercing of her heart by a dart) has fascinated artists and critics alike for centuries. Famously captured by Bernini in the seventeenth century, *The Ecstacy of Saint Teresa* was bluntly described in the 1970s by psychoanalyst Jacques Lacan: "[S]he's coming. There's no doubt about it."[51] Would Michael Field have interpreted St. Teresa's words in a similar way? St. Teresa's mystical experience involves sex, but it also involves God. The physicality of this event is undeniably vital, yet St. Teresa alters bodily boundaries and uses them to enable love of God. As Constance M. Furey explains, St. Teresa "equates experiencing God with the exhilaration caused by seeing, touching, or being pierced by another. If this should not be 'reduced' to sex, neither does it exclude sex."[52] Mystical desire is, then, "queer in its effects—exceeding and hyperbolizing its own conventionality."[53] St. Teresa's mystical sexuality and incarnational theology conveys thus all the paradoxes of Catholic decadence and accepts that "we are never wholly self-contained, never fully bounded, never fully in control of bodies or of language."[54] In a similar vein, the body is constantly present in Michael Field's Catholic verse, but the body is "not enough," as Bradley's poem "The Homage of Death" reveals:

> How willingly
> I yield to Thee
> This very dust!
> My body—that was not enough![55]

In this poem, Bradley echoes St. Teresa's lines (translated by Michael Field's contemporary, Arthur Symons), "behold me here, sweet Love; . . . See here my heart, I lay it in thy hand; my body, my life and soul, my bowels and my love."[56] As for St. Teresa, for Michael Field the sensual and spiritual spheres are inextricable in their verse:

> Beloved, I give Thee all
> This Adam's Fall,
> This my desert—
> Thy Father would not let Thee see
> Corruption, but I give it Thee.[57]

St. Teresa's religious language of female desire thus permeates Michael Field's Catholic verse, inflecting it with decadent qualities. Their verse is religious, but it speaks of an ambiguous desire, and its voice is often distinctively female: "[T]his Adam's Fall." More fundamentally, for Michael Field, St. Teresa represents a crucial duality that neither St. John nor John Gray do: she is both female and queer. Over the last two decades, critics have convincingly argued how St. Teresa's writings can be read, if not as openly homoerotic, decidedly sexually ambiguous.[58] According to Corinne E. Blackmer, "This mysterious female pleasure experienced by women mystics such as Teresa of Ávila . . . exceeds . . . heterosexuality and the symbolic order of masculine language."[59] Paola Marín also claims that, in Teresa's writing, it is possible "to find an explicit 'anti-straight' attitude in the sense that she puts at stake the paradigms of a social organization based on heterosexuality—that is, a phallocentric regime."[60] Drawing from Paul Julian Smith's proposal that St. Teresa's visions could be seen as acts of disavowal, a refusal to internalize the phallic order, Marín claims that St. Teresa's *Transverberation* could thus be read "not as a penetration by a ghostly phallus, but as a denial of sexual differences: indeed, the agent who holds the dart that enters her heart is a (sexless) angel."[61]

St. Teresa's ambiguous female-male wound is central to Michael Field's articulation of their equally ambiguous desire. In contrast to the patriarchal gender binary that defines sexual identities via the genitals, Marín proposes that mystical discourse is "queer and differs from courtly love, because it points toward the instability of sexual difference."[62] This instability is clear, for instance, in St. Teresa's *Meditations on the Song of Songs* (1566–71), in which she represents God simultaneously as husband and mother with divine breasts.[63] Michael Field's persona and relationship is equally ambiguous. As Virginia Blain notes, "although they played husband-wife games modelled on heterosexual marriage, it was only one of a range of intimacies . . . it could (also) be argued that they

modelled themselves after their idea of a same-sex male couple."[64] More than
with St. John, Michael Field could thus identify with the ambiguous femininity of St. Teresa, a *female* religious figure who transgressed gender, sexual,
and literary boundaries. When Julia Kristeva writes on St. Teresa, she stresses
the radical novelty of this transgression: "By the hand for the first time of a
European woman, pleasure unto death is conveyed with a sensual exactitude
that defies decorum."[65] St. Teresa's rebellious and sensual "exactitude" is reflected
in Michael Field's poetry, and it also "defies decorum"; it is used to present female
same-sex desire within a religious framework.

Equally important for Michael Field was St. Teresa's female language of
the crucifix. Following Ruth Vanita's assertion that women often depict female
sexuality through floral imagery, scholars such as Roden and Cauti argue that
Michael Field feminize Christ in poems such as "A Crucifix" through an association with flowers.[66] I would add that, more fundamentally, Michael Field
were using the mystical female language of St. Teresa. Tracing Michael Field's
debt to another female poet is as vital as acknowledging their feminine reinterpretation of male homoerotic tropes. In "Before the Crucifix," St. Teresa
addresses the image of Christ in the following way:

> On rose and jasmine fair;
> On *Thee* I gaze and see
> A thousand gardens there.
> Thou Flower all seraph-bright.[67]

By describing the crucifix as a flower, existing among rose and jasmine, St.
Teresa is transforming it into a virginal female figure. In "A Crucifix," Bradley
uses the same device: "As a lily Thou art among thorns, / As a rose lies back
against his briar."[68] What is more, while St. Teresa uses the metaphor of the garden to allude to the female genitalia, Bradley describes the crucifix as a "welcoming open fruit," thus embracing and expanding St. Teresa's feminine description.

St. Teresa's sensual concept of *self-oblation* is also borrowed by Bradley in
poems, such as "The Five Sacred Wounds," in which the poet gives herself to the
ambiguous Other: "Have compassion on me / . . . / God, for my hardness pity
me!" writes Bradley, replicating St. Teresa's "Lord, I am thine, for I was born for
Thee! / . . . / O Bounty, showing Pity on my soul!"[69] Like in St. Teresa's writing,
the pain of ecstasy is constantly regarded in Michael Field's Catholic poems
as "the grace of mystical contact with one another and with the transcendent
God."[70] In "Purgatory," Cooper establishes a dialogue with St. Teresa's most famous works in which the notion of self-oblation is also explored: *The Way to
Perfection* (1566–67) and *The Interior Castle* (1577). In the former, the Spanish

mystic describes ways of attaining spiritual perfection through prayer and its four stages: meditation, quiet, repose of soul, and perfect union with God. *The Interior Castle* presents the soul as a castle containing seven mansions or dwelling places, which she interprets as the journey of faith through seven stages, ending in union with God. Both stanzas in Cooper's poem "Purgatory" begin with the word "perfection," the first one alluding to the perfection of God and the second to the perfection of one's soul. In the second stanza, the poet writes,

> Perfection of my soul!—
> How shall I reach my goal,
> Unless I leave His Face,
> Who is my dwelling-place,
>
> . . .
>
> Unless, deprived of Him,
> I may achieve Him, . . .
> Bearing consummate pain,
> Supremely to attain?[71]

With this exclamation, Cooper embraces St. Teresa's description of the arduous journey of the soul to attain perfection and the supreme dwelling place which is God, or Love, only finally gained through self-oblation: complete pain and death.

Michael Field's identification with St. Teresa's sensual doctrine only intensified with their illness. Both rejected drugs (opium) to alleviate their pain because they wanted clear minds in order to continue writing, as if they were offering their own self-oblation.[72] M. Lynn Seitz notes that Bradley's agony "over the suffering of her niece was intense, but of a peculiar quality that seemed to almost welcome the sacrificial torment they underwent."[73] Just one month after Cooper's death, Bradley annotated in their mutual diary, "I gave thanks for my twain—the one on the left hand & the other on the right—thanks that they died Catholic, St. Theresa's <u>dying</u> thanks."[74] This quotation is of twofold importance. First, it alludes to St. Teresa's self-oblation in death. Yet it may well be a reference to the crucial fact that the saint died in the arms of another female figure, Anne of St. Bartholomew (1550–1626), her inseparable companion for the last five years of her life. As Anne describes in her *Autobiography* (1584–1622), at the moment of her death, St. Teresa does not call for the priest but the sister:

> The day of her death she was unable to speak from early morning:
> in the evening, the Father who was attending her . . . told me to
> go take some nourishment. But scarcely had I left than the Saint
> became restless. . . . The Father asked her if she wished me near
> her. She answered yes, by signs. . . . As soon as she saw me, she

smiled at me, showed me such condescension and affection that she caught me with her two hands and rested her head in my arms. I held her thus in my embrace until she expired.[75]

The intensity and religious ecstasy of the Spanish mystic poetry of St. Teresa and St. John of the Cross provided a method for Michael Field to reconcile the sensuous pagan poetry of their past with a still sensuous yet sacred verse. Spanish mysticism opened a newly liberating rather than repressive religious path. The Spanish mystics' combination of paradoxes, profane and sacred love, and homo-erotic and natural imagery contributed to Michael Field's exploration of their own identity, gender, religion, and writing after their conversion. As pagan symbols had served them to express their mutual love, after their conversion the vigor of the Spanish mystic doctrine and language enabled Michael Field to transform religious space into a stage for their mutual unconditional love.

Through Spanish mysticism, Michael Field were able to create a religious, sensual language of love, which spoke of their past interest in the senses but that also surpassed bodily boundaries. By using the sexualized imagery of the Spanish mystics—and in particular the female language of St. Teresa—they could dislocate their embodied self and reimagine it in spaces and forms not regularly inhabited. Like John Gray, Michael Field found in St. John of the Cross peace and a means for transforming their desires. In St. Teresa, they found a figure with whom they could identify. She also offered them a female and sexually ambiguous language of ecstasy and love both adequate and necessary to express their unusual union in Catholic terms. In their religious verse, Michael Field replicated, in Kristeva's terms, St. Teresa's "extremes of being": "oscillation, flux, body and soul, flesh and word, the inception of the imaginative faculty and the ardent desire to share it."[76]

Ultimately, Michael Field's engagement with Spanish mystic poetry also enriches our understanding of the relationship between aestheticism, decadence, modernism, and Catholicism. The fact that many decadent writers like Michael Field, John Gray, Arthur Symons, and George Moore were attracted to the Spanish mystics was not incidental, nor was the modernists' interaction (through figures like Ezra Pound, Gertrude Stein, and T. S. Eliot) with Spanish mysticism. Michael Field's later spirituality and engagement with the Spanish mystics points toward modernism in its experimentation with symbols, its linguistic freedom that incorporates the paradoxes of decadence, but also in its passionate fire. Before Sackville-West and Stein, Michael Field had already placed St. Teresa in the pantheon of religious lesbian icons. The mystical sexuality of Michael Field's Catholic verse, borrowed from Spanish mystic poetry, can be at times wonderfully hyperbolic, dynamic, experimental, queer, and protomodernist.

Notes

1. Michael Field, "Works and Days," BL Add MS 46804A, fol. 37v (September 16, 1914) [K.B.]

2. Mary C. Sturgeon, *Michael Field* (London: George G. Harrap, 1922), 197.

3. Mark Knight and Emma Mason, *Nineteenth-Century Religion and Literature* (Oxford: Oxford University Press, 2006), 191.

4. Knight and Mason, 197.

5. Frederick S. Roden, *Same-Sex Desire in Victorian Religious Culture* (Basingstoke, UK: Palgrave Macmillan, 2002), 224.

6. Marion Thain, "'Damnable Aestheticism' and the Turn to Rome: John Gray, Michael Field, and a Poetics of Conversion," in *The Fin-de-Siècle Poem*, ed. Joseph Bristow (Athens: Ohio University Press, 2005), 313.

7. Ursula King, *Christian Mystics* (London: Routledge, 2004), 143. For a more detailed account of the efflorescence of mysticism in sixteenth-century Spain, see also E. Allison Peers, *Studies of the Spanish Mystics*, 3 vols. (London: SPCK, 1951); Andrés Martín Melquiades, *Historia de la mística de la Edad de Oro en España y América* (Madrid: Biblioteca de Autores Cristianos, 1994); and *Faith and Fanaticism: Religious Fervour in Early Modern Spain*, ed. Lesley K. Twomey (Aldershot, UK: Ashgate, 1997).

8. Julia Kristeva, *Teresa, My Love: An Imagined Life of the Saint of Avila* (New York: Columbia University Press, 2014), 44.

9. E. Allison Peers, *Studies of the Spanish Mystics*, vol. 1 (London: SPCK, 1951), xvii.

10. Terence O'Reilly offers a fascinating exploration of courtly love and mysticism in Spanish poetry in *From Ignatius Loyola to John of the Cross* (Aldershot, UK: Variorum, 1995).

11. Corinne E. Blackmer, "The Ectasies of Saint Teresa: The Saint as Queer Diva from Crashaw to *Four Saints in Three Acts*," in *En Travesti: Women: Gender Subversion, Opera* (New York: Columbia University Press, 1995), 326. Blackmer argues that for queer twentieth-century artists, such as Vita Sackville-West and Gertrude Stein, among others, Teresa became a lesbian icon, a figure of societal, artistic, and sexual transgression. Sackville-West wrote a dual biography of St. Teresa of Ávila and St. Thérèse of Lisieux entitled *The Eagle and The Dove* (1943), in which she associates the figure of St. Teresa with Sappho and hints at lesbian practices. Stein wrote the libretto for the opera *Four Saints in Three Acts* (1934), which features St. Teresa.

12. *Michael Field, the Poet: Published and Manuscript Materials*, ed. Marion Thain and Ana Parejo Vadillo (Peterborough, Ontario: Broadview, 2009), 161.

13. See Roden, *Same-Sex Desire*; Marion Thain, "'Damnable Aestheticism'" and '*Michael Field*': *Poetry, Aestheticism and the Fin de Siècle* (Cambridge: Cambridge University Press, 2007); Thain and Vadillo, *Michael Field, the Poet*; and Camille Cauti, "Michael Field's Pagan Catholicism," in *Michael Field and Their World*, ed. Margaret D. Stetz and Cheryl A. Wilson (High Wycombe, UK: Rivendale, 2007).

14. Michael Field, *Works and Days: From the Journal of Michael Field*, ed. T. Sturge Moore (London: J. Murray, 1933), 313.

15. Field, 314.

16. For a more detailed account of the relationship between Gray and Michael Field, see, for example, Roden, *Same-Sex Desire*, and Thain, "'Damnable Aestheticism'" and '*Michael Field*.'

17. Thain, '*Michael Field*,' 171.

18. Katharine Bradley [K.B.] to John Gray [J.G.] (spring 1907), quoted in Thain and Vadillo, *Michael Field, the Poet*, 339.

19. K.B. to J.G. [1911], Dep. 372, N20, f. 28, Gray & Raffalovich Papers, National Library of Scotland (h,ereafter NLS).

20. K.B to J.G. [1907], Dep. 372, N17, f. 34, NLS.

21. Michael Field, "Works and Days," BL Add MS 46801, fol. 66v (April 9, 1911) [E.C.].

22. J.G. to K.B., October 24, 1908, quoted in Peter J. Vernon, "The Letters of John Gray" (PhD diss., University of London, 1976), 280.

23. Thain and Vadillo, *Michael Field, the Poet*, 346.

24. Thain and Vadillo, 346.

25. St. John of the Cross, *The Dark Night of the Soul*, ed. Benedict Zimmerman, trans. David Lewis (London: T. Baker, 1908), 62–63.

26. Cooper testifies to her postconversion celibacy in "Works and Days." In 1907 she wrote that, since converting, "I have never fallen into fleshly sin." In 1908 she added that "When I came into this Church a year ago [I gave] a gift that was a vow of chastity," quoted in Chris White, "'Poets and Lovers Evermore': The Poetry and Journals of Michael Field," in *Sexual Sameness: Textual Differences in Lesbian and Gay Writing*, ed. Joseph Bristow (London: Routledge, 1992), 40.

27. Michael Field, "Holy Cross," in *Poems of Adoration* (London: Sands & Co, 1912), 30.

28. K.B. to J.G. [1913], Dep. 372, N19, f. 68, NLS.

29. St. John of the Cross, *Dark Night of the Soul*, 118.

30. K.B. to J.G. [n.d.], Dep. 372, N17, NLS.

31. Michael Field, "Works and Days," BL Add MS 46801, fol. 2v (ca. January 1, 1911) [K.B.].

32. K.B. to J.G. [November 23, 1908], Dep. 372, N18, f. 15, NLS.

33. K.B. to J.G. [1909], Dep. 372, N17, NLS.

34. K.B. to J.G. [n.d.], Dep. 372, N17, NLS.

35. Michael Field, "Words of the Bridegroom," in *Poems of Adoration*, 93.

36. See Thain, "'Damnable Aestheticism,'" 327–31.

37. Michael Field, "Fregit," in *Poems of Adoration*, 5 (my italics).

38. K.B. to J.G. [1913], Dep. 372, N19, f. 16, NLS.

39. K.B. to J.G. [1909], Dep. 372, N17, NLS.

40. "This life of S. Theresa—I find, examining it is sought in itself." K.B. to J.G. [1907], Dep. 372, N17, f. 18, NLS.

41. K.B. to J.G., September 15 [1907], Dep. 372, N20, NLS.

42. St. Teresa of Ávila, *The Autobiography of St. Teresa of Avila*, trans. E. Allison Peers (London: Sheed and Ward, 1979), 192–93.

43. J.G. to "Michael Field," January 20, 1908, quoted in Thain, '*Michael Field*,' 193.

44. Thain, '*Michael Field*,' 193–94.

45. Thain, 185.

46. Michael Field, "Prophet," in *Poems of Adoration*, 64.

47. Michael Field, "Viaticum," in *Poems of Adoration*, 106–7.

48. Thain and Vadillo, *Michael Field, the Poet*, 161.

49. Female language understood henceforth as écriture feminine, a theory developed by Hélène Cixous in "The Laugh of the Medusa" (published originally in French in 1975). In this work, Cixous affirms that "woman must write her self: must write about women and bring women to writing." Cixous herself identified with St. Teresa and linked her figure with female transgression: "I was St. Teresa of Avila . . . that madwoman who knew a lot more than all the men. And who knew how to become a bird on the strength of loving." Hélène Cixous and Catherine Clément, *The Newly Born Woman*, trans. Betsy Wing (London: I. B. Tauris, 1996), 99.

50. Joy Dixon, "Introduction" to "Religion and Sexuality," special issue, *Victorian Review: An Interdisciplinary Journal of Victorian Studies* 37, no. 2 (2011): 41.

51. Jacques Lacan, *On Feminine Sexuality, Book XX: Encore, 1972–73*, trans. Bruce Fink (New York: Norton, 1998), 76.

52. Constance M. Furey, "Sexuality," in *The Cambridge Companion to Christian Mysticism*, ed. Amy Hollywood and Patricia Z. Beckman (Cambridge: Cambridge University Press, 2012), 335–36.

53. Karma Lochrie, "Mystical Acts, Queer Tendencies," in *Constructing Medieval Sexuality*, ed. Karma Lochrie, Peggy McCracken, and James A. Schults (Minneapolis: University of Minnesota Press, 1997), 183.

54. Furey, "Sexuality," 336.

55. Michael Field, "The Homage of Death," in *Mystic Trees* (London: Eveleigh Nash, 1913), 94–95.

56. St. Teresa, "What Would'st Thou Do with Me?" trans. Arthur Symons, in "The Poetry of Santa Teresa and San Juan de la Cruz," *Contemporary Review* 75 (1899): 542–51.

57. Michael Field, "The Homage of Death," 94.

58. For more on St. Teresa and her reputedly homoerotic attachments, see Blackmer, "Ecstasies of Saint Teresa," and Paola Marín, "Teresa de Ávila (Teresa de Jesús)," in *Spanish Writers on Gay and Lesbian Themes*, ed. David William Foster (Westport, CT: Greenwood, 1999).

59. Blackmer, "Ectasies of Saint Teresa," 308.

60. Marín, "Teresa de Ávila," 161.

61. Marín, 160.

62. Marín, 160.

63. St. Teresa, *The Collected Works of St. Teresa of Avila*, trans. Kieran Kavanaugh and Otilio Rodriguez, vol. 2 (Washington, DC: ICS, 190), 207–63, quoted in Marín, "Teresa de Ávila," 160.

64. Virginia Blain, "'Michael Field, the Two-Headed Nightingale': Lesbian Text as Palimpsest," *Women's History Review* 5:2 (1996): 252.

65. Kristeva, *Teresa, My Love*, 4.

66. See Ruth Vanita, *Sappho and the Virgin Mary: Same-Sex Love and the English Literary Imagination* (New York: Columbia University Press, 1996); Roden, *Same-Sex Desire*; and Cauti, "Michael Field's Pagan Catholicism."

67. St. Teresa, "Before the Crucifix," in *Minor Works of St. Teresa*, ed. Benedict Zimmerman (London: Thomas Baker, 1913), 60.

68. Michael Field, "A Crucifix," in *Mystic Trees*, 35.

69. Michael Field, "The Five Sacred Wounds," in *Mystic Trees*, 33; St. Teresa, "Self-Oblation," in *Minor Works*, 3.

70. Edward Howells, "Early Modern Reformations," in *Cambridge Companion*, 122.

71. Michael Field, "Purgatory," in *Poems of Adoration*, 31.

72. On December 4, 1913, Cooper testifies in her last entry in "Works and Days" how she refused to take drugs: "All through my time of special prayer for clearness of mind up to the End—all through my little sacrifice of the help of poppy, . . . I had received already such marked & amazing response," quoted in Thain and Vadillo, *Michael Field, the Poet*, 295.

73. M. Lynn Seitz, "Catholic Symbol and Ritual in Minor British Poetry of the Later Nineteenth Century" (PhD diss., Arizona State University, 1974), 179.

74. Michael Field, "Works and Days," BL Add MS 46804A, fol. 8r (January 28, 1914) [K.B.]. The "twain" Bradley refers to seems to be Edith Cooper and her younger sister, Amy (who had passed away in 1910 and was also a Catholic convert).

75. Ana de San Barlotomé, *Autobiography of Anne of Saint Bartholomew*, trans. Sister Mary Anna Michael (St. Louis: HS Collins, 1916), 41–42.

76. Kristeva, *Teresa, My Love*, 214.

TEN

Michael Field's Eric Gill

Radical Kinship, Cosmopolitanism, and Queer Catholicism

KRISTIN MAHONEY

IN JUNE 1913, MICHAEL FIELD WROTE TO THE SCULPTOR
Eric Gill (1882–1940) to thank him for a small statuette, *Madonna and Child*
(1912–13) (fig. 10.1), which had been sent to them after they admired a plaster
cast from the same plasticine original in the home of their friend William
Rothenstein. Though they acknowledge that "early French Madonnas have
smiled freakishly as [his] creation," they state that the statuette seems to them
"more of the East than of the Church," with a "Chinese forthrightness in dealing with a religious subject, a squareness of imagination that takes one East-
ward, where belief is too calm to own to any vagueness of emotional appeal."[1]
They make note of the warmth and corporeality in Gill's depiction of the *Madonna and Child:* "Feeling is of the very essence of religion—that your figurine
expresses solidly—with the sparseness of the fundamental art in the giver of
food & the vivid joy & vivid love of the little mouth that has received the gift
from the breast."[2] They seem to feel that Gill's work stresses Christ's body, his
hunger, and Mary's emotions, her maternity in a manner that is "solid" and
"sparse" rather than ethereal. This is, in their eyes, a highly embodied form of
Catholic worship that accentuates the fleshliness of the both Virgin and child,
a mode of representation that, to them, speaks with an "Eastern" inflection.

While they note that they are strangers to Gill, they seem to believe that
their shared status as artists and converts to Catholicism grants them the right

Figure 10.1. Eric Gill, *Madonna and Child* (1912–13), William Andrews Clark Memorial Library, University of California, Los Angeles.

to speak frankly and with a certain degree of intimacy about his art and their common faith. They "cannot write Dear Sir," they insist, so they open the letter with the salutation "Artist to artist," and they close by acknowledging that they have engaged in "frank speaking" around the topic of the figurine.[3] The letter is strikingly familiar. Bradley and Cooper congratulate Gill "that the best thing that can arrive to one by God's grace has been brought to [him] by that mysterious agency of godhead." They wish that he may "be as happy & sustained as [they] have been through the heaviest trial!" And they express the hope that Gill's art might "give to the Church what it so needs, reality of beauty in its images" and that the Church might "give to [his] art its own true unction!"[4] As fellow converts, fellow artists, they feel that they may converse freely and openly with Gill about the matter of faith as well as his artistic practice, as they are, though they have never met, deeply linked through their common religion.

I would like to use Michael Field's strange letter and the figurine it describes as a starting point from which to initiate a reconsideration of Gill's aesthetic practice, his religious faith, and his approach to kinship. Michael Field, I argue, might have been Gill's most astute audience. This is perhaps not surprising given their sculptural poetic practice and their agalmatophilia, as Ana Parejo Vadillo has argued in an earlier chapter of this book. They locate in Gill's work a devout Catholicism with an "Eastern inflection," a highly embodied "freakishness" and "forthrightness" that they find immensely appealing. And they seem to feel that their shared status as artists and Catholic converts unites them and places them together within a community of dissident devotion. What they see in Gill is exactly what I wish to foreground. Michael Field's strange yet perceptive reading of this image of the *Madonna and Child* highlights Gill's sexual dissidence, his integration of "Eastern" and Catholic aesthetics, and his fleshly approach to the divine. Noting that his work appears to be "of the East," they gesture toward his strange positioning in relationship to the Indian and Egyptian sculptural traditions with which he was engaging at the time, a relationship at once Orientalist and cosmopolitan, emerging simultaneously from a fetishistic vision of "the East" as sensual and exotic and an authentic desire for knowledge of Indian and Egyptian art history. The manner in which this image circulated also demonstrates Gill's connection to an aestheticist and sexually dissident strain of Catholicism, as well as the cosmopolitan aesthetic vision that Michael Field claims registers so clearly in the image itself. Copies of the original sculpture cast in bronze were given to the Ceylonese art historian Ananda Coomaraswamy and to Oscar Wilde's literary executor and friend Robert Ross, who in turn presented the work to the Johannesburg Art Gallery.[5] Plaster copies were sold to William Rothenstein (for himself and for Michael Field) and to the

Meynells, a Catholic family with strong ties to the aestheticism of the 1890s, and plaster copies of a very similar sculpture from the same period, *Madonna and Child, Suckling* (1913), were bought by Marc-André Raffalovich and John Gray, two Catholic converts with connections to the decadence of the fin de siècle.[6]

While Gill is often thought of as a "distinctly heterosexual" figure with a circumscribed and highly localized vision, during the teens he affiliated himself with a group of authors and artists whose nonnormative sexual identities were deeply intertwined with their Catholic religious identity, and he exhibited a tremendous thirst for information about global artistic practices, writing frequently to Coomaraswamy and engaging extensively with Indian art.[7] This figurine, then, along with Michael Field's reading of it, places Gill within a queer and cosmopolitan network, which in turn allows for new insight into his aesthetic and sexual practices. Recent work on Gill has tended to represent him as a provincial paterfamilias, one who wished to withdraw from the world into a fantasy rural English pastoral, whose incestuous relationships with his sisters and daughters amount to an amplification of patriarchal ideology with a stress on the ownership of women and the exaggeration of conventional masculinity.[8] However, reading Gill as Michael Field's letter tells us to, within the context of their queer Catholic network and global art history, brings to light a markedly different Eric Gill, a Gill whose strange (and at times disturbing) ideas about sexuality, the family, and the representation of the body are inflected by a cosmopolitan aesthetic vision as well as queer, decadent approaches to the practices of love and affiliation.

The reconsideration of Gill's work initiated by Michael Field's letter necessitates, in turn, a reconsideration of their significance as well as the influence of decadence in the early twentieth century. While Michael Field are often understood to have been increasingly neglected as the century turned, the interest that they held for Gill indicates that their work and the queer decadent community of which they were a part remained influential during the modernist period. As I hope to demonstrate here, the pairing of Gill and Michael Field is doubly rewarding, as it enriches our understanding of aesthetic history and queer history, allowing us to see the manner in which fin-de-siècle aesthetics remained present within the modernist moment and, in addition, providing insight into the manner in which the sexual dissidence of the 1890s informed highly disruptive forms of sexual radicalism in the twentieth century. Furthermore, just as seeing Michael Field's Eric Gill allows for insight into the afterlife of aestheticism during the modernist period, examining the manner in which these aestheticist connections engendered transnational engagement for Gill allows us to perceive the role of transhistorical communication in the development of modernist forms of cosmopolitanism and sexual dissidence. Fin-de-siècle figures like William Rothenstein facilitated Gill's exposure to Indian art, aestheticist writers like Michael Field admired and encouraged the evidence of this exposure in his artistic output, and his interest in Indian and Egyptian sculpture flourished while collaborating with Jacob Epstein on Wilde's tomb, a monument to the most significant figure associated with British aestheticism. Reading Gill through Michael Field's eyes brings to light Gill's complex historical positioning, as well as the manner in which his connections with decadence opened into a cosmopolitan engagement with Indian and Egyptian aesthetic traditions. Examining the manner in which Eric Gill read, responded to, and engaged with Michael Field draws out the persistent influence of these poets during the modernist moment and locates their integration of decadence, Catholicism, and sexual dissidence at the heart of British modernist practice.

I want to be careful to say here that, while I am trying to situate Gill's vision of desire and his aesthetic practices within a larger cosmopolitan and sexually dissident ethos that sought to rethink kinship and community, I am not condoning Gill's abuse of his daughters. Since the publication of Fiona MacCarthy's biography of Gill, which revealed that he had sex with his sisters and his dog and sexually abused his daughters, it is Gill's sexual practices that have attracted the most attention and caused the most discomfort in discussions of his work and career. While the UK's Survivors Trust as well as the National Association for People Abused in Childhood have called for the removal of Gill's sculptures from the façade of the British Broadcasting Corporation, his work remains on display there and at Westminster Cathedral and the League of Nations. As his work continues to be so public and prominent, his ideas about kinship and desire should be directly addressed, as they are central to his larger vision. In addition, reading his vision of divine eroticism within the decadent context from which it emerged highlights the extent to which the dissident decadent ethos, which we tend to associate with a more progressive and pleasing politics, could be repurposed and implemented within a program of abuse. This deserves to be considered, as engaging only with those elements of queer history that we find politically appealing results in a flattening of our understanding of the complex and divergent directions in which radical sexual practice moved in the late nineteenth and early twentieth centuries.[9] Situating Gill's work and career within the contexts to which Michael Field's letter directs us highlights the influence of queer Catholicism and transnational and transhistorical networks on his peculiar mode of British modernism, allowing us to see how he transmuted the influence of Indian sculpture and a late-Victorian aestheticist strain of sexually dissident faith into a startling, highly disruptive, and iconoclastic approach to kinship and desire. Highlighting the connections between Gill's vision of sexuality and the queer cosmopolitan networks from which it emerged allows us to see that the contestation of heteronormative social relations on the part of queer subjects working within a decadent and cosmopolitan tradition did not always result in just or liberatory practices.

"Vivid Joy & Vivid Love": Eric Gill and Queer Catholicism

Recent critical treatments of Gill by, for example, Fiona MacCarthy, Anthony Hoyland, and Michael Yorke have highlighted his preoccupation with sexuality.[10] However, as much as these critics stress Gill's unconventional ideas about desire and the family, they nevertheless disregard evidence that might counter or complicate their representation of Gill as "heterosexist," conventionally gendered, and deeply patriarchal.[11] The criticism of Gill, then, seems to be operating in a complex and conflicted manner, advertising itself as honest and unabashed in its treatment of sexual content while suppressing or disregarding Gill's interest in same-sex desire. The rich archive of material related to Gill's personal life in the Eric Gill Collection at the William Andrews Clark Memorial Library allows, however, for the emergence of a very different vision of his ideas about desire. In 1913, inspired by his reading of Havelock Ellis, Gill composed a set of case studies concerning his own sexual development and asked his wife Ethel to do the same. Each wrote one narrative about their heterosexual experiences ("He & She") and another about their same-sex experiences ("He & He" and "She & She"). Gill begins "He & He" by discussing the sexual experiences he had with other boys when he was young, and he concludes by noting that these desires have persisted in his adult life, stating, "Since the age of twenty I have had several loves & sometimes the affair has lasted for several years together. I usually prefer young men, grooms, or young soldiers with strong smooth limbs."[12] The sense of Gill's sexuality that emerges here is far more fluid and polymorphous than the aggressively heterosexual portraits painted by Yorke, Hoyland, and MacCarthy.

Gill's decision to create a document recording his sexual experiences with men two months after he converted to Catholicism seems noteworthy.[13] While MacCarthy's biography emphasizes the contradictions between Gill's Catholicism and his "urge to experiment with social conventions," the two are in fact linked and in accord with one another.[14] Gill's sexual practices need to be understood within a queer context, as motivated by a queer desire to undermine stable ideologies governing sexuality and affiliation and as occurring in conversation with the queer Catholicism of the turn of the century.[15] Catholicism's status as a dissident faith attracted Gill, and his initiation into the faith occurred in relationship to figures with ties to a particularly queer strain of Catholicism.

During this phase of his career when he was most actively engaged in sexual experimentation and theorizing, he was drawn to a religious practice that Marion Thain, drawing on the work of Ellis Hanson, has referred to as a "container" for sexual dissidence and a community whose sexual dissidence was articulated through their practice of that faith.[16]

Soon after his conversion and the composition of "He & He," Gill came to know two figures with strong ties to late-Victorian aestheticism and the queer Catholicism of the 1890s, Marc-André Raffalovich and John Gray. Gray, who is often thought to have been the inspiration for Wilde's Dorian Gray, wrote decadent poetry in the 1890s and had been ordained as a Catholic priest in 1901.[17] He was responsible for Michael Field's conversion to Catholicism in April 1907, having met Bradley in 1906, on the very day that their beloved dog Whym Chow died, an event that was tied directly in their own personal narrative to their turn to Catholicism.[18] Raffalovich, a French writer who had composed decadent poetry as well as a defense of Uranian love in the 1890s, had converted to Catholicism and moved to Edinburgh to be with Gray as he served as the parish priest at St. Peter's Church. Gill first visited Raffalovich's home in 1914. Following this visit, Raffalovich wrote to express his pleasure at their developing friendship, setting the tone for an intimate and playful correspondence that continued for years. During the next six years, Gill executed a series of sculptures for Raffalovich, as well as a portrait and a bookplate. He became increasingly intimate with the pair and received frequent visits from Gray at his home in Ditchling.

Gill's intimacy with Gray and Raffalovich in the years immediately following his conversion ensured that he was aware from the first of the rich possibilities Catholicism offered for the braiding together of eroticism and faith. As Frederick Roden notes in his discussion of sexuality and religious faith in Victorian England, Catholicism was understood as "culturally queer" during this period and attracted figures like Raffalovich and Gray, who found in Catholic rhetoric concerning the longing for Christ a useful framework for the sublimated expression of same-sex desire.[19] Ellis Hanson argues, "Raffalovich and Gray both learned to master that slight and subtle shift of the lens by which sexual desire is re-envisioned as Christian or Platonic *agape*."[20] Gill's friendship with Raffalovich and Gray, practitioners of what Raffalovich referred to as "sublime inversion," would have exposed him to models of the integration of Catholicism and sexual dissidence, and his correspondence with and work for the pair reveals that he took great pleasure in the erotic possibilities such an integration might offer.[21] The sculptures he executed for Raffalovich revel in the beauty of the male form. In 1915 he completed a sculpture, *Acrobat*, for Raffalovich. The location of this sculpture is unknown, but the pencil sketches

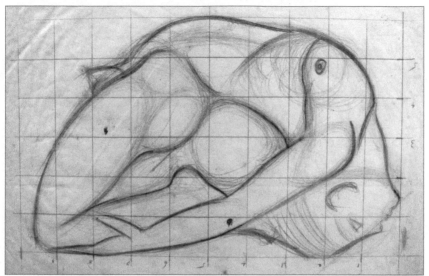

Figure 10.2. Eric Gill, *Sketch for Sculpture: Acrobat* (ca. 1915), William Andrews Clark Memorial Library, University of California, Los Angeles.

of the sculpture at the Clark Library depict a nude male figure resting on his stomach with his back arched and his legs bent behind his back (fig. 10.2). In 1920, he completed a similarly erotic treatment of the male form, a sculpture of Saint Sebastian with his hands behind his head and a long lean torso (fig. 10.3). In a letter to Raffalovich, Gill notes, "You will be amused to hear that the study from which I did the carving was made from myself in a mirror."[22] This sculpture, like the *Madonna & Child*, linked Gill to a community of sexually dissident Catholics and, in addition, placed his own physique on display, thereby entering his body into an erotic exchange with queer Catholic men, surrendering his own form to their gaze. At times, Gill's fusion of the carnal and the divine could even exceed his sexually dissident patrons' sense of propriety. Gray once asked Gill to carve a small statue of a man weeping for his sins. The resultant sculpture, which was deemed too "fleshly," was displayed on Gray's mantel "shrouded from head to foot."[23]

Through Raffalovich and Gray, Gill came to know another figure linked to aestheticist strains of queer Catholicism, Father Vincent McNabb. McNabb, confessor to Michael Field, was a Dominican priest with ties to the doctrine of Distributism, a doctrine Gill, with his previous interest in socialism, found immensely appealing.[24] While preserving the concept of private property, Distributism insisted that property ownership should be distributed as widely as possible so each family and individual might have access to the means of production. McNabb also argued that Catholics should return to the land and exist

Figure 10.3. Eric Gill, *Saint Sebastian* (1920), Tate Britain, London.

on self-sustaining farms. McNabb and his thinking played a central role in the development of the utopian community in the Sussex countryside of which Gill was the center. Eric Gill, Hilary Pepler, Desmond Chute, and Joseph Cribb became lay tertiaries of the Order of St. Dominic and founded a guild of Catholic craftsmen, the Guild of St. Joseph and St. Dominic, in Ditchling, East Sussex, a small village about fifty miles south of London. McNabb was frequently present at Ditchling in the teens and twenties, taking Gill's confession and spending long days talking with him about the Catholic faith and the future of the guild. This was the period in Gill's life and career when he was most open to and interested in radically experimental forms of connection, desire, and cooperation, and his diary demonstrates that he spent hours during this period speaking with Father Vincent about the "project of a religious order of artists," "Beauty & Work," and Irish nationalism.[25] McNabb had an immense effect on Gill's ideas about community, politics, and art, and he should be understood as one of the most crucial influences in the development of Gill's vision of affiliation in the teens and twenties.

McNabb's intense closeness with and reverence for Michael Field indicate that Gill would have found in McNabb a progressive confessor comfortable speaking frankly to bohemian artists about their dissident sexuality. McNabb first met Bradley and Cooper in 1908, and his treatment of Cooper during their initial meeting was seemingly quite open and kind. Cooper reported that there was "no shyness" between them.[26] When Cooper insisted that "he must know broadly the truth if he [was] to be of help to [her]" and spoke to him "of the ancient wrong, of the wild sinning & wild penances-in-vain," he responded, "You have known Christ's Redeeming Love" and spoke "of all the apostles—sinners, traitors to their Lord, chosen to reveal Him."[27] He seems to have operated as a patient and accepting spiritual advisor to the pair. As Marion Thain notes, Bradley and Cooper struggled with how to integrate their previous pagan aesthetic with their new faith, and this struggle is reflected in a palimpsest version of their volume *Wild Honey from Various Thyme* (1908), in which they pasted new Catholic poems over the most pagan verses.[28] This volume was presented to McNabb in 1911 and, according to a letter Bradley wrote to John Gray, elicited his approval: "Now the Church has welcomed the Honey-book. Fr. Vincent amazes me."[29] They composed a lyrical, mystical preface to a collection of McNabb's sermons, *The Orchard Floor* (1911), which attempts a similar integration of their pagan and Catholic passions, comparing the "Spirit of Revelation" that might pass through McNabb's sermon fragments to the wind passing through leaves to form an oracle.[30] McNabb seems to have accepted their peculiar integration of ancient and Christian forms of devotion as well as their passion for each other. In an introduction to a posthumous collection of Michael Field's poetry, *The Wattlefold* (1930), he speaks admiringly of the intimacy between Bradley and Cooper:

> I was given a priest's entry to their home life. To have that rare
> privilege was to witness a fellowship in life and love all too rare if
> not indeed unique in the history of letters. The full self-effacement
> of each in the life and life's work of the other was to my way of

thinking the essential drama from which the drama of their pen
was kept alight. . . . These two poets who elected to be known as
one had achieved a unity which if Plato is to be believed, is the
divinest attribute of the . . . Maker of the Universe.[31]

McNabb read their partnership as a model of sublime inversion. He remained
close with the pair during their illness and until their deaths in 1913 and 1914.
Cooper was diagnosed with cancer in 1911. When Bradley was diagnosed with
cancer two years later, she told only McNabb and John Gray.[32] McNabb wrote
to his brother Laurence after Cooper's death that it had been a "privilege to know
this gifted woman."[33] After Cooper died, Bradley moved to Hawkesyard Priory
to remain close to McNabb and, according to Mary Sturgeon, spent one of her
final afternoons reading to him the poetry of her deceased beloved.[34] On the
day Bradley died, McNabb immediately noted her absence from the chapel in
the morning and "had a sudden certainty of the end."[35] He "ran down the grassy
slopes to the house" to find her "stretched on the floor of her room, dead."[36] This
does not seem to have been a detached or conventional relationship between
priest and penitent but an extremely intimate friendship.

As Gill's friend, McNabb would have operated as another strong link to
an aestheticist tradition of Catholic sexual dissidence, and, as his confessor, he
would have represented a tolerant listener accustomed to the frank discussion
of nonnormative sexual practices, including same-sex desire and incest. Gill first
met McNabb in June 1914, a few months before Bradley's death, and he was at
the time, as his diary indicates, engaged in a sexual relationship with his sister
Gladys. McNabb moved, then, very quickly from serving as the confessor to a
set of writers involved in an incestuous relationship to operating as the confi-
dante of another artist engaged in comparably dissident sexual practices.[37] The
"unity" of Bradley and Cooper's incestuous "fellowship" would have been quite
fresh in McNabb's mind. It seems likely that McNabb exhibited the same kinds
of permissiveness and understanding in his treatment of this new penitent as he
had when speaking to Cooper of her "wild sinning."[38]

Michael Field's relationship, as well as the manner in which their "fellowship" was reverenced by McNabb, may have operated as points of reference
during the later phases of Eric and Gladys's relations with one another. In 1929,
Gladys and Eric rekindled their sexual relationship. Glady's first husband had
died, she had divorced her second, and she was living in a small cottage with her
daughter where Gill would frequently come to visit.[39] The Wattlefold was published the following year, and Gill would have been well aware of McNabb's ap-
proving description of the love between these two "princesses of English song."[40]
Gill's "working library" is housed at the Clark Library and includes a copy of

The Wattlefold. Did Gill recognize in Bradley and Cooper fellow practitioners of a radical form of sexual dissidence? As Kate Thomas argues, the incestuous nature of Bradley and Cooper's relationship has been politely avoided in much recent criticism.[41] But was it something Gill and his sister actively discussed? Perhaps they found comfort in McNabb's endorsement of Bradley's and Cooper's "fellowship in life and love."[42] Perhaps they saw in the fellowship between these two rebels who nevertheless received Christ's redeeming love a model of sexual dissidence that remained in contact with the divine.

The Catholic community with which Gill engaged in the teens and twenties exposed him to new ways of conceiving of kinship and desire. Catholicism itself could be said to enable a queer approach to kinship. The rhetoric of Catholicism certainly does something queer with familial language, undoing the stability of our understanding of what maternity is, of the division between fathers and sons, facilitating a series of substitutions and sublimations that blur and redefine kinship roles and the primacy of blood ties. Within his new community of Catholic sexual dissidents, Gill was surrounded by figures who drew upon this element of Catholic rhetoric in rethinking and remaking their own bonds with others, resolving their own nonnormative kinship inclinations by integrating their approach to affiliation with their faith. The familial rhetoric of Catholicism allows for the blurring of boundaries between biological and divine connections. Kinship and religious adoration can be intertwined and exchanged for one another. Gray, Gill, and Michael Field drew upon this model of substitution in renaming and redefining their connections with friends and mentors. As Chris White notes, Bradley and Cooper chose to exclude "the language of blood relatives" from the vocabulary concerning their union, turning to classical scholarship and then the language of Catholicism to rename their "Sacred Relation."[43] Marion Thain argues that Bradley and Cooper chose to figure their relationship with their dog Whym Chow as a Holy Trinity in order to deal with repressed incest anxiety. According to Thain, their identification with the Father and the Son within that Trinity "is a familial identification that neutralises and legitimises the intense erotic bond between aunt and niece."[44] Raffalovich referred to himself as Gray's "father & mother," and Gill referred to McNabb and Father John O'Connor, another Dominican priest with close ties to the community at Ditchling, as his "spiritual father and mother."[45] Drawing on the rhetoric of Catholicism, incestuous ties could be renamed as divine, and same-sex desire and friendship could be remade as familial. The Catholicism with which Gill was engaging in the teens offered numerous alternative models of affiliation and allowed for the conceptualization of all manners of nonnormative kinship and sexuality.

Gill's interest in incest is an outgrowth of his more general interest in undoing conventional conceptions of desire and affiliation. During the teens and twenties, when Gill was most actively engaged in violating the norms that govern the conceptualization of home, community, and desire, he was drawn to the sexual practices that most violently unsettle and redefine these concepts. As Gayle Rubin and Judith Butler have argued, the incest taboo plays a crucial role in the stabilizing of kinship systems and gender roles.[46] If the incest taboo operates as the centerpiece of the gender system and the stability of kinship structures, the practice of incest could be understood as one of the most radical forms of sexual dissidence.[47] Butler has raised questions about how the incest taboo demonstrates the persisting interest in recognizing certain social arrangements and not others as legitimate love.[48] Gill's sexual experiments refuse the boundaries delineating legitimate and illegitimate love and call into question the most fundamental laws governing the expression of desire. Gill's wish to contest foundational sexual ideologies and test out new ways of conceiving of kinship should be understood as an offshoot from his engagement with queer Catholicism, and his radical kinship practices should be understood as inflected by his contact with aestheticism and decadence.

This tendency to radically contest the most fundamental norms governing sexual arrangements is similarly reflected in Gill's "experiments" with animals. If the incest taboo is, as Lévi-Strauss argues, "the fundamental step because of which, by which, but above all in which, the transition from nature to culture is accomplished," the taboo against bestiality might be understood as similarly foundational, "maintaining the ontological boundary between human and animals."[49] While rethinking affiliation between humans, Gill also became interested in testing and reconsidering the division between humans and nonhuman animals. At Ditchling, Gill seems to have become increasingly fascinated with the sexuality of animals. In 1915, he recorded in his diary that a doe rabbit had been "put to buck in noon. V. interesting process. Two copulations in less than five minutes."[50] In a 1916 entry, he notes that he had "examined & compared specimens of semen from [himself] & a spaniel dog under microscope."[51] Gill brings to his investigation of animals and their bodies a scientific curiosity, as well as an apparent desire to set up equivalences as much as to establish difference. In a 1929 entry (that has been struck through), Gill records "experiments with dog in eve."[52] A few entries later, he states that he "continued experiment with dog after & discovered that a dog will join with a man."[53] Bestiality, like incest, violates the limits of conventional subject positions. While incest may contest the stability of kinship structures and the gender system, bestiality contests the structures that define what it is to be human. To transgress these boundaries is to call into question some of the most fundamental elements of our understanding of identity. Gill's sexual practices in the teens and twenties are united by a desire to attack at their very core those concepts of identity that seem most inviolable and unquestionable. And again, these practices should be understood as of a piece with Gill's drive toward rethinking community and the concept of affiliation and his ties to queer Catholicism. What is troubling and disappointing is the fact that, while a utopian desire to reconceptualize basic human activities, such as love and work, unites his thinking during this period, many of the experiments inspired by these utopian desires result in abuse and the disregard of involved subjects' capacity to consent. His violations of sexual norms point to the fact that as much as these norms might delimit and discipline, they can at times provide forms of protection for disempowered or silenced subjects. His utopian impulses result at times in appealing experiments like the guild, but his radical attempts at complete liberation and freedom just as often result in exploitation and disregard for the freedom of others.

As startling and strange as Gill's behavior during this period might seem, members of the queer Catholic community with which Gill was affiliated were engaged in similarly radical experiments concerning the process of affiliation. Michael Field's devotion to their dog Whym Chow also called into question the distinction between human and nonhuman animals, placing the dog in a series of erotic and kinship positions and undoing the fixity of the boundary between species. Ruth Vanita argues that Whym Chow served as an erotic proxy for Bradley and Cooper.[54] Jill Ehnenn's reading of Michael Field's elegiac poetry stresses the poets' creation of an "eroticized narrative of their beloved dog as conduit for queer desire and interwoven subjectivity."[55] Frederick Roden asserts that their "devotion to their 'son,' a progeny who was not biologically procreated," allowed "the two women [to] come to God not as brides of Christ but as mothers and lovers of their dog."[56] Positing Whym Chow as proxy, conduit, son, and lover, Bradley and Cooper demonstrate their intense desire to cross species lines in the expression of intimacy. While readers have often struggled with how seriously to take their impassioned statements concerning their dog, their wish to be united with him can be linked conceptually to their interest in collaboration and their dissident approach to desire. Bradley and Cooper, like Gill, were drawn to ways of working and loving that necessitated a dramatic shift in the conception of identity and the boundary between self and other. Their queer approach to affiliation also seemed to facilitate a dissident understanding of the kinship between human and nonhuman animals. And, as Roden and Thain have noted, Michael Field's devotion to their dog is also bound up with their Catholicism. Catholicism's queer approach to kinship, its tendency to substitute and sublimate kinship positions and allow earthly contact to stand in for divine connection, also allowed them to translate their intimacy with their pet into a form of worship. In their poems about Whym Chow, the dog is compared to the Holy Spirit and to Christ. Loving Whym Chow became a way to love one another and a way to love God. Due to Gill's intense fascination with sexual acts, it was perhaps unavoidable that his practices would take on a more sexual valence than Michael Field's.[57] However, in the case of Gill as well as in the case of Michael Field, the radical questioning of kinship structures engendered by queer Catholicism opened into the contestation of the fundamental otherness of nonhuman animals.

While at first glance the aesthetics of Eric Gill and Michael Field could not seem more opposed to one another, Bradley and Cooper's work, their thinking, and the members of their community provide an incredibly useful framework for understanding Gill's thinking about kinship and desire in the teens and twenties. Gill expressed deep admiration for their writing. In a 1914 letter to William Rothenstein, Gill thanks Rothenstein for sending him Bradley's *Mystic Trees* (1913) and notes that he has also acquired Cooper's *Poems of Adoration* (1912). The poetry has, he states, "the extraordinary atmosphere of a shrine," and "to read ten or more of the poems one after the other is to feel that you are . . . in a place where precious things are ritually preserved & worshipped."[58] The poetry has for him a physicality. It places you somewhere, makes you feel as if you are coming into contact with divine things. Nevertheless, he notes, they seem "withdrawn from the mess and dirt of this admirable world." However, while their extraordinary nature places them above the material world, that same nature places them on intimate terms with Christ. The two poets are, he insists, "completely enfolded in the everlasting arms."[59] Their mysticality and ethereality places them in a highly embodied embrace with Christ. They are in his arms.

This element of Michael Field's work must have held great appeal for Gill, as his work in the teens and twenties expresses intense enthusiasm for the idea of entering into true intimacy with Christ. In a letter to Rayner Heppenstall from the early 1920s, he actually describes conversion as a form of intercourse: "Joining the Church is not like joining the I.L.P. or the 3rd International. It's like getting married and, speaking analogically, we are fucked by Christ."[60] His *Nuptials of God* engraving from the same period places a similar emphasis on the erotic valence of the relationship between Christ and the faithful, showing Christ in the embrace of his bride, the Roman Catholic Church. And his countless sketches of a nude Christ on the cross lavish great attention on the contours of Christ's body and the details of his genitalia. Gill's representations of a nude Christ integrate a queer appreciation for the beauty of the male form with desire for true contact with the divine. In conversation with queer Catholicism, Gill developed a vision of faith that was highly eroticized, embodied, and sexually dissident.

"More of the East than of the Church"

Gill's interest in braiding together dissident eroticism and religious faith must also be understood in relationship to the element of his aesthetic that Michael Field seemed most interested in highlighting, its "Easternness." Gill's engagement with Indian art was in part initiated by Bradley and Cooper's friend William Rothenstein. Rothenstein operated as a contact point between Gill and an array of transhistorical and transnational aesthetic influences. As Arrowsmith notes, Rothenstein's "home generally served as an unofficial nexus point for various artists, poets, and scholars."[61] The longevity of Rothenstein's career as well as the breadth of his contacts meant his home was a site where one was just as likely to encounter either Max Beerbohm or Roger Fry. While he brought Gill into contact with modernist artists including Jacob Epstein and Lucien Pisarro, he was, of course, also a link to the 1890s and to late-Victorian aestheticism. Bradley and Cooper first encountered the *Madonna and Child* statuette that they so adored in Rothenstein's home, and he actively encouraged Gill to think of himself in relationship to Michael Field, writing to him about the pair's Catholicism during the period when Gill had begun toying with the idea of converting: "Your own hankerings and longings for [some kind of traditional discipline] & your expressed interest in Roman Catholicism made me think of my friends the Michael Fields & the comfort & guidance they have been able to get from submitting themselves to a tradition of ritual."[62]

Rothenstein sat at the point of tension between the Victorian and the modern in Gill's career, carrying his eye backward to the aestheticism of the fin de siècle while pointing him forward to the emergent avant-gardism of the teens. In addition, he broadened the geographical boundaries of Gill's aesthetic. Rothenstein participated in the founding of the India Society in 1910, an organization that aimed to promote Indian fine arts to the British public, and he transmitted his enthusiasm for Indian art to Gill. He wrote to Gill during a trip to India that he wished that Gill were there with him to see the carvings of "archaistic figures of naked Gods & Goddesses" on the cliff below Gwalior Fort in Rajasthan.[63] By 1913, Rothenstein seems to have shared with Michael Field the opinion that Gill's work had begun to exhibit evidence of "Eastern" influences. Michael Field notes in a letter to Rothenstein following their receipt of the *Madonna and Child*, "I have had a letter from Eric Gill, wondering that we all find his work has an

Eastern element in it."[64] If this element was present, it was due to the influence of Rothenstein and the manner in which he operated as a contact point between Gill and one of his most significant mentors, Ananda Coomaraswamy, the art historian who was largely responsible for the transmission of Indian art history to England at the turn of the century.

According to Gill, it was probably Rothenstein who first introduced him to Coomaraswamy, and, as Arrowsmith's discussion of the influence of Indian aesthetics on the work of Gill demonstrates, Coomaraswamy's writings and photographs had a considerable impact on his approach to artistic production.[65] While, as Arrowsmith reveals, contact with Indian traditions transformed Gill's technique, leading him to embrace the direct carving technique used by Indian sculptors, his engagement with Indian sculpture and his ongoing correspondence with Coomaraswamy also impacted his theories concerning faith and desire. As Sarah Victoria Turner has recently argued, Coomaraswamy's particular vision of the "vein of deep sex-mysticism" and the reconciliation of the sacred and the profane in Indian sculpture held intense appeal for Gill, "who was exploring the fusion of the sacred and the sexual in his own carvings."[66] In conversation with Coomaraswamy, Gill further developed his vision of a divine eroticism. As Richard Cork notes, Coomaraswamy's call for a "frank recognition of the close analogy between amorous and religious ecstasy" was enormously influential for Gill.[67] He found in the works that Coomaraswamy showed to him models of how the sculptor might integrate eroticism with worship, along with a demonstration, as Coomaraswamy would later put it, of the extent to which spirituality and sensuality are "inseparably linked," "merely the inner and outer aspects of one and the same expanding life."[68]

Rothenstein, then, linked Gill to Coomaraswamy and Indian art history as well as to Michael Field and the fin-de-siècle past, and, in addition, he "fostered the friendship" between Gill and Jacob Epstein, securing Gill's connections with both British modernism and the production of the Oscar Wilde memorial.[69] Gill's work with Epstein on Wilde's tomb, for which Gill designed the inscription and, according to Michael Pennington, carved the wings, enfolds his interest in sexual dissidence and his interest in global aesthetics.[70] It seems likely that Gill would have been eager to participate in the memorial project, as he was an admirer of Wilde's work.[71] Wilde's growing reputation as a martyr for the cause of sexual freedom probably held great appeal for Gill as well. His participation in the construction of the tomb was a logical extension of his interest in queer Catholicism and the aestheticism of the fin de siècle. In addition, his work on the project provided an opportunity to integrate his interest in that tradition with his developing interest in "Eastern" art.

Epstein received the commission to produce Wilde's tomb from Robert Ross in 1908, and his initial designs followed suggestions he received from "Wilde's admirers" to employ a Grecian aesthetic.[72] However, Gill and Epstein had begun to frequent the British Museum and the Victoria and Albert Museum in order to admire Indian, Assyrian, and Egyptian sculpture, and, due to the influence of Commaraswamy, they became increasingly enthusiastic about the possibility of integrating these influences into their modernist sculptural practice. As a result, Epstein's vision for the monument transformed. As Arrowsmith notes, Epstein "[brought] the Wilde tomb from Classical Greece, through archaic Lykia, then Assyria, and finally Egypt" (95).[73] The face of the winged sphinx that Epstein produced exhibits, Pennington argues, "a peculiar affinity to the face of the hieratic Egyptian pharaoh, Akhenaton (1300 B.C.)," and Arrowsmith's reading of the work highlights evidence of the influence of a fourteenth-century bust of Akhenaton that Epstein would have encountered at the Louvre.[74] The time Gill and Epstein spent admiring Indian and Egyptian sculpture in London museums and in Coomaraswamy's photographs also informed their thinking about the frank representation of sex and the body. The new sensuality of their shared aesthetic registers in Epstein's representation of the pronounced genitalia of the "flying demon angel," which caused such enormous scandal when the sculpture was placed in Père Lachaise in 1912.[75] The memorial that Gill and Epstein produced and the scandal it elicited honored the most famous sexual dissident with an act of aesthetic dissidence that violated the norms governing the representation of the male body, as well as prioritizing European artistic traditions, turning purposefully away from Europe and to India and Egypt for inspiration.

Gill's collaboration with Epstein and his cosmopolitan engagement with global art history also informed his treatment of kinship, resulting in one of his best-known works, *They* (or *Ecstasy*, 1910–11) (fig. 10.4), an attempt (in Gill's mind) to hallow incestuous desire and transform the most radical form of sexual dissidence into an expression of divine love. As Arrowsmith argues, Gill and Epstein's work of this period suggests that Coomaraswamy probably showed them pictures of the temple of the Hindu sun god Surya at Konark, which is decorated with sculpture inspired by the Tantric belief that "formalized sexual acts" might act as "an ecstatic shortcut to spiritual enlightenment."[76] Gill and Epstein discussed plans to construct a temple of their own on the grounds of a property named Asham House, a "twentieth century Stonehenge," to be decorated with carvings similar in both style and content to this type of Indian temple sculpture.[77] The project, according to Pennington, was meant to "celebrate the primal and the sexual on a grand scale."[78] Epstein's Asham sketch,

Figure 10.4. Eric Gill, *They* (or *Ecstasy*, 1910–11), Tate Britain, London.

One of the Hundred Pillars of the Secret Temple (1910–11), which represents a man and woman engaged in sexual intercourse, registers clearly the influence of the sculptures at Konark, as does Gill's contemporaneous *They*, which also represents a man and woman standing and engaged in sexual intercourse.[79] Judith Collins asserts that *They* was intended to stand in Gill and Epstein's "open-air temple dedicated to love."[80] Gill's sister Gladys and her husband Ernest Laughton were the models for *They*, and Gill's diary reveals that he was actively engaged in a sexual relationship with Gladys during this period. An entry in 1911, for example, notes that he slept with her at Epstein's home.[81] This work emerges directly from Gill's radical sexual experimentation and his attempts to rethink categories of kinship and the practice of affiliation. Representing his own sister engaging in sexual intercourse—making material evidence of his own longing for her in the style of temple sculpture that links sex acts with worship—operates here as a method for sanctifying sexually dissident behavior. Gill titled a drawing for the work "Christ and the Church."[82] Gill so believed in the divinity of even the most radically dissident forms of sexual practice, he thought he might use his own incestuous desire as the source material for a representation of Christ's relationship with his followers. Roger Fry's response to the sculpture highlighted these elements of Gill's thinking. On first seeing a photograph of the work, Fry wrote to say, "This is real religious art."[83] A few days later, he wrote to request additional photographs of the work, stating, "I want to send one to Ed Carpenter who will welcome it immensely."[84] Fry comprehended immediately that Gill wished to fuse the erotic and the divine and, in addition, that Gill's work would be of interest to one of the best-known proponents of sexual dissidence. *They* can be understood, then, as an integration of the multiple strands of influence and experimentation under discussion here. A representation of radical sexual dissidence informed by Gill's contact with queer Catholic communities and stylistically inflected by his engagement with Hindu temple sculpture, *They* reflects Gill's belief in the holiness of sexual acts and the divinity of erotic union.

In their correspondence with Gill, Michael Field stress the "Eastern" quality of his work and the highly embodied quality of his faith. Reading his work from their perspective, and with their influence and the influence of members of their circle in mind, allows for a very different and much more accurate picture of Gill to appear. As Bradley and Cooper indicate, he integrated his faith with his interest in the body, and Indian sculpture along with the work of decadent Catholics made it clear to Gill that he was, in his desire to perform this integration, part of a larger community of erotic artists and iconoclasts. During the teens and twenties, when Gill seemed so determined to extricate himself from every ideology that might structure or inhibit his desires, to abolish all norms and customs governing sexual practice, queer Catholicism along with his engagement with Coomaraswamy's reading of Indian sculpture inflected his thinking and enabled his contestation of conventional sexual ideologies. Memorializing Wilde in an erotic sculpture with an Egyptian inflection, consecrating his love for his sister in a carving inspired by Hindu temple sculpture, Gill braided together sexual dissidence, religious faith, and global aesthetics. This Gill, a queer, decadent, Catholic, and cosmopolitan Gill, is Michael Field's Gill, a sculptor who highlights the "vivid joy" of faith and the "feeling" that is the "essence" of religion. And this vision of Gill only emerges clearly when we see him through their eyes. Looking at Gill's sculptures with Bradley and Cooper reveals how fruitful it can be to think and read across boundaries of periodization. The insights afforded by the unlikely pairing of Eric Gill and Michael Field indicate what is to be gained when we allow for the interplay between the Victorian and the modern, acknowledging the cross-pollination and conversation that occurred between figures and movements that have for too long been considered in isolation from one another. Reading Gill through Michael Field, we see the manner in which his engagement with late-Victorian decadent Catholicism and Coomaraswamy's vision of Indian sculpture's "sex-mysticism" engendered the "vivid love" in his religious and erotic sculptures, as well as his investment in radical, disruptive, and taboo sexual practices. And reading Michael Field through Gill, we see how their queer and erotically inflected Catholicism, the manner in which they understood their incestuous love for one another as well as their transgressive love for Whym Chow to be "completely enfolded in the everlasting arms" of Christ, operated as a significant and vital influence on modernist practice in the twentieth century.

Notes

1. Michael Field to Eric Gill, June 3, 1913, Collection on Eric Gill, MS. Gill, William Andrews Clark Memorial Library, University of California, Los Angeles. (Transcriptions from manuscript sources are my own.)

2. M.F. to E.G., June 3, 1913. 3. M.F. to E.G., June 3, 1913.

4. M.F. to E.G., June 3, 1913.

5. Judith Collins, *Eric Gill: The Sculpture* (New York: Overlook, 1998), 79.

6. Collins, 80, 87–88.

7. Anthony Hoyland, *Eric Gill: Nuptials of God* (Kent, UK: Crescent Moon, 1994), 63.

8. Fiona MacCarthy, for example, stresses Gill's "sexually possessive attitude to his own daughters" and his tendency to "retreat," evident in the move to Ditchling and Capel-y-Ffinn. See MacCarthy, *Eric Gill: A Lover's Quest for Art and God* (New York: E.P. Dutton, 1989), xi, 84, 187. She also refers often, in the same book, to the "Englishness"

of his work and his character (see 22, 272). Rupert Arrowsmith, however, has recently troubled this vision of Gill as provincial and removed from the international scene. See Arrowsmith, *Modernism and the Museum: Asian, African, and Pacific Art and the London Avant-Garde* (New York: Oxford University Press, 2011).

9. Kadji Amin's recent work on Jean Genet similarly calls for an acknowledgment of the fact that, while certain figures and moments resist the idealizing tendencies of queer studies, scholarship should nevertheless engage with "forms of transgression" that "do not necessarily provide the payoff of either utopian world making or progressive politics that scholars might desire." Amin addresses the "injunction" within queer studies "that queer collectivities, kinships, coalitions, and counterpublics operate as a utopian model of more just, egalitarian, and caring social forms" and "interrogates the unstated assumption that a heroic and even ascetic agency animates queer relations." See Kadji Amin, *Disturbing Attachments: Genet, Modern Pederasty, and Queer History* (Durham, NC: Duke University Press, 2017), 13.

10. See MacCarthy, *Eric Gill*; Hoyland, *Nuptials*; and Michael Yorke, *Eric Gill: Man of Flesh and Spirit* (New York: Universe Books, 1981).

11. Hoyland, *Nuptials*, 57.

12. Eric Gill, "He & He," in bound collection of various manuscript items, 1910–14, Collection on Eric Gill, MS. Gill, William Andrews Clark Memorial Library, University of California, Los Angeles.

13. Gill converted to Catholicism in February of 1913. The "He & He" and "He & She" entries in the bound notebook at the Clark Library are dated April 1913.

14. MacCarthy, *Eric Gill*, xi.

15. I borrow the term "queer Catholicism" from Patrick O'Malley's investigation of the manner in which "the formulation and articulation of Catholic subjectivity in Britain comes to be particularly related to that of nonnormative sexual subjectivities." See O'Malley, "Epistemology of the Cloister: Victorian England's Queer Catholicism," *GLQ: A Journal of Gay and Lesbian Studies* 15, no. 4 (2009): 541.

16. Marion Thain, *'Michael Field': Poetry, Aestheticism, and the Fin de Siècle* (New York: Cambridge University Press, 2007), 169.

17. For a discussion of John Gray's connections to Wilde's novel, see Jerusha McCormack, *The Man Who Was Dorian Gray* (New York: St. Martin's, 2000), 39–102.

18. According to Emma Donoghue, "Canon Gray, whose past had overlapped with the Michaels', could understand their hunger for something more, now Whym Chow was dead, some consolation no human friend could give" (Donoghue, *We Are Michael Field* [Bath, UK: Absolute, 1998], 123).

19. Frederick Roden, *Same-Sex Desire in Victorian Religious Culture* (Basingstoke, UK: Palgrave Macmillan, 2002), 2.

20. Ellis Hanson, *Decadence and Catholicism* (Cambridge, MA: Harvard University Press, 1997), 323.

21. As Hanson notes, Raffalovich used the term "sublime invert" in his discussion of "the capacity for intense religious feeling among inverts" (323).

22. Eric Gill, *Letters of Eric Gill*, ed. Walter Shewring (London: Jonathan Cape, 1947), 138.

23. McCormack, *Man Who Was Dorian Gray*, 258.

24. McNabb would often insist that he was not a proponent of Distributism, but there are many resonances between the ideas expressed in his own lectures and writings and the doctrines of Distributism, and he engaged enthusiastically with G. K. Chesterton and Hilaire Belloc and their expression of Distributist ideals.

25. Diary of Eric Gill, October 5, 1917, Collection on Eric Gill, MS. Gill, William Andrews Clark Memorial Library, University of California, Los Angeles (hereafter cited as Diary of Eric Gill); Diary of Eric Gill, October 8, 1917. In a July 18, 1922, entry, Gill notes that he had a "discussion with Fr. Vincent about Sinn Fein."

26. Marion Thain and Ana Parejo Vadillo, eds., *Michael Field, the Poet* (Peterborough, Ontario: Broadview, 2009), 283.

27. Thain and Vadillo, 285–86.

28. For further discussion of this palimpsest version of *Wild Honey from Various Thyme*, see Thain, 'Michael Field,' 171–72.

29. Quoted in Thain, 'Michael Field,' 172. The book is inscribed "To the Very Revd, the Prior of Holy Cross" (171). McNabb was prior of the Holy Cross Priory from 1908 to 1914. See Ferdinand Valentine, *Father Vincent McNabb, O.P.: The Portrait of a Great Dominican* (London: Burns and Oates, 1955), 237.

30. Michael Field, preface to *The Orchard Floor: Selected Passages from Sermons by the Very Rev. Vincent McNabb, Compiled by Miss E.C. Fortey* (London: R. & T. Washbourne, 1912), vii.

31. Vincent McNabb, introduction to *The Wattlefold: Unpublished Poems by Michael Field, Collected by Emily C. Fortey* (Oxford: Basil Blackwell, 1930), v–vi.

32. See Roden, *Same-Sex Desire*, 198.

33. Valentine, *McNabb*, 384.

34. Mary Sturgeon, *Michael Field* (London: George G. Harrap, 1922), 57.

35. Sturgeon, 61.

36. Sturgeon, 61.

37. While Gill does not state explicitly in his diaries that he informed McNabb about his incestuous relationships, he does make note of McNabb taking his confession, and in a 1921 entry he records that he made a "confession to Fr. O'Connell in eve. And talk after supper re Eliz. & my 'affairs,'" presumably referencing his sexual abuse of his daughter Elizabeth (Diary of Eric Gill, July 25, 1921). This would seem to indicate that he spoke to his Catholic confessors about his incestuous sexual practices.

38. McNabb and Gill did eventually fall out with one another. In 1935, Gill published an article in the *Sun Bathing Review* that McNabb found objectionable, and McNabb wrote to Gill to ask him to inform those who coupled their names that "we are no longer one." Vincent McNabb to Eric Gill, January 20, 1935, Collection on Eric Gill, MS. Gill, William Andrews Clark Memorial Library, University of California, Los Angeles.

39. MacCarthy notes that Gill recorded in his diary on November 1, 1929, "Bath and slept with Gladys" (MacCarthy, *Eric Gill*, 239).

40. McNabb, introduction to *Wattlefold*, vi.

41. Kate Thomas, "'What Time We Kiss': Michael Field's Queer Temporalities," *GLQ: A Journal of Lesbian and Gay Studies* 13, no. 2–3 (2007): 329. A recent notable

exception to this tendency is Carolyn Tate's "Lesbian Incest as Queer Kinship: Michael Field and the Erotic Middle-Class Victorian Family," *Victorian Review* 39, no. 2 (2013): 181–99.

42. McNabb, introduction to *Wattlefold*, v.

43. Chris White, "Poets and Lovers Ever More: The Poetry and Journals of Michael Field," *Sexual Sameness: Textual Difference in Gay and Lesbian Writing*, ed. Joseph Bristow (New York: Routledge, 1992), 34. The relationship is referred to as a "Sacred Relation" in their journals. See Ivor Treby, *Uncertain Rain: Sundry Spells of Michael Field* (Bury St. Edmunds, UK: De Blackland, 2002), 27.

44. Thain, *'Michael Field*,' 193.

45. Hanson, *Decadence*, 318; Eric Gill, *Eric Gill: Autobiogaphy* (New York: Devin-Adair, 1941), 219. 46. See Gayle Rubin, "The Traffic in Women: Notes on the Political Economy of Sex," in *Toward an Anthropology of Women*, ed. Rayna R. Reiter (New York: Monthly Review Press, 1975), 157–210; Judith Butler, *Antigone's Claim* (New York: Columbia University Press, 2002).

47. This is not to say that incest is always necessarily destabilizing or oppositional. As Elizabeth Barnes notes, while some critics have argued that incest transgresses normative kinship relations, others have argued that "incest is an *effect* of these sexual and familial norms, a patriarchal privilege of particular (read: white, middle class) nuclear family lives." See Elizabeth Barnes, introduction to *Incest and the Literary Imagination*, ed. Elizabeth Barnes (Gainesville: University Press of Florida, 2002), 9–10.

48. Butler, *Antigone's Claim*, 21.

49. Claude Lévi-Strauss, *The Elementary Structures of Kinship* (Boston: Beacon Press, 1969), 24; Kathy Rudy, "LGBTQ . . . Z?" *Hypatia* 27, no. 3 (2012): 607.

50. Diary of Eric Gill, April 12, 1915.

51. Diary of Eric Gill, October 25, 1916.

52. Diary of Eric Gill, December 8, 1929.

53. Diary of Eric Gill, December 13, 1929.

54. See Ruth Vanita, *Sappho and the Virgin Mary: Same-Sex Love and the English Literary Imagination* (New York: Columbia University Press, 1996).

55. Jill R. Ehnenn, "'Dragging' at Memory's Fetter': Michael Field's Personal Elegies, Victorian Mourning, and the Problem of Whym Chow," *Michaelian* 1 (2009), n.p. http://www.thelatchkey.org/Field/MF1/ehnennarticle.htm.

56. Roden, *Same-Sex Desire*, 194.

57. For further discussion of Gill's belief that "the erotic and the spiritual are not opposites or separable" and that "human love is a participation in Divine Love," see Yorke, *Eric Gill*, 120–22.

58. Gill, *Letters*, 58.

59. Gill, *Letters*, 58.

60. Quoted in MacCarthy, *Eric Gill*, 162.

61. Arrowsmith, *Modernism and the Museum*, 53–54.

62. William Rothenstein to Eric Gill, November 30, 1911, Collection on Eric Gill, MS Gill, William Andrews Clark Memorial Library, University of California, Los Angeles.

63. Rothenstein to Gill, November 26, 1910, Tate Gallery Archive. Quoted in Arrowsmith, *Modernism and the Museum*, 79.

64. Quoted in William Rothenstein, *Men and Memories* (New York: Coward-McCann, 1932), 280.

65. Walter Shewring, "Ananda Coomaraswamy and Eric Gill," in *Ananda Coomaraswamy: Remembering and Remembering Again and Again*, ed. S. Durai Raja Singam (Kuala Lumpur, 1974), 189. Quoted in Arrowsmith, *Modernism and the Museum*, 53.

66. Sarah Victoria Turner, "The 'Essential Quality of Things': E. B. Havell, Ananda Coomaraswamy, Indian Art and Sculpture in Britain, c. 1910–14," *Visual Culture in Britain* 11, no. 2 (2010): 255.

67. Richard Cork, *Wild Thing: Epstein, Gaudier-Brzeska, Gill* (London: Royal Academy of Arts, 2009), 37.

68. Ananda Coomaraswamy, typescript of lecture, "Understanding the Art of India," 1935, Collection on Eric Gill, MS Gill, William Andrews Clark Memorial Library, University of California, Los Angeles.

69. Robert Speaight, *The Life of Eric Gill* (London: Methuen & Co., 1966), 48. Gill had contact with Epstein and his work prior to Rothenstein's "fostering" of the friendship. He had defended Epstein's controversial frieze for the British Medical Association building in the Strand. However, according to Rothenstein's memoirs, it was Rothenstein who "sent Gill down to Epstein, thinking he might work with him for a time, and the two became friends" (Rothenstein, *Men and Memories*, 195).

70. According to Pennington, "The wings, with their machine-like accuracy of line, form and repetition, owe more to the expert carving techniques of Gill than the expressiveness of Epstein. Recent evidence has come to light in a letter from A. Mola to J. Stern (in the possession of Richard Buckle), which confirms that Gill was seen working on the wings in Epstein's studio." See Michael Pennington, *An Angel for a Martyr: Jacob Epstein's Tomb for Oscar Wilde* (Reading: Whiteknights, 1987), 42.

71. According to Rene Hague, he could not read *The Ballad of Reading Gaol* without weeping. See Douglas Cleverdon, "Portrait of Eric Gill," compiled by Douglas Cleverdon and Guy Brenton, for BBC program, typed manuscript, May–July 1961, Eric Gill Collection, Harry Ransom Center, University of Texas, 9.

72. According to H. Montgomery Hyde, "Wilde's more enthusiastic admirers would have liked a Greek youth standing by a broken column, or some scene from his works, such as *The Young King*, which was suggested many times" (Hyde, *Oscar Wilde: A Biography* [London: Farrar, Strauss, and Giroux, 1975], 382).

73. Arrowsmith, *Modernism and the Museum*, 95.

74. Pennington, *Angel for a Martyr*, 42; Arrowsmith, *Modernism and the Museum*, 94.

75. Jacob Epstein, *Epstein: An Autobiography* (New York: E. P. Dutton, 1955), 51.

76. Arrowsmith, *Modernism and the Museum*, 80.

77. Gill, *Letters*, 32–3.

78. Pennington, *Angel for a Martyr*, 27.

79. See Arrowsmith, *Modernism and the Museum*, 80–81.

80. Collins, *Eric Gill*, 72.

81. Diary of Eric Gill, January 12, 1911.

82. "Catalogue Entry: *Ecstasy* (1910–11), Eric Gill," tate.org.uk, accessed June 9, 2014, http://www.tate.org.uk/art/artworks/gill-ecstasy-t03477/text-catalogue-entry.

83. Roger Fry to Eric Gill, February 15, 1911; quoted in "Catalogue Entry."

84. Roger Fry to Eric Gill, February 18, 1911, Collection on Eric Gill, MS Gill, William Andrews Clark Memorial Library, University of California, Los Angeles.

ELEVEN

"Betwixt Us Two"

Whym Chow, Metonymy, and the Amatory Sonnet Tradition

SARAH E. KERSH

KATHARINE BRADLEY AND EDITH COOPER BEGAN THE WORK for a volume of poems that would eventually be entitled *Whym Chow, Flame of Love* in 1906. The volume as a whole, however, was not printed until April 1914—four months after the death of Edith Cooper. *Whym Chow* praises the poets' dramatic and spiritual connection with their furry chow dog named Whym that lived with them from 1898 until his painful death in 1906. Varying in length from six to eighty-eight lines, the thirty verses mourn the loss of their pet and—at first glance—look neither like a sonnet sequence nor like amatory poetry. The sequence, printed in a limited edition through Eragny Press, was bound in soft, russet suede reminiscent of the beloved chow's own coat and acted as a relic for the lost companion. Even from the opening line—"I call along the Halls of Suffering!"—the book grieves for Whym Chow; however, its publication also served as an elegy for Edith Cooper herself.

Although it is usually read, and rightly so, as a volume of elegiac poems, scholars such as Jill R. Ehnenn have argued that the poems in this volume are "personal elegies" and provide "exceptional and important examples of Victorian elegy, examples that deserve study because, both within and against dominant discourses of death and mourning, they shed light on their era's literary elegiac forms and other practices of grief."[1] While the volume's engagement with the elegiac tradition is perceptively articulated by Ehnenn, she also suggests that the work of mourning done through the elegy fails, according to Freudian terms, because Michael Field are unwilling to let go of the companion in the verses, instead articulating "inconsolable loss, along with pleas for Chow's return, throughout the collection's thirty poems."[2] It is in part due to this failure as elegy that I suggest *Whym Chow, Flame of Love* might revise both elegiac tropes and poetics of the amatory sonnet tradition. Drawing on both traditions, the volume is invested in troubling an understanding of dyadic bonding in the late nineteenth/early twentieth century; *Whym Chow* shatters the understanding of lover and beloved as a bond between two—and only two—interlocutors. Primarily, I turn to metonymy as the rhetorical device central to Michael Field's revision of the two-person bond associated with amatory poetics of the Victorian era. Metonymy in *Whym Chow*, and its work of contiguity, allows the volume to disrupt and reconfigure a tradition of amatory poetics as well as an understanding of intimacy at the turn of the century.

While the title of the volume of poems, *Whym Chow, Flame of Love*, is a reference both to Walter Pater's "hard, gemlike flame" of aestheticism and, as Leire Barrera-Medrano shows in another chapter of this book, to St. John's *The Living Flame of Love*, the dog himself was named in honor of Edward Whymper, the mountaineer who helped recover the remains of James Cooper, Cooper's father and Bradley's brother-in-law.[3] The death of the father figure was a site of inherited wealth and independence, but it was also the scene of traumatic and heartbreaking entries in the poets' joint journal, "Works and Days."[4] While named after Whymper and therefore a reminder of James Cooper's death, Whym is also a homophone of "whim" or caprice, suggesting a name more evocative of the puppy's initial charm (such as the "Bacchic cub" of verse IV) than the rugged mountaineer.

Whym Chow, as noted, entered the lives of Bradley and Cooper in 1898. Cooper writes at the top of a page of "Works and Days," "Michael Scribbles—" and follows with the text of a poem entitled "A Dog's Sigh."[5] On the following page, Bradley titles the entry "Whym Chow" and records the following:

> Friday evening, January 28th. Whym Chow arrived—a dusky sable—a wolf with civilization's softness, an oriental with musky passion—white-rolling eyeballs, & the power of inward frenzy— velvet mariners and little savages of eastern armies behind.
>
> I suppose our new love of animals is a desire to get into another Kingdom—we reach after the Kingdom of the dead—we can penetrate into the Kingdom of animals.[6]

From his entrance into their lives, Whym Chow evoked feelings of deep love and desire, as well as the grief pangs for those lost to death. Here, the details of the small puppy's fur and playfulness contrast with the longing to cross "kingdoms" to that of the dead. While crossing the boundary of death is impossible, Whym Chow, and the interspecies love he represents, is a temporary substitution bringing softness and love even while an embodied reminder of death and loss. Death and desire, love and mourning are intertwined in the final volume of Michael Field's poems. The very name of the volume, *Whym Chow, Flame of Love*, evokes whimsicality even as it memorializes the figure of death, and, in form, it fuses the elegiac and the amatory. As Joseph Bristow argues, "some of the finest 1890s lyrics look back to the authority of the poetic past to embrace, sometimes shockingly, the desirability of death."[7] Indeed, to read love poems in tandem with the elegiac is not all that unusual in Victorian poetry—many scholars agree that Tennyson's *In Memoriam* (1850) draws on the tradition of amatory sonnet sequences even while it is the most famous of Victorian elegies.[8] Moreover, the amatory tradition of courtly love is predicated on the unavailability of the beloved to the lover. In the sonnet sequences of Petrarch and Ronsard, the beloved is always unattainable either because of status or engagement, whereas in elegy the beloved is unattainable because of death. Both poetic forms long for and desire an impossible union or reunion. Amatory poetics are "predicated on the absence or unattainability of a beloved addressee," as is elegiac address.[9]

What makes *Whym Chow* so interesting, however, is the figure of metonymy within the volume. The poems rely on a juxtaposition of poetic traditions, elegiac and amatory, that suggest a melding of poetic forms. However, it is both the literal and rhetorical figure of Whym Chow that melds Cooper and Bradley's past grief and their hope of a happy future. The dog—and in turn the poetry about the dog—functions as part of a metonymic chain of meaning only made obvious when read across both traditions of elegy and amatory; in other words, across desire *and* grief. In his famous articulation of metaphor and metonymy, Roman Jakobson writes, "The development of a discourse may take place along two different semantic lines: one topic may lead to another either through their similarity or through their contiguity. The metaphoric way would be the most appropriate term for the first case and the metonymic way for the second, since they find their most condensed expression in metaphor and metonymy respectively."[10] Drawing on Jakobson's articulation of metaphor as constructed through similarity and metonymy as built on contiguity, I argue that metonymy in these poems provides a way for Michael Field to create a linguistic chain of connected meaning through the figure of Whym Chow that spans the elegiac and the amatory.

Returning to the diaries once more, Cooper writes of Whym Chow and his namesake in an entry entitled "Palm Sunday." Here, she discusses the many images of the "furry sweet" arranged in their home; specifically, she describes a collage of pictures hung on the wall "opposite our bed." Even the very design of the decor draws attention to the link between Whym Chow and Edward Whymper:

> We have the furry sweet in seven different pictures. At the same time my Love [Bradley] has given me pictures of herself—one with Whym is perfect in solemn protectiveness to the little creature and beyond him to all her Beloved few . . . To Henry, to the thought of the dead, left to the living in trust. It stands under Whymper's great photograph of the way up the Vale to Zermatt—it has the same gravity of tone and light on the brow like snow-celestialness that shines over the unseen Weishorn [. . .] at every moment our dogs claiming the care of our hands, the watchfulness the admiration of our eyes, the service of our feet—& always behind us thought of that Valley of the Shadow of Death.[11]

The inscription on an image of Bradley and Whym Chow, which reads, "To Henry, to the thought of the dead, left to the living in trust," is suggestive of the link between love and death for Michael Field. While the dogs (and in this entry Cooper also references their other dog, a basset hound named Musico) demand the "care of our hands" and "service of our feet," they are also always in the shadow of death. In this record, love and death are juxtaposed, quite literally, on the bedroom wall. To put it another way, the collage of images is a visual representation of the linguistic associations created by the juxtaposition of amatory and elegy and played out through the rhetorical figure of metonymy in the poems. In his analysis of Jakobson's argument, Hugh Brendin suggests, "Metaphor creates knowledge of the relation between objects; metonymy presupposes that knowledge."[12] In my reading, the presupposition of knowledge is vitally important to the analysis of *Whym Chow* insofar as the volume of poems requires the reader to previously understand how such visually contiguous images representing love, death, mourning, and hope not only make sense to Bradley and Cooper but are also reanimated rhetorically, rather than visually, in these poems. The metonymic chain becomes the site of desire that breaks the dyadic bond of Victorian marriage in favor of something more contiguous, and perhaps more queer.

Whym Chow, "The Longer Allegiance"

Turning to the poems about the furry companion, the verses in *Whym Chow, Flame of Love* were not the only poems written about Michael Field's dogs. In the journals, Bradley and Cooper compose others, notably "A Dog's Sigh," written on the occasion of Whym Chow's arrival, and then a sonnet entitled simply "Whym Chow." The first published poem dedicated to Whym Chow appears in the 1908 volume of poems *Wild Honey from Various Thyme*. "Whym Chow" is part of a section of the volume entitled "The Longer Allegiance." In this individual sonnet to the dog, the animal becomes a kind of fulcrum of poetic union as well as sensual connection. Chow, and his furry paw, stand in as muse, as saintly attribute, and as art itself:

> Nay, thou art my eternal attribute:
> Not as Saint Agnes in loose arms her lamb,—
> The very essence of the thing I am:
> And, as the lion, at Saint Jerome's suit,
> Stood ever at his right hand, scanning mute
> The hollows of the fountainous earth, whence swam,
> Emergent from the welter, sire and dam:
> While Jerome with no knowledge of the brute
> Beside him, wrote of later times, of curse,
> Bloodshed, and bitter exile, verse on verse
> Murmuring above the manuscript (in awe
> The lion watched his lord, the Vulgate grew),
> So it was wont to be betwixt us two—
> How still thou lay'st deep-nosing on thy paw![13]

Beginning as a typical Italian sonnet, the poem starts with an octave that praises the dog and melds the idea of him as a saintly attribute, like St. Agnes's lamb, and as a guard and muse, in the vein of St. Jerome's lion.[14] An "attribute" is also a metonymic suggestion—the lamb stands in as the representation of St. Agnes in a way similar to the function of Whym Chow for Bradley and Cooper.[15] But Chow is also much more, according to the poem; he is "the very essence of the thing I am," as well as the vigilant overseer of Michael Field's poetry/prophecies. Like St. Jerome's lion, Chow watches the process of writing, guarding and protecting it as well as inspiring it.[16] As part of the sequence of sonnets entitled "The Longer Allegiance," the "Whym Chow" sonnet echoes the language of deep loyalty suggested by the title and expands the notion of allegiance (fealty between lord and liege) to suggest something that crosses planes of being, that lasts "longer," like that of St. Jerome's lion.

The poem is certainly odd in its analogous positioning of the domestic pet as an eternal and mythical beast, but what is even stranger is the substitution of figures through metonymy in the last couplet. What or who is represented by "two" in "betwixt us two"? The verse does not easily distinguish between the

lion/dog and the two poets. If the "us two" refers to two people, we can imagine
the dog lying between Bradley and Cooper as they write. However, potentially,
the two women are imagined as one (male) poet making the "us two" simply the
dog alongside the composite "Michael Field." Or, possibly the two are the composite author plus the text "he" composes. It is this sliding referent of "two" that
is symptomatic of an articulation of intimacy that reconfigures a notion of dyadic bonding.[17] Michael Field use "two," but the meaning of two has proliferated
to include a variety of dyads and even troubling the notion of two through the
introduction of composite forms, like "Michael Field" himself. "Two" becomes an
unreliable sign in the poem, no longer indicating two distinct bodies or interlocutors but simply suggesting deep, eternal, intimate bonds.[18] It is also interesting
to note here that the "two" becomes most unreliable when the sonnet turns and
focuses on composition—the sestet imagines the act of writing. The final six
lines recount literary composition following Jerome as he "wrote," "verse on verse,"
of the "manuscript." Thinking about Bradley and Cooper's penchant for cocom-
posing poems, one writing and the other heavily revising, the metonymy here calls
into question the individuality of the author figure through the troubling of two-
ness.[19] This obfuscation reinforces Michael Field as both single authorial voice
and the intermingled voices of two women.

Amatory poetics have their roots in the dichotomy of the lover and beloved
in the Renaissance tradition of courtly love. In nineteenth-century amatory
poetics, the focus moves away from courtly love to take up residence in the
domestic sphere. At the center of the domestic sphere for Victorians, however, is
a legal institution founded on the union of the lover and the beloved—marriage.
George Meredith's *Modern Love* (1862) specifically interrogates marital love, and
Dante Gabriel Rossetti's *House of Life* (1881) refers to nuptials and bridal beds.
Exemplified by Elizabeth Barrett Browning's *Sonnets from the Portuguese* (1850),
scholars have "attributed a pioneering role" to Barrett Browning for the "nineteenth century revival of the amatory sonnet sequence."[20] In other words, Victorian poets play with the tropes of love and desire like earlier amatory poetics;
however, for Victorians, this love is often connected to a legal bond—the marital bond—that binds two subjects into one under the law.

Even though the "Whym Chow" sonnet does not seem to have much in
common with amatory poetics at first, it echoes many of the tropes present in
Sonnets from the Portuguese. In the seventh sonnet of the series, Elizabeth Barrett
Browning writes,

> The face of all the world is changed, I think,
> Since first I heard the footsteps of thy soul
> Move still, oh, still, beside me, as they stole

Betwixt me and the dreadful outer brink
Of obvious death, where I, who thought to sink,
Was caught up into love, and taught the whole
Of life in a new rhythm . . .
Because thy name moves right in what they say.[21]

Here the beloved stands between the poet and impending death, teaching her a new rhythm to life and possibly a new rhythm, or meter, of poetry. Barrett Browning and Michael Field deploy similar tropes: both poets engage death, imagine intercession on behalf of the speaker, and explore an understanding of space "betwixt" interlocutors of the verse.[22] However, unlike Michael Field's sonnet, Barrett Browning's has two clear interlocutors in the form of "I" and "thy," also read as the lover/speaker and the beloved. In the "Whym Chow" sonnet, it is hard to distinguish one body from another, poet from beloved and beloved from the dog, lying "deep-nosing on thy paw."[23] Michael Field revise the dyad of the lover and the beloved in the Whym Chow poems, shifting the emphasis of amatory poetics away from the binary of I/thy to something else. While it might be an inclination to see Field's move away from lover/beloved as simply a necessary shift that accompanies their pseudonym, I emphasize that the slippage of "betwixt us two" in Michael Field's sonnet is multivalent. The possibility for multiple interpretations of those interlocutors shatters any easy dichotomy of lover and beloved or poet and dog.

Articulating the necessity of "two" in Victorian understandings of marriage, Carolyn Dever writes of Bradley and Cooper, "Victorian marriage: the metaphor of two in one, by which two individuals are merged as a single—and male—subject. This metaphor is significant in every way for Michael Field. And, indeed, Bradley and Cooper retooled their partnership for the twentieth century, exploiting the metaphor by using Michael Field to turn one last great Victorian institution, the institution of marriage, against itself."[24] Michael Field revise and expand the poetic form of the sonnet as well as the institution of marriage, retooling it and turning it "against itself." In Dever's articulation, the metaphor of Victorian marriage substitutes a single, male subject for the husband and wife. Of course, for Bradley and Cooper, this marriage combines two women substituting their individual selves with that masculine pseudonym, "Michael Field."[25] However, I suggest that the 1908 sonnet "Whym Chow" playfully calls into question "twoness" present in the amatory tradition and based on the dyad of lover and beloved. If metaphor rhetorically juxtaposes two otherwise divergent objects or ideas in order to highlight some similarity, as in Dever's articulation of the metaphor of marriage, then Whym Chow as a figure in the poem performs a different rhetorical function. The number of interlocutors within the verse is unclear; instead of two, the verse engages with a polysemous chain of references. "Betwixt" becomes a space of connection, but that connection occurs between multiple composite figures that might include any combination of Whym Chow, Bradley, Cooper, and Michael Field.

To put it another way, the metonymy present draws on an understanding of "two" that depends entirely on our conception of "two-ness" as a notion of late Victorian love poetry. Elaine Freedgood writes of metonymy, saying that

> Metonymy is, rhetorically, both too weak and too strong: it tends toward the conventional, the obvious, the literal, the material. . . . Metonymy tends to be read according to habit—that is, according to a frame of reference. . . . So the seemingly mundane issue of habit is actually fraught with contingency: Whose habits? When and where? Provoked by what knowledge, memories, unconscious conflicts . . . emotional upheaval, economic vicissitudes, or religious pressures? . . . Or, perhaps, . . . metonymy arrives with the threat of a disavowed historical narrative, one whose return may be its only truly contingent aspect.[26]

In the slippage of metonymy—the difference between the expected, the conventional, and the "radical instability in its effect on literary form and meaning"—there is multivalency *and* polyphony.[27] In other words, metaphor defines its two components in order to articulate a relation of similarity. However, metonymy does not define or pin down but instead proliferates through contiguity. As indicated in the poem, Whym Chow is not just a dog but an "eternal attribute" and "the very essence of the thing I am"; as an attribute, he represents a metonymous chain of meaning. Reading the phrase "betwixt us two" suggests a context in which we see intimacy as a convention existing between two discrete bodies. The poem's metonymy disrupts this, though, suggesting that "two" does not refer to a particular number of beings unless we buy into a Victorian convention of intimacy, and all that is encoded in an understanding of "twoness"—in short, marriage.

Taking this one step further, Lee Edelman writes about metonymy as a figure of queer desire, saying, "Metaphor, that is, binds the arbitrary slippages characteristic of metonymy into units of 'meaning' that register as identities or representational presences."[28] In other words, metonymy in "two" allows Michael Field's poem to gesture toward language of intimacy and marriage, but "two" does not mean literal or numerical twoness represented in heterosexual marriage. "Whym Chow" becomes a site of queer desire only when the rhetoric of marriage as a metaphor of two is acknowledged as an insistence of heterosexuality.

Divorced from metaphor and viewed through metonymy, the "two" in the poem invokes the chain of connotations and a rhetoric of queerness because of its reliance on contiguous meanings only available to those capable of reading beyond or outside of the original metaphor. Put even more simply, metonymy allows for a proliferation of meanings that are coterminous, circumjacent, and juxtaposed. These implications only gain their rhetorical complexity through Michael Field's particular network of meaning; their formulation of authorship, devotion, and queer family.[29]

Although this chapter lays out an argument that Michael Field are challenging conceptions of intimacy, marriage, desire, and subjectivity, I want to be careful to present a full picture of their complexity. Though we can read the women's pseudonym Michael Field as a figure who deeply questions Victorian norms, scholars also argue that Bradley and Cooper were not wholly radical in their daily lives. They chose to "marry" one another and even exchanged rings, which they called "wedding bands."[30] Holly Laird recounts an exchange between Michael Field and poet Robert Browning in which they objected to Browning's claim that they defied "social conventions." Bradley quickly responded that while they did not want to be "'stifled' (or rendered speech-less) by social expectations, they had no desire to challenge the 'customs' and 'beliefs' of men."[31] From their letters and journal, it seems Cooper and Bradley deeply wanted to live in quiet domesticity together. While they exchanged rings, they could still be quite critical of wedding ceremonies, and marriages in general, in their diaries. Marion Thain points to "[p]aradox [as] the hallmark of [the aesthetic] moment. . . . Michael Field's work can best be read through Bradley and Cooper's manipulation and apparent reconciliation of conflicting concepts."[32] It is because of this tension of "conflicting concepts," however, that I suggest a reading of Michael Field that negotiates convention through revision—using the amatory understanding of twoness in order to build upon it, reframe and retool it, while still maintaining a rootedness in the tradition of amatory poetics.

The Metonymy of Twoness

While the initial 1908 "Whym Chow" sonnet does not appear in the 1914 volume, *Whym Chow, Flame of Love*, there is a similar slippage of dyads and, in particular, pronouns across the verses in the volume. If "Whym Chow" plays with metonymy in order to suggest the multiplicity of the poems' referents, then the volume of *Whym Chow, Flame of Love* takes this to a new level. The original sonnet to Whym Chow and the amatory sonnet tradition itself informs the full volume, but the poems in it are not sonnets. The sonnet's literary history lends itself to the project of memorializing Chow as well as meditating upon love for

Chow and through Chow; Bradley and Cooper continue the amatory tradition by exploring desire and longing, but they explode the sonnet as a form and, at the same time, the cult of "two."[33]

In *Whym Chow, Flame of Love*, the thirty poems range in length from six to eighty-eight lines, as noted earlier. The volume abandons any understanding of intimacy as simply dyadic in favor of a different kind of connection that spans the human/animal divide. Manipulating rhyme, line length, and poem length, these formal changes again underscore that *Whym Chow* reformulates the construct of dyadic bonding as well as ideas of individuality, authorship, and subjectivity.[34] Moving easily between pronouns and the suggestion of one, two, and three interlocutors, poem III in the volume calls out to the deceased Whym Chow: "Be our daemon, be / Guardian-angel near / To the cruel sphere / Of our destiny."[35] Here, Michael Field rely on the first-person plural to make the triangulation of the dog, Cooper, and Bradley explicit. In other poems, however, like the opening poem of the series, the first person overrides the collective voices of the women represented in "our." For example, the opening line of the volume as a whole reads, "I call along the Halls of Suffering." While the "I" in the opening verse suggests a singular speaking subject, verse V is entitled "Trinity," and in it "I" functions as a kind of chorus suggestive of two voices in a unitary refrain under the metonymy of "I":

> I did not love him for myself alone:
> I loved him that he loved my dearest love
> Oh God, no blasphemy
> It is to feel we loved in trinity
>
> . . .
>
> So I possess this creature of Love's flame,
> So loving what I love he lives from me;
> Not white, a thing of fire,
> Of seraph-plumèd limbs and one desire,
> That is my heart's own, and shall ever be:
> An animal—with aim
> Thy Dove avers the same . . .
> O symbol of our perfect union, strange
> Unconscious Bearer of Love's interchange.[36]

In V, the verse has expanded from a sonnet to an eighteen-line lyric composed of two nine-line stanzas. More than losing the sonnet form, the poem also suggests a reimagination of the women's love for one another. "So I possess this creature of Love's flame" must refer to Whym Chow—as the title of the volume suggests—but the "I" in the line, as well as the possessives, conceal any actual possession or individual. The "One desire" and the "symbol" of "our perfect union strange" may refer to the union of the women themselves, their union with the dog, or their union through the dog. It is impossible to tell given the slippage of our understanding of "union" as only ever dyadic (even while the title of the poem urges us to think in threes rather than twos). This slippage might even revise the sonnet form itself, in part because the thought/counterthought structure is so prevalent in Petrarchan sonnets. In other words, *Whym Chow* seeks to unseat the binary thinking that frames the octave/sestet structure.[37]

David Banash suggests that "here the lovers reinvent and enact their passion through the mediating body of their beloved dog. In proximity to the animal Other, the Fields find a space of possibilities to transform themselves."[38] Composed late in their career and during their conversion to Catholicism, it *does* seem that *Whym Chow* is an attempt to articulate something about their passion for one another. However, I want to build on Banash's argument to suggest that the "other" is not easily located in the poems themselves because of the impossibly shifting signifiers and problematic pronouns. Locating "the other" is particularly difficult since the location of the "other" necessitates a distinction between the self and other that is resisted in the poems. Additionally, while Whym Chow, according to Banash, is a "mediating body" insofar as the dog is named the "unconscious Bearer of Love's Interchange," Whym Chow as a name does not just refer to a dog. For Michael Field, the phrase "Whym Chow" is a homograph— Whym Chow, "Whym Chow," and *Whym Chow* are a dog, a poem, and a volume of poems, all of which share the same name. Of homographs, Edelman writes, "Bearing no singular identity, the homograph . . . precipitates into meaning by virtue of its linear, its metonymic, relation to a context that seems to validate, which is to say 'naturalize,' one denotation over another."[39] The homograph "confounds the security of the distinction between sameness and difference, gesturing in the process towards the fictional status of logic's foundational gesture."[40] Inherent in the homograph is the work of metonymy insofar as one rhetorical phrase actually represents at least three related sites of knowledge (a dog, a sonnet, and a volume of poems). Moreover, Whym Chow is labeled by the poem as a site of creative and amatory *exchange*—"Love's interchange."

Because of the multiplicity of references, it is more useful to imagine Whym Chow, the signifier in all its meaning, in light of Elaine Freedgood's theory of things. Of course, Whym Chow the dog is not a thing, but Freedgood suggests that we might want to "follow" connections outside of the texts in which they are housed. In name, "Whym" refers to Edward Whymper and the homophone "whim." However, Whym Chow is also emphatically named "an animal" (line

10), calling into question ownership and the ramifications of commodities to be traded and owned, as well as the animal familiars of pagan mythologies and, for this poem in particular, the animal incarnation of the Holy Spirit in the form of a dove (line 16).[41] Finally, "Chow" is often associated with language suggestive of the Orient in the poems. The Orientalization of Chow is strong in verse VIII, entitled "Out of the East." Here, Chow is associated with precious stones: "Jasper and jacinth, amber and fine gold / The topaz, ruby, the fire-opal, grey" (lines 1–2). The verse continues: "O Eastern Prince from fuming China hoary / That on thy orient rug celestial lay, / Thy coat a web of treasure manifold!" (lines 4–6). Whym Chow's coat is an object of aesthetic beauty and a sight of riches. Verse VIII, in conjunction with V's reminder of Whym Chow as "Love's flame," connects the figure of the dog to ideas of fin-de-siècle aestheticism and the Orientalism deeply rooted in the movement. In short, the figure of metonymy opens the possibility for all of these meanings to be present at the same moment. Derrida writes of metonymic force that it "divides the referential trait, suspends the referent and leaves it to be desired, while still maintaining the reference."[42] Whym Chow as the object of focus for the volume of poems is easily dismissed as simply the dog himself. If read only as an amatory and elegiac set of poems for the loved-but-lost family member in furry form, it is easy to scorn *Whym Chow* as a somewhat ridiculous volume evocative of the excesses of decadence. Instead, *Whym Chow* might be more than simply the metaphor of a child for the lesbian couple, a saintly talisman for the newly converted Catholics, or a mystic familiar for the once-pagan pair. As metonym, *Whym Chow* has "dizzying potential" rather than a single reading.[43] *Whym Chow, Flame of Love* is a poetic project of transformation—of formal transformations and queer transformations that attempt to reimagine a kind of connectedness and intersubjectivity that transcends a typical model of dyadic bonding, or even triadic bonding, of self and other.[44]

The only poem that approaches the traditional sonnet comes almost halfway through the sequence. Verse XIII is entitled "My Cup," and though its fourteen lines suggest a sonnet, the poem looks more like the Imagist poems of the early twentieth century than the "Whym Chow" sonnet:[45]

> Chow, thou hast drunk the bitter cup—
> Love unto death,
> That makes love free and lifts it up
> To heaven and its own breath:
> So God gave death
> To His Beloved, as we
> Gave it to thee.

Oh, 'twas a sacramental Cup—
Death given for Love!
We bade thy little spirit sup
With First and Last above,
When of our love
We made thee free
Eternally.[46]

The turn—at the repetition of the titular cup, "Oh, 'twas a sacramental Cup"—moves the poem from the death of the dog to everlasting life. Figured through language of Christ's sacrifice, the poem collapses the relationships of those involved; the relationship between God and "His Beloved" is refigured as "we" and "thee." Chow's spirit communes with "First and Last above," suggesting his transition to some new trinity only available through death and freedom from the earthly trinity of "our love."

The echo of the Victorian amatory sonnet is strong in "My Cup." In particular, Barrett-Browning's most famous of sonnets reads,

How do I love thee? Let me count the ways.
I love thee to the depth and breadth and height
My soul can reach, when feeling out of sight
For the ends of being and ideal grace.
. . .
I love thee with a love I seemed to lose
With my lost saints. I love thee with the breath,
Smiles, tears, of all my life; and, if God choose,
I shall but love thee better after death.[47]

For *Sonnets from the Portuguese*, love is figured through the expanse of the soul and through grace; moreover, love and death are bound together, making love more intense through death and blurring the lines between elegy and amatory poetics. For *Whym Chow*, Cooper and Bradley imagine "When of our love / We made thee free / Eternally" (lines 12–14). Love is both the freedom to enter eternity and the thing that is left behind in favor of eternity and death.

Though the poems cathect the grief of the poets into a variety of metaphors—Christian, pagan, and literary—the actual death of Whym Chow in 1906 was bitterly mourned by Bradley and Cooper, and the volumes of "Works and Days" that succeed his death are permeated with his presence. On her birthday in 1907—January 12—Cooper writes about Whym Chow in ways that blur family linage, birth, and death:

> This day, no longer kept as my birthday, is dedicated to the dear
> Mother who bore me. . . . On little Chow's birthday I celebrate
> that re-birth that came as the wind listeth. Steeped in my tears,
> snatched into light by the spirit of an indubitable love unto
> Death—by Chow—in him I am born again—& this can but be
> a solemn, thankful, Votive Day to my Mother—my noble mother
> who bore me of the flesh.[48]

Again, the rhetoric of metonymy is at work; the connection between birth-days, family lines, and the deceased is built around contiguity. But as with all metonymy, it relies on an understanding of association that Cooper seeks to rewrite. Cooper's own birthday does not represent her but her mother; and Whym Chow's birthday, she suggests, represents both the Chow and her own rebirth through him. "Flesh" seems to be shared across birthdays as emblematic of connection, transformation, and, even here, the nearing arrival of death. While Chow himself is a signifier in this metonymic chain of intimate relationships and understanding of the self, family, and birth, the volume of poems becomes a significant link.

In a later record of *Whym Chow, Flame of Love*'s production, Bradley writes in "Works and Days," "I have been preparing the Chow book—Hennie's from M.S. . . . how we loved one another."[49] The slide between "I" (Bradley), the volume, "Hennie" (Cooper), and their love is represented sequentially in this entry. Again on August 25, 1914, Bradley references "Hennie's" Chow book: "Europe seething in blood. On August 5th England declared war. That night I returned from Liphook there's a little book Chow bound that fills in some details between now and the operation. It is my duty now to write in the big yearbook of the big events."[50] The advent of war, "Europe seething in blood," and the duty of Bradley to record the events in the "big yearbook," serve as a parenthesis for a strange phrase that stands in for the narrative of time lost: "a little book Chow bound." Referred to here, the book again represents how Cooper and Bradley loved one another, and the book itself stands in—"Chow bound"—for details of their lives that cannot be composed in the diaries; the volume's metonymy "fills in some details." It is the stand-in for both love and mourning on a personal as well as continental scale. The "Chow book" is, as Deborah Lutz argues, a "material object" begging to be "read": "The Victorian representation of the cadaver as a special type of information- and emotion-laden artifact also influenced—and was influenced by—the literary. The body and the book intersected. . . . Matter stood in for lived presence, for the narrative of a body. As such, these mementos are the material objects that beg to be 'read' more than, arguably, any other objects."[51]

Reading *Whym Chow, Flame of Love* as a representation of the "cadaver," we see the body and book intersect in more than just titular terms for Michael Field. What would it mean to take Whym Chow as an object meant to be read not as a metaphor for the "alternative" family structure of Michael Field but as a metonymy? Metonymy would mean not a concrete understanding but endless links of information. *Whym Chow* (and hence, Whym Chow) is a representation of the domestic—the tamed pet, bought and featured within a domestic scene such as the vignette described by Cooper on "Palm Sunday." He is the object of Orientalism in verses titled the "Asian Bacchant," "Out of the East" (VIII), and "Fur for Mandarins" (XIV), as well as in Bradley's description of his arrival as "an oriental with musky passion."[52] *Whym Chow* is a sensuous fetish—"Dearer would that fur beguile / Than the pillow's tenderest fold" (XXIV, lines 60–61)—and evocative as a stand-in for physical touch as well as metaphysical connection, as evidenced in the changing pronouns and shift from one to two, to "trinity," and more (V). He is a martyr and an attribute for the tortured and misunderstood artist. Whym Chow, as a rhetorical phrase, is all of these and more.

In a final, wonderfully Michael Fieldian moment in "Works and Days," Cooper's handwriting records the content of Bradley's letter to Marie Sturge Moore:

> You, when we are alone, may speak to me of Chow, especially if you are afraid you do not know what he is to me—Not what a dog has been to any mortal before; what perhaps his lion was to St. Jerome—the lion who was far back below the Vulgate. The lion is forever with St. Jerome & so you must always think of Chow . . . Chow was not a dog at all.[53]

Here, Whym Chow, as a signifier, is both dog and "not a dog at all;" he, and the "Chow bound" volume of poetry are part of the metonymic chain that is the understanding of self, other, intimacy, and identity within the work of Michael Field. "Works and Days" in this entry enacts the metonymic chain as we read Bradley's words of intimacy to Sturge-Moore ("You, when we are alone"), via Cooper's looping hand. Here, Bradley's and Cooper's voices intertwine in the physical text of the diary. As a closing note on metonymy and the revision of literary tropes, let me point out the—perhaps too obvious—rich metonymy present in the pseudonym "Michael Field." Michael Field is both Bradley and Cooper, and yet the authorial voice they maintained was distinct from them individually. Michael Field as authorial figure engages with and revises amatory poetics through metonymy. This rhetorical device is redolent of the way their pseudonym and Whym Chow, both as book and dog, signify queer desires formulated through contiguity and revision.

Notes

1. Jill R. Ehnenn, "'Drag(ging) at Memory's Fetter': Michael Field's Personal Elegies, Victorian Mourning, and the Problem of Whym Chow," *Michaelian* 1 (2009), n.p., http://www.thelatchkey.org/Field/MF1/ehnennarticle.htm. Accessed March 26, 2019.

2. Ehnenn. According to Ehnenn, *Whym Chow* differs from Michael Field's other "representations of bereavement and the lost love object" in part because there is no move "toward the resolution of grief" in the poems, thus failing to execute "an emotional and behavioral chain of events" in which the grieving party "gradually can withdraw their attachments to the lost love object and return to everyday life." Ehnenn quips, "Instead, as if pulling on his leash, *Whym Chow* literally drags them deeper into their memories, thwarting detachment" (2009, n.p.).

3. Walter Pater writes in *The Renaissance*, "A counted number of pulses only is given to us of a variegated, dramatic life. . . . How shall we pass most swiftly from point to point, and be present always at the focus where the greatest number of vital forces unite in their purest energy? To burn always with this hard, gemlike flame, to maintain this ecstasy, is success in life" (Walter Pater and Adam Phillips, *The Renaissance: Studies in Art and Poetry* [New York: Oxford University Press, 1986], 152). Indeed, Bradley's description of Whym Chow's "power of inward frenzy" in the January 28 diary entry cited seems to echo Pater's thoughts on vital forces and purest energy. On Michael Field and Edward Whymper, see Emma Donoghue, *We Are Michael Field* (Bath: Absolute Press, 1998), 96.

4. In the journals, much of the story unfolds in the 1898 volume (see Donoghue, *We Are Michael Field*, 92–97).

5. Michael Field, "Works and Days," BL Add MS 46787, fol. 10v (January 1898) [E.C.].

6. Michael Field, "Works and Days," BL Add MS 46787, fol. 11r (January 28, 1898) [K.B.].

7. Joseph Bristow, "How Decadent Poems Die," in *Decadent Poetics: Literature and Form at the British Fin de Siècle*, ed. Jason David Hall and Alex Murray (New York: Palgrave Macmillan, 2013), 28–29.

8. Reading *In Memoriam* in conjunction with Herbert, Joseph Phelan argues, "This affinity highlights *In Memoriam*'s status as a repressed or disguised sonnet sequence" (*The Nineteenth-Century Sonnet* [Houndmills, Basingstoke: Palgrave Macmillan, 2005], 90). Mary Jean Corbett's "No Second Friend?: Perpetual Maidenhood and Second Marriage in *In Memoriam* and 'The Conjugial Angel,'" *ELH* 81, no. 1 (2014): 299–323, as well as Alec Magnet's chapter in *Queer Victorian Families: Curious Relations in Literature* (New York: Routledge, 2015) also explore Tennyson's metaphors of marriage and love within the elegiac tradition.

9. Amy Christine Billone, *Little Songs: Women, Silence, and the Nineteenth-Century Sonnet* (Columbus: Ohio State University Press, 2007), 3.

10. Roman Jakobson, *On Language*, ed. Linda R. Waugh and Monique Monville-Burston (Cambridge, MA: Harvard University Press, 1990), 129.

11. Michael Field, "Works and Days," BL Add MS 46787, fol. 14v–15 (n.d., 1898) [E.C.].

12. Hugh Bredin, "Roman Jakobson on Metaphor and Metonymy," *Philosophy and Literature* 1 (1984): 101.

13. Michael Field, *Wild Honey from Various Thyme* (London: T. Fisher Unwin, 1908), 191 (lines 1–14).

14. Saint Jerome is a figure with whom Michael Field had prior interest. In *Sight and Song* (1892), the poets compose a poem from the painting by Cosimo Tura, describing St. Jerome's penitence in the wilderness.

15. Whereas the lion is a figure from the mythology of St. Jerome, the lamb is an icon of St. Agnes. In other words, the lamb represents St. Agnes herself—in art historical terms, it is her attribute or the symbol of her character. The lamb is a symbol of chastity and purity and seems to be associated with St. Agnes in part because the Latin word for lamb, *agnus*, is so close to her name. The lion, however, is not merely an attribute of St. Jerome but a figure from the stories of the saint's mythologies.

16. The use of saint imagery and allusion to mystic traditions is not unusual for Michael Field. Both Ehnenn and Barrera-Medrano, elsewhere in this volume, more fully analyze their engagement with Catholic theory and iconography, further emphasizing the poets' deep engagement with multiple formal traditions.

17. *Sight and Song* (1892) also troubles dyadic modes of relating; however, in that volume the "two" that is reconfigured is that of the viewer and the subject viewed. The poetic voice looks at figures in paintings, such as St. Jerome and Venus, but the "I" and "you" of the poems become impossible to fully break down given the unpredictable plurality of the viewer.

18. Even the figure of the lion is a common trope in heraldry and is therefore a long-standing symbol of familial or clan connections as represented by a coat of arms. In other words, the lion often represents a connected group of people through visual representation on a crest or shield.

19. Marion Thain and Ana Parejo Vadillo write, "We know from Bradley and Cooper's own descriptions that poetry and drama were often written through a process where each woman took sections to write independently but then edited the other's work" (Thain and Vadillo, eds., *Michael Field, the Poet: Published and Unpublished Manuscripts* [Peterborough, Ontario: Broadview, 2009], 46).

20. Marianne Van Remoortel, *Lives of the Sonnet, 1787–1895: Genre, Gender and Criticism* (Farnham, UK: Routledge, 2011), 89.

21. Elizabeth Barrett Browning, "Sonnets from the Portuguese," in *Complete Poetical Works of Elizabeth Barrett Browning*, Cambridge Edition of the Poets (Boston: Houghton Mifflin, 1900), 216 (lines 1–7, 14).

22. Betwixt, according to the *Oxford English Dictionary*, can suggest betweenness either in positionality or time, but it can also refer to "more than two" in its early uses. Fairly uncommon by Bradley and Cooper's time, this earlier definition is a medieval form that disappeared toward the end of the seventeenth century.

23. Field, *Wild Honey from Various Thyme*, 191 (line 14).

24. Carolyn Dever, "Introduction: 'Modern' Love and the Proto-Post-Victorian," *PMLA* 124, no. 2 (2009): 374. I am so grateful to Dever for first introducing me to "the Michael Fields" and their work.

25. Erik Gray supports the connection between metaphor and marriage, writing, "In fact metaphor and marriage are intimately aligned. *The Book of Common Prayer*, for

example, explicitly asserts that marriage itself is a metaphor." See Gray, "Metaphors and Marriage Plots: *Jane Eyre, The Egoist,* and Metaphoric Dialogue in the Victorian Novel," *Partial Answers* 12, no. 2 (2014): 268.

26. Elaine Freedgood, *The Ideas in Things: Fugitive Meaning in the Victorian Novel* (Chicago: University of Chicago Press, 2006), 12–13.

27. Freedgood, 13.

28. Lee Edelman, *Homographesis: Essays in Gay Literary and Cultural Theory* (New York: Routledge, 1994), 8–9.

29. Edelman articulates that metaphor is privileged in language, and therefore metonymy has a grounding in metaphor. He says, "Metonymy can only generate 'meaning' through reference to a signified imagined as somewhere present to itself.... It is only within the logic of metaphor that metonymy as such can be 'identified'" (*Homographesis,* 8–9).

30. As a short aside, Michael Field actually asserted that they were "closer married" than Elizabeth Barrett Browning and her husband Robert Browning, saying, "Those two poets, man and wife, wrote alone; each wrote, but did not bless or quicken one another at their work; *we are closer married*" (quoted in Donoghue, *We Are Michael Field,* 43).

31. Quoted in "Contradictory Legacies: Michael Field and Feminist Restoration," *Victorian Poetry* 33, no. 1 (1995): 120. Laird continues, writing of their marriage and their adoption of Whym Chow as a child-substitute: "Later, after they set up house together, they became attached to a dog, Whym Chow, for whom they felt as passionately as for a child. For Bradley and Cooper, several familial relationships were simultaneously available and surely productive of complex kinds of friction. As open as they were about their mutual love, they were as markedly discreet about possible inequalities or irritating differences dividing them. They eventually hedged all this within the walls of a firmly monogamous 'marriage,' living a quiet and carefully structured domestic life together" (120).

32. Marion Thain, *'Michael Field': Poetry, Aestheticism and the Fin de Siècle* (Cambridge: Cambridge University Press, 2007), 16.

33. Reading sonnets through the lens of gender, Billone argues for the usefulness of the sonnet form for nineteenth-century women, saying, "Women poets gravitate toward the sonnet form because, with its exigent rules of meter, syllable count, rhyme scheme, and structural shifts, it offered them a readymade metaphor for the difficulties of articulation. Highly compressed and restrained, the sonnet helped to make inexpressibility visible" (*Little Songs,* 56). This seems apt for Michael Field as well, though *Whym Chow, Flame of Love* explodes the "restrained" sonnet form in favor of something different.

34. Michael Field attempted to revise love poetry in earlier lyrics as well. *Long Ago* (1889) and *Underneath the Bough* (1893) both revisit the amatory tradition through the lyrics of Sappho and the *Rubáiyát of Omar Khayyám,* respectively.

35. Michael Field, "Poem III," in *Whym Chow, Flame of Love* (London: Eragny Press, 1914), 12–13 (lines 15–18).

36. Michael Field, "Poem V," in *Whym Chow,* 15 (lines 1–4, 10–18).

37. In their chapters in this volume, Ehnenn argues for the revision of forms within the "Catholic Poems" as a connection to queer desire and disability, while Barrera-Medrano

notes their experimentation with Spanish poetic forms also in the context of queer love. My argument about form here follows a similar path in that I also want to highlight the remarkable innovation at play in Michael Field's formal experiments.

38. David Banash, "To the Other: The Animal and Desire in Michael Field's *Whym Chow: Flame of Love*," in *Figuring Animals: Essays on Animal Images in Art, Literature, Philosophy, and Popular Culture*, ed. Mary Sanders Pollock and Catherine Rainwater (New York: Palgrave Macmillan, 2005), 196.

39. Edelman, *Homographesis*, 13.

40. Edelman, 13.

41. Witches were said to have animal companions, or familiars, who did their bidding. Some mythology even suggests that witches could inhabit the body of their familiar. What is interesting is the position of Whym Chow as both pagan and Christian, especially since his death marked Bradley and Cooper's conversion to Catholicism. For scholars dealing with Michael Field's Catholic conversion, see Jill Ehnenn, "Looking Strategically: Feminist and Queer Aesthetics in Michael Field's *Sight and Song*," *Victorian Poetry* 42, no. 3 (2004): 213–60; Frederic Roden, *Same-Sex Desire in Victorian Religious Culture* (New York: Palgrave Macmillan, 2002); and Cheryl A. Wilson, "Bodily Sensations in the Conversion Poetry of Michael Field," *Victorian Review* 54, no. 2 (2016): 179–97, as well as chapters in this volume by both Ehnenn and Barrera-Medrano.

42. Jacques Derrida, *The Work of Mourning*, ed. Pascale-Anne Brault and Michael Naas (Chicago: University of Chicago Press, 2003), 61.

43. Freedgood, *The Ideas in Things*, 14.

44. My argument is informed here by the scholars who have articulated Michael Field in terms of triads and trinities including Roden, *Same-Sex Desire*, and Thain, '*Michael Field': Poetry, Aestheticism and the Fin de Siècle*, as well as Ruth Vanita, *Sappho and the Virgin Mary: Same-Sex Love and the English Literary Imagination* (New York: Columbia University Press, 1996), and Martha Vicinus, "Faun Love: Michael Field and Bernard Berenson," *Women's History Review* 18, no. 5 (2009): 753–64.

45. Sarah Parker writes of aestheticism, decadence, and Imagism as part of the modernism movement: "The late nineteenth and early twentieth century was also a period of intense artistic innovation and experimentation, characterized by three major movements of aestheticism, decadence, and modernism. All of these movements responded to the immense pace of social change by seeking new art forms that would capture, resist or provide alternatives to 'modern' life" (*The Lesbian Muse and Poetic Identity, 1889–1930* [New York: Pickering and Chatto, 2013], 3). Read in this light, it is perhaps not so unusual to see Michael Field's poetics beginning to look like those of another poetic movement, Imagism.

46. Michael Field, "Poem XIII," *Whym Chow*, 28 (lines 1–14).

47. Elizabeth Barrett Browning, "Sonnet 43," *Complete Poetical Works*, 223 (lines 1–4, 11–14).

48. Michael Field, "Works and Days," BL Add MS 46796, fol. 8v–9r (January 12, 1907) [E.C.].

49. Michael Field, "Works and Days," BL Add MS 46804 A, fol. 7r (January 27, 1914) [K.B.].

50. Michael Field, "Works and Days," BL Add MS 46804 A, fol. 34r (August 25, 1914) [K.B.].

51. Deborah Lutz, *Relics of Death in Victorian Literature and Culture* (London: Oxford University Press, 2014), 2.

52. Michael Field, "Works and Days," BL Add MS 46787, fol. 11r (January 28, 1898) [K.B.].

53. Michael Field, "Works and Days," BL Add MS 46795, fol. 44r (n.d., 1906) [E.C.].

Selected Bibliography

Bashant, Wendy. "Aesthetes and Queens: Michael Field, John Ruskin and *Bellerophôn*." *Journal of Pre-Raphaelite Studies* 15 (2006): 74–94.

Bickle, Sharon. "Disability and Gender in the Visual Field: Seeing the Subterranean Lives of Michael Field's *William Rufus*." *Victorian Literature and Culture* 40, no. 1 (2012): 137–52.

———, ed. *The Fowl and the Pussycat: Love Letters of Michael Field 1876–1909*. Charlottesville: University of Virginia Press, 2008.

———. "'Kick[ing] Against the Pricks': Michael Field's *Brutus Ultor* as Manifesto for the New Woman." *Nineteenth Century Theatre and Film* 33, no. 2 (2006): 12–29.

Blain, Virginia. "'Michael Field, the Two-Headed Nightingale': Lesbian Text as Palimpsest." *Women's History Review* 5, no. 2 (1996): 239–57.

Bristow, Joseph, ed. *The Fin-de-Siècle Poem: English Literary Culture and the 1890s*. Athens: Ohio University Press, 2005.

———. "Michael Field: In Their Time and Ours." *Tulsa Studies in Women's Literature* 29, no.1 (2010): 159–79.

———. "Michael Field's Lyrical Aestheticism: Underneath the Bough," in *Michael Field and Their World*, edited by Margaret D. Stetz and Cheryl A. Wilson, 49–62. High Wycombe, UK: Rivendale Press, 2007.

Conley, Susan. "'Poet's Right': Christina Rossetti as Anti-Muse and the Legacy of the 'Poetess.'" *Victorian Poetry* 33 (1994): 365–86.

Donoghue, Emma. *We Are Michael Field*. Bath: Absolute Press, 1998.

Ehnenn, Jill R. "'Drag(ging) at Memory's Fetter': Michael Field's Personal Elegies, Victorian Mourning, and the Problem of Whym Chow." *Michaelian* 1 (2009), n.p.

———. "Looking Strategically: Feminist and Queer Aesthetics in Michael Field's *Sight and Song*." *Victorian Poetry* 43, no. 1 (2005): 109–54.

———. "'Our Brains Struck Fire Each from Each': Disidentification, Difference, and Desire in the Collaborative Aesthetics of Michael Field." In *Economies of Desire at the Victorian Fin de Siècle: Libidinal Lives*, edited by Jane Ford and Kim Edwards Keates, 180–203. New York: Routledge, 2016.

———. *Women's Literary Collaboration, Queerness, and Late-Victorian Culture*. Aldershot, UK: Ashgate, 2008.

Evangelista, Stefano. *British Aestheticism and Ancient Greece: Hellenism, Reception, Gods in Exile*. Basingstoke, UK: Palgrave Macmillan, 2009.

Fletcher, Robert P. "'I Leave a Page Half-Writ': Narrative Discoherence in Michael Field's *Underneath the Bough*." In *Women's Poetry Late Romantic to Late Victorian: Gender and Genre, 1830–1900*, edited by Isobel Armstrong and Virginia Blain, 164–82. Basingstoke, UK: Macmillan, 1999.

Fraser, Hilary. "The Religious Poetry of Michael Field." In *Athena's Shuttle: Myth Religion Ideology from Romanticism to Modernism*, edited by Franco Marucci and Emma Sdegno, 127–42. Milan: Cisalpino, 2000.

———. "A Visual Field: Michael Field and the Gaze." *Victorian Literature and Culture* 34, no. 2 (2006): 553–71.

———. *Women Writing Art History in the Nineteenth Century: Looking Like a Woman*. Cambridge: Cambridge University Press, 2014.

Gallagher, Rob, and Ana Parejo Vadillo. "Animating Sight and Song: A Meditation on Identity, Fair Use, and Collaboration." *19: Interdisciplinary Studies in the Long Nineteenth Century* 21 (2015) DOI: http://doi.org/10.16995/ntn.754.

Gray, Erik. "A Bounded Field: Situating Victorian Poetry in the Literary Landscape." *Victorian Poetry* 43, no. 4 (2003): 465–72.

Harrington, Emily. "Michael Field and the Detachable Lyric." *Victorian Studies* 50, no. 2 (2008): 221–32.

Hughes, Linda K. "Michael Field (Katharine Bradley and Edith Cooper) and Significant Form." In *The Oxford Handbook of Victorian Poetry*, edited by Matthew Bevis, 563–78. Oxford: Oxford University Press, 2013.

Ireland, Kenneth R. *Sight and Song*: A Study of the Interrelations between Painting and Poetry." *Victorian Poetry* 15, no. 1 (1977): 9–20.

Laird, Holly. "Contradictory Legacies: Michael Field and Feminist Restoration." *Victorian Poetry* 33, no. 1 (1995): 111–27.

———. *Women Coauthors*. Urbana: University of Illinois Press, 2000.

Leighton, Angela. *Victorian Women Poets: Writing against the Heart*. New York and London: Harvester Wheatsheaf, 1992.

Locard, Henri. "Works and Days: The Journals of 'Michael Field.'" *Journal of the Eighteen Nineties Society* 10 (1979): 1–9.

London, Bette. *Writing Double: Women's Literary Partnerships*. Ithaca, NY: Cornell University Press, 1999.

Lysack, Krista. "Aesthetic Consumption and the Cultural Production of Michael Field's *Sight and Song*." *Studies in English Literature, 1500–1900* 45, no. 4 (2005): 935–60.

MacDonald, Jan. "'Disillusioned Bards and Despised Bohemians': Michael Field's *A Question of Memory* at the Independent Theatre Society." *Theatre Notebook: A Journal of the History and Technique of the British Theatre* 31, no. 2 (1975): 18–29.

Mahoney, Kristin. "Michael Field and Queer Community at the Fin-de-Siècle." *Victorian Review* 41, no.1 (2015): 35–40.

Maxwell, Catherine. "Michael Field, Death, and the Effigy." *Word & Image* 34, no. 1 (2018): 31–39.

———. *Scents and Sensibility: Perfume in Victorian Literary Culture*. Oxford: Oxford University Press, 2017.

Mitton, Matthew. "Before Michael Field: Katherine Bradley as 'Arran Leigh.'" *Philological Quarterly* 89 (2010): 311–35.

Moriarty, David J. "'Michael Field' (Edith Cooper and Katharine Bradley) and Their Male Critics." In *Nineteenth-Century Women Writers of the English-Speaking World*, edited by Rhoda B. Nathan, 121–42. New York: Greenwood, 1986.

Olverson, Tracy. "Michael Field's Dramatically Queer Family Dynamics." In *Queer Victorian Families: Curious Relations in Literature*, edited by Duc Dau and Shale Preston, 57–76. New York: Routledge, 2015.

———. *Women Writers and the Dark Side of Late-Victorian Hellenism*. London: Palgrave, 2010.

Parker, Sarah. "Fashioning Michael Field: Michael Field and Late-Victorian Dress Culture." *Journal of Victorian Culture* 18, no. 3 (2013): 313–34.

———. *The Lesbian Muse and Poetic Identity, 1889–1930*. London: Pickering and Chatto, 2013.

Prins, Yopie. "Greek Maenads, Victorian Spinsters." In *Victorian Sexual Dissidence*, edited by Richard Dellamora, 43–81. Chicago: University of Chicago Press, 1999.

———. "A Metaphorical Field: Katherine Bradley and Edith Cooper." *Victorian Poetry* 33, no. 1 (1995): 129–48.

———. "Sappho Doubled: Michael Field." *Yale Journal of Criticism* 8, no. 1 (1995): 165–86.

———. *Victorian Sappho*. Princeton, NJ: Princeton University Press, 1999.

Roden, Frederick S. *Same-Sex Desire in Victorian Religious Culture*. Basingstoke, UK: Palgrave Macmillan, 2002.

Saville, Julia F. "The Poetic Imaging of Michael Field." In *The Fin-de-Siècle Poem: English Literary Culture and the 1890s*, edited by Joseph Bristow, 178–206. Athens: Ohio University Press, 2005.

Stetz, Margaret D., and Cheryl A. Wilson, eds. *Michael Field and Their World*. High Wycombe, UK: Rivendale Press, 2007.

Sturge Moore, Thomas, and D. C. Sturge Moore, eds. *Works and Days: From the Journal of Michael Field*. London: Murray, 1933.

Sturgeon, Mary. *Michael Field*. London: Harrap, 1922.

Taft, Vickie L. "The Tragic Mary: A Case Study in Michael Field's Understanding of Sexual Politics." *Nineteenth-Century Contexts: An Interdisciplinary Journal* 23, no. 2 (2001): 265–95.

Thain, Marion. "'Damnable Aestheticism' and the Turn to Rome: John Gray, Michael Field, and a Poetics of Conversion." In *The Fin-de-Siècle Poem: English Literary Culture and the 1890s*, edited by Joseph Bristow, 311–36. Athens: Ohio University Press, 2005.

———, ed. *Michael Field and Fin-de-Siècle Culture and Society: The Journals, 1868–1914, and Correspondence of Katharine Bradley and Edith Cooper from the British Library London*. Marlborough, UK: Adam Matthew, 2003 (thirteen reels of microfilm).

———. *Michael Field and Poetic Identity, with a Biography*. London: Eighteen Nineties Society, 2000.

———. *'Michael Field': Poetry, Aestheticism and the Fin de Siècle*. Cambridge: Cambridge University Press, 2007.

———. "Perspective: Digitizing the Diary—Experience in Queer Encoding (A Retrospective and a Prospective)." *Journal of Victorian Culture* 21, no.2 (2016): 226–41.

Thain, Marion, and Ana Parejo Vadillo, eds. *Michael Field, the Poet: Published and Manuscript Materials.* Peterborough, Ontario: Broadview, 2009.

Thomas, Kate. "'What Time We Kiss': Michael Field's Queer Temporalities." *GLQ: A Journal of Lesbian and Gay Studies* 13, no. 2–3 (2007): 327–51.

Treby, Ivor C., ed. *Binary Star: Leaves from the Journal and Letters of Michael Field, 1846–1914.* Bury St. Edmunds, Suffolk: De Blackland Press, 2006.

———, ed. *The Michael Field Catalogue.* London: De Blackland Press, 1998.

———, ed. *Music and Silence: The Gamut of Michael Field.* Bury St. Edmunds, Suffolk: De Blackland Press, 2000.

———, ed. *A Shorter Shīrazād: 101 Poems of Michael Field.* Bury St. Edmunds, Suffolk: De Blackland Press, 1999.

———, ed. *Uncertain Rain: Sundry Spells of Michael Field.* Bury St. Edmunds, Suffolk: De Blackland Press, 2002.

Vadillo, Ana Parejo. "Aestheticism and Decoration: At Home with Michael Field." *Cahiers Victoriens et Edouardiens* 74 (2011): 17–36.

———. "Another Renaissance: The Decadent Poetic Drama of A.C. Swinburne and Michael Field." In *Decadent Poetics: Literature and Form at the British Fin de Siècle,* edited by Jason Hall and Alex Murray, 116–40. Basingstoke, UK: Palgrave, 2013.

———. "Living Art: Michael Field, Aestheticism and Dress." In *Crafting the Women Professional in the Long Nineteenth Century: Artistry and Industry in Britain,* edited by Kyriaki Hadjiafxendi and Patricia Zakreski, 243–71. Farnham, UK: Ashgate, 2013.

———. "A Note upon the 'Liquid Crystal Screen' and Victorian Poetry." *Victorian Poetry* 41, no. 3 (2003): 531–36.

———. "Outmoded Dramas: History and Modernity in Michael Field's Aesthetic Plays." In *Michael Field and Their World,* edited by Margaret Stetz and Cheryl Wilson, 237–49. London: Rivendale Press, 2007.

———. "Poets of Style: Poetries of Asceticism and Excess." In *The Cambridge Companion to Victorian Women's Poetry,* edited by Linda K. Hughes, 230–49. Cambridge: Cambridge University Press, 2019.

———. "Sight and Song: Transparent Translations and a Manifesto for the Observer." *Victorian Poetry* 38, no. 1 (2000): 15–34.

———. "'This Hot-House of Decadent Chronicle': Michael Field, Nietzsche and the Dance of Modern Poetic Drama." *Women: A Cultural Review* 26, no. 3 (2016): 195–220.

———. "Walter Pater and Michael Field: The Correspondence, with Other Unpublished Manuscript Materials." *Pater Newsletter,* no. 65 (Spring 2014): 27–85.

———. *Women Poets and Urban Aestheticism: Passengers to Modernity.* Basingstoke, UK: Palgrave Macmillan, 2005.

Vadillo, Ana Parejo, and Rob Gallagher. "Animating Sight and Song: A Meditation on Identity, Fair Use, and Collaboration." *19: Interdisciplinary Studies in the Long Nineteenth Century* 21 (2015) DOI: http://doi.org/10.16995/ntn.754.

Vadillo, Ana Parejo, and Marion Thain, eds. *Michael Field, the Poet: Published and Manuscript Materials.* Peterborough, Ontario: Broadview, 2009.

Vanita, Ruth. *Sappho and the Virgin Mary: Same-Sex Love and the English Literary Imagination.* New York: Columbia University Press, 1996.

Vicinus, Martha. "Adolescent Boy: Fin de Siècle Femme Fatale?" *Journal of the History of Sexuality* 5, no. 1 (1994): 90–114.

———. *Intimate Friends: Women Who Loved Women, 1778–1928*. Chicago: Chicago University Press, 2004.

———. "Sister Souls: Bernard Berenson and Michael Field." *Nineteenth-Century Literature* 60, no. 3 (2005): 326–54.

White, Christine. "Flesh and Roses: Michael Field's Metaphors of Pleasure and Desire." *Women's Writing* 3, no. 1 (1996): 47–62.

———. "The One Woman (in Virgin Haunts of Poesie): Michael Field's Sapphic Symbolism." In *Volcanoes and Pearl Divers: Essays in Lesbian Feminist Studies*, edited by Suzanne Raitt, 74–102. London: Only Women Press, 1995.

———. "'Poets and Lovers Evermore': Interpreting Female Love in the Poetry and Journals of Michael Field." *Textual Practice* 4, no. 2 (1990): 197–212.

———. "The Tiresian Poet: Michael Field." In *Victorian Women Poets: A Critical Reader*, edited by Angela Leighton, 148–61. Oxford: Blackwell, 1996.

Wilson, Cheryl A. "Bodily Sensations in the Conversion Poetry of Michael Field." *Victorian Review* 54, no. 2 (2016): 179–97.

Editions of Michael Field's Diaries

Editors' note: Michael Field's manuscript diaries are held in the British Library, London, Add. MS. 46776: vol. 1 (October 1868) to Add. MS. 46804A: vol. 30 (1868–1914). Full details of these and other archival holdings can be found in Ivor C. Treby, *The Michael Field Catalogue* (London: De Blackland Press, 1998).

The following sources are also available:

Michael Field Diary Archive [online], *Victorian Lives and Letters Consortium* (Center for Digital Humanities, University of South Carolina): http://tundra.csd.sc.edu/vllc/field.

Sturge Moore, Thomas, and D. C. Sturge Moore, eds. *Works and Days: From the Journal of Michael Field*. London: Murray, 1933.

Thain, Marion, ed. *Michael Field and Fin-de-Siècle Culture and Society: The Journals, 1868–1914, and Correspondence of Katharine Bradley and Edith Cooper from the British Library London*. Marlborough: Adam Matthew Publications, 2003. [13 reels of microfilm]

Texts by Michael Field

Editors' note: These sources have been arranged chronologically for ease of reference. These texts were published as "Michael Field" unless otherwise indicated. Verse dramas have been indicated with an asterisk.

The New Minnesinger and Other Poems. London: Longmans, Green, and Co., 1875, by Arran Leigh. [K.B. alone]

Bellerophôn. C. Kegan Paul, 1881, by Arran and Isla Leigh. [K.B. and E.C.]*

Callirrhoe. Fair Rosamund. London: George Bell & Sons, 1884.*

The Father's Tragedy, William Rufus, Loyalty or Love? London: George Bell & Sons, 1885.*

Brutus Ultor. London: George Bell & Sons, 1886.*

Canute the Great, The Cup of Water. London: George Bell & Sons, 1887.*

Long Ago. London: George Bell & Sons, 1889.

The Tragic Mary. George Bell & Sons, 1890.*

Sight and Song. London: Elkin Mathews and John Lane, 1892.

Stephania, a Trialogue. London: Elkin Mathews and John Lane, 1892.*

A Question of Memory. London: Elkin Mathews and John Lane, 1893.*

Underneath the Bough. London: George Bell and Sons, 1893. (Also published as a second, revised and decreased edition later in 1898)

Attila, My Attila! A Play. London: Elkin Mathews, 1896.*

Underneath the Bough. Revised and decreased edition. Portland, ME: Thomas B. Mosher, 1893.

The World at Auction. London: Hacon & Ricketts, 1898.*

Noontide Branches: A Small Sylvan Drama. Oxford: Henry Daniel, 1899.*

Anna Ruina. London: David Nutt, 1899.*

The Race of Leaves. London: Hacon & Ricketts, 1901.*

Julia Domna. London: Hacon & Ricketts, 1903.*

Borgia. London: A. H. Bullen, 1905. (Published anonymously)*

Wild Honey from Various Thyme. London: T. Fisher Unwin, 1908.

Queen Mariamne. London: Sidgwick and Jackson, 1908.*

The Tragedy of Pardon, and Dian: A Fantasy. London: Sidgwick and Jackson, 1911. (By the "author of *Borgia*")*

Tristan de Léonois, The Accuser, A Messiah. London: Sidgwick and Jackson, 1911. (By the "author of *Borgia*")*

Poems of Adoration. Edinburgh: Sands & Co, 1912.

Mystic Trees. London: Eveleigh Nash, 1913.

Whym Chow: Flame of Love. London: Eragny Press, 1914.

POSTHUMOUS PUBLICATIONS

Dedicated. London: George Bell & Sons, 1914.

Ras Byzance, Deirdre, A Question of Memory. London: Poetry Bookshop, 1918.*

In The Name of Time. London: Poetry Bookshop, 1919.*

A Selection from the Poems of Michael Field. Edited by T. Sturge Moore. London: Poetry Bookshop, 1923.

Above Mount Alverna, Iphignia in Arsacia, The Assumption. Oxford: Basil Blackwell, 1930.*

The Wattlefold: Unpublished Poems. Collected by Emily C. Fortey, with preface by Vincent McNabb. Oxford: Basil Blackwell, 1930.

Contributor Biographies

LEIRE BARRERA-MEDRANO is a teaching fellow in Spanish at the University of Bath. She has recently completed a PhD in English at Birkbeck, University of London entitled "Spain and British Decadence, 1880–1920: Aesthetics of Extremes." Her publications include "'Inarticulate Cries': Arthur Symons and the Primitivist Modernity of Flamenco," *Volupté: Interdisciplinary Journal of Decadence Studies* 1 (2018), and "'Dolls in Agony': Vernon Lee in Southern Spain," *Cahiers Victoriens et Édouardiens*, 83 (2016). She is also coeditor of Girasol Press.

JOSEPH BRISTOW is a distinguished professor of English at the University of California, Los Angeles. His recent books include (with Rebecca N. Mitchell) *Oscar Wilde's Chatterton: Literary History, Romanticism, and the Art of Forgery* (Yale University Press, 2015) and an edited collection, *Oscar Wilde and the Cultures of Childhood* (Palgrave Macmillan, 2017). He is completing a study of the Crown prosecution of Oscar Wilde.

JILL R. EHNENN is a professor of English at Appalachian State University, where she teaches Victorian Studies and in the Gender, Women's, and Sexuality Studies Program. She is the author of *Women's Literary Collaboration, Queerness, and Late-Victorian Culture* (Ashgate/Routledge, 2008), articles on nineteenth-century women authors such as Dorothy Wordsworth, Elizabeth Siddal, Vernon Lee, and Lucas Malet, and multiple articles and chapters on the female coauthors who wrote as "Michael Field." Her current book project is *Michael Field's Revisionary Poetics*, under contract with Edinburgh University Press.

SARAH E. KERSH is an assistant professor in the Department of English at Dickinson College in Carlisle, Pennsylvania, where she teaches courses on Victorian literature and culture, queer studies, and digital humanities. Her current book project is a collaboration with Pearl Chaozon Bauer, which argues for the political worth of nineteenth-century poetry during a time of changing marriage and property laws. She recently collaborated with Dickinson undergraduates to create an online, annotated version of Michael Field's volume of ekphrastic poems, *Sight and Song* (1892). This project can be found at michaelfield.dickinson.edu.

KRISTIN MAHONEY is an associate professor of English at Michigan State University. She has published essays on aestheticism and decadence in *Victorian Studies, Criticism, English Literature in Transition, Literature Compass, Nineteenth Century Prose, Victorian Review,* and *Victorian Periodicals Review.* Her book *Literature and the Politics of Post-Victorian Decadence* was published by Cambridge University Press in 2015. She is currently working on a project entitled *Queer Kinship after Wilde: Transnational Aestheticism and the Family.*

CATHERINE MAXWELL is a professor of Victorian Literature at Queen Mary University of London and author of *The Female Sublime from Milton to Swinburne: Bearing Blindness* (Manchester University Press, 2001), *Swinburne* (Northcote House, 2006), *Second Sight: The Visionary Imagination in Late Victorian Literature* (Manchester University Press, 2008), and numerous articles on Victorian literature. She was a Leverhulme Major Research Fellow for 2014–16, during which time she completed *Scents and Sensibility: Perfume in Victorian Literary Culture* (Oxford University Press, 2017), which received the 2018 ESSE (European Society for the Study of English) award for Literatures in the English Language.

ALEX MURRAY is a senior lecturer in Modern Literature at the Queen's University, Belfast. His most recent monograph is *Landscapes of Decadence: Literature and Place at the Fin de Siècle* (Cambridge University Press, 2016) and he is coeditor with Kate Hext of *Decadence in the Age of Modernism* (Johns Hopkins University Press, 2019).

SARAH PARKER is a lecturer in English at Loughborough University. She is the author of *The Lesbian Muse and Poetic Identity, 1889–1930* (Pickering and Chatto/ Routledge, 2013). Her other publications include articles and chapters on Constance Naden, Edna St. Vincent Millay, Amy Levy, Djuna Barnes, and Sarah Waters. Her current research project focuses on the post-1900 careers and afterlives of women poets associated with the fin de siècle, arguing that these figures were still active and significant in the twentieth century.

MARGARET D. STETZ is the Mae and Robert Carter Professor of Women's Studies and professor of Humanities at the University of Delaware. In 2015, she was named by the magazine *Diverse: Issues in Higher Education* to its list of the twenty-five top women in U.S. higher education. She has published several books, including *British Women's Comic Fiction, 1890–1990* (2001; reissued by Routledge in 2018), and more than 120 peer-reviewed articles on a range of topics. She has also been curator or cocurator of thirteen exhibitions on late nineteenth-century print culture at venues such as Harvard University, Liverpool Central Library, and the Rosenbach Library and Museum in Philadelphia.

KATE THOMAS is the K. Laurence Stapleton Professor of English at Bryn Mawr College. The author of *Postal Pleasures: Sex, Scandal and Victorian Letters* (Oxford University Press, 2012), she has also published articles on queer temporality, Matthew Arnold's diet, wax queens, and nineteenth-century potboiler fiction. She is currently working on a monograph titled "Victorians Fat and Thin."

ANA PAREJO VADILLO is a Reader in Victorian Literature and Culture at Birkbeck College, University of London. She is the author of *Women Poets and Urban Aestheticism: Passengers of Modernity* (2005) and coauthor of *Michael Field, the Poet: Published and Manuscript Materials* (2009) and *Victorian Literature: A Sourcebook* (2011). She has coedited a special issue of *Victorian Literature and Culture* (On Literary Culture and Women Poets). She has also coedited "Science, Literature and the Darwin Legacy," *19: Interdisciplinary Studies in the Long Nineteenth Century* 11 (2010) and "The Nineteenth-Century Digital Archive," *19: Interdisciplinary Studies in the Long Nineteenth Century* 21 (2015). She is currently working on a book entitled "Cosmopolitan Aestheticism."

Index